victorian

afterlife

John Kucich and Dianne F. Sadoff, Editors

victorian
afterlife

Postmodern Culture Rewrites the Nineteenth Century

University of Minnesota Press   Minneapolis / London

Lines from "A Postcard from the Volcano," by Wallace Stevens, from *The Palm at the End of the Mind,* edited by Holly Stevens (New York: Vintage Books, 1972), page 127, are reprinted by permission of Alfred A. Knopf, Inc.

Published by the University of Minnesota Press
111 Third Avenue South, Suite 290
Minneapolis, MN 55401-2520
http://www.upress.umn.edu

Library of Congress Cataloging-in-Publication Data

Victorian afterlife : postmodern culture rewrites the nineteenth century /
    John Kucich and Dianne F. Sadoff, editors.
        p.   cm.
    Includes bibliographical references and index.
    ISBN 0-8166-3323-1 (alk. paper)—ISBN 0-8166-3324-X (pbk. : alk. paper)
    1. English literature—19th century—History and criticism—Theory, etc.
2. Literature and history—Great Britain—History—19th century. 3. Literature
and history—Great Britain—History—20th century. 4. Great Britain—
History—Victoria, 1837–1901—Historiography. 5. English fiction—Film
and video adaptations. 6. Great Britain—Civilization—19th century.
7. Great Britain—Civilization—20th century. 8. Postmodernism.
    I. Kucich, John. II. Sadoff, Dianne F. III. Title.
    PR461 .V5 2000
    820.9'008—dc21
                                                                00-008492

Printed in the United States of America on acid-free paper

The University of Minnesota is an equal-opportunity educator and employer.

11 10 09 08 07 06 05 04 03 02 01 00   10 9 8 7 6 5 4 3 2 1

We approach the final stage in the conditions of historical learning.

Lord Acton, *Lectures on Modern History* (1895)

One of the most popular genital piercings today, the Prince Albert—in which a ring is inserted through the urethra and out the underside of the head of the penis—is named after Queen Victoria's consort. The prince reportedly got the piercing to tether his penis to his leg, in order to fit into the tight pants that were the fashion of the day.

Marilee Strong, *A Bright Red Scream:*
***Self-Mutilation and the Language of Pain* (1998)**

The one duty we owe to history is to rewrite it.

Gilbert, *The Critic as Artist,* by Oscar Wilde (1890)

contents

Introduction
Histories of the Present
Dianne F. Sadoff and John Kucich   ix

mystifications

Modernity and Culture, the Victorians and Cultural Studies
John McGowan   3

At Home in the Nineteenth Century: Photography, Nostalgia,
and the Will to Authenticity
Jennifer Green-Lewis   29

The Uses and Misuses of Oscar Wilde
Shelton Waldrep   49

Being True to Jane Austen
Mary A. Favret   64

A Twentieth-Century *Portrait*: Jane Campion's American Girl
Susan Lurie   83

Display Cases
Judith Roof   101

engagements

Found Drowned: The Irish Atlantic
Ian Baucom   125

The Embarrassment of Victorianism: Colonial Subjects and the
Lure of Englishness
Simon Gikandi   157

Hacking the Nineteenth Century
Jay Clayton   186

Queen Victoria and Me
Laurie Langbauer   211

Sorting, Morphing, and Mourning: A. S. Byatt Ghostwrites Victorian Fiction
Hilary M. Schor   234

Asking Alice: Victorian and Other Alices in Contemporary Culture
Kali Israel   252

Specters of the Novel: *Dracula* **and the Cinematic Afterlife of the Victorian Novel**
Ronald R. Thomas   288

Postscript
Contemporary Culturalism: How Victorian Is It?
Nancy Armstrong   311

Contributors   327

Index   331

Introduction
Histories of the Present

Dianne F. Sadoff and John Kucich

A scene from *Clueless,* Amy Heckerling's campy 1995 film version of *Emma,* handily identifies the crisis of postmodern historiography that *Victorian Afterlife* addresses. From the backseat of a car, Cher watches Josh and his intellectual poseur girlfriend critique their university creative-writing class. "Like Hamlet said," the long-haired, beret-wearing girlfriend proclaims, "to thine own self be true." Cher pipes up: "[Hamlet] didn't say that. That Polonius guy did." Girl laughs: "I think I remember *Hamlet* accurately"; Cher: "Well, I remember Mel Gibson accurately."[1] Tongue in cheek, *Clueless* follows Cher in undoing literary history and placing twentieth-century cultural icons in the position of textual originals. Heckerling's allegorical scene, in which the 1990s meet the 1950s, flaunts a manic historical insouciance, like Cher's, that foregrounds the dysfunctions of cultural memory in the construction of postmodern identity. What leverage does the concept of periodization provide for cultural self-awareness in this film? Heckerling suspends the question by charming us with a heroine who has no sense of history at all. Named after a "great singer . . . of the past who now does infomercials," Cher lives in a Beverly Hills mansion with pillars that date "all the way back from 1972"; when asked if she likes Billie Holliday, Cher replies, with a teasing glance at the camera, "I love him." Heckerling speaks to and seemingly for Cher's contemporaries in her audience, who presumably have no sense of how a historical moment represents itself to itself. At the same time, Heckerling trumps such ignorance by burying within her film enigmatic "clues" about the ironic origins—whose import is undecidable—of Cher's life story in Austen's novel.

Clueless thus confirms—albeit in a forgiving spirit—the view of post-modern historiography associated with Fredric Jameson, who begins *Postmodernism, or, the Cultural Logic of Late Capitalism* by declaring: "It is safest to grasp the concept of the postmodern as an attempt to think the present historically in an age that has forgotten how to think historically in the first place."[2] In Jameson's analysis, modernism is also obsessed with the concept of "the New," as it strives compulsively to watch its own coming into being. Postmodernism, however, looks for more radical disruptions—for "breaks, for events rather than new worlds, for the telltale instant after which [history] is no longer the same" (ix). But the complete victory of commodification in the postmodern age—an age in which the image suffers no constraints outside those of the marketplace—has turned postmodern history, according to Jameson, into "the random cannibalization of all the styles of the past," creating a "loss of historicity" that becomes both a cultural pathology and the grounds for neurotic historical fantasy of the most spectacular and extravagant kind. This deficit (which Jameson tries not to privilege as a periodizing concept, though he sometimes does just that) provokes "a series of spasmodic and intermittent, but desperate, attempts at recuperation" (x–xi).[3] Postmodern theory—which drives Jameson's work, as well as our own—is, in his view, one of those recuperative efforts.

Armed with this knowledge of postmodern historical crisis, how does the cultural critic confront the recent explosion of postmodern Victoriana? For despite the recent blockbuster popularity of Shakespeare and Elizabeth I movies, films of Victorian novels have saturated the middlebrow and art-house movie circuit since the early 1990s. *Clueless* is part of a fascination with the nineteenth century that inhabits late-century postmodernism's obsession with the telltale instants of historical rupture, with the "shifts and irrevocable changes in the *representation* of things" (ix). Oddly, however, the prominence of the nineteenth century for postmodernism has yet to become the subject of rigorous scholarly analysis; that is to say, postmodern fixation on the nineteenth-century past as the specific site of Jameson's "break," in which the present imagines itself to have been born and history forever changed, is a cultural phenomenon that itself needs to be historicized—needs, indeed, simply to be acknowledged. The origins of this book lie in our surprised awareness of this critical gap: there has been very little scholarly work that has attempted to historicize postmodern rewritings of Victorian culture.[4] By bringing together a diverse and noted collection of cultural critics, we have attempted to begin a discussion of postmodernism's privileging of the Victorian as its historical "other."

An intense historiographical curiosity, we believe, drove 1980s and 1990s Victorian revivalism and located the Victorian age as historically central to late-century postmodern consciousness. The scale of the phenomenon itself is enormous. Merchant and Ivory, Iain Softley, Ang Lee, and Patricia Rozema have filmed and marketed E. M. Forster and Jane Austen novels, as the groundless postmodern imagination projects a "Victorian feel" into Regency and early high-modern texts alike. A. S. Byatt's postmodern-Victorian pastiche, *Possession,* won the Booker Prize, vaulting her into the first rank of highbrow novelists. The mainstream popularity of Caleb Carr's *The Alienist,* E. L. Doctorow's *The Water-Works,* Neal Stephenson's *The Diamond Age,* and the cult success of William Gibson and Bruce Sterling's cyberpunk *The Difference Engine* map an extraordinary consumer demand for Victorian instances of "historiographical metafiction," as Linda Hutcheon has labeled the genre.[5] The stage and screen—both big and small—supply postmodern-Victorian cultural goods: Tom Stoppard's *Indian Ink, Arcadia,* and *The Invention of Love;* hit Broadway extravaganzas such as *Jekyll and Hyde, Marie Christine,* and *In the Blood;* the recent spate of films and plays about Oscar Wilde; and the lavish and seemingly endless made-for-TV adaptations of *Middlemarch, Pride and Prejudice, Wuthering Heights, Vanity Fair,* and others. Victorian sexuality, in particular, seems made for such retellings. Alices in and out of wonderland abound in popular fiction and film, in photography and manuscript exhibits on both sides of the Atlantic at, for example, the Pierpont Morgan Library and the National Portrait Gallery; at a corporate display space, the Equitable Gallery, Carroll's eroticized girls and scenes of fathers and daughters invite the lobby-stroller's gaze. Photos and paintings of Victorian fairies, Cameron daughters and other virgins, and tableaux of mythological, high-camp Victorian girls show in New York and Chicago. Victoria herself has recently been eroticized in a filmic revision of history, *Mrs. Brown.* As our examples suggest, these nineteenth-century returns are produced by even as they manifest the explosion and diversification of the cultural marketplace since the emergence of visual and media technologies. These remakes also recall a time when high culture was "popular," as the postmodern-Victorian mode both reifies a lost era of high culture and popularizes its imitations.

But high and middlebrow art are hardly alone in their obsession with the Victorians, for the historical reimagining of the nineteenth century seems to be reflected in almost every domain of contemporary culture. In mainstream politics, a small-scale "culture war" has opened up a front here: the Victorians, according to the now-deposed Newt Gingrich, cannily represented the mewling and whining poor even as they regulated their diets and controlled their getting, spending, and reproduction.[6] Indeed, a battle over the ideological implications of nineteenth-century culture has been enjoined by those who, led by Gertrude Himmelfarb, have argued that conservative Victorian ideals can cure us of our current social ills.[7] Although she berates critics influenced by Michel Foucault for bureaucratizing the Victorians, Himmelfarb's popular version of the nineteenth century also represents the Victorian social system monolithically, as she attempts to subsume social conflict in a universalized set of moral values. Despite its pervasive "class-conscious[ness]," Victorian England was "remarkable," she claims, for its "common ethos"; for Himmelfarb insists that most Victorians, "including a majority of the working classes, subscribed to even if they did not always abide by" these commonly held values. Characterizing the Victorians as though they were a homogeneous society, Himmelfarb portrays nineteenth-century laborers as emulating the virtues of their betters, mimicking duty, piety, industry, prudence, temperance, cleanliness, and, above all, respectability. In Himmelfarb's scenario, these Victorian workers viewed "life" (or social position?) as "natural, right, and, for the most part, happy." Himmelfarb's adjective "remarkable"—which chimes throughout her book—identifies her fable as a postmodern fantasy of Victorian working-class heroism, in which every "tedious, backbreaking task" is a moral victory over poverty. In Himmelfarb's paean to an "orderly and satisfactory" past, then, the triumph of morality over poverty becomes a model for postmodernism's nostalgic retrospective look at its own origins.[8]

Consumer culture has shared in postmodern nostalgia for the nineteenth century, but—in contrast to Himmelfarb's politicized nostalgia—it uses the Victorian past to aestheticize contemporary reality. Victorian fashions and furnishings are enjoying a resurgence that has spawned magazines such as *Victoria* and *Victorian*. Home-decorating books and magazines teach twentieth-century homeowners how to load a mantel with curios and kitsch, people a wall with elaborately framed and sepia-toned family photos, and choose for the drawing room a patterned wallpaper or chintz. One such periodical follows a feature on "William Morris at Kelmscott Manor" with "Morris in America" and with advice about arts-and-crafts decoration for the home office.[9] Through consumer culture, moreover, we might trace a curious difference between our own postmodern relation with the Victorians and the moderns' vexed version of their immediate precursors. Whereas, Jameson maintains, the modernists appropriated the Victorian past to criticize cultural commodification, postmodernism fashions commodities that make the process of consumption glamorous and pleasurable. In this formulation, however, the term *postmodern* itself overvalues the (very real) ideological and aesthetic tensions between the contemporary and modern periods. Given the centrality of historical emergence that contemporary culture locates in the nineteenth century—as our collection seeks to demonstrate— aspects of late-century postmodernism could more appropriately be called "post-Victorian," a term that conveys the paradoxes of historical continuity and disruption that this anthology seeks to bring into focus.

Unprecedented in their scale and glamour, the recent high and popular cultural movements to rewrite the nineteenth century seek to create self-awareness in the present by reworking the past. Academic scholarship itself has not been immune to postmodernism's historical and self-reflective constructions of knowledge. The resurgence of interest in the nineteenth century is related, for example, to the emergence of cultural studies, which now dominates English departments and has made significant inroads into other humanistic disciplines. The field of cultural studies is often said to owe its origins to two critical revisions of nineteenth-century culture: Raymond Williams's *Culture and Society* and E. P. Thompson's *The Making of the English Working Class*. As John McGowan points out in his essay for this collection, moreover, the field of cultural studies owes its expanded notions of culture to repressed nineteenth-century figures such as Matthew Arnold, figures who argued for what appears culturally conservative from the perspective of postmodernism: the touchstone, the canon; the best that has been thought and said; the aesthetic superiority of high cultural contents and philosophies to those of the masses. New academic historicisms have enabled a wide range of theoretical revisionings—not just those of cultural studies— and although this work has been done in all historical periods, the nineteenth century has been a particularly fertile area for consideration. The period has been marked by major critical texts that claim to have found in the nineteenth century the origins of contemporary consumerism (Baudrillard), sexual science (Foucault), gay culture (Sedgwick et al.), and gender identity (Gilbert and Gubar, Showalter, Armstrong). Ethnography, economics, science studies, the history of medicine, and other popular areas of scholarly inquiry have focused on the nineteenth-century materials that they view as anchoring their respective disciplinary paradigms.

These contemporary cultural critics, like this book's contributors, construct a history of the present by writing about rewritings of the Victorian past. For if historicity can be defined in the postmodern era as "a perception of the present as history," the present becomes a moment that locates the individual doubly in historical time. Immersed in the present, we experience what poststructuralism once derided as "presence," even as we sense that the present is "defamiliarized," as Jameson argues; we feel a "distance from immediacy" that resembles a "historical perspective" (284). Through a process of reification, we step back to conceptualize and date this present as itself a historical period: the 1980s, for example, becomes "the Reagan era," or the 1990s, the millennial fin de siècle. In postmodern historicity, then, any present moment is also always already a historical moment, located within a self-reflexive and periodizing temporality. Closely linked to this sense of the historicized present, moreover, is a "buried or repressed theory of historical periodization" (3). Momentarily stabilizing but perhaps anxiously disavowing historical change, these periodizing hypotheses, Jameson argues, prevent late-twentieth-century individuals from sensing present history as "sheer heterogeneity" (6). Seized within these temporal systems, individuals sense themselves as placed in history, and theorize themselves as situated within moments of national emergence or dominance or crisis.

This move retrospectively to constitute a history of the present has been criticized by some theorists as fraught with ideological dangers. Raymond Williams argues, for example, that such retrogressive structures, infinitely regressive and in search of ever-earlier historical origins, serve to idealize a periodized historical past. Williams traces the ways in which British poets and novelists, in successive historical periods, relocate England's golden age to serve their self-representing needs. From Williams's critical perspective, Himmelfarb's history of the present as a degraded version of Victorian social stability seems yet another retrospectively idealized narrative of the past, fabricated in light of present needs. Either in Jameson's Marxist or Himmelfarb's postliberal and moralist history of the present, this monolithic thinking renders the nineteenth century static in comparison with a dynamic postmodernism.[10]

But why, exactly, has contemporary culture preferred to engage the nineteenth century—not the modern period or the eighteenth century—as its historical "other"? This question, perhaps the most pressing issue for our volume, resists a single, reductive answer. Rewritings of Victorian culture have flourished, we believe, because the postmodern fetishizes notions of cultural emergence, and because the nineteenth century provides multiple eligible sites for theorizing such emergence. For the postmodern engagement with the nineteenth century appears to link the discourses of economics, sexuality, politics, and technology with the material objects and cultures available for transportation across historical and geographical boundaries, and thus capable of hybridization and appropriation. Here, we make a periodizing claim of our own: that the cultural matrix of nineteenth-century England joined various and possible stories about cultural rupture that, taken together, overdetermine the period's availability for the postmodern exploration of cultural emergence. Despite the ideological dangers of periodizing hypotheses, then, we and our contributors launch here a periodizing project.

Jameson, too, participates in a periodizing project of this kind by privileging the historical novel in his version of narrative emergence and innovation. He locates in the nineteenth century the emergence of a modern sense of historicity; in the 1950s, the "flowering and exhaustion" of high modernism and a concomitant "waning or blockage" of historicity; in the 1980s and 1990s, the emergence of the postmodern "crisis and paralysis" (284) of historicity. Jameson explains this periodization as grounded less in our experience of history than in the socioeconomic structures in place at any given time. Thus he locates the nineteenth century as a privileged site of emergence for postmodernism because the "conditions of possibility" in which the historical novel emerged articulated those socioeconomic forces with the cognitive mappings they made available to the writers of the period. In the early nineteenth century, Jameson maintains, it was practicable for members of the middle class to engage in self-representation, to portray their notion of their class's past and future, to articulate a "social and collective project" in a historically new form, temporal narrative (283–84). The formal innovations since Sir Walter Scott—like the science fiction and nostalgia films on which Jameson focuses in this section of his book on postmodernism—depend on Scott's having originated the historical novel. The historical novel's emergence, then, is symptomatic of the economic sphere's penetration into the aesthetic that Jameson regards as a key feature of industrial capitalism's inaugural stage.

Jameson's Marxist explanation of the Victorians as central to postmodern historicity overlaps, to some extent, with Andreas Huyssen's developmental cultural history. Huyssen maintains that "postmodernism has always been in search of tradition while pretending to innovation."[11] Thus, Huyssen argues that late-century postmodernism has had to leap over the modernist avant-garde to create a tradition in the wake of modernist cultural exhaustion. In Huyssen's chronology, "the 1960s can be regarded as the closing chapter in the tradition of avant-gardism"; postmodernism in the late 1970s and beyond thus "appears much more traditional than it did in the 1960s," because "postmodernism itself can now be described as a search for a viable modern tradition . . . outside the canon of classical modernism" (164–69). Although Jameson and Huyssen say little about the *significance* of the nineteenth-century past as the emergent site for late-century postmodern historicity, their shared perception that avant-garde, high-modern culture has been eclipsed offers one explanation for the recent return to the nineteenth century as a locus of historical self-understanding. Yet Williams might put these retrospections into a larger cultural perspective. Redefining tradition and innovation in terms of historical structures of feeling more inclusive than either Jameson's or Huyssen's, Williams's critique demonstrates that these related but somewhat contradictory explanations are insufficient to answer the central cultural question this volume asks. The same could be said of many hypotheses now current: that postmodernism's revival of narrative has evoked nostalgia for nineteenth-century aesthetic forms; that the rise of women into positions of cultural authority as both producers and consumers has sparked a return to representations of nineteenth-century domesticity as an emergent "women's world"; and so on.

The post-Victorian panorama our contributors provide here portrays as overdetermined postmodernism's obsession with the Victorian age. While our contributors locate postmodern fantasies of emergence in the Victorian past, they also enlarge our sense of "historical emergence" by scrutinizing a range of post-Victorian borrowings. The critics whose work appears in this book view various forces and tropes at work in postmodern culture: vampirizations of the Victorian cultural past; uncanny hauntings of our moment by its historical self-representations; returns of the repressed; morphings of Victorian narrative and illustrative forms; nostalgic misreadings of an already nostalgic visual scenario; costumings and imitations of political authority; productive imitations of colonial cultural ethics, and more. Taken together, these essays illustrate the workings of overdetermination within the post-Victorian and, as such, they complicate Jameson's analysis of economic and historical causality, or Huyssen's notion of developmental cultural traditions. Indeed, this book proposes that multiple historical narratives of emergence, organized in different meaningful sequences, each coherent at a particular level of interpretation, create an appropriate paradigm for the postmodern/Victorian conjunction. In this model, economic, psychosexual, technological, and political determinants have joined in a matrix of forces that constitute late postmodernism's obsession with the Victorians. These multiple determinants insist that any answer to the question "Why does postmodernism return to the nineteenth century as the site of a crucial historical break?" must be a heterogeneous one.

Economics provides one powerful (and often sublimated) focal point for reflections on the emergence of the postmodern, as several contributors to this volume point out. Giovanni Arrighi's massive history of the three "long centuries" of capitalism provides perhaps the most comprehensive analysis of both the differences between Victorian Britain's economic arrangements and those of late capitalism, and the similarities that allow us to see the nineteenth century as the originary site of our economic situation.[12] In nineteenth-century Britain, Arrighi argues, machine-extractive and manufacturing activities became the means by which capitalism expanded; yet when trade (via the railroads or colonizing joint-stock charter companies, such as the East India Company) could no longer create markets and therefore expand capital and production, an increased specialization in financial speculation gradually emerged as a mode of British national economic dominance. In the twentieth-century United States, massive industrial production, vertically organized corporations, the pursuit of stable currencies, and the end of the gold standard led to the creation of governmental organizations to manage the world money supply. The global and transnational corporation enabled more flexible modes of capital accumulation and disabled or eclipsed colonial and imperialist expansion as modes of national economic dominance. In the postmodern imaginary, then, the "break" between economic production and economic reproduction, between technologies of manufacture and technologies of the production and control of value itself, becomes a key to understanding the relationships among nationalism, industrialism, and technological development.

Arrighi's analysis would draw our contributors' general assent; for although few of the essays in this book specifically examine economics, many assume the necessary imbrication of their key terms—such as *commodification, fetishization, consumption,* even *politics*—with economic systems. John McGowan raises the question, perhaps more forcefully than the other contributors, of the economic grounds on which totalizing concepts such as "modernity" and "culture" rest. In his critique of zeitgeist thinking, McGowan argues that the concepts of the modern, which anchors and organizes time (and so contemporary anxieties about change), and of culture, which organizes space (and provides a sense of coherence that modernity cannot), began with the Victorians. Basic political categories, McGowan argues, also derive from the notion of the modern and from the Victorian *liberal,* itself an economic label and position. In McGowan's view, postmodernism represents the political left's recognition that it must argue beyond the necessity to change modernity's economic arrangements, beyond the current vogue for new totalizing concepts, such as "global economy." McGowan concludes that what he calls "pragmatic particularism" must replace monolithic thinking within postmodernism. He argues for an overdetermined model of intellectual work that posits engagements with the local and specific as central to historical recuperation.

But the contributors to this volume have also traced the discourse of sexuality as another nineteenth-century site of postmodern emergence. Foucault's history of sexuality locates the Victorians as a convenient yet unreliable "other" for late-twentieth-century sexed individuals. Were the Victorians on the other side of "repression" from us sex-saturated postmoderns, or did they successfully struggle to overcome that repression and so unleash the powerful sexual and emotional forces that some critics have called the "truth of the self"? *The History of Sexuality* actually collapses both propositions together. Although the Victorians "produced" sexuality, rather than repressing it—sponsoring an explosion of discourse about sex that is often located at the origins of contemporary sexual knowledge—that eruption only suffocated agency, according to Foucault, in a disciplinary apparatus that makes the twentieth-century notion of "sexual liberation" itself a ruse of power. Hence, the media spectacle of an American president, who in popular mythology is "addicted" to secretive and illicit sex, resembles a retold Victorian story in which sexuality serves as the key to "character." In this spirit, John Fowles's *The French Lieutenant's Woman* (as well as Karel

Reisz's 1981 film version, starring Jeremy Irons and Meryl Streep) has figured our contemporary contemplation of Victorian sex as a dizzying hall of mirrors, in which it seems impossible to decide whether Victorian sexuality lies behind us in the dust, or whether, in their passionate struggles with sexual repression, the Victorians were somehow the harbingers of sexual self-realization. In either case, contemporary culture struggles to identify a nineteenth-century sexual "break" that might be said to initiate and alter the history of sexuality for postmodern individuals.

Several contributors to *Victorian Afterlife* explore the history of our present sexualities as post-Victorian rewritings. Shelton Waldrep examines recent films and plays about Oscar Wilde that portray the poet and playwright as gay martyr. Noting that these works always see Wilde as a split figure—both Victorian and contemporary—Waldrep argues that the privileging of Wilde's sexuality, and the flaunting of candid talk about homosexuality, reflect postmodernism's nostalgia for the real and its search for "authenticity." Waldrep claims that in recent academic representations of Wilde as queer rather than gay—as disrupting sexual and other interrelated binaries—Wilde continues to be seen as the genuine, originary figure for contemporary "gay definitional systems." These visions of Wilde as the first martyr for contemporary sexual heuristics disregard Wilde's *difference*: the difficulty of recognizing his iconoclasm in Victorian rather than contemporary terms. Depicting another hybrid and diffuse sexual figure, Kali Israel surveys the proliferation of Alices in contemporary fiction, museum exhibits, and criticism. Critical polemics about the "denial" of sexuality in discussions of Dodgson and his "little girls," she discovers, conceal how postmodernism remains haunted by the threat of sexual emergence and nonnormativity Alice represents. Fiction and scholarship about Alice, she shows, participate in ongoing arguments about agency and victimhood, survival and damage, that revolve around the figure of the newly sexualized but still "innocent" juvenile woman. Israel argues that Alice stories of resilience and triumph risk colluding with backlash politics—in demonizing any suggestions about female victimage, in celebrating the autonomy of the liberal subject, and in linking female rebellion with sex. Nevertheless, Israel argues that skepticism toward such stories threatens to undermine the productive accounts of rebellion that we locate in Victorian female sexuality and associate with resourceful female heroines in any age. Alice's mobility as a figure compels

Israel to see "wondering" as a structural necessity of her tales, whether of Victorian "originals" or postmodern daughters.

Postmodern political struggles of race as well as gender have identified the nineteenth century as a site of origin and rupture, a moment of emergence. Post-Victorian political narratives can thus reorganize official representations of the nineteenth-century past's liberal or conservative legacies. Postcolonial constructions of national subjectivity, for example, which often revolve around the nineteenth-century emergence of the national subject and which foreground the political interests of minority groups and non-Western cultures, have sometimes been occluded by Marxist analyses that tie features of postmodernism closely to Western economic models. Jameson himself has been accused of creating a series of binaries between First and Third Worlds, and excluding the latter from postmodern cultural models because he regards its economical foundations as distinct from capitalism's.[13] Postcolonial theory, however, finds in marginalized societies' complex engagements with the West the intertextual histories, fluid subjectivities, and multiplicitous cultures that mark postmodernism as possessing a specific political instrumentality. Such theorizing consistently attempts to recuperate the nineteenth-century birth of postcolonial politics.

Simon Gikandi and Ian Baucom provide striking—though very different—accounts of the construction of postcolonial subjectivity through imaginary nineteenth-century political pasts. Baucom's compelling discussion of the Irish Great Famine sees the "completion" of historical process and national consciousness in the efforts of a postmodern poet, Paul Muldoon, to conceive the Famine as actively present in late-century, diasporic Irish identity. Baucom demonstrates how Muldoon's personal and psychological poetry covertly invokes traumatic nineteenth-century events to rehistoricize and politicize Irish subjectivity. Using a "situated psychoanalysis"—a term borrowed from Anne McClintock—Baucom reads postmodern revisitations of the Famine, whether poetic or ritualistic, not as an effort to repress history but as an attempt to absorb and integrate Irish historical events into contemporary culture, that is, to "introject" rather than to "incorporate" them. Finding a complex historical perspective in a poet whose work has been viewed as deeply subjective, Baucom shows that Muldoon grounds postmodern, non-unified Irish subjectivity in a particular diasporic political history. Like Baucom, Gikandi rereads the supposed "repression" of nineteenth-century history to discover the political efficacy of post-Victorian subjectivity. How could important native anticolonialists, he asks, also promote dominant features of Victorian ideology? Gikandi argues that the prominence of Victorian moral codes in C. L. R. James's and in Alexander Crummel's work reveals Victorianism to be not just a repository of "traditional values" but also the irruption of modernity—and, therefore, of ideas crucial to revolutionary struggle. This perspective transforms official histories of Victorianism, as it promotes the stature of popular intellectuals and practices. The language of Victorian moral authority, Gikandi shows, enabled the struggle to overthrow colonialist rule; thus, Victorianism's imperial "embarrassment" consists in the fact that its own values helped to reverse its global conquests. Gikandi restores historical continuity to Victorian and contemporary anti-colonialist subjectivities by tracing the beginnings of this reversal in the mid-nineteenth century, showing how this redeployed Victorianism was—and continues to be—indispensable to what has now come to be called postcolonial culture.

Alongside these political movements, feminism has enjoyed a vexed yet fascinated struggle with its Victorian origins. Laurie Langbauer examines the politics of gender identity and emancipation as focused on the figureheads who adorn those movements. The current feminist scholarly interest in Queen Victoria, Langbauer argues, derives from the tensions she stands for, between an impossible privacy and the "public persona required by institutional needs." Like Victoria, senior feminist faculty find themselves in positions of institutional power and capable of leveraging authority; like Victoria, they perform autobiographical acts of self-sovereignty, seeking to reach out to other women who could never be like—or identify with—themselves. For Langbauer, then, Queen Victoria functions not as a convenient scapegoat for contemporary feminist scholars but as the very model of female identity with which late-twentieth-century women must battle and, ultimately, accept. Susan Lurie demonstrates the ways feminist overvaluations of nineteenth-century sexual enlightenment in the novels of a writer such as Henry James can obscure the profoundly repressive and heterosexist values of such precursors. In her essay on Campion's rewriting of James's homosocial appropriation of feminism, Lurie argues that Campion's uncanny use of discourses that sexualize James's desexualized nineteenth-century feminist heroine nevertheless serves to regulate "female sexuality in the interest of homogenizing U.S. culture and bloodlines." In Campion's film, figures of exoticized immigrant women thus serve to whiten and Americanize femininity. Yet Lurie argues, as well, that Campion critiques her own feminist countererotics, which ironically deploys powerful, even violent, masculine sexuality to introduce Isabel to a proper heterosexuality. Here, the postmodern rewriting of unconventional Victorian sexualities itself becomes capable of being rewritten, as postmodernist cultural texts turn on—or trope—their own move toward revivalism.

Other contributors to *Victorian Afterlife* argue that post-Victorian technologies and modes of cultural production and reproduction mimic or rewrite their nineteenth-century models. From this perspective, postmodern historiography has been profoundly conditioned by the material forms through which it represents or thinks about the past. As Mark Poster has argued elsewhere, postmodern culture emerges, at least in part, through the "dissemination of technologies that reconfigure space and time, the relation of human to machine and mind to body." These technologies, he claims, drastically change "the conditions under which the subject is constituted, indeed even the subject who writes history." In Poster's postmodern epistemology, which focuses on contemporary media, historiographic practices, like technologies of the self, shape the individuals who deploy them. Poster's argument, that technology rescripts the individual and alters historiography, dovetails nicely with Jameson's notions about the historical novel's emergence; for, like nineteenth-century print culture's role in constituting bourgeois individuals, media culture manufactures postmodern selves. "Just as the emergence of the capitalist mode of production promoted stories through which the entire past could be rethought and its history rewritten," Poster argues, "so the emergence of electronics and now digital modes of information opens new positions and instantiates new viewpoints about the past."[14] In addition, post-Victorianism can "reimagine" stories about nineteenth-century technology in order to defamiliarize clichés about Victorian humanism or about technological gradualism.[15] Although the contributors to this volume do not regard these technological shifts as monolithic, a number of them examine contemporary cultural production and reproduction as appropriating Victoriana forcefully to fashion these new viewpoints and positions.

Several of these contributors trace the complex and repressed relationships between contemporary technologies and the Victorian machinery they seem self-evidently to have displaced. As Judith Roof shows, for example, computer technology surprisingly draws its semiotic systems from Victorian graphic design. These graphological appropriations deflect late-twentieth-century anxieties about technology, she argues, making computer users feel that technology is "safe and familiar." In these ways, Roof demonstrates, material culture, too, is embedded in historicity, in textuality, in graphology. This illustrative and graphic rewriting, moreover, which markets information technologies as a matter of "consumer choice," ultimately sustains the economic structures of late-twentieth-century capitalism. For Jay Clayton, postmodern rewritings of the Victorian fascination with information technologies or proto-computers—with "difference engines"—revisit a period when the boundary between science and culture was unstable, when new technologies "troubled the human/machine interface." The "mechanical devices" and "alternative histories" he examines revise received notions of nineteenth-century temporality, foregrounding anachronism and figures of the untimely as a historical mode capable of policing the boundary between what he calls escapism and a "politics of the future," the two primary ideological uses of postmodern fascination with Victorian technology. Thus Victorian technical forms continue to rewrite the present even as some theorists have tried to close their history by affirming, in extravagant terms, the radical newness of postmodern knowledge and computing technology.

Other contributors argue that the technologies of postmodern media culture fetishize or are haunted by Victorian cultural documents. As Jennifer Green-Lewis points out, visual culture has currently identified the bewhiskered, top-hatted, and hoopskirted Victorians as appropriate objects for accumulating and expressing postmodern anxieties about authenticity. Because photographic technologies produce texts replete with "documentary assertiveness," she says, we can "see the Victorians." For Green-Lewis, the currently popular Victorian photograph nurtures postmodern nostalgia even as it sentimentalizes images already nostalgic in the nineteenth century. The aesthetic of visual realism, then, enables us to view the Victorians as confirming our own desires for certainty even as we indulge our pleasures in loss. Like the still camera's framings, twentieth-century cinematic technologies both revive and interrogate the Victorians. Ronald Thomas's study of film's meditations on the signifying potentials of its own technological origins reveals how a Victorian text such as *Dracula* projected a cultural materialist analysis that only postmodern sensibilities can adequately decode. Showing that Victorian illustrative and graphic technologies refigure the visualized, spectacular nature of postmodern culture, Thomas argues that nineteenth-century representational technologies sought to shore up the concept of selves that were increasingly under attack. Early cinema, deploying figures of the "undead," seemed to spellbind its spectators; postmodern

filmic re-visions and hauntings, however, display cinema's power to transform modern subjectivities and our sense of historicity. These essays, then,
examine the ways postmodern modes of reproduction manage contemporary fears about the unstable selves, asynchronous lives, and asymptotic
spaces created by the practices that technology introduces into late-twentieth-
century lives.

Taking the concept of overdetermination to its limits, two contributors
have written about the nineteenth-century emergence of historical reanimation itself. In a self-reflexive, even playful mood, Mary Favret and Hilary
Schor examine the postmodern forms and tropes of "revival" that parody
the popular Victorian obsession with death. Favret foregrounds the trope
and ethos of fidelity in two film adaptations of Jane Austen's novels. Here,
questions of fidelity to Austen's texts, to Austen as icon, to the referent of
classical realism, and to the sourcetext behind the novel-as-film overlap
with questions of sexual fidelity in Austen's plots. This eroticization of the
retrospective imagination, and its figural fixation on the body of a (lost)
lover, produces a meditation on history itself as a form of, or an attempt to
escape, mortality. In postmodern representations of Austen as Victorian,
fidelity to the past might be seen as either "an animating or mortifying
process"; whether the loyal heroine suffers domestic entombment and objectification or achieves worldly (though merely conjugal) success is a question that remains suspended for her contemporary spectators. The ambiguities of reanimation, Favret suggests, compel postmodern culture to link a
passion for the past with the libidinal opposition of Eros and Thanatos.
Hilary Schor traces A. S. Byatt's "resurrection-work"—her shadowy inhabi-
tations of Victorian literary forms and psyches—to argue that postmodern
culture uses Victorian fears of immateriality as a mirror for our own queasi-
ness about resuscitating the past. Reviving and rewriting Victorian interests
in spiritualism, evolution, archaeology, and other excavations of mortality,
Byatt embodies the "ghostly" forms of the past in fictional pastiche, seeing
literary form itself as the encryption of vitality. Schor links three Victorian
responses to physical and formal immateriality—which she calls sorting,
morphing, and mourning—to contemporary concerns with the seemingly
insubstantial yet historically haunted materials worked over by contemporary culture. For Favret and Schor, postmodern resurrections of Victorian
reflections on mortality attempt to locate in the nineteenth century the origins of the historiographical uncertainties plaguing postmodernism.

In the aggregate, then, the essays in *Victorian Afterlife* propose that the network of overdeterminations shaped by economics, sexuality, political struggle, and technological forms privileges the Victorian period as the site of historical emergence through which postmodernism attempts to think its own cultural identity. Yet questions about the political implications of the post-Victorian remain. Indeed, is the political prognosis for the post-Victorian mode, as a form of historical consciousness, as limited as Jameson would have us believe?[16] Is postmodern historicity lost in the prison house of marketable images? Jameson's pessimism about the voracious gobbling up of culture by the system of late capital is shared, in some fashion, by analysts who regard the post-Victorian as a mystified historicist project. Some cultural critics, however, view the post-Victorian mode as politically productive, as offering effective strategies for the fashioning of political positions, values, and subjectivities. This anthology does not offer a definitive answer to these political questions, but stages a sharp debate.

In this debate, half of the contributors have argued that post-Victorianism is, in various ways, a collective misrepresentation not simply of "history itself," but of the very nature of historical knowledge. They have focused on the roots of postmodern historiography in commodification, but they have also defined a variety of particularized epistemological failures within postmodern historiography: the fallacious nature of periodization itself, a project that, as John McGowan points out, postmodernism has inherited, ironically, from the Victorians; the retrospective projection of contemporary anxieties about authenticity into the nineteenth century, which Green-Lewis finds to be yet another symptom of postmodern "nostalgia for the real"; the coercive demand of contemporary sexual politics for teleologies of liberation, as diagnosed by Waldrep, Lurie, and Favret; the management of technological anxiety through faux Victorian display graphics, which Roof views as serving the interests of consumer capitalism. In this set of essays, then, the postmodern "loss of history" is indicted for a range of analytic dysfunctions. These include simple misreading of the events of history, as well as more complex forms of ideological complicity with postmodernism's efforts to read the past only as the self-congratulatory story of its own emergence. This volume itself, moreover, and its attempt to define postmodern "culture" on the basis of period generalizations, however qualified, is not exempt from this critique of historical mystification.

The other half of the contributors, however, have argued that the post-Victorian can reread history in socially and politically progressive ways. This potency appears most commonly in the intertextuality of postmodern historiography, in which contemporary epistemological convictions can be seen to have enabled a dialogic, rather than a positivist, vision of history as text. It may also appear through instances of current mythmaking that, in the irredeemable absence of a genuinely "historical" ground of any kind, productively use fictions of the Victorian past as pragmatic instruments within political struggle. Although none of the contributors presents a full-fledged theorization of postmodern history as intertextuality, several have defined potentials for historicized self-understanding in post-Victorianism, potentials that argue for the ideological efficacy of postmodern image-production. They illustrate as well the concomitant dangers of interpretively reducing such images to causal origins in commodification, nostalgia, or epistemological narcissism. These essays ascribe to the postmodern conviction that history is always already discursive, and, in that sense, always changing. They subscribe, however implicitly, to versions of intertextual historiography affirmed by postmodern theorists and neopragmatists, from Dominick LaCapra to Hayden White to Richard Rorty. Arguing for the interdisciplinary and intertextual nature of history, LaCapra defines the historical project as "a 'dialogic' exchange both with the past and with others inquiring into it."[17] This belief can be ideologically enabling if the search for historical origins—Jameson's "nature"—is replaced by a historical project that, as Foucault puts it, "disturbs what was previously considered immobile," "fragments what was thought unified," and "shows the heterogeneity of what was imagined consistent with itself."[18] These projects, then, counter a totalizing political pessimism about postmodern culture in the age of global capital.

This volume as a whole suggests that any intertextual historical analysis of this kind must come to terms with postmodern historicity's emphasis on nineteenth-century emergence. In other words, it must confront the historically specific questions of economic, psychosexual, material, and political emergence that haunt postmodern identity. Essays in the second half of this volume do precisely that, taking up the political question of postmodern emergence not as a compulsive vision, doomed to a circularity in which anything like "the past" is forever lost, but instead as a terrain of intertextual exploration deeply engaged with nineteenth-century textuality in local and particular cases. Gikandi thus documents how elements of Victorian ideology can be turned back against themselves to counter imperialism; Langbauer and Baucom remythologize Victorian events and icons to make them newly available for politically self-conscious subjectivities; Israel excavates the political ambiguities embedded in discourses of Victorian sexuality; Schor represents literary form, particularly pastiche, as actively engaging the problematics of postmodern historiography; Clayton foregrounds anachronism and figures of the untimely as historical modes appropriate for postmodern rewriting; and Thomas displays the power of emergent cinematic technologies for transforming Victorian characters into modern subjects. Documenting how the present reads the past, and also how the past can read the present, these essays demonstrate that postmodern reflections on emergence can generate the discovery of differences, and possibly beginnings—if not origins. They can replace a search for Jameson's "breaks" with a more Foucauldian search, patient and documentary, for "beginnings, atavisms, and heredities."[19] These essays recognize that it is impossible to decode postmodern historicity only in the light of a nondiscursive historical formation, and instead seek to interrogate the discursive complexities of postmodern interest in historical emergence as the condition for our own cultural critique and our own historical knowledge.

Nancy Armstrong's "Postscript" concludes by defining the conditions for our own cultural critique and historical knowledge. A polemical tour de force, Armstrong's essay articulates the political implications of asking what is, and what is not, "Victorian" about postmodernism, showing in the process how the contemporary reemergence of Victorian conventions and rewritings parallels resurgent anxieties about the erosion of culture itself. Armstrong reframes this collection's concerns and obsessions by equating appprehensions about free-floating postmodern discursivity with fears about national identity: what imagined community does postmodern culture— with all its apparent disregard for the social or historical referents of cultural products—effectively legitimate? Armstrong argues passionately for the value of a postmodern theoretical knowledge that specifies how dominant systems of representation produce social groups. Citing 1960s political theater as initiating a strategic cultural politics, she claims that postmodern cultural understanding can contribute to social change. In the absence of a recovered "original" behind the social classification of individuals, she argues, the differential system of social types itself should be our primary critical object, because "how people are represented may well be who they are." In her own historical rewriting, Armstrong constructs a post-Victorian cultural politics by locating in the 1960s an alternative periodized moment in which postmodern awareness can be said to have emerged.

The debate about the political meaning of historical rewriting—about the mystifications or the productivity of the post-Victorian as a historiographic practice—is not one this book pretends to resolve. The contributors themselves have often not marked out their positions declaratively but have rendered them implicit in the critical choices they have made about their Victorian subject material and their historicizing arguments. To some degree, contributors in the first half of the volume have chosen to critique postmodern culture through readings of Victorian culture, whereas contributors to the second half have chosen to produce a new post-Victorianism by reading the nineteenth century through a postmodern analytics—although this would be too reductive a distinction. At stake on both sides of this debate is a sense that history matters, even if its narrativization in postmodern culture is plural and diffuse. None of the contributors, for example, subscribes to the liberatory, ahistorical view of postmodernism trumpeted most loudly perhaps by Jean-François Lyotard, in his rallying cry that the postmodern "in whatever age" is the shattering of belief in master narratives and the "discovery of the 'lack of reality' of reality, together with the invention of other realities."[20] We see the emergence of the debate that structures this anthology, rather, as an opening for the profoundly important analysis of the conditions of postmodern historicity and of postmodernism itself as a reflection on historical knowledge. *Victorian Afterlife* thus takes up but does not complete the challenge to define the fantasies of postmodern emergence that have privileged the nineteenth century as the essence of the past. We hope to provide instead multiple ways to measure the ideological motives and effects of a postmodern history that inevitably "forgets" the past, or remembers it by trying to imagine it as present, or fashions its past by retelling the history of its present.

Notes

1. *Clueless,* directed by Amy Heckerling, with Alicia Silverstone, Paul Rudd, Stacey Dash, and Brittany Murphy. Paramount, 1995.

2. Fredric Jameson, *Postmodernism, or, the Cultural Logic of Late Capitalism* (Durham, N.C.: Duke University Press, 1991), ix.

3. Jameson has, in fact, come under fire for the more totalizing aspects of his work on postmodernism, including his attempts at periodization. For a good summary, see Michael Walsh, "Jameson and 'Global Aesthetics,'" in *Post-Theory: Reconstructing Film Theory,* ed. David Bordwell and Noël Carroll (Madison: University of Wisconsin Press, 1996), 481–500.

4. A recent anthology of essays that addresses this postmodern historicity is Stephen Baker, *Signs of Change: Premodern, Modern, Postmodern* (Albany: State University of New York Press, 1996), but this collection charts historical change straightforwardly, reading the postmodern largely in terms of its discontinuities with earlier periods, rather than exploring the dynamics of historical mystification and/or intertextuality that is at the heart of this volume's project. Robert Kiely's *Reverse Tradition: Postmodern Fictions and the Nineteenth-Century Novel* (Cambridge: Harvard University Press, 1993) performs its own hybridization of nineteenth-century and postmodern texts, rather than analyzing texts devoted themselves to such hybridization. Frederick M. Holmes's *The Historical Imagination: Postmodernism and the Treatment of the Past in Contemporary British Fiction* (Victoria, B.C.: University of Victoria Press, 1997) explores figurations of nineteenth-century subject matter in postmodern fiction, but not the engagement of postmodern texts with nineteenth-century texts. Elizabeth Deeds Ermarth, *Sequel to History: Postmodernism and the Crisis of Representational Time* (Princeton, N.J.: Princeton University Press, 1992), uses a few contemporary texts to advocate the elimination of history as a referent for temporal imaginings. Many shorter studies touch on various questions about postmodern returns to Victorian texts; two of the most substantial are Carole Siegel, "Postmodern Women Writers Review Victorian Male Masochism," *Genders* 11 (1991): 1–16; and Garrett Stewart, "Film's Victorian Retrofit," *Victorian Studies* 38.2 (1995): 153–98.

5. Linda Hutcheon, *A Poetics of Postmodernism: History, Theory, Fiction* (London: Routledge, 1988), 5.

6. The "welfare debate" of 1995–96 in the United States, for example, repeatedly invoked the Victorians. Politicians and political scientists on both ideological sides of the struggle raised the specter of Charles Dickens, *Oliver Twist*, and the social problems of drunkenness, illegitimate births, poverty, and filth that could be cured by the "Victorian virtues." See, for example, Katherine Q. Seelye, "Gingrich Looks to Victorian Age to Cure Today's Social Failings," *New York Times*, 14 March 1995, A19; Frances Fox Piven, "From Workhouse to Workfare," *New York Times*, 1 August 1996, A27; Jerry Gray, "Federal Budget Finally Emerges" (rpt. *New York Times*), *Portland Press Herald*, 25 April 1996, A1, A16. In the last of these three, Representative Pat Williams, D-Montana, is portrayed as holding a small bowl aloft, "as though he were an orphan begging for food. 'Please Mr. Gingrich, may I have some more?'" he intones, suggesting the inadequacy of nineteenth-century welfare institutions to address late-twentieth-century social needs—and apparently failing to understand his own reference to Dickens's melodramatic polemic against the workhouse (A16).

7. Some literary critics have followed in Himmelfarb's tracks by seeing forms of post-Victorianism as a reassertion of stable concepts of morality and personal agency against a degenerate postmodernism. See Kelly A. Marsh, "The Neo-Sensation Novel: A Contemporary Genre in the Victorian Tradition," *Philological Quarterly* 74 (1995): 99–123; or Frederick M. Holmes, "The Historical Imagination and the Victorian Past: A. S. Byatt's *Possession*," *English Studies in Canada* 20 (1994): 319–34. This moral totalization of periods is more often played the other way, however, with

postmodern "open-mindedness" seen as a liberation of moral sensibility from the reductive constraints of Victorian ethics. See, for example, David W. Landrum, "Rewriting Marx: Emancipation and Restoration in *The French Lieutenant's Woman*," *Twentieth-Century Literature* 42 (1996): 103–13.

8. Gertrude Himmelfarb, *The De-Moralization of Society: From Victorian Virtues to Modern Values* (New York: Alfred A. Knopf, 1995), 34, 77, 80–81.

9. *Old-House Interiors* 2.2 (fall 1996): 42–57.

10. John McGowan sums up Jameson's theory as the "insistence that postmodernism as a temporal term designates a historical period that is to be identified by a set of characteristics that operate across the whole historical terrain" (*Postmodernism and Its Critics* [Ithaca, N.Y.: Cornell University Press, 1991], 181).

11. Andreas Huyssen, *After the Great Divide: Modernism, Mass Culture, Postmodernism* (Bloomington: Indiana University Press, 1986), 170.

12. Giovanni Arrighi, *The Long Twentieth Century: Money, Power, and the Origins of Our Times* (London: Verso, 1994), 159–300.

13. The best critique remains Aijaz Ahmad, "Jameson's Rhetoric of Otherness and the 'National Allegory,'" *Social Text* 17 (1987): 3–25.

14. Mark Poster, *Cultural History and Postmodernity: Disciplinary Readings and Challenges* (New York: Columbia University Press, 1997), 12.

15. See, for example, Herbert Sussman, "Cyberpunk Meets Charles Babbage: *The Difference Engine* as Alternative Victorian History," *Victorian Studies* 38 (1994): 1–23.

16. See Patrice Petro, "After Shock/Between Boredom and History," in *Fugitive Images: From Photography to Video,* ed. Patrice Petro (Bloomington: Indiana University Press, 1995), 265, for an important argument with Jameson's claim that "nostalgia art neither annihilates history nor completely effaces its ideological relationship to the past" (279). Petro argues instead that the prominence of boredom with historical reproductions that is inscribed in much postmodern "nostalgia art" denaturalizes the falsification of history through repetitive and banal images, making possible a metacritical interrogation of the relationship between past and present.

17. Dominick LaCapra, *History and Criticism* (Ithaca, N.Y.: Cornell University Press, 1985), 9.

18. Interview in Allan Megill, *Prophets of Extremity: Nietzsche, Heidegger, Foucault, Derrida* (Berkeley and Los Angeles: University of California Press, 1985), 235.

19. Michel Foucault, "Nietzsche, Genealogy, History," in *Language, Counter-Memory, Practice,* ed. Donald Bouchard (Ithaca, N.Y.: Cornell University Press, 1977), 145.

20. Jean-François Lyotard, *The Postmodern Condition: A Report on Knowledge,* trans. Geoff Bennington and Brian Massumi (Minneapolis: University of Minnesota Press, 1984), 81.

mystifications

Modernity and Culture, the Victorians and Cultural Studies

John McGowan

John Stuart Mill begins his 1831 essay "The Spirit of the Age" with the conviction that his very subject matter is new:

> The "Spirit of the Age" is in some measure a novel expression. I do not believe that it is to be met with in any work exceeding fifty years in antiquity. The idea of comparing one's own age with former ages, or with our notion of those which are yet to come, had occurred to philosophers; but it never before was itself the dominant idea of any age.[1]

My thesis in this essay is, in some ways, a simple one. I will argue that the very enterprise of this book marks our Victorianism. We inherit the proclivity to characterize eras, to read the events and fashions of a particular historical moment, as indices of an era's "spirit," its profound way of being, from a group of German-influenced English writers who were the first literary (or artistic) intellectuals cum social critics: Samuel Taylor Coleridge, John Stuart Mill, Thomas Carlyle, John Ruskin, Matthew Arnold, Harriet Martineau, George Eliot, and William Morris, to name just a few.[2] These intellectuals had basically the same ambitions and followed the same methods characteristic of cultural studies at the end of the twentieth century: they aimed to intervene in their society by explaining the age to itself.

But my thesis is complicated by the fact that I want both to trace the consequences of proceeding from the assumption that an era has a spirit and to try to be skeptical about that assumption. My exploration of this terrain

3

will unfold in three sections. The first connects the notion of a zeitgeist to the corollary concepts of the "modern" and of "culture." The second considers how the basic categories describing political orientation—left, right, center—since the French Revolution derive from the concept of the modern. Finally, I want to turn back upon my whole essay and speculate on what the critical enterprise would look like if we somehow managed to dispense with the "modern" and "culture" as signposts. This last move is crucial because I am guilty, throughout these pages, of the very patterns I wish to question. I am operating close to the limits of my own intellectual paradigms—which, of course, following zeitgeist logic, I deem others' paradigms as well.

The Modern and Culture

Mill's "The Spirit of the Age" is a great place to start because it offers just about every notion entailed in the belief that time is divided into "ages" in its first five pages and because its identification of searching out the zeitgeist as itself "the dominant idea of [the] age" already pushes almost to the point of parody the whole enterprise. Mill provides a new way of doing intellectual work, and the concept of "the dominant" is essential to this new paradigm. The spirit of any era cannot be described unless the plurality of actions, motives, and beliefs of human beings is organized according to a rubric that identifies the dominant, the truly determinative. What explains, what gives meaning to, the individual event or utterance? The answer, since 1800, has very often been "modernity," understood as a relational matrix within which particulars are held.

Isobel Armstrong follows Mill's characterization of his age almost exactly when she stresses the "modernism" of the Victorians, a modernism best indicated by their attention to change:

> Victorian modernism . . . describes itself as belonging to a condition of crisis which has emerged directly from economic and cultural change. In fact, Victorian poetics begins to conceptualise the idea of culture as a category and includes itself within the definition. . . . [T]o be 'new' or 'modern' . . . was to confront and self-consciously to conceptualise *as* new elements that are still perceived as the constitutive forms of our own condition.[3]

To understand ourselves—or those from the past whom we study—is to examine the "dominant" or "constitutive" lineaments of thought, belief, values, and practices. And part of being "modern" is to have self-consciously taken up this critical task.

Mary Poovey's work offers a sophisticated and highly influential contemporary version of reading particulars in relation to an overarching modernity. Her theoretical goal is to avoid a simplistic mapping of part to whole; adopting Louis Althusser's definition of ideology, she wants, like him, to short-circuit an "expressive" model in which the part expresses unproblematically the qualities of the modern matrix.[4] Rather, the part stands in tension with that matrix, which it both contests through the inadvertent mobilization of contradictions and "reproduces" through the symbolic resolution of those contradictions (123). The novel *David Copperfield* thus "construct[s] the reader as a particular kind of subject—a psychologized, classed, developmental individual" that "*is* the modern subject," *and* also indicates "the contradictions inherent in this subject" (90). The both/and relationship of *David Copperfield* to the ideological constitution of the social field is generalized to all literary texts: "'Literature' cannot exist outside a system of social and institutional relations, and in a society characterized by systematic class and gender inequality, literature reproduces the system that makes it what it is" (123). But literary texts can also "expose the operations of ideology within class society" because "they provide the site at which shared anxieties and tensions can surface as well as be symbolically addressed" (124). (Poovey does not consider whether "exposure" might be a subset of "reproduction." In other words, must exposure always threaten an ideology? Is an ideology consciously held always more vulnerable than one that is unexposed? If so, why?)

I want to highlight three features of Poovey's work. First, the significance of *David Copperfield* rests on its connection to "shared anxieties" and the construction/exposure of the modern subject. In other words, both meaning and knowledge here rely on identifying an overarching constitutive framework (historically limited though it be to one era and one place) to which the literary text is related. Second, the critic's work is absolutely vital because that framework is "the very condition of its [the novel's] intelligibility . . . even if the reader is not conscious of this pattern" (90). The epistemically privileged critic describes these conditions of intelligibility.[5] Third, despite Poovey's insistence that "causation is never unidirectional," it is hard to see how texts are more than reactionary in her view (18). *David Copperfield* "reproduces" (not *produces*) modern subjecthood, which seems inevitable because there is no sense in Poovey that a text could rewrite the very terms of intelligibility. Textual reproductions do introduce differences, but the processes by which fundamental changes (from a premodern to a modern subject, say) would occur are less clear, although we are told "that the conditions that produce both texts and (partly through them) individual subjects are material in the ever elusive last instance" (17). These (material) "conditions of intelligibility," then, are the container within which the parts are held or, to switch metaphors, the subbasement on which all particulars rest. Only this working assumption justifies the general statements about the Victorian context that undergird all the individual readings in Poovey's book. For example, within the general contention that the movement from the eighteenth to the nineteenth century can be characterized by "the consolidation of bourgeois power," she can claim that during the Victorian era, "as the liberal discourse of rights and contracts began to dominate representations of social, economic, and political relations . . . virtue was depoliticized, moralized, and associated with the domestic sphere, which was being abstracted at the same time . . . from the so-called public sphere of competition, self-interest, and economic aggression" (10). This dominance of liberal discourses could be and was contested in all kinds of ways in Poovey's readings; what is not possible is to write a text that is not related to the framework of intelligibility created by that dominant discourse. The priority of framework to text justifies the vocabulary of Poovey's literary criticism: texts "expose" contradictions that are "inherent" in the modern subject and in modern ideology" (124, 90).

My uneasiness with this type of criticism stems somewhat from a skepticism about generalizations. To characterize Victorian ideology is always ham-handed—and generates both endless revisionist histories that contest previous generalizations by way of citing specific counterinstances and repeated efforts to stake out ever wider conceptualizations of the fundamental conditions so that everything will be caught in their net. Such generalizations become more vacuous, less perspicacious, the wider they become. The irony of Poovey's work is that she recognizes the need for and brilliantly exemplifies focused engagements with the specific, yet still can only theorize the significance of such engagements through anchoring them in the wide generalizations. What I really want to question is not historical accuracy, but the models of meaning, knowledge, and the social that zeitgeist thinking implies. Must we assume that the meaning of individual acts and texts unfolds against or in relation to the backdrop of a containing social context? What kind of knowledge does work like Poovey's claim to provide and what does it imagine the consequences of producing such knowledge? Must we know the conditions of intelligibility to alter them? Does knowing the conditions of intelligibility in 1850 impact on our relation to the conditions of intelligibility in our own day? Is there any way to keep identified contexts from spiraling out into concatenated relations with other contexts to eventually form a totalized image of the social field? I want to ask: Is pluralism possible? And I also want to know why pluralism is so hard. The logic of criticism seems to push us to ever widening fields of relation. What would it take to argue that some one thing is not related in any way to some other thing? Any criticism that talks of "shared anxieties" or, even more globally, of "conditions of intelligibility" that are beyond conscious awareness is not likely to recognize unrelated spheres of human endeavor, except across the gulf that separates one era or one culture from another. Spice up your totality with tensions and contradictions to the max, there will still be a container postulated as guarantor that the bits are in relation to one another.

Before tackling the pluralist question, however, I want to examine the assumptions of zeitgeist thinking a bit further. For starters, such work is oriented toward questions of power and identity. It seeks to answer the question "who are we" and to identify what or who made us that way. We express our identities through what we produce and consume, but such expression is constrained (at least) and determined (at worst) by the matrix within which we live. Thus the project of a book like this one: the various authors collected here will identify various characteristics of the 1980s and 1990s on the basis of contemporary productions and consumptions of "the Victorian."

The names offered for the constitutive framework vary—culture, ideology, habitus, lifeworld, national character. The social critic's task is to describe us to ourselves; we live the life underwritten by the present age, but only half consciously. We are the very stuff of culture, but not fully aware of how culture is the very stuff of each one of our individual selves. We suffer from delusions of individuality.

Of these various names, I am particularly interested in modernity and culture, because of the current prominence of cultural studies, multiculturalism, and the like, and because the terms *modernity* and *culture* have a complicated history, sometimes related, sometimes not. Zeitgeist discourse is ostensibly temporal. The division of time into "then" and "now," into "pre-modern" and "modern," has been a primary organizing device of intellectual analysis since the end of the eighteenth century. The whole rhetoric of "development" as applied to nations and to children relies on a unified, holistic model of time in which all humans can be tracked and the location of various behaviors as "modern" or "advanced" is not taken as problematic. This diachronic scale assumes continual change, so that what was modern yesterday will not be particularly modern tomorrow. Change does not necessarily sweep the old away entirely, and so we get Althusser's "uneven developments" or Raymond Williams's "residual, emergent, and dominant."[6] Such concepts try to explain why the "modern" is not everywhere present in modern times.

Culture enters because once temporal analyses admit different paces of change, it is tempting to isolate the differential spatially in order to still be able to identify the modern. In other words, if the modern is inextricably mixed in with the premodern everywhere, then how does it effectively act out its modernity? The holistic assumptions in the term *modernity* discourage analyses that cannot separate out the modern from the nonmodern. Grafted on top of the temporal differentiation of modern/nonmodern, then, is a spatial differentiation. These two things both exist in the same moment in time, but one is modern and one is not. How can that be? Culture provides the answer. Some places and the people who inhabit them are less modern, more resistant to change, than others. It is their culture—a set of habits, beliefs, and practices that characterizes them as a group—that explains this resistance.

We can see immediately that the concept of "culture" makes the same unified and holistic assumptions that inform the concept of zeitgeist.[7] But culture stands in an ambiguous relation to temporal discourses. In Johann Gottfried Herder's work, "culture" serves to resist the yardstick of modernity; his arguments for the incommensurability of cultures claims that modernity does not give us a way to judge all cultures together.[8] Certainly in our own time raising the banner of culture has been a persistent and perhaps the most successful (if never fully so) strategy in battles against modernization. But the holism of culture has also made it easier to characterize peoples as "backward," "primitive," "underdeveloped," and the like; in such cases, the discourses of modernity and of culture work hand in glove.

I am even more interested, however, in how a discourse of culture supplements the temporal discourse of modernity imagistically. If all humans now live in a modern moment, their different relations to the modern can only be figured in spatial terms. The temporal, it seems to me, is inevitably abstract in a way the spatial is not. The modern is an abstract notion to which we are all held accountable. We are judged in terms of our relation to the cutting edge, the up to date. But the image of that most current thing is always out ahead of us; it must be continually produced (at various sites from the Hollywood studios to corporate research and development units to "original" academic research) because it is so seldom (if ever) lived. The modern is rarely concretely possessed—and only fleetingly before it becomes obsolete. The spatial is what we live, that messy compromise between the traditional/habitual and the new. If the modern has its own abstract unity by virtue of an imagined development that is not "uneven," then the spatial has the unity of its messy mixture of old and new secured by the concept "culture." Here, we say, is a lived life that coheres, that functions. The unity and holism that informs the notion of zeitgeist attains local habitation and a name in culture, understood in the anthropological sense as "a whole way of life."

Modernity in its full purity is never lived anywhere; thus the (presumed) unity of the lived must be designated otherwise. In some discourses, culture then becomes a way to explain the modern's inability to fully install itself. Proponents of modernization will talk (as does Edward Burnett Tylor in his 1871 classic *Primitive Culture*) of "survivals," pieces of the past that a culture cannot or will not give up.[9] Dystopic views of modernization will insist that its predilection for endless change dissolves various stabilities (designated as "traditional" and "cultural") necessary to life.

Mill takes a more middle-of-the-road position: "The first of the leading peculiarities of the present age is, that it is an age of transition. Mankind have outgrown old institutions and old doctrines, and have not yet acquired new ones" (30). It is commonplace to quote Matthew Arnold's "Stanzas from the Grande Chartreuse" at this point—"Wandering between two worlds, one dead, / The other powerless to be born, / With nowhere yet to rest my head"—and to attribute Victorian melancholy and doubt to the fact that Mill was right. The Victorians exist in an uneasy transition from Romanticism to Modernism (if you are doing literary history) and from the premodern to the modern (if you are doing history history). But my claim is that the very notion of the modern inevitably places us in a moment of transition. The modern is always out in front of us. The abstract ideal of the modern leads us to ask anxiously in every moment, "Are we being modern yet?" And the answer, inevitably, is "not quite yet."

This anxiety can be assuaged somewhat (never fully) by shifting the focus from the temporal (modernity) to the spatial (culture). One strategy is to celebrate what we have now: our culture. Here an attempt is made to escape the tyranny of temporal judgments by affirming what is and has been over what is to come. Culturalism of this sort is a hallmark of Lyotardian postmodernism, which sometimes pursues a policy of trying to value the local and particular apart from the master narrative of progress and development.[10] It is worthwhile to note that culturalism is hardly a new strategy; arguably, the majority of the world's population since 1500 on (meaning, in large part, the non-European populations who had to confront the imposed presence of Europeans) has never been modern if being modern entails a fundamental valuation of change as continual and as an improvement. What is new in postmodernism is only the first adoption by leftist intellectuals of spatial over temporal priorities.

Culturalism, however, seems only fitfully successful. The lure of the modern is not easy to cast aside. Syncretism—various deals with the devil—seems the order of our day. Even the most fervent attempts to maintain cultural integrity tolerate various kinds of accommodation with the modern, while a self-conscious theatricality inflects many efforts to live traditional cultures. The prefix "re" becomes crucial: cultural practices are reenacted, revitalized, reproduced, represented. The staged, ritual character of these events marks their quaintness. They exist only within the charmed space of reenactment.

I do not want to trivialize all attempts to maintain traditional cultures. Many such efforts are (all too) deadly earnest. But earnest efforts will inevitably court fanaticism because only constant vigilance, an obsession with purity, can keep out all traces of the new. At one end of the spectrum, culturalism is weekend playacting, dressing in clothes you would never wear during the week, and performing/watching "traditional" activities that have no part in daily modern life. At the other end of the spectrum, culturalism is an attempt to say a thunderous "no" to modernity in all its forms. Not surprisingly, most expressions of culturalism fall somewhere between these two extremes, leaving us in a hybrid space that feels both unsettled and peculiarly (postmodernly?) ours. When I name my children Kiernan and

Siobhan, I really do not know what I am doing, since I long ago opted out of the last piece of my Irish heritage (Roman Catholicism) that marked me as in any way Irish. So why this ethnic gesture in naming my children? What bit of Irishness beyond pretty names am I wishing upon them?

A certain kind of contemporary humor plays this doubleness to the hilt. We love the image of the Navaho rug maker who tells us she can only weave while watching TV because the weaving is so monotonous. Tourism and Hollywood play this doubleness somewhat differently. The staged past both calls us to a quaint life less hectic, less comfortable, less complex than our own *and* reassures us of our modernity. We get to be proud of being modern (at least, more modern than they) while also indulging in the fantasy of sloughing off the burden of modernity. The fate of the Victorian as marker of the past in the late twentieth century reveals that our current time sense not only involves a modernity always fading out in front of us into the far future, but also the receding of the past. If my students are any indication, the past today comes in two flavors: Victorian and then some obscure, undifferentiated far past beyond the Victorian, a time when people lived in castles (or was it caves?) and knights in armor tilted at dinosaurs.

Although their period was the modern for Mill, Carlyle, and Ruskin, the Victorian is now quintessentially the past, the period against which we gauge our own modernness. The Bloomsbury group played a large role in this transformation of the Victorian into the nonmodern by introducing the (subsequently) endlessly repeated narrative of our (ambivalent) progress around sexuality. No restaging of Victorian life is complete without reassuring us that we are more enlightened sexually than those repressed Victorians. (For my students, interestingly, the salient belief is not that the Victorians were sexually repressed, but that all their marriages were arranged by tyrannical parents.) Yet many of these restagings also ruefully contrast the complexities of our sexual world against the simplicities of the Victorian (when men were men, and women were women—and they liked it that way). The film version of *A Room with a View* offers a perfect example. For starters, it pushes E. M. Forster's tale from Edwardian times firmly back into the Victorian. Then it ridicules Victorian prudishness throughout. But we also get the joyous innocence of the men's naked bathing, untroubled by the threat of homosexuality (either Forster's or our own).

I much prefer the film version of Henry James's *Wings of the Dove,* located in a transitional period, between the Victorian and the modern. From my point of view, of course, the issue is not whether such a transitional time ever really existed, but that viewing any time as transitional is one of the hallmarks of the problematic of the modern. The film, however, locates that transitional moment in the past, not in the here and now (as Mill and Arnold do). Still, it is trying to break down the easy assumption that we know who the Victorians are (repressed premoderns) and who we are (enlightened moderns). And it tries to make us see that James's characters, although dressed in ways we associate with simpler times, occupy a social landscape every bit as complex, as unscripted and undernormed, as our own. The rules of the game, which designate social standing and suitable sexual partners, are all changing in the world the film presents, so that the possibilities for and significance of actions are radically unclear. The film suggests that things are often in flux, that our assumption of simpler, more innocent, times is backward projection, not historical accuracy. But it, like *A Room with a View,* is still structured around the comparative question of our modernness against theirs.

Cultural studies, it seems to me, continually traverses the same ground, albeit with a different orientation. It posits features of modernity generally seen as negative—the development of capitalism (whether monopoly or late or global) and of the bureaucratic state—and then considers the relative positioning of various groups ("subcultures") in relation to that modernity, gauging which groups are better equipped to resist it. In both the films and cultural studies, a fundamental ambivalence about modernity is probed; modern sexual mores, modern styles, modern music, and modern secularism are generally (although not always) affirmed, while modern corporatism (whether economic or political) and modern anomie are condemned via nostalgia for past communities or celebration of the solidarity of subcultures.

Modernity also fosters ambivalence because the only possible answer to the question of whether we are being modern yet is "Yes and no." No, we will never be fully modern, because the modern is out in front of us. Yes, we are modern because immersed in constant change, the surest sign of modernity. If we live in a world where change is the norm, then we live in the modern world. The modern is its own continual negation. Anything substantial, no matter how advanced, will yield in its turn to the even further advanced. We cannot, substantively, be modern. But we can (must?) have the *form* of modernity, a form that requires an odd ascesis, a withholding of full investment in any substantial thing. Computers offer an extreme version of this relationship to things and time. A computer is outdated a month after its purchase. This obsolescence is not simply a result of our cultivated craving for the new, but stems also from the need to be in touch with our contemporaries.[11] We cannot communicate with others if we lag behind them. We all need to be on the same page in the book of (modern) time. But how can we be on the same page in a speed-reading world of constant change? *Culture* is a term that taps the brakes. We can say something about the here and now, identify regularities and stabilities within the horizon of change, through the concept of culture. It is our pole star within the swirling heavens.

Let me summarize the argument thus far before taking up the way we chart political positions in relation to this narrative of modernity. What interests me is the organization of much intellectual work around two concepts that I see as related to each other supplementally. The temporal concept judges events, practices, and social structures according to their modernity, their development. But this model also posits a holistic matrix within which change occurs. Modernity is a dynamic whole, nowhere fully present, but a process that figures prominently (often determinately) in the constitution of particulars. The spatial concept "culture" gives the here and now a coherence that modernity (always in transition) cannot provide. Various elements of culture can be judged as more or less modern. Culture can be a rallying point against the blackmail of the modern, but it also assuages the anxiety of not being modern enough. Maybe we are not fully modern yet, but that culture over there is even less modern than we.

"Modernity" and "culture" between them organize a huge amount of our intellectual landscape (most prevalently in the humanities and the social sciences). Mapping the particular to the modern and/or to the cultural began with the Victorians and has become particularly prominent among American academics since the early 1980s.[12] Current efforts to map the Victorian (either to characterize a shared Victorian culture or to identify the clashing forces within a contradiction-ridden social matrix) hoist certain Victorian writers (Mill, Carlyle, and Ruskin especially) on their own petard.

The Modern and the Political

I want to turn now to the use of modernity as a political measuring rod. The terms *left* and *right* in their political sense are contemporaneous with the "discovery of time" and the birth of the term *culture*.[13] Dating from the French Revolution, left and right are coordinated with responses to change.

Actually, there are three possibilities: left, right, and liberal. The liberal is the champion of modernity, at home in its cities, and a proponent of its economic and social arrangements, which are legitimated as the best possible (in an imperfect world) ways to approach justice (on the basis of meritocracy) and freedom (civil rights and free enterprise). Mill is, of course, the great spokesman for liberalism in the Victorian age. And he, along with Arnold, points toward one version (the Ted Kennedy variety) of twentieth-century liberalism when he abandons laissez-faire positions in favor of state interference in training, protecting, and rewarding citizen-workers. Nowadays, we think of laissez-faire liberals as conservatives or rightists, sometimes called neoconservatives, less often called neoliberals. The last label is the most accurate historically. The important point here is that the definition of left and right today in the United States (things are different in other parts of the world) represents the complete triumph of liberalism, which has split in two since 1789, thus giving us our current internecine struggles between interventionist liberals and laissez-faire liberals. Both groups are proponents of modernity, which means they favor economic and technological growth, change, and innovation; they support rights-based democracy; and they are adherents of market economics.

Liberalism's middle-aged paunch has pushed nonliberal versions of left and right to the margins. Nonliberal positions are characterized by attempts to reject modernity *tout court.* (As with culturalism, such attempts in politics are often compromised in one way or another, which yields the usual obsessions with purity and the inevitable schismatic breakdowns into splinter groups asserting their integrity against the complicities of their erstwhile allies.) The rightists can be characterized as premoderns, nostalgic for premodern social and economic arrangements. During the Victorian era, rightists were often medievalists, pointing to that age of faith and social hierarchies as a model for a just and well-ordered society. The defining concern of true-blue rightism is order. The right's prime objection to modernity is its chaos, its anomie, its individualistic anarchy. (Thus, when a liberal such as Arnold plays the anarchy card in a text like *Culture and Anarchy,* he is halfway to becoming a reactionary.) In this view, modern political and social arrangements undermine all authority and leave the unchecked individual to do as he or she pleases, while modern economic arrangements promote the war of all against all in unbridled competition. Modern society lacks any "social glue," principles of authority or bonds of affection, respect, or obligation that establish relations beyond interest-driven give-and-take in political and economic bargaining. Patriotism, and its cousins ethnic and racial loyalties/ hatreds, have, in practice, proved the most potent elixirs concocted to prevent modern societies from dissolving into the individualistic war of each against all. Perhaps if we could reassess the threat and lose this fixation on the bogeyman of anomie, we would be spared cures that have been disastrous while addressing a disease that has never manifested itself.

In our own day, premodernism flourishes fitfully among "cultural conservatives," a group the Republican Party in the United States managed to incorporate and exploit during the 1980s, but which damaged that party in presidential elections in the 1990s. The increased visibility of culturalism and various fundamentalisms in religion during the last quarter of the twentieth century demonstrates that abhorrence of modernity and all of its works still exists. For much of the world's population, modernity has brought no palpable benefits, and the program of jettisoning the modern entirely in favor of the premodern "survivals" that have persisted alongside the modern has gained new and vocal adherents. Such movements have highlighted the extent to which modernity is the province of (primarily professional) elites. Workers in the West were brought into modernity's fold before World War II through nationalistic patriotism, racism, or brute force, and after World War II through economic participation in prosperity. But the move toward a global economy has widened the economic gap between professional (upper) middle classes and less skilled (lower) middle classes, a widening that has made the cultural gaps (which had never disappeared) between these two groups prominent once again.

There are various litmus tests for attitudes toward the modern, for marking the gulf between the sophisticated elites who feel at home in modernity and the much larger numbers who have never experienced modernity as anything more than a threat. Three such tests are attitudes toward religion, toward cities, and toward ethnic identities. The liberal proponent of modernity (whether Democrat or Republican) is likely to be a-religious, at ease in large cities (even if living in the suburbs), and unlikely to take ethnic identity very seriously (professional identity is probably primary; family life, though crucial, is not organized ethnically for elites, who marry along class lines, not ethnic ones). The elites—and the two political parties—are not going to roll back modernity significantly. But each party needs to court constituencies that are hostile to modernity in ways the elites are not. And when, as has happened in the Republican Party, the nonelites manage to move from being the foot soldiers to being elected representatives, disarray can follow as the modernism of the business class clashes with the premodernism of the cultural right.

But what of the radical left? If the radical right are premodernists, does that make the radical left postmodernists? If only it were that simple. The nineteenth-century radical left divides between the Marxists and the anarchists.[14] Marxism's great strength and its great flaw as a political program (I am bypassing its theoretical and/or factual accuracy altogether here) are one and the same: it ignores all cultural objections to modernity, all protests against how modernity destroys "ways of life." Marxism is only interested in modernity's economic sins, how it creates "poverty amid plenty." The typical Marxist is the engaged intellectual (not the proletariat he tries to woo to the party) and, like other elites, is at home in modernity and its godless, frenetic cities. He does not so much reject modernity as he expects to come out on its other side. Modernity is a stage on the way to socialism—and much of modernity will survive into the socialist future. Marxism, in other words, can only appeal to those who are temperamentally modern, not to premodernists. A leftist political party can only attract premodernists if it succeeds in getting them to check all their cultural allegiances at the door and focus political activity on the sole issue of a bigger slice of the pie. The cultural recidivism of our times followed from the discovery by Ronald Reagan's Republicans and Margaret Thatcher's Conservatives that certain hot-button cultural issues (flag burning, for instance), if played right, could trump economic interest. (Of course, it did not hurt that Reagan was playing off the oil-crisis inflation of the 1970s and Thatcher off the same energy crisis, symbolically centered on the coal miners in Britain.)

Anarchism is less easy to track, but the energies of the *enragé* must be noted because they are also with us today. Tapping into culturalist energies via the themes of hostility to the state, reverence for religious and social authority, abhorrence of modern cities (figured as a-religious, homosexual, and the home of nonworking nonwhites), and traditional family values has unleashed a rage that has spawned paramilitary groups, violent confrontations with federal agencies (especially out West), and "domestic terrorism" (the Oklahoma City, Atlanta, and abortion clinic bombings). The left's engagement with these energies has been troubled. Starting with the civil rights and student movements of the 1960s, but accelerating with the "identity politics" of the 1970s and 1980s, the left has tried to face up to the fact that economic issues are not primary for some constituencies still willing to associate their politics with the left. It turns out that the indignities most crucial to many people willing to take vigorous political action involve issues of equality, recognition, appreciation, respect, and tolerance more than economic concerns. For people who want to be taken seriously on their own terms—and want to resist changes that seem to threaten those terms—traditional leftist economic issues and tactics (the ballot, strikes, revolutions) are less compelling than cultural issues (or representation and recognition) and symbolic tactics (demonstrations, civil disobedience, media access and coverage).[15]

If this analysis is correct, then postmodernism (as an intellectual movement) can be read as the left's attempt to process the fact that its political agenda cannot simply be the transformation of modernity's economic arrangements within the context of a general acceptance of the modern. Rather, the left has to reinvent itself, first by grasping just what are the complaints/grievances of the groups crudely lumped under the inadequate label of "identity politics," and second by thinking through a social vision that gets at the root causes of the abuses that underlie those grievances. I think this work has hardly begun. Old (economist) ways of thinking are hard to put aside, although I would say the most progress has been made on this front. Less successful has been the attempt to understand fully the stakes in cultural politics for groups on both sides. For example, despite all the current focus (both theoretical and historical) on racism, analyses of intolerance are never going to get us very far until the powerful appeal of racism can be presented in nonpathologized terms. So long as leftist intellectuals provide descriptions of *their* (whatever population is in mind) benightedness, the gap between those intellectuals and their purported allies cannot be closed.[16]

Along with its repudiation of Marxist economism, postmodern theory has (more fitfully) considered the left's entire relation to modernity. Various bits and pieces of the modern (its addiction to universalist arguments and solutions, for example) have been questioned, and there have also been repeated flirtations with anarchistic jettisoning of the modern altogether. But neither total rejection nor Jürgen Habermas's attempted embrace of modernity's unfinished emancipatory project has proved attractive to many. The dramatic choices the postmodernist debate of the 1980s appeared to offer have faded into a more meticulous project of picking through, piece by piece, the modernist heritage, figuring where and how each piece might be useful or harmful. Such salvage work is hardly heady; it yields few moments of stunning, all-illuminating epiphany. As a result, we entered the millennium in a peculiarly undramatic way. The ending of the twentieth century was accompanied by neither a whimper nor a bang. Perhaps we peaked too soon, but that's fine by me. (I am prone to semiserious baby-boom determinism, so the fact that we hit the millennium in middle age may account for its not living up to its hype.) The year 1989 put the apocalyptic East–West face-off to bed in an inconclusive nonending that was at least semitriumphant given the possible scenarios. The big one was never dropped. If our current situation is innumerable intractable local conflicts, each of which requires sustained, fine-grained attention with a minimum of general commitments/ beliefs if any solution is to be found, should we bemoan the lost clarity of global schemes, globally envisioned progress, and enemies identified as evil empires? I don't think so.

The political stakes, then, in my desire to question the Victorian heritage that has us gauge political positions and possibilities in relation to modernity lie in my conviction that the terms *left* and *right* have lost their usefulness and that holistic covering terms such as *modernity, capitalism, disciplinary society, patriarchy, socialism,* and their ilk are likewise an argumentative hindrance rather than a help. We need more nuanced, more particularist, analyses that consider situational utility, situational harm. Progress here would be greatly enhanced by abandoning the belief that modernity is of a piece, that each element of contemporary life stands in relation to other elements more or less modern, and by acknowledging that modernist themes (such as "universal rights") cannot be judged apart from the situations in which they are deployed. Current appeals to the "global economy" are the blackmail of the modern in a new guise. "Survivals" (in Tylor's sense) like France's social safety nets cannot survive long; only streamlined modern economies will be able to compete; retaining any local differences that hamper productivity or subtract the cost of social goods from the shareholders' bottom line will prove shortsighted and self-destructive. The price paid for local difference, of uneven development, is too high.

The left would do better to resist such holistic analyses and the prescriptions they warrant. Its political analyses and programs should be decoupled both from a sensibility that says "yes" or "no" to modernity *tout court* and from theories that identify any new practice as the thin edge of the wedge. Production for export markets is not necessarily bad, does not necessarily destroy local communities. All the grounds for judgment and decision are in the details of the particular situation. Instead of trying to hold out against modernity, or of "outing" oneself or others as already complicit in some way with the modern, the left might try to stop taking the modern as a yardstick. Certain actions (for example, rural electrification) need not carry certain inevitable consequences. Modernization does not everywhere take the same form and have the same results. If we can disconnect individual actions from the overarching matrix of the modern, we can be more attentive to the very different consequences that can follow from similar actions taken at different times in different places and handled differently. We should cherish what works, but recognize how much does not—while recognizing that modernity does not prescript results. Yes, there are various pressures of various sorts, including the pressures of a world economic situation, but various creative responses to those pressures are always a possibility.

Such pragmatic particularism comes with its own attendant risks. The temptation can be to cultivate one's garden, to build enclaves (restricted, "intentional" communities) against the general uncertainty. The watchwords can become "family" and "community," two local forms of relatedness that eschew connection or intervention in wider social structures named "state," "corporation," or "United Nations."

In such a climate, images of the Victorian can function to reinforce a certain sheltered ideal of community. All the recent films set in that generalized English past that covers from Jane Austen to E. M. Forster are essentially drawing-room comedies or melodramas. These films ignore the hungry forties specifically and the working classes generally, while presenting an astoundingly insular view of England when we consider that the time period in question saw England at its most expansive, ruler of the empire on which the sun never set. We get England only; even the recent spate of (vaguely anti-English) films set in Scotland and Ireland all avoid the 1850 to 1910 time period. (The counterexample, *Mrs. Brown,* gives us the ultradevoted Scottish servant to the British monarch, not the Scottish rebel.) The golden age of Victoria provides a very popular contemporary image of domestic felicity— domestic in both its senses of confined to the family home and confined to the home country. Contented relatedness is a function of sealed-off relations, in unremarked tension with the outward-directed imperial grasp of the actual historical period. The Victorian figured in this way in these films dovetails with a prominent isolationist mood in a prosperous America and England disinclined to take much responsibility for or remediating action toward the less well off either abroad or at home.

My point in this section has been that our way of understanding the political categories left and right has shrunk since the early part of the Victorian period because political and intellectual elites (for the most part) have lost the sense that these categories chart fundamental orientations to modernity itself. Modernity is not at stake in our politics; left and right are defined within a framework that takes modernity as the unalterable given, and thus focuses only on possible maneuvers within modernity. The narrow focus of contemporary filmic representations of the Victorian replays this narrowing of possible political positions and political options in contemporary two-party democracy in both England and the United States. To re-ask the question of modernity gives us a useful alternative vision of what is at issue in contemporary politics and on the vicissitudes of the two major parties in both countries since the 1960s. Postmodernism can be seen as the intellectual discourse that attempts (especially from the left's point of view) to reconfigure the primarily economic view of politics that prevailed before the 1960s. However, we can also view postmodernism as calling us to eschew the fixation on modernity altogether, to organize our thinking along entirely different lines, to stop being modernists in exactly the way the Victorians were modernist: that is, in taking modernity as the key reference point when examining allegiances, beliefs, practices, and outcomes. In other words, I believe that my raising the question of modernity in the way I do in this essay is part and parcel of an effort to rethink the whole political landscape, to get beyond inherited (and currently very confused) configurations of left and right.

The Postmodern and the Left

The reader will have noted that my essay, thus far, commits the very sin it strives to describe. I have characterized a certain type of cultural criticism as modern and have claimed that we and the Victorians are both modern because we practice that type of criticism. To say that critical generalization since 1800 is usually temporally and/or culturally organized is to enact the very critical move to which I am trying to draw attention. As recent (1975–95) criticism geared toward uncovering ideological taken-for-granteds amply demonstrates, even tonally descriptive accounts of unacknowledged assumptions convey a skeptical, if not downright denunciatory, relation to the material described. Some positions, it seems, are hard to occupy self-consciously. If, as an ideology or a zeitgeist critic, you are doomed to be no different from those whom you critique, does the critique lose all its value? Or is there some payoff for self-consciousness, for the examined life? Is there any way to use self-consciousness about the intellectual paradigm this essay discusses?

For starters, let's acknowledge a fascinating, if perhaps, infinite regress here. Zeitgeist thinking would suggest we pose this question: "What about the current moment allows the paradigm of zeitgeist thought to become a consciously raised issue?" What in the temper of our times or in our current intellectual situation allows us to identify, as Walter Benn Michaels does, a belief in culture as our prevailing myth and to examine the structures and consequences of that belief? And, to be fair, I need to acknowledge that cultural studies is not everywhere guilty of simple assumptions about culture; the work of Stuart Hall and Paul Gilroy, in particular, tends in directions that I pursue here.[17] I have, as you can imagine, various thoughts on this "why now" question that I would love to try out on you, the gentle reader, for plausibility. But that path leads back into the labyrinth just when I want to consider if we can bypass the labyrinth. Can we do our intellectual work in other ways?

One solution, of course, is to opt for pure particularity, for singularity. Certain strains in poststructuralism (especially in Jacques Derrida, Gilles Deleuze, and Michel Foucault) point us in this direction.[18] These writers indicate a tension between the particular and the categories by which we envelop it, and consider (at least tentatively) the possibility of encountering the specific thing without subsuming it under a more general term. The problem of such an approach is dramatically conveyed by the Jorge Luis Borges story "Funes the Memorius." The title character has perceptions so fine that today's tree is completely different to him than yesterday's, so much so that they cannot be identified by the same name or grouped in a single category. Funes is an idiot; the narrator tells us he "suspect[s] . . . that [Funes] was not very capable of thought. To think is to forget a difference, to generalize, to abstract."[19] Funes finds the world overwhelming and ends up in bed in a darkened room, the only way he can survive in a world of countless singularities impressing themselves upon him.

Still, it is tempting to pursue the Foucauldian dream of taking appearances as all there is, thus eschewing our habitual mapping of appearances to identity, essence, causal matrices, or deep foundational regularities such as culture. Yes, singularities are inflected by, gain significance through, their relations and interactions with other singularities. And many of these relations may exist over fairly long stretches of time, institutionalized and maintained by various social arrangements, some of which are enforced against opposition. But there is no reason to think that these various relations and arrangements map onto some deeper and unifying reality that is acquired differently, is possessed unconsciously and thus more tenaciously, and is more fundamental than any of our other beliefs about the world and our place in it. The systematic relationships and fiercely held commitments that do exist are human products, no more and no less than my casual preference for blue over yellow shirts. Depending on context, what is casual now could become all-important and vice versa; there are a variety of ways in which we acquire beliefs and commitments, none of which is more fundamental or exists on a deeper level than any other. Similarly, there are many different kinds of social pressure (power) brought to bear on individual belief formation and such pressure is brought to bear in many different ways, but none operates on a different level than any of the others, and they form cohesive or contradiction-ridden wholes only as a result of specific human actions aimed at establishing such encompassing relations among things. We live in a world in which lots of energy is expended trying to change each other's minds and actions; such efforts often involve attempts to rescript the meaning of things through recontextualization and to forge new connections. The results of such efforts are mixed.

Because the results are mixed, my argument throughout this essay has been skeptical of any easy generalizations about what constitutes either Victorianism or our own moment. My argument suggests that it makes sense to identify various specific conditions of specific historical moments; we might even claim that some of these conditions are "modern," meaning that they did not exist prior to some designated date (say, 1600). But we should avoid thinking that there is some substrate called "modernity" or "Western (or American or English) culture" that actively structures the relations of all of these conditions to one another. The elements of the modern exist in contingent, problematic, and ever-changing relation to one another. In other words, the elements are not necessarily related to one another at all. We live in a modern world, but it is not systematic in the way that terms such as *modernity* would have us believe. My approach suggests that we ask: Who (in any particular historical or cultural analysis) is trying to make what kind of connection between what elements of the past and what elements of the present, and how, and why? Relationships and meanings are forged through various (contingent) human actions, one of which is the telling of stories in fiction and film, another of which is making interpretive arguments in criticism. In other words, the Victorians as a group characterized by certain shared features do not exist except insofar as they are produced in that similarity by a discourse that has aims on its audience. The right question is not whether the Victorians were really like that or not, but the Bakhtinian question of whom this discourse addresses (answers, contests, affirms) and to what ends.

I will close by indicating, all too briefly, that Hannah Arendt's thoughts on storytelling and judgment might help us reorient our notion of what criticism can accomplish. Arendt, especially in the posthumous *Life of the Mind*, was committed to an ontology of appearances.[20] The real for Arendt is that which exists between humans in publicly apprehensible forms. But the real is not purely singular in Arendt because of the requirements of storytelling and judgment. Storytelling is necessary for two reasons: to maintain the reality of that which is not itself apprehensible now and to consider the meaning of the real. Things appear. Many of these "things" are human deeds (action) or the products of human efforts (work). Action and work would seem futile if they left no ongoing impress on the world. Work's legacy is very often the things it creates which now furnish our world. But action that does not create a material object depends on stories for preservation—and for an impact on future deeds.

Stories, however, do more than just memorialize. Appearances are not self-evident; their possible meanings unfold over time through a process of pondering and retelling. Storytelling records, but it is also productive. The story elaborates and speculates; it ponders possible ways of being in the world as exemplified by the actions it relates. Here is where story connects to judgment. Each of us has to decide how to live a life. Or, if that is too grand, each of us has various decisions to make in various situations. We are guided, certainly, by the particulars of the situation, which include our particular purposes as well as the possibilities afforded by the situation and our estimate of possible success. In other words, judgment involves gauging what is possible in these circumstances in relation to what I desire to achieve. Any situation offers a number (more than one but less than infinity) of options for action. Judgment entails both identifying the options and choosing among

them. Stories often offer examples of creative or otherwise extraordinary actions that invite us to expand our notions of the possible.

What has this model of the interaction among situations, stories, and
judgments to do with academic work that explains *Bleak House* through
mapping it to typical Victorian attitudes or (in the more sophisticated version of this kind of work) to a constitutive Victorian social field? Primarily,
I think it shifts the focus of our mapping efforts. Judgment aided by stories
still must decide which stories (among many) are relevant to the situation at
hand—and in what ways those stories are instructive. No fit is perfect; we
are always proceeding by analogy and approximation. The fluidity of the
process is crucial because the absence of exactitude keeps judgment supple
and creative in the attempt to respond to novel circumstances. My suggestion, then, is to reorient our relationship to various elements of the past.
Instead of understanding the element's meaning as a function of its dynamic
relation to the defining discourses, ideology, or beliefs of its age or culture,
we should be considering what elements of the past can mean in relation to
our purposes in the present. Instead of viewing things that appear as indices
of who they (the Victorians) were and/or who we (postmoderns?) are, those
things would be elaborated through stories that ponder what we might become. Instead of asking (anxiously) "Are we being modern yet?" and looking over our shoulders for the precept who bears the report card that registers how well we have passed the test, we would see in stories of the past
images of being in the world that tell us there are multiple ways to be
human and that we are engaged in the project of living out some of those
ways. And we could recognize retellings precisely as meditations on ways of
being in the world, not claims about the determinate structures of reality
(be it natural or social) or the fixed identity of groups past or present.

Whether such an approach would lessen the pressure on the "we" that I
invoke in the previous sentences is an open question. I hope that a focus on
the future we are trying to make possible instead of on describing the lineaments of the past might make images of the "we" more fluid, less a group
solidarity we necessarily share or can be blamed for not accepting than
forms of human relatedness that must be continually re-created.[21] The "we"
is precisely what the storyteller, the user of discourse, is trying to create
through the appeal to an audience, with success in that endeavor blessedly
hard to achieve and only temporally stable even when achieved. Just as the
elements of the modern do not cohere into an all-encompassing "modernity"

that organizes them once and for all in one way, so individual human existences touch each other in some ways and in some times, but not in others. Just exactly what connections are made and when is the product of human action, not the result of systematizing unities that lurk beneath or behind or beyond that contact of humans, one with another.

Notes

My heartfelt thanks to John Kucich, who whipped this essay into any shape it can purport to possess.

1. J. S. Mill, *Mill's Essays on Literature and Society*, ed. J. B. Schneewind (New York: Collier Books, 1965), 28.

2. For venerable, but still valuable, studies of Victorian intellectuals, see John Holloway, *The Victorian Sage* (New York: Norton, 1965); Patrick Brantlinger, *The Spirit of Reform: British Literature and Politics, 1832–1867* (Cambridge: Harvard University Press, 1977); Eugene Goodheart, *The Failure of Criticism* (Cambridge: Harvard University Press, 1978); and Thais Morgan, ed., *Victorian Sages and Cultural Discourse: Renegotiating Gender and Power* (New Brunswick, N.J.: Rutgers University Press, 1990).

3. Isobel Armstrong, *Victorian Poetry: Poetry, Poetics and Politics* (London: Routledge, 1993), 8.

4. See Mary Poovey, *Uneven Developments: The Ideological Work of Gender in Mid-Victorian England* (Chicago: University of Chicago Press, 1988), 3, for her definition of ideology. Subsequent references from this text are noted parenthetically in the body of the essay. See Louis Althusser, *For Marx* (New York: Vintage Books, 1969), esp. 200–218, for the critique of "expressive totality" and the notions of "uneven development" that Poovey adopts. See also Louis Althusser, "Ideology and Ideological State Apparatuses," in *Lenin and Philosophy* (New York: Monthly Review Press, 1971), 127–86, for the understanding of ideology on which Poovey draws. Poovey's more recent *Making a Social Body: British Cultural Formation* (Chicago: University of Chicago Press, 1995) makes much more extensive use of the terms *modernity* and *culture* (especially in chapter 1) than *Uneven Developments* and, thus, might seem even more suited to my concerns in this essay. My choice of the earlier book has been governed by the neatness of the example of how she reads *David Copperfield*. I do think the more recent work evidences the same intellectual paradigm, although admittedly stretched to the breaking point since Poovey strives mightily to accept "that modern culture's imaginary totality" is not "effective" (14) *and* to argue that in "early nineteenth-century Britain . . . the groundwork was laid" for "this representation of a single culture [mass culture]" that "competed with and then gradually replaced another representation, which emphasized the differences among various groups within England" (*Making* 2, 4).

5. The contradictions in the conditions of intelligibility provide the possibility that readers, as well as critics, "can achieve" some "distance" from the matrix, Poovey tells us (*Uneven* 90). But she also says that her "reading" of *David Copperfield* "is not an interpretation that a nineteenth-century audience would have been likely to devise" (*Uneven* 89).

6. Raymond Williams, *Marxism and Literature* (New York: Oxford University Press, 1977), chapter 8.

7. Much of what I have to say about culture has been influenced by Christopher Herbert's superb *Culture and Anomie: Ethnographic Imagination in the Nineteenth Century* (Chicago: University of Chicago Press, 1991), which traces English notions of "culture" from 1770 to 1870.

8. See J. G. Herder, *Herder on Social and Political Culture*, ed. F. M. Barnard (Cambridge: Cambridge University Press, 1969), as well as Isaiah Berlin, *Vico and Herder* (London: Hogarth Press, 1968).

9. Edward Burnett Tylor's *Primitive Culture* (*The Collected Works*, vol. 3 [London: Routledge/Thoemmes, 1994]) offers the foundational definition of "culture or civilization, taken in its wide ethnographic sense" as "that complex whole which includes knowledge, belief, arts, morals, law, custom, and any other capabilities and habits acquired by man as a member of society" (1). This definition is followed very quickly by the assertion that various cultural stages "may be consistently arranged as having followed one another in a particular order of development" (14) and by the introduction of the concept of "survivals," which are defined as the "customs, opinions, and so forth, which have been carried by force of habit into a new state of society . . . [and] remain as proofs and examples of an older condition of culture out of which a newer has been evolved" (15).

10. Skepticism about modernity necessarily entails skepticism about postmodernity. For the most part, I think *postmodernism* is a word that has outlived its usefulness; for a while during the 1980s it did serve to focus attention on a set of intellectual debates and choices. Jean-François Lyotard's influential *The Postmodern Condition: A Report on Knowledge* (Minneapolis: University of Minnesota Press, 1984), specifically, poised the local as incommensurate against larger frameworks that would subsume it. His strategy is culturalist, although his argument is couched in rather different terms. The local in his book abides in "language games" rather than in cultures or subcultures.

11. See Mary Douglas and Baron Isherwood, *The World of Goods: Towards an Anthropology of Consumption* (New York: Norton, 1979), for an argument that consumption is always about social involvement and thus primarily oriented toward gaining information and establishing social relations. We must buy computers in order not to be poor, if we accept their assertion that "the rightful measure of poverty . . . is not possessions, but social involvement" (11).

12. Walter Benn Michaels, "'You Who Never Was There': Slavery and the New Historicism, Deconstruction and the Holocaust," *Narrative* 4 (1996), writes: "[I]f we return to the revised version of the question with which we began—which

myths do Americans believe—we can see that culture, not visitors, races or even history, is the correct answer. Americans, especially American academics, believe in the myth of culture; indeed, with respect to American academics, the point could be put more strongly—we do not simply believe in the myth of culture, many of us have accepted as our primary professional responsibility the elaboration and promulgation of the myth" (13–14).

13. For an argument that historical paradigms of thought are a late-eighteenth-century and nineteenth-century phenomenon, see Stephen Toulminn and June Goodfield, *The Discovery of Time* (New York: Harper and Row, 1965). For accounts of "culture" as a concept dating from the same period, see Chris Jenks, *Culture* (London: Routledge, 1993); Raymond Williams, *Keywords* (New York: Oxford University Press, 1976); and A. L. Kroeber and Clyde Kluckhohn, *Culture: A Review of Concepts and Definitions* (New York: Vintage Books, 1960).

14. What, you might ask, about left Hegelians and their descendants, later in the century, the social democrats? In *Postmodernism and Its Critics* (Ithaca, N.Y.: Cornell University Press, 1991), I have tried in chapter 4 to delineate a left Hegelian position that is neither Marxist nor liberal. Such a position dovetails with some (but hardly all) elements of contemporary communitarianism (of the Charles Taylor rather than the Alisdair MacIntyre variety) while also utilizing some hints from attempts to resuscitate a republican civic-virtue tradition. But I think now that left Hegelianism is more liberal than not—and certainly liberal in its attitudes toward modernity, change, and individual rights. Liberalism is a capacious house and I think we need to come to terms with its variants, instead of believing that we can reject it wholesale. We can no more banish liberalism by fiat than we can make the modern disappear. Liberalism and the modern are the horizons within which we operate, and the clean choice of affirmation/rejection should be swapped for the messy task of working through the details of what opportunities (for good and for evil) our past, our intellectual and emotional predilections, and our present afford us (fully recognizing that different groups and individuals located within this horizon have different purposes that inflect their assessment of possibilities). All of which is to say that I remain a left Hegelian (or a "radical democrat" in today's parlance), but that I think this position stands in a more complex relationship to liberalism than "it is" or "it isn't" can encompass.

15. My characterization of these leftist, but noneconomically motivated, political agents connects up to long-standing controversies about the "New Left," "the new social movements," and "identity politics." Readers will find the essays collected in Linda Nicholson and Steven Seidman, eds., *Social Postmodernism: Beyond Identity Politics* (New York: Cambridge University Press, 1995), and in Charles Taylor, K. Anthony Appiah, Jürgen Habermas, Steven C. Rockefeller, Michael Walzer, and Susan Wolf, *Multiculturalism: Examining the Politics of Recognition* (Princeton, N.J.: Princeton University Press, 1994), a good place to start.

16. I am attracted to, without having worked out all the implications of, the "principle of symmetry" promoted by Barbara Herrnstein Smith in chapter 3 of *Belief*

and Resistance: Dynamics of Contemporary Intellectual Controversy (Cambridge: Harvard University Press, 1997). The principle recommends that we take as a starting assumption that others with whom we disagree have as reasonable a basis for their beliefs as we have for ours. The difficulty of enacting the principle becomes apparent when that other is someone who strongly believes in racial differences. But it is equally hard to imagine progress in an argument in which the only move is my repetition that you are wrong—really, truly, and fundamentally wrong.

17. See especially Stuart Hall's essays "Gramsci's Relevance for the Study of Race and Ethnicity" and "New Ethnicities," in *Stuart Hall: Critical Dialogues,* ed. David Morley and Kuan-Hsing Chen (New York: Routledge, 1996); and the first chapter of Paul Gilroy's *The Black Atlantic: Modernity and Double Consciousness* (Cambridge: Harvard University Press, 1993).

18. See Michel Foucault, *Discipline and Punish: The Birth of the Prison,* trans. Alan Sheridan (New York: Vintage Books, 1979), 251–55, and *The History of Sexuality,* vol. 1, *An Introduction* (New York: Vintage Books, 1980), 42–45, for passages that indicate his attempt to disconnect appearances from a "depth hermeneutic" that locates their meaning in essences or identities hidden from view.

19. Jorge Luis Borges, *Ficciones* (New York: Grove Press, 1965), 115.

20. I discuss Arendt's notions of storytelling and judgment in detail in chapter 3 of my *Hannah Arendt: An Introduction* (Minneapolis: University of Minnesota Press, 1998). On Arendt's ontology, see Kimberley Curtis's wonderful essay "Aesthetic Foundations of Democratic Politics in the Work of Hannah Arendt," in Craig Calhoun and John McGowan, eds., *Hannah Arendt and the Meaning of Politics* (Minneapolis: University of Minnesota Press, 1997), 27–52. Arendt's own texts on these topics are widely scattered, from the essays on Gotthold Lessing, Isak Dinesen, and Walter Benjamin in *Men in Dark Times* (New York: Harcourt Brace Jovanovich, 1968) and the essay "Truth in Politics" in *Between Past and Future* (New York: Penguin Books, 1977) to the posthumous *Lectures on Kant's Political Philosophy* (Chicago: University of Chicago Press, 1982). See Hannah Arendt, *Life of the Mind* (New York: Harcourt Brace Jovanovich, 1981), 42–46, for the most succinct statement of Arendt's ontology of appearances.

21. I highly recommend Iris Marion Young's "Gender as Seriality: Thinking about Women as a Social Collective" in Nicholson and Seidman, *Social Postmodernism,* 187–215, for a way of thinking about the existence of groups that gets us beyond the stalemate of essentialized identities versus mobilized differences.

At Home in the Nineteenth Century
Photography, Nostalgia, and
the Will to Authenticity

Jennifer Green-Lewis

What is this narrative of origins? . . . It is not a narrative of the object; it is a
narrative of the possessor.

Susan Stewart

Until the 1970s, as Raphael Samuel has noted, there really was no market
for Victorian photographs, few readers for those images that currently
crowd the pages of popular and academic journals, weigh down coffee tables
in vast tomes, perform new (and revisit old) narratives along the walls of
contemporary art galleries, and provide, in short, visual accompaniment to
just about any reference to the word *Victorian*.[1] For more than a century,
pictorial photography was considered merely testament to the bad taste of
the Victorians; today, with our sophistication as readers apparently indexed
to our liberation from the burdens of realism, it is the artifice of barefoot
Alice against an Oxford wall, H. P. Robinson's consumptive fourteen-year-
old, and Julia Cameron's tousled cupid that excite academics and media
alike, while the general classificatory shift of the found photograph from a
fragment or bit of a thing (junk) to an icon or part of a thing (antique), has
taken images of the nineteenth century to market as conveyors of identity
and authenticity.

Desire for those twinned commodities sustains a thriving business that
services its customers' nostalgia in the manner of photography itself: with the
promise of access; with the solace of retrieval; with the pleasures of loss. Our

fin-de-siècle romance with Victorian culture is played out in representational and technological forms that, thanks to the primary semantics of photography and film, are themselves always tempered by endless deferral. Moreover, and somewhat ironically, the very realism we are supposed to have outgrown—an ideologically bound, historically contingent way of seeing—is increasingly privileged as a path to the site of authenticity and identity, if not itself, even, the object of our desire.[2]

In this essay I take as a given Richard Terdiman's assertion that "how a culture performs and sustains [its recollection of the past] is distinctive and diagnostic," for if, as I have argued elsewhere, "The canon of images to which we are so attached reveals as much and perhaps more about the intervening century and a half of readers as it does about the original seconds photographed," recent noncanonical re-presentation of the nineteenth century is equally instructive about postmodernity.[3] Our relentless memorialization of the Victorians will provide an extraordinary amount of material to future historians of the twentieth century, not least because what we popularly define as Victorian is frequently coterminous neither with the life of its monarch, nor even with the beginning and end of her century; it designates an aesthetic, rather than a precisely historical, concept. Contemporary cultural allusions to the Victorians sweep generously if inaccurately from the late eighteenth and early nineteenth century (Romantics and Jane Austen therefore included) right up to the outbreak of the Great War (the death of Victoria herself thereby ignored).

The past, one might point out, has always maintained some cultural authority that supports, among other things, the activity of reproducing and purchasing objects past their prime. The current authority of the past, though, is especially acute, a fact that alone deserves some scrutiny; and the popular shape of the authoritative past is identifiably Victorian. Past, of course, is past, the 1800s really no more so than the 1950s and no less than the 1660s, yet something vaguely Victorian is what advertisers usually mean now when they say (equally vaguely) "yesteryear," "olde worlde," or even "olden times." We re-create the past in response to popular demand, that much seems clear; less apparent are the reasons why such a generalized demand exists to be satisfied with a *Victorian* product. Or, to put it another way: why, when we want to reinvent and revisit the past, do we choose the nineteenth century as the place to get off the train? What is it about the look of this past that appeals to the late-twentieth-century passenger?[4]

The Visible Nineteenth Century

The first answer to these questions is both obvious and subtle: We can see the Victorians. Not just imaginatively, but really—or at least as really as we see anyone through the agency of photography, an art invented, perfected, and practiced by them. No matter how conscious we may be that "the causative link between the pre-photographic referent and the sign [is] highly complex, irreversible, and can guarantee nothing at the level of meaning," the evidentiary force of photography nevertheless offers "the consolation of a truth in the past which cannot be questioned."[5] The Victorians are visually real to us because they have a documentary assertiveness unavailable to persons living before the age of the camera. Further, though they may appear in their hoops, top hats, and whiskers, and as much as photography affirms the strangeness of the Other, so it emphasizes the shared ordinariness of its human subjects, in this case Victorians, only by historical accident rather than evolutionary difference.

Precisely because we see them in photographs, Victorians have all the pathos and appeal of photography itself; whatever attractions the Victorian period has for consumers are actually compounded by their existence in photographs, rather than just in words or paintings. The Victorians continue to exist in the absolute and paradoxical present of the photograph, always there yet gone forever; both in, and out, of history; always already dead— yet still alive. Yet, although much has been made about the distinctively Victorian characteristics of photography, how it so perfectly embodies the obsessions of the period, there is a far more obviously postmodern quality to the frustrations of our relationship with it. No effort, however extraordinary, will ever yield access to a photograph and permit the viewer, Alice-like, to climb through its frame into another world. Quite apart from the irony contingent on our every encounter with the paradox of the photograph, and at odds with photography's promise of interiority and penetration, is the hard surface of mirror images that will not melt into air. Nonetheless, we have determined the Victorians to be accessible thanks to their recognizably familiar representational status, while access itself has been enabled by the cultural invisibility of the photograph qua photograph, the apparent absence of trace within the picture of its own making such that in our day-to-day dealings with photographs we rarely make distinction between a photograph and its subject, and often efface agency altogether. The referent, as Barthes says, "adheres," with the consequence that in re-presenting the nineteenth century to us, Victorian photographs have become like "what we said of it . . . A part of what it is"—old texts, inseparable as objects from our way of reading them.[6] And just as other historical artifacts affirm for many people a connection with a previous human intelligence, so old photographs, their negatives (and subjects) long gone, assume the aura of originals, not merely in terms of their economic value, but as points of reference or departure.

Those departure points, the sites and sources of authenticity, tend to be located with the human rather than the object world. Searches for authenticity are at base searches for signs of life, the indices of other human beings—thumb marks in the pottery, hair caught in oil paint on a canvas, light on glass that glanced off a human face. When I look back to photography's earliest days, it is not the precision of Daguerre's fossils and shells or Fox Talbot's mistier impressions of Lacock Abbey that most fascinate me, stunning as these different images are for their detail and achievement (figures 1 and 2). Instead, it is by the small and accidental sign of an unknown human being that I am most moved: Daguerre's "Boulevard du Temple, Paris," of 1838 or 1839 (figure 3), in which an anonymous subject appears unwittingly before us, by virtue of having stopped to get his boots cleaned on a Paris street—stopped, that is, long enough to have his presence recorded on a daguerreotype and thus to be taken out of history, while the rest of the people crowding the street that day simply disappeared into it.

Figure 1. Louis Jacques Mandé Daguerre, *Collection de coquillages et divers*, 1839. Musée des Arts et Métiers. CNAM, Paris. Reprinted by permission.

Figure 2. Fox Talbot, *A Courtyard Scene*, ca. 1844. Photographic History Collection, National Museum of American History, Smithsonian Institution. Reprinted by permission.

Figure 3. Louis Jacques Mandé Daguerre, *Boulevard du Temple, Paris*, ca. 1838. Bayerisches Nationalmuseum, Munich. Reprinted by permission.

With that mark on the glass plate (the double mark, really, for the boot-black too, though less clear, was partially secured by his labor), humanity stepped into the contemporary frame of visual realism. For it is the fundamental visibility of the Victorians *on our own terms*—that is, through the reality-conferring camera—that accounts in part for their cultural persistence. Our subjection to an increasingly image-proscribed world, a world with more mirrors (or screens) than there are rooms to climb into, has produced a market for images that seeks differentiation in the hierarchy of age. Thus, over the years Victorian photographs have increased in status and value as they have accumulated histories and meanings. Given that we are used to characterizing modernist culture as, in Stephen Connor's words, "the moment when self-consciousness invaded experience," it seems plausible that photographic images offer the same kinds of consolations as the larger aesthetic of Victoriana generally: a refuge, however illusory, from the self-consciousness of our time; some escape, perhaps, from the "unresolved steering problems" of what Habermas calls the "legitimation crisis" of contemporary society, defined by Connor as the sense that there no longer "seems to be access to principles which can act as criteria of value for anything else"; some respite from our "consciousness of the discontinuity of time . . . [the] break with tradition, [the] feeling of novelty, of vertigo in the face of the passing moment."[7]

The moralizing and occasionally grandiose visions of Victorian photographers as, for example, Rejlander's *The Two Ways of Life* (figure 4), like

Figure 4. Oscar Gustav Rejlander, *The Two Ways of Life*, 1857. The Royal Photographic Society, Bath. Reprinted by permission.

Figure 5. H. P. Robinson, *Autumn*, 1863, from *Pictorial Effect in Photography*, 1869. The Art Museum, Princeton University. The Robert O. Dougan Collection, gift of Warner Communications, Inc. Photograph credit: Bruce M. White. Reprinted by permission.

Robinson's unabashedly sentimental anachronisms (figure 5), reveal none of the self-doubt or irony that characterizes modern art and photography. Such images are in fact popular now *because* of their ostensible confirmation of premodern certainties and have become scholastically of interest thanks to their ludicrousness—as a kind of proof of a world once free from self-consciousness, at once naive or desirable (depending on one's viewpoint). There is a crude assumption of superiority in many such readings of the photographs that fails to recognize the serious artistic purpose of the works, and that cannot account for their contemporary success other than by granting to the Victorians an even greater share of tackiness than previously supposed.[8] Sentimental; sexually repressed (the photo-histories that accompany *The Two Ways of Life* almost always draw attention to the naked breasts and note what a scandal they caused); humorless realists about to be shattered by modernism and the cubist war—such essentialization of the Victorians has become a way of organizing, in strikingly Victorian fashion, the great wealth of materials and ideas they left behind.

Essentializing the Victorians runs counter to postmodernist practice, of course, and maybe that is why so many consumers of Victoriana have tried to steer clear of postmodernism; loyal to their period, they prefer to believe themselves out of, rather than in, the moment under analysis. It is one of the attractions of the nineteenth century that it is fixed and over, done with, definable in terms of dates and monarch and things that happened. After all, nothing will ever happen there again, so at least, theoretically, the possibility exists of a totalizing classification. Moreover, if theory itself is the mediator of postmodernity, it is hardly surprising that Victorianists have tended not to be theorists, because theory and authenticity are at opposite ends of a Victorianist's spectrum. Victorianists are vaguely censorious, in fact, of the proliferation of theory; Charles Newman speaks for many of them when he claims that postmodernism is only the representative system of an "inflation of discourse" across all levels of society but most notably in the spheres of culture and communication.[9] By contrast to the ballooning instability of postmodernity, the nineteenth century in its finitude and fixity appears to the cranky Victorianist both continent and authentic. And one proof of its authenticity, in a peculiar twist of logic, is its photographs of real people doing real things in identifiably real places.

In the search for authenticity the existential connection between photograph and referent is thus readily identified as a necessary, even natural, relation. Joel Snyder notes that "Photographs make a special claim upon our attention because they are supposed not only to look realistic . . . but also to derive from or be caused by the objects they represent. This 'natural connection' has been taken as a reinforcement and even as a guarantee of realistic depiction."[10] John Tagg is right to remind us, however, that what causes the connection between photograph and referent is *un*natural, insofar as it is the result of a discriminatory process "in which particular optical and chemical devices are set to work to organise experience and desire and produce a new reality"; photographs themselves are not mystical emanations but instead the "material product of a material apparatus set to work in specific contexts, by specific forces, for more or less defined purposes. . . . That a photograph can come to stand as evidence . . . rests not on a natural or existential fact, but on a social, semiotic process" (3–4). Despite this, modern accounts of photography frequently emphasize, as Snyder laments, "the unique way that photographs come into being. . . . a photographer uses a camera which 'captures' a 'trace' of the object itself. . . . The world delivers itself to the film" (224).

Phenomenologies that reference the causal links between photographs and their objects thus efface the simplest of truths regarding photography: before it is anything, every photograph is a picture; a construction, made, not begotten. As readers we accept the realism of the photograph, not *because* a photograph is so astonishingly like the thing it depicts, but in fact *despite* "its failure to substitute for a visual experience" (Snyder, 228). When I look at the *Boulevard du Temple,* I do not care that the man having his boots cleaned is a blur at best; that I would have seen a very different view that day had I looked out upon the crowded boulevard; that this daguerreotype, as a sign of a real world, is profoundly unlike the reality it represents. None of this matters, for in his signal transference to the daguerreotype the man has become, to revisit Barthes, "neither image nor reality [but] a new being, really: a reality one can no longer touch" (87).

In the next section I will focus on the "social, semiotic process" of meaning in photographs, by considering what kinds of Victorian images we have endowed with value, and to what ends. But I should probably note before I do, that while acknowledgment of that process should demystify the relation between a photograph and its referent, for me it does not fully eradicate, nor indeed even seriously trouble, its realist appeal. My consciousness of the larger culture of photographic meaning and my response to the iconic assertiveness of a given image exist in uneasy suspension. Much as I am aware of the organizing principles of "experience and desire" in the act not merely of photographing but of making sense of photographs in the larger culture of images, much as I attend to the materiality of the product and its specific, material purpose, I cannot deny that my fascination with the bootblack and his customer on the Parisian boulevard has to do with knowing— or *wanting* to know—that "the thing of the past, by its immediate radiations (its luminances) has really touched the surface which in its turn my gaze will touch" (Barthes, 81).

Unnatural Images: The Victorians Preserved

The following brief list constitutes a sort of contemporary top twenty (or so) of nineteenth-century British photographs, compiled simply by cross-referencing popular books of the coffee-table variety, including exhibition catalogs, that profess to deliver the history of photography. A similar list could, with different consequences, be made of American photographs. It need hardly be added that I am not concerned here with the aesthetic or technological merits of these pictures, but only with what we might conclude about ourselves from the results of a brief poll on contemporary taste.

My questions are simple, but indicate the direction that a fuller accounting of photography's history might take: Of what kind of nineteenth century are we fondest? What images—whose images—are our preferred sightings of the persons who lived there?[11]

My list of currently popular Victorian photographs includes the following: Thomas Annan's pictures of Scottish closes; just about anything by Cameron, but particularly *Whisper of the Muse (George F. Watts)* (1864–65); her photographs of Mary Hillier; and the portraits, especially Thomas Carlyle (1867), Mrs. Herbert Duckworth (1867), and Sir John Herschel (1867); Lewis Carroll's Alice as a beggar maid (1859); the Cottingley Fairy photographs (now revisited in movie version as a "true story"); Emerson's pictures of the Norfolk Broads, especially *Poling the Marsh Hay* (1886), *Gathering Water-lilies* (1886), and *Osier-Peeling* (1888); Hugh Diamond's portraits of his insane female patients; Frederick Evans's French and English cathedrals, notably *The Sea of Steps—Wells Cathedral* (1903); Roger Fenton's English landscapes, but more popularly the Crimean *Valley of Death* (1856); Francis Frith's photographs of Egypt; Clementina Hawarden's pictures of her daughters in the studio at Princes Gardens; David Octavius Hill and Robert Adamson's collaborative work representing middle-class Edinburgh, such as *The McCandlish Children* (1845), but also their documentation of the fisherfolk of Newhaven; John Edwin Mayall's pictures of Queen Victoria; Rejlander's composite morality tableaux, especially *Hard Times* (1860) and *The Two Ways of Life* (1857); Robinson's *Fading Away* (1858) and the pastorals, especially *Bringing Home the May* (1862); Fox Talbot's early calotypes of Lacock Abbey, and *The Open Door* (1843); Frank Sutcliffe's naked *Natives* (1895); John Thomson's *The Crawlers* (1877–78).

It is worth considering what kind of world these frequently reproduced photographs depict, for, as Foucault has noted, a "period only lets some things be seen and not others," and our visual selection of the Victorians is a means of charting postmodern desire.[12] To what kind of Victorian things do we give visibility? What do we want to see?

There is an imbalance in the list in favor of the pastoral (Emerson, Fenton, Robinson) over the urban (Annan, Thomson): Victorian England in popular photographs tends to be rural and southern. And there is a similar emphasis on the mid-century at the expense of the late, which might explain the overrepresentation of the upper classes who could afford, in the 1850s and 1860s, the expensive equipment and leisure time necessary. Of course, another way of explaining this is to wonder whether the view from the upper classes is not the preferred view of the 1990s, which would make the incarnation of the 1850s and 1860s as the definitively Victorian age somewhat incidental. To note that Victorian England in photographs is predominantly pastoral, southern, and mid-century is in fact to note what is really the common denominator of the photographs listed above: the perspective afforded by class. What is represented in these photographs is not as instructive as *how* it is shown. Pictures of the outdoors, garden or countryside, tend to reflect the elevated viewpoints of the landed gentry at home (Talbot, Fenton) or the colonial traveler abroad (Fenton, Frith). What social difference is represented is frequently sentimentalized (Robinson, Rejlander) or of anthropological and inherently nostalgic interest (fishwives by Hill and Adamson; Norfolk farmworkers by Emerson). The working classes tend to be obscured: portraits of the poor are often fabrications with middle- or upper-class sitters as models (Carroll, Robinson), or, if real, the laborers are sufficiently distanced to permit abstraction and mythologizing (Emerson). Only Thomson's famous image of a beggar woman with a baby disrupts the apparent harmony.

The list overrepresents pictorial and art photography, images theatrically conceived and designed to illustrate some particular moral theme or viewpoint. The photographs of the Victorians that have greatest currency today seem to be those, in fact, that represent them pretending to be something other than themselves: dressed as figures from history or poetry, as dairy maids or mythical characters; undressed in pornographic or pseudoclassical pose; or, with the later art photographs, looking as though they are in paintings and not photographs at all. Few of the pictures hint at social unrest or inequity; what social documentary there is, with the notable exception of Thomson, presents itself as picturesque. Almost all photographs here enact what social difference they record. Almost all are elegiac in their invitation to look back—they already have, that is to say, a relationship with the past that is itself an expression of the way in which they are used today.

For there is a good deal of celebrating of these images, from individual displays of a photographer's work, to more lavish shows marking anniversaries of dates in photography's history. One popular exhibition of 1984 demarcated the period 1839–1900 as "The Golden Age of British Photography," years that closely approximate the tenure of Victoria and add a convenient twist to the catalog's insistence on the Victorian-ness of photography itself.[13] With its identification of the age both *as* age, and as "golden," the exhibition assumed the familiar nostalgic perspective (after the golden age, after all, we become simply but less glamorously "modern"). The canon of Victorian photographs, it should be noted, as represented in this or any other exhibition, does not include anything approaching the horror or the lyricism of the American Civil War photographs.[14] There is little in most Victorian photography books to startle or disturb the casual viewer: scenes of comfortable domesticity, bourgeois family life; forays into moral questions in Pre-Raphaelite garb. As they are preserved in these images, at least, it seems that the Victorians we like best to look at inhabit a world of moral absolutes, sentimentalism, and confidence in their visual powers somewhat at odds, one would have thought, with the rather troubled climate of philosophical, scientific, and religious debate.

It is not within the scope of this essay to attend to the variety of ways in which our present mode of seeing the Victorians departs from the historical truth of who those people were (even if such a task were possible); my interest is rather in the use we make of the photographs left to us and the aesthetic we have created from them: for a taste for antiquity in the guise of the Victorian has expression now far beyond the formal presentation of images in exhibitions and books; and, as Wendy Wheeler notes, because "it is modernity that troubles us, what comes 'after' modernity is to be found written upon the features of our contemporary cultural life as the return of those things which are excluded, lost or repressed as a condition of modernity and of the subjectivity it produces."[15]

Take, for example, family photographs. Perhaps yours are not yet sufficiently old, but now thanks to the services of the mail-order catalog you can "transform family photos into heirloom originals"—a curious simultaneity of forward and backward planning. Pictures supplied by you can be reproduced on "cotton muslin in old-fashioned sepia tones, then combined with trinkets, buttons and vintage postcard reproductions in an evocative 36" square Family Photo Quilt" for a mere $295.[16] What exactly will be evoked by the quilt or the now sepia-colored images is by the way, for to be evocative here is to be only vaguely suggestive of an imprecise past commercially identified as "yesteryear." In nostalgia, specifics (including the specifics of the truly authentic) are unimportant, even a hindrance; one can be nostalgic for something one never experienced, or about which one has the vaguest impression or sketchiest memory. The word *vintage,* once meaning a specific and special year, now gestures loosely in the direction of a world in which we probably were not alive, or that we remember only from the perspective of childhood, and makes no claim to fact or specificity in its reference to the past.

The same catalog that can bring us the quilt offers us also a "personalized wedding certificate" to bring "old world romance to modern couples." Once again, it is not the thing itself that is old, because, like the quilt, the certificate will be made to order; here it is the process that endows the certificate with authenticity because it "dates back to medieval times." By virtue of using that process, the catalog implies, the wedding certificate is elevated to a higher art:

> Now you can have your own hand made testimony. We will send you a kit to include your wedding date and location, as well as signatures of both husband and wife. Each affidavit will be painstakingly rendered on parchment paper by an English artisan. After an individual hand aging process, the parchment paper is gilded, signed by the artist and stamped for authenticity. Your heirloom arrives ensconced in this rich gold frame ready to hang. (41)

Naturally, it helps that the artisan is English; so does the individuality of the aging process (authenticity promised in the synecdoche of the hand; parchment with its pedigree worth more than mere paper). Here, as with the quilt, instant lineage is projected. We may not have the ancestors but we can be them, and have the heirlooms ready to pass on down to anticipated future generations. Of course, it would be picky to note that heirlooms are usually new when they are original—that is, before they become heirlooms. These made-to-order heirlooms come instead prematurely aged, a mere invention to get them going, so to speak, to give them a leg up on the last hundred or so years of history. Now they are ready to be passed down, because they *look* as if they are old enough to be worth something, to have memories in tow. A whole line of projected begetting can even justify the $395 this last one costs.

One way of reading desire for these products of prefabricated history would be to argue that the aesthetic to which the quilt and the certificate appeal is actually ahistorical, developed out of a past emptied of history whose dialogic noise has been muffled. Certainly it is hard to quarrel with the viewpoint that the commodification of the past necessarily promotes image at the expense of word. The mess that is history is traded in for flat images that elide conflict and contradiction because, as Connor puts it, there is something of an "enshrined belief in the metaphysical priority of images over words, the belief that an image directly shows us the reality which words can only communicate in a fragile and untrustworthy manner" (97).[17] The quilt looks old and that is sufficient, because appearance constitutes reality and history is an expensive irrelevance.[18]

It certainly would come as no surprise to learn that producers of the postmodern have rid themselves of history and thus ended it, given the multitude of voices currently proclaiming the end of art, the death of the author, the end of literature (you name it, it's over).[19] But it is not quite true. History cannot be done away with because, like Barthes's referent, it *adheres*; the structures of thought that permit the essentializing of the Victorians are, as I have already noted, those inherited from the nineteenth century; the fudging of the past and the vague inaccuracies in the service of style represented by the wedding certificate and the newly minted heirloom quilt do not constitute a refusal to encounter the realities of the past so much as they suggest a vague but widely felt longing for a communion with it, even if it means having to make it first. The existence of the fake quilt does not mean that other quilts are not also crafted that people sleep under, keep for years, and pass down the family. The significance of the simulacrum in the catalog lies not in its substitution for the real but rather in its *self-consciousness* about that act, a self-consciousness about and a desire to "do" history that no more eradicates history than thinking about literature does away with it. As Linda Hutcheon argues, "We are not witnessing a degeneration into the hyperreal without origin or reality, but a questioning of what 'real' can mean and how we can *know* it."[20] What is occurring is neither the end of history nor an erasure of history from consciousness, but rather *a rethinking of what history itself is* even (and perhaps especially) in the experiencing of a commodified desire to visit it.

Heightened contemporary attention to photography of all kinds may thus be understood in this light as "a tangible symptom of an omnipresent, omnivorous and well-nigh libidinal historicism" (Jameson, 66); for just as in the crisis of legitimation, "questions of value and legitimacy do not disappear, but gain a new intensity" (Connor, 8), so through the obsessive historicism of contemporary visual taste, what history actually is—how we know it and whether we can—becomes increasingly pertinent. Re-creating the past, in our own or others' images, does not signify the dissolution of a real, fact-based history as much as it forces its reassertion (nor should we blush to use the word *real* occasionally unadorned by quotation marks).

Postmodern history need not find us, as academics, perched uncomfortably between the camps of either/or: either Baudrillard's collapse of difference and destruction of meaning in the age of the simulacra (easy to argue but depressing to live); or history-is-fact-not-text (into which camp it might harm one's career to fall).[21] Rather, it can push us into a new and vigorous consideration of all that the production of history entails, a task enabled by the play of the postmodern that highlights, as Hutcheon points out, "the modes of historiography we had come to consider 'natural': continuous narrative, inevitable development, universal (in other words, recognizable) patterns of action" (225). The magnetic field or "cultural dominant" that is postmodernism should in fact be understood as forcing discussion of the limits and uses of historical knowledge, through its continual and obsessive play between the authentic and the inauthentic (Jameson, 56).

Nostalgia and the Will to Authenticity

Desire for authenticity may be understood in part as a desire for that which we have first altered and then fetishized, a desire, perhaps, for a past in which we will find ourselves; but it is most frequently experienced and figured as a desire, or a sickness, for home. Whence this longing for home? Roger Rouse sees in contemporary society a sort of metaphorical mass dislocation, resulting from the fact that in modernity "we have all moved irrevocably to a new kind of social space"—the "social space of postmodernism"; Angelika Bammer argues that the old paradigms within which we used to situate ourselves are no longer operative, with the result that we have created the idea of home as the "imaginary point where here and there—where we are and where we come from—are momentarily grounded."[22] Recent critical discussion constructs home as a place where the self is initially defined, a place you cannot go back to but keep trying to revisit; a place of safety, "the last frontier," as Marianna Torgovnik calls it.[23] But home has its darker side: a desire for it may reflect the modernist will to origins, but in the postcolonial period it is frequently perceived as symptomatic of an elegiac mode of cultural vision complicit with domination—what Renato Rosaldo calls "imperialist nostalgia."[24] Home from this perspective is the "locus of regressive nostalgia . . . [a] rallying ground for reactionary nationalisms . . . linked from the very beginning to the particular pathology of violence and loss that marked the colonialist venture" (Bammer, x–xi).

The contemporary identification of home with notions of what is real has yet to be fully explored. Just a cursory glance at random home furnishing magazines shows a virtual obsession with the notion of authenticity, an authenticity frequently defined as Victorian.[25] *Country Living*'s house of the year, for example (February 1998), is a gothic revision, an "updated version" of a "picturesque style," every last detail "gothic inspired." Another featured house in the same edition, although built in 1983, boasts an "authentic feeling" by virtue of being stuffed with old objects. The irresistible ambiguity of the phrase "authentic feeling" promises to deliver real feeling as much as (or along with) authenticity—authenticity, that is, defined by longevity. What is inauthentic is the present, defined by default as fake, a replica or simulacrum of an absolute past.[26]

"If we are to build places for ourselves, we need to know who we are," writes David Kolb in a study of postmodern architecture.[27] But Kolb has it backwards; it is the places we build for ourselves that define who we are. Desire for identity, rather than identity itself, fuels in turn the desire that there *be* a there there where we can be at home—where we can be like, if we cannot be, ourselves. And, as Susan Stewart observes, "it is in [the] gap between resemblance and identity that nostalgic desire arises."[28] It is not because of who we are, but rather out of a desire for what we believe we *once were* that the inhabitants of the Disney-created town of Celebration, Florida, are driven to perform their civic identity in a willed re-creation of lost small-town America; just as it is nostalgic desire—more self-consciously ironic, perhaps, but no less performative—that unites the mock audience of the mock band Spinal Tap as it plays at being an audience.[29]

What we have today is a nostalgia for what is, in fact, already nostalgic: a desire for shared desire; a will toward an authenticity determined by communal consent. Academic treatments of nostalgia tend to dismiss it as reactionary and politically suspect, a combination of poor history and narcissistic imaginings, but nostalgia is not merely a symptom of massively retrogressive fantasies, nor, despite its association with the conservatism of the picturesque, is it an expression of underlying hatred for social change. To the student of cultural studies, nostalgia may well be "not really about the past but about its erasure by democratic mass society," as Elinor Fuchs claims—but the student of cultural studies forgets the postmodern complexities of history and indeed threatens a new essentialism by inferring a retrievable primary past to be subverted or erased by the falsification of nostalgic imagination.[30] Nostalgia cannot be said to essentialize history so much as it seeks its own; and, as Wheeler notes, in its construction of the past, nostalgia "offers no barriers to our understanding because it does not appeal in the first place to critical understanding but to experience and affect" (98). This is presumably part of the perceived danger, as much as it is the appeal of commercial nostalgia: its artifacts—the heirloom quilt, the wedding certificate, the house stuffed with authenticity, the lost small-town America town, the mock rock concert—*look* authentic, just as they appear to reference an authentic lived experience. Thus the absent original becomes ever more fetishized, for its authority must be distinguished from subsequent imitations.

It is the sense of dislocation from primary experience figured in such remakes of history that photography embodies and simultaneously promises to heal. If, as Susan Sontag has written, "everything exists to end in a photograph," then everything may also be said to begin its afterlife at that point—to achieve authenticity in a sort of post-real representational world.[31] Loss, after all, is the precondition of nostalgia, and whatever is feared lost is fetishized by its association, at times its conflation, with the imagined primary experience that initially shaped identity. Photographs of the past have thus come to signify a kind of last resort—Torgovnik's last frontier—the final resting place of the truly authentic. And although they cannot cure our *nostos algos,* our sickness for home, Victorian photographs find a place and a time for it.

Notes

1. Raphael Samuel, *Theatres of Memory* (London: Verso, 1994), 1:337.

2. Realism, of course, has a history of collision with notions of what is real, and its association with Victorian culture seems to have made it especially vulnerable to the notion that the world revealed to us by its microscopes and telescopes is somehow the product or the consequence of its outlook; as though empiricism were nothing more than an affirmation of relations between words and things.

3. Richard Terdiman, *Present Past: Modernity and the Memory Crisis* (Ithaca, N.Y.: Cornell University Press, 1993), 3; Jennifer Green-Lewis, *Framing the Victorians: Photography and the Culture of Realism* (Ithaca, N.Y.: Cornell University Press, 1996), 16.

4. The nineteenth century has a great many places to alight: thanks to recent movies, one can make quite specific stops in nineteenth-century America from Hawthorne to Henry James; in England, the track stretches between Jane Austen and Thomas Hardy, current final destination E. M. Forster. Here I make little or no distinction between what are clearly very different destinations, because my subject—the creation of a past that is only generally "Victorian"—presupposes a lack of precision.

5. John Tagg, *The Burden of Representation: Essays on Photographies and Histories* (Amherst: University of Massachusetts Press, 1988), 3, 1.

6. Roland Barthes, *Camera Lucida* (New York: Farrar, Straus and Giroux, 1981), 6; Wallace Stevens, "A Postcard from the Volcano," in *The Palm at the End of the Mind,* ed. Holly Stevens (New York: Vintage Books, 1972), 127.

7. Steven Connor, *Postmodernist Culture: An Introduction to Theories of the Contemporary* (Oxford and Cambridge: Basil Blackwell, 1991), 4; Jürgen Habermas, *Legitimation Crisis,* trans. Thomas McCarthy (London: Heinemann, 1975), 4; Connor 8; Michel Foucault, *The Foucault Reader,* ed. Paul Rabinow (Harmondsworth, England: Peregrine/Penguin, 1986), 39.

8. On its display at the Art Treasures Exhibition of Manchester in 1857, *Humphrey's Journal of Photography* found *The Two Ways of Life* to be "[A] magnificent picture, decidedly the finest photograph of its class ever produced" (9:1857, 93; qtd. in Beaumont Newhall, *The History of Photography* (New York: Museum of Modern Art, Little, Brown, 1982), 74, a comment possibly tempered by the fact that the queen purchased it. Victoria's artistic tastes were considered by some to be lamentably middlebrow. See Stanley Weintraub, *Victoria* (New York: Truman Talley, 1992), 117.

9. Charles Newman, *The Post-Modern Aura: The Act of Fiction in an Age of Inflation* (Evanston, Ill.: Northwestern University Press, 1985), 10.

10. Joel Snyder, "Picturing Vision," in *The Language of Images,* ed. W. J. T. Mitchell (Chicago and London: University of Chicago Press, 1980), 224.

11. To ask these questions is, of course, to assume that a photographic canon may be used as an index of contemporary as well as historical taste, and to further assume that works will be marginalized if they do not satisfy or confirm current beliefs about any given period.

12. Michel Foucault, *Discipline and Punish: The Birth of the Prison,* trans. Alan Sheridan (New York: Vintage Books, 1979), 217.

13. See Mark Haworth-Booth, ed., *The Golden Age of British Photography 1839–1900* (New York: Aperture Press, 1984).

14. The notable absence of drama from the nonetheless very popular Crimean War photographs (1854–56) was less a technical consequence than an indication of taste on the part of Roger Fenton, his patrons, and his public. See Green-Lewis, 97–144.

15. Wendy Wheeler, "Nostalgia Isn't Nasty—The Postmodernising of Parliamentary Democracy," in *Altered States: Postmodernism, Politics, Culture,* ed. Mark Perryman (London: Lawrence and Wishart, 1994), 96.

16. *Exposures* catalog (winter 1998): 40.

17. It need hardly be said that the most theoretically inclined of photography's recent critics do not share this view. See, for example, the work of Victor Burgin, which is driven by an understanding of photography's immanent textuality: "the intelligibility of the photograph is no simple thing; photographs are texts inscribed in terms of what we may call 'photographic discourse'" (*Thinking Photography,* ed.

Victor Burgin [London: Macmillan, 1988], 144); see also Alan Sekula (in Burgin); Snyder; Tagg; and, more recently, Eduardo Cadava, *Words of Light: Theses on the Photography of History* (Princeton, N.J.: Princeton University Press, 1997).

18. See Carol Mavor for discussion of our "tradition of infantilizing history" by remaking the Victorians "into lost, innocent children" in a past "free from wear and tear" (*Pleasures Taken: Performances of Sexuality and Loss in Victorian Photographs* [Durham, N.C.: Duke University Press, 1995], 3).

19. Fredric Jameson finds the widespread sense "of the end of this or that" (which he rather suggestively terms "inverted millenarianism") to be, indeed, a defining element of postmodernism ("The Cultural Logic of Capital," *New Left Review* 146 [1984]: 53).

20. Linda Hutcheon, *A Poetics of Postmodernism: History, Theory, Fiction* (London: Routledge, 1988), 223.

21. See Jean Baudrillard, *Simulacra and Simulation,* trans. Sheila Faria Glaser (Ann Arbor: University of Michigan Press, 1994).

22. Roger Rouse, qtd. in *New Formations* 17, ed. Angelika Bammer (summer 1992): viii; Bammer, ix.

23. Marianna Torgovnik, "Slasher Stories," *New Formations* 17 (summer 1992): 145.

24. Renato Rosaldo, *Culture and Truth: The Remaking of Social Analysis* (Boston: Beacon Press, 1989), 69–70.

25. The lingerie store Victoria's Secret is obviously also in the business of authentication, assuming that its products are what "real" women wear, just as femininity seems to be what is on offer at *Victoria* magazine, a glossy potpourri (a word they like a lot) of Anglophilia in the shape of home furnishings, clothing, recipes, and wedding-day fantasies.

26. Of course, there is a hierarchy of (in)authenticity; not for readers of *Country Living* the made-to-order antique wedding certificates or the newly minted heirloom quilts; the 1983 house is presumably more "authentic," if the price tag is indexed to authenticity.

27. David Kolb, *Postmodern Sophistications: Philosophy, Architecture and Tradition* (Chicago and London: University of Chicago Press, 1990), 159.

28. Susan Stewart, *On Longing: Narratives of the Miniature, the Gigantic, the Souvenir, the Collection* (Durham, N.C., and London: Duke University Press, 1993), 145.

29. Spinal Tap, the parodic heavy metal rock band created for a 1984 mock documentary, was so popular that it actually went on tour twice: "We get to go on stage and pretend that we're Spinal Tap. And the fans get to play too, because they get to pretend that they're real Spinal Tap fans." Identity as it is performed in the social space of the mock concert depends on the self-consciousness of parodic remove, in that the audience is united by its mass identification of what is not real—all of which raises a question voiced by one of the band's creators, Rob Reiner: "So what are the criteria for what is a real band?" (*Washington Post,* 15 March 1992, G11).

30. Elinor Fuchs, "Postmodernism and the Scene of Theatre," in *Signs of Change: Premodern-Modern-Postmodern,* ed. Stephen Barker (Albany: State University of New York Press, 1996), 33. I am aware that I must answer to the same charge as that student, of course, in consequence of my contention that there is, indeed, such a thing as a real past as distinguished from re-creations of it. Sensitive as we may be in theory to the textuality of all history, in practice, teachers, scholars, and readers make judgments between historical texts, judgments that have in large part to do with their accuracy as much as their utility. How we go about making those judgments (and, indeed, distinguishing between what is useful and what is accurate) is one of the more pressing questions urged by postmodernism.

31. Susan Sontag, *On Photography* (New York: Doubleday, 1977), 24.

The Uses and Misuses of Oscar Wilde

Shelton Waldrep

Perhaps beginning as early as Sir Peter Hall's 1992 revival of the play that Wilde thought his masterpiece, *An Ideal Husband,* Wilde has been reappearing with a vengeance. Wilde's wife, Constance Lloyd (later Wilde, then Holland), has a play devoted to her, and Tom Stoppard's latest effort, *The Invention of Love,* has Wilde show up in the last act only to steal the show. Stephen Fry plays him in the film *Wilde* and Liam Neeson stars as Wilde on Broadway in *The Judas Kiss* and may play him in another biopic. Off Broadway, Wilde appears as the suffering victim of Victorian morality in Moises Kaufman's *Gross Indecency: The Three Trials of Oscar Wilde.* In essentially all of these versions of Wilde one sees a familiar portrait of the artist as a condemned man with the Victorian press as the enemy—the Marquess of Queensberry, the father of Wilde's aristocratic lover, Lord Alfred "Bosie" Douglas, becomes the embodiment not so much of the Victorian population's superego, but its id. The courts become the unwitting supporters of Queensberry's paranoia and insane patriarchal urgings just as Wilde remains the figure who refused good advice at almost all stages of his own tragedy.

Indeed, the most recent version of Wilde has changed little from the Wilde we have seen since at least the 1940s; that is, Wilde is represented primarily as a tragic figure incapable either of removing his own inaction in the face of the criminal trials or going against Bosie's wishes to make them into a comeuppance to his father. In spite of the fact that the Labouchère amendment, under which Wilde was convicted for gross indecency with another man, was in effect until 1967, Wilde's plight is made to seem, nonetheless, a peculiarly Victorian one, and the other Victorians in Wilde's life are largely portrayed as hypocritical moral police who destroyed a man of genius. Within this unvarying scenario, Wilde was not only the first fully formed gay martyr, but also the last Victorian one. In both cases, Wilde seems to grow in cult status even as he becomes better known than he could have ever imagined (and he could imagine a lot). Wilde continues as that rare exception: a well-known marginalized person; a star famous for his exclusion.

It is telling that for all of the cult of personality that Wilde's influence seems to contain, the Wilde we get in much recent work is a rather remote version of the man himself. Indeed, many of the reviews of the recent portrayals of Wilde remark the fact that we do not get a very good look into the mind of Wilde. Even in the most ambitious deconstruction of his myth, Kaufman's play, Wilde appears as a distant figure whose set speeches—mainly in court—are overdetermined dramatic moments in which the audience is supposed to be overwhelmed by what appear to be the mere facts of the story. For those who might already know the plot—even the bare outline— the play depends too much on our shock at the evil treatment he receives, even though the writer plays with the idea that Wilde lied on the stand about the true nature of his homosexuality. But to reduce the trial to this fact alone is to miss the point of everything else that the trials might have meant. That is, Wilde is still being encoded as a gay martyr, with this idea containing much of the dramatic punch for recent versions of Wilde's life. Plays and films may now be able to treat Wilde's homosexuality with less delicate gloves than in the past, but it is still the mere fact of this activity that the versions can never escape. To make the activities "everyday" ones is not really an option as it is the emergence of Wilde's queerness that makes him "mean" in this historical context at all.

This is not to say that the recent popular version of Wilde is without anything new to add to the legend. In Kaufman's play especially an attempt is made to wrestle with the way in which we represent Wilde. Kaufman's solution is to fashion a play made up wholly of the discourses that attempt to explain him—from the biographies written by Wilde's contemporaries to new literary or cultural scholarship on him. Likewise, the commentary of some critics on the recent explosion of representations of Wilde cautions that we should not make him signify only as a gay martyr (or Irish national-ist, as in Terry Eagleton's *Saint Oscar*). Rather, we should think about how it is that we are playing Wilde.[1] Although this awareness that Wilde is some-how being misrepresented is a sign of a problem with the popularity of Wilde, there really is not a current representation of Wilde that actually challenges the usual version. Even Kaufman, while raising the question of just how one should define Wilde, makes this important point into a joke placed at the beginning of the second act when a somewhat shy and befuddled English professor is made to discuss the meaning of Wilde's trials with the author. The interview comes across like a parody of a local TV talk show—with the professor as the rube—though the real point is not only how preposterous academics are supposed to be, but how incapable they are of seeing just what Wilde really represents: a homosexual who was imprisoned because he was gay. At one point, the author asks the expert, "And what happens in the trial?" to which the character, Marvin Taylor, replies: "Well, what happens in the trial is he [Wilde] comes head on up against legal discourse, and perhaps I would even say legal-medical discourse. And he begins to lose to this sort of patriarchal medical discourse that makes him appear to be a homosexual as opposed to hum . . . someone who had desire for other men." Kaufman goes on to question Taylor about the use of the modern definition of the term *homosexual* as applied to Wilde, and what one should do about the question of Wilde's lying on the stand about his own homosexuality—a key moment in the play's plot. The interview concludes with Taylor noting that "what they [the prosecutors] were trying to do I think was to fix homosexuality, to contain the disruption which Wilde presented, and this is a disruption of all kinds of things, of class, of gender, of hum sexuality, hum and they did that, very successfully."[2]

Although presented parodically here, the same point is made by the gay actor Stephen Fry in an essay on preparing for the part of Wilde in the new film version. Fry describes Wilde as a "messianic" figure who "rose again to become within a short time after his death the most widely read and trans-lated English-language author in Europe after Shakespeare, and he lives with us now in boxer shorts, playing cards, coffee mugs, coasters, and pencil sharpeners."[3] Fry points out that for him—and by implication for other gay men—he and/or the times have changed and what should be of interest as concerns Wilde is not his ability to act as a poster boy for gay liberation, but something else instead:

I still retain affection for that luxuriantly poisonous style, but it is, I suppose, not much more than literary drag, and, like so many drag acts, it can become tiresome. At any rate, it has nothing whatever to do with Oscar Wilde or his works. Indeed, such images are only part of what the current jargon labels the "self-oppression" to which we are all prey. Wilde's courage lay not in his "alternative sexuality" but in the freedom of his mind. To picture him primarily as a gay martyr *avant la lettre* is, I think, to play into the very hands of those who brought him down a hundred years ago. (87)

Both of these writers make gestures toward understanding the complexities of Wilde's signification. The reality, however, is that Wilde once again gets presented as an example of what the 1990s saw as important about Wilde: his role as gay martyr.[4] The representation of Wilde as an iconoclast is ultimately subordinate to this idea. What is lost, in fact, is almost any sense of Wilde as anything but the representation of an ideological struggle between the forces of repression and rebellion. One could posit that this recent idea of Wilde is not only reflective of its particular times, but also particularly sterile in its ability to get at any of the complexity of Wilde. One can, in fact, compare some of the recent versions to earlier incarnations of Wilde existing well within the postmodern, though reflecting generational or decadal differences, to see that Wilde has been better handled before. Like the Victorian period itself, Wilde is often treated like a period piece in which certain rules of "authenticity" seem to be in effect. Sometimes in the retelling of Wilde's life, however, the opposite also seems to obtain as Wilde is made to represent the particular mood of the times that create him.[5] Although the directors of two planned film versions of *An Ideal Husband* were unaware of each other's film before they had committed themselves to the project, it is interesting that the two films differ in their settings: one approaches the play as a period piece set in London in the 1890s, while the other sets the story in the contemporary period in the shires outside of London.[6] The purported reason to do the latter instead of the former is to show the "relevance" of Wilde's work. Viewing Wilde both as a contemporary and as a part of history—though as a version of relevant history that may see that history as the beginning of our own—is part of a schizoid split in the use of Wilde. Why would we want Wilde to be both historical and contemporary? What can be said about these twin impulses, and how is it that Wilde is the figure who most embodies our own split consciousness about things Victorian?

In a general discussion of the representation of the Victorian period on film, Garrett Stewart offers a possible explanation:

> If more films treating Victorian subjects have been produced in the last few years than at any other point in recent memory, they are also very different from historical biography on film, let alone from Civil War pictures or Indian colonial adventures. Whether adaptations of famous novels or not, they are concerned less with the historical than with the personal, the intimate, or the psychosexual.[7]

He later concludes: "In the age of the digitalized generation rather than the chemical registration of images, there is a growing nostalgia for the real itself—and for the way the real once gave itself up to film, first to photography and then to cinema" (184). The filmic representation of the Victorian, in other words, has replaced photography, which used to act as a real link to a past that some could still remember. We now suffer nostalgia for the real, which Stewart also refers to as "social memory" as opposed to the "kind of cultural fantasy" that movies about the Victorian period offer instead. If this is the case, then the biographical nature of many of the recent cultural representations of Wilde functions, at least in part, to allow us to explore our own present—what Stewart refers to as the "psychosexual"—as an attempt to rediscover our primal scene of originary technological fetishism. What is perhaps most striking is that the process for understanding the present involves looking backward, not forward, in time. As Stewart finally notes: "The modernist 'make it new' has become a postmodernist revamping: the resuscitating of history in an image of the present—and of the present's own image systems. To borrow a term from the photochemical medium itself, this is the true double exposure of Victorian culture in contemporary film" (194).

Although it is Coppola's version of Dracula that Stewart uses as his example of this effect, the 1997 film *Wilde* seems to follow his formula perfectly in its attempt to summon a "real" version of Wilde for the screen. The film opens with the wonderful conceit of showing Wilde in Colorado during his visit to the silver mine at Leadville, where the miners dedicated a new vein to him called "The Oscar." This scene is well played by Fry, who establishes Wilde as someone who responds sincerely and genuinely to generosity in others; that is, when a young Adonis-like miner asks him questions about Benvenuto Cellini while filling Wilde's glass with liquor, Wilde is not only touched by the genuineness of the hospitality but is also quite comfortable to be at the bottom of a mine shaft rather than in a salon in London. This scene is fanciful in its depiction of the miners, but it is key to understanding the rest of the film—especially the ways in which the scene illustrates Wilde's ability to cross class lines with ease, and acts as a contrast to Wilde's later discomfort in the male brothel to which Douglas will take him and where similar manners are not in place. Indeed, Wilde's inability to fit it in at Taylor's has less to do with his role as a family man than with Douglas's flagrant attempts to embarrass him and show off in front of him by making love to one of the renters. The tension within Wilde's life, then, comes not from Wilde's loyalties being divided between Douglas and his wife but from Douglas and his own sense of how one should treat others.[8]

As even the trailers for the film proclaim, this version of Wilde is supposed to be the most accurate one so far. Although this claim seems to refer to the more candid depiction of gay sex, Fry's article on preparing for the role suggests that at least part of what the producers wanted to accomplish was to present the complexity of Wilde's life by showing not only that he was gay, but just how this fact took its toll on Wilde's marriage—most especially his relationship with his children, which is shown to be of great importance to him. The desire on the part of the film to posit a more family-oriented Wilde at the same time that it candidly represents Wilde's (and Douglas's) sexuality comes out of a scholarly approach that repositions Wilde as queer, not gay, or, as Fry and others see him, as someone who struggled against categorization on all fronts—not just the sexual.[9] The film follows logically from this reevaluation of Wilde. What the film fails in, however, are two things: (1) it tries too hard to be a biopic, to fill in the various gaps in Wilde's life (homosexual and heterosexual); (2) it does not really recognize the extent to which it is indebted to the history of the cinematic portrayal of Wilde and his work. The former is much more of a problem in that by struggling mightily to make the film correct factual inaccuracies in the story of Wilde's life, the film's creative team fails to give us a story with any real drama. As a film, *Wilde* never takes the risks it needs to in order to avoid being simply the fairly reliable capsule summary of Wilde's downfall that it essentially is. Rather than risk radically challenging the notion of Wilde's gayness—or, the opposite, making that the main theme of the film—the director and/or writer has opted instead for a version of Wilde that will probably please no one. The film contains few moments like the opening scene in

Colorado—a gambit that pays off. Most scenes are instead tastefully under-played by Fry and stick to Richard Ellmann's biography fairly scrupulously. In other words, the film can be quite dull.

There are, however, two moments—entirely visual ones—that work well and that suggest just what our collective interest in Wilde might be all about. The first scene occurs early in the film when Wilde is settled in London after returning from America and takes to the street in a sumptuous butter-colored outfit that advertises his neo-dandy look. As Wilde walks through a square he runs into a group of barristers that part for him much like a school of dull fish encountering a barracuda (see figure 1). The irony, of course, and it is all visual, is that Wilde will find himself head-to-head with the legal es-tablishment in a few years' time, and during that battle he will be the one who is knocked off course. The second image comes at the end of Wilde's fa-mous speech after the curtain drops on the premiere of *The Importance of Being Earnest*—Wilde's greatest theatrical success. As Wilde seems almost overcome by the audience's spontaneous reaction to the play, the camera pans back at a high angle showing Wilde alone on the stage—and in the

Figure 1. Confident after his American tour, a young Wilde strides against the legal establishment that will later bring him down. Stephen Fry in *Wilde* (1997). Copyright 1997 Samuelson Entertainment Limited, N.D.F. International, Ltd. Photograph by Liam Daniel. Reprinted by permission.

Figure 2. Triumphant on opening night, Wilde is alone in a crowd at the cusp of his tragic fall. Stephen Fry in *Wilde* (1997). Copyright 1997 Samuelson Entertainment Limited, N.D.F. International, Ltd. Photograph by Liam Daniel. Reprinted by permission.

frame (see figure 2). The effect is to remind us that even during the height of the applause, Wilde is shouldering a great number of burdens and might be alone in facing them. Wilde has no one to turn to and is on a path that will ultimately find him abandoned by the very people who would, literally, applaud him. Both of these images from the film are premonitions of the fall to come, yet both emphasize our enjoyment in seeing Wilde as both a flamboyant rogue and, paradoxically, a tragic figure. The film fails to generate enough of a sense of the former—the times when Wilde was able to conquer London on his own terms and present a challenge to the establishment. To take this aspect away from Wilde—or de-emphasize it—does as much of a disservice to him as making the tragedy seem like the inevitable birth of gay identity via the sacrifice of and mourning for a brilliant man.

Wilde's meaning for us now, then, is relatively little changed. We can hope to see him as a multifaceted thinker and writer ahead of his time, but in fact we keep reinventing him each time he reappears. The popular representations of Wilde that are currently in vogue emphasize some of the complexity of representing Wilde, yet fail as works of art to function apart from mere biography. It may well be that we are still underestimating Wilde. The production of *An Ideal Husband* playing, as I write, in the West End has the dandy figure, Lord Goring, played by the actor Christopher Cazenove made up to look like Wilde—a mistake not only of age, but also in interpreting the play. Wilde may have toyed with the public's perception of him via his dandies in *Dorian Gray* and in the plays, but he certainly meant for these figures to do more than function simply as stand-ins for himself. Wilde would never be so vulgar or simplistic, and popular representations of Wilde should strive to do something of the same rather than settling for a convenient caricature of his myth.

Paralleling the representations of Wilde on the stage and screen has been an equally active reassessment of Wilde in the academy. Perhaps because of the activist nature of much of their work, queer studies scholars fashion a Wilde that is much the same as the one found in the popular representations of him. For example, Wayne Koestenbaum argues that the postprison Wilde that Ellmann's biography seems to ask us to reexamine is a Wilde who has accepted his homosexuality and attempted, in his last two works, *De Profundis* and *The Ballad of Reading Gaol,* to posit a reader who would by today's definition be called gay. Koestenbaum argues that the result of Wilde's "hard labor" was the "birth of gay reading," the polemical aspects of which may be discerned in Wilde's interest in the design and printing of his last published works (which included, e.g., *The Importance of Being Earnest*). In this romantic, if not primarily personal, reading of Wilde, he sends his books on into the century he was never to see with the encoding of an identity that would surface with a vengeance—yet not know full collective political identity until after Stonewall. Koestenbaum's reading suggests that Wilde's last three years after prison were, if not productive of text, at least of subtle signs designed to show that he was not only aware of his new definitional power, but attempted to turn it into something that we would now recognize as an early sense of identity politics. Although one might welcome Koestenbaum's early attempt at the revival of Wilde as an agent in his own reconstruction, this take on Wilde assumes not only that he gave up his own earlier attempts at avoiding sexual binaries, but also that he prophesied a movement and a cause that, in fact, he may well have never accepted. Koestenbaum seems to depend for his solution to the Wildean conundrum on the idea that the political activism that affected Wilde vis-à-vis prison reform could be, or was, wedded to his interest in same-sex desire. The resulting birth, though

Koestenbaum does not put it quite so bluntly, was the gay reader. Wilde's works, therefore, only awaited the correct audience of the future.[10]

Much scholarly work on Wilde's sexual meaning since Koestenbaum has attempted to paint him as a "queer" presence rather than a "gay" one. The subtle distinction is both the difference between the work and the man or the genuine undecidability about the importance he would have placed on the sexual as opposed to (or distinct from) other axes of his identity. Does "queer," in other words, allow us to connect some of the dots? For Eve Kosofsky Sedgwick, a queer Wilde is a Wilde who is very aware of many more binaries than the homo/hetero divide—no matter how troubling that particular one would become for him; that is, Wilde's confusing of auto/allo sexuality in *The Picture of Dorian Gray*—Dorian's self-love as a way to displace male-male desire into an aesthetic realm or register or Wilde's Proustian pseudonationality as an Irish Protestant in exile—is as important to understand as is the moment that his work crystallizes as the "invention" of homosexuality.[11] More recently, Jonathan Dollimore and Alan Sinfield, along with Joseph Bristow and others, have labeled Wilde "queer" for the similar reason that he represents for them both the codification of a regime of signs—whether pregiven, self-selected, or a little of both—and a space, inherently political and/or theoretical, in which an opposition to oppression could be articulated and staged. Wilde's individuality, his refusal of any phallocentric reading, makes visible an identity whose time has finally come—queer, not straight. As Sinfield explains:

> For us, it is hard to regard Wilde as other than the apogee of gay experience and expression, because that is the position we have accorded him in our cultures. For us, he is always-already queer—as that stereotype has prevailed in the twentieth century (for the sake of clarity, I write "queer" for that historical phase—not contradicting, thereby, its recent revival among activists—and "gay" for post-Stonewall kinds of consciousness). But Wilde's typicality is after-the-effect—after, I believe, the trials helped to produce a major shift in perceptions of the scope of same-sex passion. At that point, the entire, vaguely disconcerting nexus of effeminacy, leisure, idleness, immorality, luxury, insouciance, decadence and aestheticism, which Wilde was perceived, variously, as instantiating, was transformed into a brilliantly precise image.[12]

That moment of transformation is both the moment that "queer" becomes visible in Wilde and something that comes into formation as the structural equivalent of "gay"—that is, what will be called "gay" after Stonewall. Sinfield's definition seems to suggest that the differences between "queer" and "gay" are only a matter of philology. In fact, the deployment of a queer Wilde instead of a gay one would help us to understand that queer can mean, as Scott Wilson argues: "that which is and is not 'gay' and 'lesbian,' it would take into account and affirm a certain heterogeneity that overflows the terms 'gay' and 'lesbian,' takes into account the slippage into negative being, into a non-identity that has the potential to inaugurate different modes of being, different forms of identity."[13]

Yet Wilde continues, in much of this type of scholarship, to function as the gay avatar and to be thought of as the originary moment for the gay definitional systems of the next century. The dangers involved with making Wilde into a gay figure are recognized early by Neil Bartlett in his prescient memoir/fable, *Who Was That Man?*, when he writes of the contradictory nature of claiming Wilde as a hero if one is a gay man:

> If I read this story in a certain light, I begin to wonder, in what sense of the word was this most famous of homosexuals actually a homosexual? He was married. His best and most successful play, *The Importance of Being Earnest* . . . celebrates the triumph of marriage over all adversity, brings down its curtain on a trio of engagements, and was deliberately premiered on St. Valentine's Day. . . . Nothing in the texts themselves demands that we read them otherwise; why should we, for instance, regard the love letters to Lord Alfred Douglas as more authentic or more important then the (lost) love letters to Constance Lloyd, Mrs. Oscar Wilde? Why should the hints of slumming or possibly homosexual scandal in the story of Dorian Gray be so carefully traced, treated as more significant or more interesting than Gray's openly declared heterosexual interest in beautiful powerless women, actresses and farm labourers? . . . So much for our lovingly constructed images of Wilde as martyr and hero. So much for the life that we imagine the handsome stranger may lead after dark. We were wrong to believe that a hidden meaning would necessarily be a subversive one, one that would help us to identify or liberate ourselves.[14]

Bartlett immediately offers another version: "The second method of interpretation appears to be a simple reverse of the first. Instead of criticizing the text (burrowing into it, attacking it, pursuing its obscure connections), I celebrate it. I do not dwell unnecessarily on the contradictions of Oscar's social position, or on the peculiarity of my choice of him as father and guide to the city [London]" (35). In other words, Bartlett constructs his own personal Wilde. His book itself is half fan letter written by a late-twentieth-century gay Londoner and half academic treatise. Bartlett understands the porousness of forms and identities where Wilde is concerned, but also that Wilde asks that one take the same approach to him that he took toward the homosexual type:

> Last night I tried to convince him [Wilde] that the real theory being proposed in *The Portrait of Mr. W. H.* does not concern the origin of Shakespeare's sonnets at all. The theory that Wilde is proposing is about our origins as homosexual men. At the very moment at which, historically, we begin to exist, he created a biography of a homosexual man in which the fake and the true are quite indistinguishable. He proposed that our present is continually being written by our history; that the individual voice can hardly be separated from the historic text which it repeats and adapts. If that is true, then we must choose our words with as much invention as care. (209)

Bartlett has learned to use Wilde only by understanding that Wilde makes the homosexual forever an impossible invention: something that can only be theorized but never represented. Wilde is unable, or unwilling, to make the figure of the homosexual a stable entity within his texts. Likewise, Bartlett is never able to bridge the contradictions inherent in having Wilde as a hero in his own life. His own book ends with him slashing the portrait of Wilde in an echo of the ending of *Dorian Gray*. Prior to this moment, however, Bartlett writes letters to Wilde in which he refigures the contradictions of Wilde as a gay martyr. Reproduced in Sinfield's book on Wilde, these letters are described by Wilson:

> The first letter expresses the great debt owed to Wilde as the sacrificial father-figure of the gay community, and celebrates the relative freedom of gay men unknown in Wilde's time. In the second, more disturbing letter, however, Oscar Wilde is perceived as a "fat bitch." He has an obscene, suffocating cadaverous presence, as if his were the stultifying, even murderous corpse of that homosexual identity. (245)

The anxiety provoked by Wilde in some gay men is part of the problem of celebrating him as his very ability to "mean" so much is what dooms him in court. Wilson goes further to question whether using Wilde as a gay martyr at all might not also mean that twentieth-century gay male identity has forever connected itself to the work of mourning; that is, if Wilde's incarceration and ruin brought forth the birth of the gay man, then what are the effects of positing his death as a martyr at the heart of one's definitional matrix? If we celebrate Wilde, are we not also celebrating death itself? Wilson explains:

> The great problem for a gay community that would authorize its existence by realizing Wilde's life and death as a gift in the very act of receiving it, is the degree to which, as a martyr, Wilde becomes canonized. That is, Wilde is made not merely a saint, but is of necessity positioned as the standard by which a gay life and identity is measured. In this case, the gay community instantly places itself in perpetual debt; its communal identity can only be established, if it ever can be established, within a system of exchanges in which death is the ordering principle, within an economy that requires each member to return what Wilde has given in order continually to realize, as his own, the communal identity. Thus, such a community becomes morbid: a community defined by, identified with and identical to, death. (240–41)

One way out of this logic is to realize that Wilde's sexuality represents, as Wilson says after Derrida, "another name for the impossible because the very conditions that make a gift possible annul the possibility of a gift. For a gift to be truly a gift it cannot take part in any exchange or economy" (241). We can never know if Wilde intended to give his life as a gift, to give it up to an identity that he was never to know. We do not know what he intended, or whether he ever really felt that the identity the courts were in the process of making for him was one he would ever have wanted to name. By giving his life he did bring about an identity that we think we know yet never actually realize. Throughout his work Wilde suggests that homosexuality—what we might now say is homosexuality—is not something that we can ever really name. Wilde's life is sacrificed to unknowing in a way that complements his work. Rather than attempt to know what he might have intended, it may well be that the use to which Wilde should be put is in the service of better understanding the conflictual nature of gay community itself: another impossible identity that gives more to us than we know how to return.

As Wilson notes about *The Portrait of Mr. W. H.,* the identity of Cyril Graham, "the inexorably doomed homosexual," is, like the portrait of Willy Hughes, a fake (237). This fact does not mean that Wilde's essay does not make desire real, but naming the desire—and perhaps realizing it fully—is something about which the author seems indifferent. The homosexual desire in Wilde's piece is everywhere present, nowhere named, and is finally negated like the story of Hughes. The desire to find what is true is subordinated to the simulacra created by the trope of interpretation itself. Wilde hides nothing, yet he cautions against making the obvious into the quantifiable, and this is precisely what happens to him both at his trials and in the next century.

Certainly Wilde's current popularity has much to do with his proto-postmodernism, his ability to place himself, whenever possible, into the systems of exchange brought about via technology, advertising, and the canniness of posing. His subsequent fame, however, says more about us than him and mirrors our desire to look into the past for the present. If the 1950s and 1960s were the decades of futurology, then the 1990s were times of looking back in order to see ahead. Wilde proclaimed his own '90s as the period of the modern, yet he also looked to Romanticism and Medievalism for inspiration in correcting what he saw as blights on the present: whether factories or Naturalist novels. The modern times he lived in were, he hoped, ones in which the spirit and form of ancient Greece could be reborn. We seem to wish that Wilde himself could be reborn and his late-Victorian era brought back so that we could better understand how he was to author the transformation of his own body into a text. Our nostalgia is for him, but our representations of him betray our own anxieties about our origins and structures for knowing ourselves.

Notes

1. For example, see Adam Gopnik, "The Invention of Oscar Wilde," *New Yorker* (18 May 1998): 78–88.

2. Moises Kaufman, "Gross Indecency: The Three Trials of Oscar Wilde," *American Theatre* 14 (1997): 35–36.

3. Stephen Fry, "Playing Oscar," *New Yorker* (16 June 1997): 85.

4. We have to consider not only the idea that this martyrdom was not necessarily chosen by Wilde, but also that it is only in the next century that his suffering is made to mean homosexuality via a system of signification that is heterosexist. To claim Wilde as a gay saint—in a sort of reverse move similar to the reclamation of *queer*—is also to risk reinscribing the very system that Wilde may have wanted most to foil.

5. For example, in the two film versions of Wilde's life that opened in 1960, one starring Peter Finch and one Robert Morley, the producers chose to tell the

story of Wilde as a period piece. The version of *Dorian Gray* from 1970, while based on Wilde's novel, sets the events in the present and uses the novel as a way to comment on the sexual mores of the burgeoning decade of the 1970s.

6. Appearing too late to receive adequate comment here, Oliver Parker's 1999 film of *An Ideal Husband* is especially successful at transferring a long, talky play into cinema. The casting of Rupert Everett as Goring is inspired, though Jeremy Northam as Chiltern almost steals the show. Northam also appears in David Mamet's film version of Terence Rattigan's *The Winslow Boy,* a production that seems indirectly influenced by Wilde just as Mamet's play *Boston Marriage* is directly a result of Mamet's experimenting with writing in Wilde's own style.

7. Garrett Stewart, "Film's Victorian Retrofit," *Victorian Studies* 38.2 (1995): 183.

8. In a further example of the way in which the film makes differences in class visible, the boys at Taylor's are objectified in a wholly other way than the miners are in Wilde's (and the film's) tacit comparison of them to Cellini's models. I thank Jane Kuenz for pointing this difference out to me.

9. In some ways, we are back to the binary of Kaufman's play: Did Wilde lie? If so, why? Or to an even more relevant debate within gay male culture: Should gay men attempt to "normalize" themselves, or maintain an unassimilability—an outsider's identity? Recent debates between queer theorists such as Michael Warner and pro-marriage gay activists such as Gabriel Rotello possibly replay some of the same questions.

10. Wayne Koestenbaum, "Wilde's Hard Labor and the Birth of Gay Reading," in *Engendering Men,* ed. Joseph Boone and Michael Cadden (New York: Routledge, 1990), 176–89.

11. Eve Kosofsky Sedgwick, *Epistemology of the Closet* (Berkeley: University of California Press, 1990).

12. Alan Sinfield, *The Wilde Century: Effeminacy, Oscar Wilde and the Queer Moment* (New York: Columbia University Press, 1994), 2–3.

13. Scott Wilson, *Cultural Materialism: Theory and Practice* (Cambridge: Basil Blackwell, 1995), 211.

14. Neil Bartlett, *Who Was That Man? A Present for Mr. Oscar Wilde* (London: Serpent's Tail, 1988), 34.

Being True to Jane Austen

Mary A. Favret

In choosing this title for my essay, I mean to invite questions about fidelity in the recent mass-media presentations of Jane Austen's novels. The cinema and TV appearances of Austen's works, as well as the glossy new versions of the novels in our local Barnes and Noble, are all putting their faith in our faith in Jane Austen, or at least they aim to make converts of us all; for in these versions of Austen, and in our obsessive measuring of their devotion—either to the literal "facts" of the written works, to the historical details of Regency England, or to an ideal that is "Austen"—our own rituals of devotion are exposed. Our being or not being true to Austen is on the line.

In this sense, the most interesting of the recent tributes to Austen's work, Ang Lee's *Sense and Sensibility* and Roger Michell's *Persuasion,* are uncannily attentive to the sorts of fidelity currently demanded of Austen's faithful. Both films understand the work of adaptation to be intimately tied to questions of fidelity, and both understand fidelity as, in some way, an encounter with the past and death. In both cases, film itself becomes a meditation on faithfulness, history, and mortality. In what follows I will be taking instruction from these two productions on what being true to a woman, a woman who died almost two hundred years ago, might demand of us under the cultural logic of late capitalism.

At the heart of these films is the question, made redundant by the plot of each novel, of whether or not being true is an animating or mortifying process. This question brings together a predominantly female audience's devotion to Jane Austen with both Anne Elliot's devotion to Wentworth and Marianne Dashwood's devotion to Willoughby ("an attachment formed so late in life as at seventeen").[1] Being true also links the difficulties of bringing a classic novel to film with the problem of realist filmmaking itself. For all the historical accuracy of its costumes and buildings, for all the cherished objects of its world, no moving picture can fix these things as enduring artifacts. Film can only show the beloved object "dissolving back into an irrevocable passage of time."[2] The "truth" of filmmaking is its revelation of this ever-retreating world.

Writing about filmic realism, Fredric Jameson suggests that the still photographic image is predicated on death, "in which history is subject to confusion with finitude and with individual biological time." Film, by contrast, has the capacity to reveal and absorb the limits of the still image, "thus liberating the contents of the image itself" from sentimental, individual death, freeing it "for a more historical and social intuition of Being" (192). In Jameson's account, filmmaking itself seems to adopt the sense of Austen's *Sense and Sensibility*: it absorbs death, loss, and the passage of time, and moves on. As Susan Morgan has written, Austen's heroines—and here Marianne Dashwood and Anne Elliot seem exemplary—learn to live to change, to live in time, which is to say that they live in the nineteenth- rather than the eighteenth-century novel.[3] Jameson advances Morgan's logic from the nineteenth-century realist novel to twentieth-century film this way: "in film . . . the realities of the 'existential'—time and death, the very death of the image in question—are drawn back into the formal process, so that they do not need to be added in as content and message." With an intuition of its own ephemerality and historicity, film has the capacity to present the past "with the lively energy of radical difference, rather than with the melancholy of mortality" (193).

The question of *being true* to the past becomes, in terms of film realism, what Jameson might call a question of the "historical" (the moving, lively energy of difference) subsuming the "existential" (the still melancholy of mortality). In the two films considered here, Jameson's "historical" and "existential" vie with one another to construct for current audiences a relationship to the past and to that ever-retreating image, Jane Austen. *Sense and Sensibility* tends toward melancholy and finitude, insisting on its distance from us. Yet this distancing, as we shall see, promotes fetishization of the past and cultural repression. Where the film does strive for animation, it relies not on "the lively energy of radical difference," but on currents of avidity and consumerism familiar to its audience. The impulse to mourn, to fetishize the past so that it remains fixed, pervades *Persuasion* as well. But this film and its heroine resist the impulse, prying open a space for living and moving within a world of otherwise inert things. If *Sense and Sensibility* leans toward mortification and repression, *Persuasion* pulls in the opposite direction, finding animation and expression for Austen's work by wrenching it from its moorings.

Although the past wears various guises in both these films, two particular pasts perform central roles: the Regency period represented by Austen's major works (1811–17) and the subsequent Victorian period, which absorbed those works into its own cultural profile. Austen, who lived and died before the reign of Victoria, was created as a cultural icon in the Victorian age. In 1870 her nephew published his *Memoir of Jane Austen,* promoting a transatlantic vogue for the novelist's works and launching the "Austen industry." Victorian culture made Austen, and made her in a way that denied her association with such Regency vices as satire, irreverence, and a fascination with gossip and the human body; it simultaneously produced Austen as a model of domestic virtue, piety, and familial devotion at odds with what might look like the professionalism, social ambition, or nonnormative sexuality of her life. In taking up Austen, late-nineteenth-century readers were already torn between imagining her as the representative of a lost time before the full incursions of an industrial society (her nephew nostalgically compares the virtues of Austen's hand sewing to machine work) and seeing her as untainted by the "ugliness" of her own time—its global wars, political turmoils, and social instability.[4] In the first instance, Austen offered an ideal lost to the Victorians; in the latter, she gave the Victorians an identity through which they might fancy themselves distinct from their precursors. The late twentieth century could not help but replay these gestures: Austen arrives as the representative of a pre-Victorian era, the last gasp of a pastoralism, paternalism, and homogeneity long lost to us. But in being pre-Victorian, she also figures the post-Victorian: a society that has sloughed off the "ugliness" (call it urbanism, repressed sexuality, commodity culture, imperialism) of a legacy we would like to disown. In recuperating Austen, then, we mimic the Victorians even as we try to move past them. In both the films under consideration here, being true to Austen involves a recourse to things Victorian.

In Austen's *Sense and Sensibility* the dynamics of animation and mortality are elaborated in a story of sexual longing. The 1995 film *Sense and Sensibility* narrates this complicated dynamic, bringing what might otherwise have been absorbed by the form of film ("time and death, the very death of the image") back as content, and linking it with the question of a sexualized fidelity. Directed by Ang Lee and written by Emma Thompson, *Sense and Sensibility* begins with a deathbed scene (the death of the father, Dashwood senior, witnessed by his son) and ends in a church cemetery, while its most affecting moment shows Elinor Dashwood grieving over the pale, still body of her sister. Thus the movie, in its attempt to bring Austen's text to life, attends upon death with highly gendered forms of devotion.

The opening scene of the movie, where the father exacts a deathbed promise from his son, offers one quick lesson in fidelity to the past. Mr. Dashwood's wish does not survive his death; it is diminished, distorted, and finally discarded in the course of conversation between his son and daughter-in-law. But the father's will haunts the film in another form: the elegiac melody that Marianne plays at her piano, the one that makes her mother and Elinor cry, is her father's favorite. It is the movie's favorite as well, repeated often to add emotional texture to a scene. More generally, the movie gives the father's death more affective power than does Austen's novel. When Edward Ferrars chides his sister Fanny for being rude to these women who "have just lost their father," he explains that "their lives will never be the same again." Later Edward catches Elinor weeping while Marianne plays their father's favorite song; it is their first intimate moment together. If it seems strange to commence this adaptation of Austen's novel by inscribing the death of the father as its initial affective code, that strangeness intensifies if we recall that the novel *Sense and Sensibility* opens not with the death of the father, but rather with the death of Mr. Dashwood's maiden aunt. Here we depart from what has gone before with a radical, if not obviously enlivening, difference.

The emotional weight given to the dead father might, of course, serve as a displacement and repression of the movie's feelings for the dead author, Jane Austen, another maiden aunt. And an analogue for the favorite song might be the novel *Sense and Sensibility* itself. When Elinor (played by Emma Thompson) asks Marianne (Kate Winslet) to play "something less mournful" than the offending, recurring song, we hear the script straining to jolly up what is, in fact, a rather melancholy novel. But what does it mean that faithfulness to the past, especially the textual past, is continually figured as the daughter's mournful fidelity to the father?

Marianne's attachment to a paternal past extends from her piano playing to her reading. Her romance with Willoughby is clearly predicated on her passionate attachment to books. Austen tells us that Marianne effectively wooed Willoughby "by dwelling upon" her favorite authors "with so rapturous a delight, that any young man of five and twenty must have been insensible indeed, not to become an immediate convert" (47). In the novel, Marianne's favorites are writers more or less contemporary with Austen: Cowper and Scott. Older, dead writers—Marianne explicitly dismisses Pope—hold no attractions. But the movie allies Marianne with poets of an anterior past, especially Shakespeare, whose Sonnet 116 she first recites with Willoughby in an erotically charged scene. Here again, the emotional power associated with the words of a dead man seems to overwrite the audience's attachment to Austen. Both Willoughby and Marianne love Shakespeare and, we suspect, it will not be long before they love each other. But whereas Willoughby, like John Dashwood, proves false to the words of a man now dead, Marianne aims to live the words she has read. Eventually this sense of life as quotation or reproduction endangers Marianne, yet it remains central to the essentially mortifying project of this film.

The scene from the screenplay that convinced Ang Lee to direct *Sense and Sensibility* highlights the overlapping desires of emotional and textual fidelity, fixing them in the figure of Marianne.[5] In that scene, Marianne, deranged with despair, wanders like a zombie out of the garden and, ascending a steep hill in a downpour that nearly obliterates our view of her, gazes at Willoughby's house in the distance. Facing the audience, Marianne recites again from Shakespeare's sonnet: "Love is not love / Which alters when it alteration finds / Or bends with the remover to remove. / O, no! It is an ever-fixe'd mark." These lines serve as Marianne's credo. They could also be read as a motto for the film project itself.

So what if this scene has no warrant in the novel (where, in fact, Marianne prudently if reluctantly stays indoors when the rain hits)? What sort of love for Austen would balk at alterations? True love "is an ever-fixe'd mark, / That looks on tempests, and is never shaken." Yet, ironically, the very repetition of the lines inscribes a love for the text: indeed, Marianne's fidelity to Shakespeare's poem leads her to "bear [Time] out even to the edge of doom." We are expected to witness how Marianne would not "admit impediment" between her mind and the poet's. Being wed to Shakespeare's text (and through it to a paternal past) brings her to death's door; reciting her inherited text in the tempest, she surrenders up bodily health.[6] Yet her faithful quotation of Shakespeare paradoxically asks us to forgive the script's freewheeling alterations of Austen's text: "Love is not love that alters when it alteration finds."

This scene exposes and simultaneously covers over the film's difficulty with textual fidelity and the female audience's allegiance to Austen. On the one hand, Marianne enacts for us the dangers of following a favorite text too faithfully, of making ourselves the ever-fixe'd mark that guarantees the life of the text. The lesson, taught by the film for its own sake, wants the audience to overlook alterations in the name of love. On the other hand, the burden of Shakespeare's words shifts uneasily from Marianne to the audience. The intervention of Shakespeare keeps us from getting too fixed on Jane Austen.

You would think that once she has moved past the edge of doom and pulled free from her relationship to Willoughby, the film, like the novel, would have Marianne abandon books altogether.[7] Instead the film keeps feeding Marianne with the words of old male writers: Colonel Brandon, an older man himself, successfully courts Marianne by reading to her from Spencer and giving her a Ben Jonson song to sing (the Jonson song supplants the father's song from earlier in the film). Visually too, the film quotes from old masters—Vermeer in particular, but also Constable, Turner, Bouchet, and Greuze; more often than not, it is Marianne who is captured in their canvases.[8] In this way the film not only masculinizes the textual and cultural past, but also suggests a female audience's heterosexualized relationship to it. And though such a relationship to the past proves mortifying (turning its devotees into ever-fixe'd marks), it never leaves the film. It remains as a buffer against our attractions to another type of history.

The danger for Marianne (and through her, for a devoted female audience) is that the past will claim her, like Pluto abducting Persephone to the realm of the dead. This danger is underscored in a scene from the screenplay that was suppressed in the final version of the film. There Marianne, after her rainy recitation, is put to bed with an "infectious fever." As Elinor wipes her sister's fevered brow, Marianne suddenly becomes alert, points to the foot of her bed and tells her sister, "Look, look!" When Elinor protests that she sees nothing, Marianne replies, "It is Papa. Papa has come. . . . dearest Papa!"[9] The stage notes here read: "The dead are coming for the dying."[10] The implication of this gothic scene evidently could not be risked by the film. It too closely aligns the fatalism associated with the father with the film's project: Marianne sees a beloved image from the past reanimated before her eyes, and though for a moment it awakens her, it ultimately threatens to take all animation from her. Rather than spectral images simply bringing the past to life, they seem here to seduce those who love them to death.

Over and over in the film, passionate fidelity is presented as fidelity to a lost past, and figured as a daughter's death-dealing love for the paternal. Yet precisely because of the repetition of this dynamic in the film, because of the array of father substitutes that push the story of *Sense and Sensibility* into a antecedent time (Renaissance poetry, seventeenth- and eighteenth-century art), one senses a counterpressure, as if the film were deflecting the demands of the history before it as well as disavowing its own movements.

In this light I want to examine the movie's second deathbed scene, its affective core, featuring the two sisters Elinor and Marianne. We might too easily read this as the feminist cure to a mortifying relationship to the past: one woman's devotion to her sister brings that sister back to the land of the living. Or we might conjecture that Marianne chooses dearest (living) sister over dearest (dead) Papa during a dark night of the soul. We might say, pace Jameson, that Marianne and the film turn from the "still melancholy" of heterosexual and generational "difference" to the "lively energy" of sisterly sameness. But sisterly sameness turns out to be just as invested in death as the father-daughter bond. The gender games at work do not fully explain why this scene suddenly transports us from Austen's England into a lurid vampire flick.

Let me explain: the firelit sequence opens with a leeching of Marianne's blood; Elinor carries the blood out of the room and into the darkness of the darkness offscreen. When she returns, Marianne is absolutely still, as "pale as wax," according to the screenplay. A high, oblique camera angle, together with lurid lighting, gives an exaggerated significance to the white sheets of the bed and the deep V neck of Marianne's white nightgown. A full-tilt shot of the room from on high reproduces that V in the composition of her bed and the wall. Next, as the camera tracks in close-up the movement of Elinor's hands and eyes up Marianne's leg, halting as she presses her mouth against Marianne's hand, we witness (at last!) the older sister's emotional rapacity. The entry of Victorian sensationalism here (Marianne looks extremely Pre-Raphaelite), with a bow to the film legacy of Dracula, announces the fear repressed in the previous, cut scene: the past, through the undead images of film, threatens to drain us of life. That fear, however, is rescripted and dispersed: here the vampire is clearly not the past but the attentive sister, feeding off of, and emotionally animated by, her dying counterpart. In a Victorian moment, the vamp becomes her sister's devourer/redeemer and we are given a new mode for our fidelity.

Fidelity is reoriented in this scene through a figure Diana Fuss has labeled the "lesbian vampire," so that, instead of the mortification of an attachment to the past, we seem to arrive at a sort of sisterly consumerism.[11] But Elinor's affective consumerism is no less predicated on death: instead of animation *of* we partake of a parasitic animation *by* the dying beloved and the history embodied in her. The scene condenses the whole series of Marianne's attachments to the past into one visible object for consumption. It recalls Jameson's comments on film in his *Postmodernism*: "Contemporary culture is irredeemably historicist in the bad sense of an omnipresent and indiscriminate appetite for dead styles and fashions, for all the styles and fashions of a dead past."[12] For Jameson, this postmodern appetite for aspects of a dead past marks a departure from and denial of the historical vision of "being in time" that distinguished Austen's novels from those of her predecessors. Such an appetite runs counter to film's capacity for the "lively energy of radical difference" or for any truly creative refashioning of the past. In films like *Sense and Sensibility*, we do not experience history; but we avoid a fatal attachment to it by repeatedly consuming it. Elinor, the faithful sister, shows us how to be true: watching her bend over Marianne's bedside, we consume consumption itself.

In *Sense and Sensibility*, the moment of consumption looks fully Victorian, as if to dissociate itself from both Austen's world and ours while it works as a not quite invisible mediator between them. After the vampire scene, an enormous cross appears on the screen, sacralizing the encounter, as if we had just watched the climactic moment of "Goblin Market." This consumerism, focused on "dead fashions and styles . . . a dead past," calls forth its own version of animation or energy—in the form of expenditure, emotional and otherwise. The film's most exuberant moment, the "money shot" near the end, when Colonel Brandon tosses into the sky a golden shower of coins, can be read together with Elinor's gushing tears and Mrs. Dashwood's prodigal purchase of beef to wed emotional liveliness to images of spending.[13] But if, in the logic of the movie, faithful consumption of the past warrants emotional and economic outpouring, it nevertheless remains within the frame of death, unable to survive without the "melancholy of mortality." At the end of the film, the camera pulls back to a long shot, revealing all the characters moving about and receding into a church graveyard, as if, with this gesture, the spectral images now return to their tombs. And, as the lights come up in our local theater, we return to the realm of the living, having spent the last two and a half hours with those specters, still, quiet, and in the dark.

Roger Michell's *Persuasion,* first telecast by the BBC in England, then released in 1996 as a feature film, translates its concerns with animation and mortality into patterns of mobility and immobility, travel and stasis, activity and a stagnant status quo. If not fatal, as in *Sense and Sensibility,* being true to the past in *Persuasion* threatens to be paralyzing, anathema to the very motion of film. The motion picture thus works to outrun its source, as if eager to leave Jane Austen's world behind. But in fact it relies on the plot of *Persuasion* to justify its peculiar manner of being true: because the past is not recuperable, one should, from its very loss, create something new.

Whereas Lee's *Sense and Sensibility* frames its work with deathbed and graveyard, Michell's *Persuasion* begins and ends with movement. Opening with alternating shots of churning oars and spinning carriage wheels, it closes with the image of a navy frigate rolling on a vast oceanic expanse. In these movements we see the film's dedication to a kind of animation that puts things in motion, releasing a restlessness, a potential for upheaval. Following hints in the novel, the film sets the narrative during the momentary peace of 1814, under the false impression that Napoleon has been conquered and peace secured.[14] Like the men of the navy, the film itself seems to chafe at this false calm and the inactivity it brings; the return to the sea at its finale, though probably a return to battle, comes as relief. In perhaps its greatest departure from the novel, *Persuasion* sends its heroine off in the departing ship with her husband; it sends them both into a turbulent world beyond its own—and Austen's—horizon. *Persuasion* thus invites us to weigh the attractions of danger and mobility (its version of animation) against the stability and peace (or mortality) we might otherwise attribute to Jane Austen's world.

Stability and peace, the film seems to suggest, entail a particular lifelessness, especially when, in contrast to the ocean, they are identified with domestic interiors. *Persuasion's* punctilious re-creation of period clothes, rooms, and furniture registers oppression: in the scenes at Bath especially, an inert domestic setting promises to sap the life from its inhabitants, who seem incapable of moving from their elegant chaises longues. To be true to this very material version of the past, it seems, is to be trapped by objects and immobilized by the status quo (epitomized by Lady Dalrymple's hushed, swaddled, and static receiving room). The film's faithful re-creation of this world only propels a desire, shared by the heroine with the camera itself, to flee. The problem for the film is finding a way to spring its heroine from the mortifying world it has, with exactitude, recaptured. How can Anne Elliot overcome the past made present? How can she find a future? The problem involves Anne Elliot's creator as well: in being true to Jane Austen, will we allow her to move beyond historically accurate houses and interiors?

Film has two necessities, Stanley Cavell suggests, and both bear on *Persuasion*'s relationship to its heroine. "First, movie performers cannot project, but are projected. Second, photographs are of the world, in which human beings are not ontologically favored over the rest of nature, in which objects are not props but natural allies (or enemies)."[15] Michell finds a story fit to realize these two necessities: a heroine in need of animation and in danger of not being able to project herself into the world surrounding her; and a world where objects—platters of food, capes, hats—bear at least as much if not more weight than Sir Walter and his associates. The ontological equity between characters and objects is made in *Persuasion* uncomfortably apparent, as when the camera lines up sailors' and servants' faces for inspection, or when Mr. Shepard argues that a woman without children "is the very best preserver of furniture." If the overstuffed armchairs at Uppercross seem, like the bodies of its master and mistress, to smother Anne with their padding, the fashionable pieces of her father's rooms at Bath allow only an astringent soullessness. At their most extreme, objects and "the rest of nature" threaten not just to eclipse, but to imperil, human life. Captain Wentworth tells a dinner party that the British Admiralty "likes to entertain itself by sending a few hundred men to sea in a ship hardly fit to be employed." The entertainment value of watching men struggle to survive the objects that define them is not restricted to war (any disaster movie knows this). It continues, *Persuasion* tells us, as a possibility within film itself, where objects can contest the significance of the human, and introduce a sort of death.

In the wartime economy, the Admiralty uses its ships as it uses its men: till they both drop. Her family seems to have applied this mode of amortization to Anne Elliott as well. The passage of time has diminished her value on the marriage market; her sister's first words in the film ("Anne? Why?")

communicate her precariousness. Written off by her family, it appears she can only escape this world by gradually dying to it. The film's job is to move Anne and the audience away from this mortifying existence, to offer another mode of exit. If Anne is to have any future life, if she is to be projected beyond this world, the camera will have to intervene, as Cavell insists.

A strange moment early in *Persuasion* explains and corrects Anne's amortization. Sir Walter and his oldest daughter have left for Bath, abandoning Anne along with Kellynch Hall. The servants are preparing to close down the house until the new tenants arrive. Covering the furniture with white sheets, a servant lets one sheet fly across the lens of the camera, enshrouding our view. Though Anne herself has been covered over for a period of years, a ghostly presence, the effect at this instant is to render not Anne but the camera, and thus the viewer, another piece of furniture left behind by the Elliots. When the white sheet overcomes our vision, reducing us for a claustrophobic moment to an object, we share Anne's position. But she also shares ours: we learn that she exists as we do, an outsider in this world. We also learn that furniture can have eyes, and with eyes, a soul: our identification with Anne bestows animation upon what had been objects, but in a distinctly unfetishized manner.[16]

The gesture with the sheet reminds us that to the world presented before us we are not present, we cannot intervene.[17] Yet the predicament introduced by that sheet is also a choice: either to remain behind, futilely stuck in a prior moment, while the world (or the film) continues on its round, or to escape a world that rejects us. To stand apart from this world, to watch it recede before one's eyes until a blank screen appears, to be in the place of the film's spectators, this might offer some hope to Anne Elliot. Amortization locates full value in an irretrievable past, and marks off "a gradual extinction" from what was; it gives a sort of history to lifeless objects, but empties out human existence.[18] To join Anne Elliott with the audience and the future, by contrast, redirects the accounting of time, and offers her an alternative way to be true to what she loves.

In its own tracing of the past, the camera leaves room for alternatives by suggesting what could have been or might still be. It supports Anne when she tells a protesting Lady Russell (and us) that she "should have been happier" if the past had been different. Of course, the story Anne has to tell, of her love for Wentworth, is forgotten by her father, unknown to her in-laws, and forbidden by Lady Russell, her one confidante. In a way, the film colludes in this suppression, insofar as it (like the novel) offers no flashbacks, no re-creation of what their love had been. That story, that past, is lost. But now that Wentworth has returned from war, Anne is offered the option to forge, anew and apart from the expectations of her world, her fidelity to Wentworth. That the camera encourages such a move can be seen early in the film, when Anne remains at home tending her nephew while the rest of the family dines at Uppercross with Captain Wentworth. The camera effectively gives movement to Anne's unexpressed desire: though she has chosen to remain at a distance, it travels to Uppercross, circles around the dining-room windows, and, not daring to enter the room, stares from outside at the back of Wentworth's head. The next shot returns to Anne, alone at home, staring at the embers in the fireplace. With a few quick strokes we learn that the camera does something the novel does not: it projects Anne in the direction of, if not immediately to, where she "should have been happier."[19]

The camera opposes Anne's tendency to fade away or retire into furniture, turning these moves back upon her and offering her other ways to leave her surroundings. Elsewhere, the film works to overcome other potentially fatal modes of leaving the past and the world behind. Wentworth's desire for a termination to all past feeling draws him to Louisa Musgrove, a young girl with no past to burden her and, unlike himself, no experience of death or loss.[20] He applauds Louisa's devotion to immediate desire, telling her to remain always true to what she has determined for herself. Being true to her own feelings, however, leads Louisa to venture beyond the constraints of the physical world. In the scene in Lyme at the Cobb, Louisa appeals to Wentworth by calling out three times from the top of the stairs, "I am determined!" Leaping forward, she nearly puts an end (de-termination) to her life.

In the novel, Louisa's fall, though pivotal to the plot, comes and goes in one abrupt, choppy sentence (129). On-screen, it affords the film's most prolonged and lyrical moment. We watch as, in slow motion, each layer of Louisa's clothing cascades upward, color after rapturous color, then white. This moment could be read as Louisa's gambit for transcendence, her leap from the world. All else is hushed and we hear only the twittering of birds and cloth (or wings?) rustling. Indeed, the image seems to endorse lyricism itself, which slow motion identifies as a desire to step out of time and color identifies with the intensity of Louisa's desire.[21] In the suspension of this gorgeous image the film deconstructs itself, peeling away all the trappings of dramatic color until, again, we are faced with a flash of white screen—as if Louisa had succeeded in leaping beyond and putting an end to the motion picture. But in *Persuasion,* "There is never an end to it," as Wentworth complains earlier. The next shot pulls back to reveal Louisa's crumpled body on the stony beach, a would-be Icarus returned to earth. Here is a flight that stops movement and nearly stops animation.

The "damned foolishness," as Wentworth dubs Louisa's transcendent flight and his endorsement of it, follows Austen's logic in the novel. But in its lingering presentation of the fall, the film departs from the novel, raising questions about its use of motion, history, and its source. It seems as if Louisa in her leap has, unlike Anne, been able to project herself and her desires heedless of the regular movement of film. *Persuasion* foregrounds this possibility in order to undermine it. Louisa's fidelity to herself, which the film joins to a disregard for "being in time," proves more mortifying to her than animating. The film resumes its own rhythm and rolls past the flash of white screen. And Louisa's fall, her moment of self-expression, turns out to belong to someone else. The lyrical fall copies a scene near the end of Jane Campion's *The Piano* (1993) in which the heroine falls from a ship and is dragged deep under the sea by the ship's falling anchor: the same fluttering upward of clothing, the same slowly sinking body, only this time under water. After a long moment of suspense, Adelaide, in *The Piano,* decides not to surrender to this beautiful death and struggles successfully to the surface. Faced with this fatally lyrical moment, "My will had chosen life," she reports.[22]

The quotation of Campion's film, itself the study of a nineteenth-century Scottish woman, serves a complex function in *Persuasion.* First, it presents Louisa's gesture of self-determination as, in fact, determined by a prior film. With this attempted leap out of time and space, moreover, the film calls another world and history—Campion's Brontë-esque version of a British woman in 1850s New Zealand—into Regency England. This insertion opens up the world of *Persuasion,* patching it to the British colonies but also extending it forward in time, to a late-twentieth-century version of Victorian gothic.[23] The impossibility of a lyrical escape from history thus forces itself upon us at the same moment that we are asked to view Austen's novel through the lens of a broader, intervening past. It is difficult to know what the Victorian signifies here, except perhaps a site where women's desire and the lure of other worlds (transcendent for Louisa, supernatural for Brontë's Catherine, down under for Adelaide, Regency England for contemporary women?) are fatally linked; but it also serves as an opening or extension of Austen's world to match our own (presumably) global perspective.

Louisa's fall performs a function similar to Marianne Dashwood's illness in *Sense and Sensibility.* That film portrays the encounter with death by reference to Pre-Raphaelitism and vampire films, fusing sisterly love with a voracious consumption of the past. In *Persuasion,* the encounter with death is also given to a young woman and hints (via Campion) at the gothic. Yet in contrast to the vampiricism of *Sense and Sensibility, Persuasion* shows the desire for death—Anne's amortization and Louisa's solo flight—as respectively a fixity or transcendence anathema to the animating movement of film. It answers the desire for death with openings onto other worlds: the world of the viewer, in Anne's case, or, in Louisa's case, the larger world of the British Empire in the nineteenth century. Where one adaptation uses the promise of consumption to shape our emotional investment in the past, the other exploits motion itself to get past the finitude of the past, forestalling consumption with reminders of its own work. (The scene following Louisa's fall is shot with a handheld camera that intensifies our sense of frantic activity as it breaks the illusion of detached observation.)

One more scene completes *Persuasion*'s efforts to project its heroine beyond the world created on-screen, a world already showing hints of something more than what we might call "Austen's world." This scene is triggered by Anne's assertion that women remain true to love long after hope is lost and Wentworth's response in a letter that his heart now belongs to Anne "even more" than it did eight years ago. These two statements, and the shared future they imagine for the pair, speak the novel's stern truth about fidelity over time: on the one hand, faithfulness may persist in the face of hopelessness or irretrievability; on the other, it may return, even increase, if we try to put the past behind us. The first truth, of a hopeless faithfulness, makes possible the second, of devotion's greater return over time. Precisely because past attachments cannot be recaptured, they have the possibility of becoming something more than they were. That "something more" underwrites the vision of a new world for the two characters; it also explains to the audience the film's lesson about its attachment to Jane Austen.

In the subsequent scene, when the two lovers kiss in broad daylight on a Bath street, we are reminded of the mutuality of the audience's and Anne's desires. In fact, the public kiss belongs to us and the movies: it brings the couple into a different world. The kiss—the visual equivalent of Anne and

Wentworth's rediscovered love—supplies the sign that they have moved beyond the limits of Regency England. The irony of this scene is that it satis-
fies the desires of the lovers along with most of the filmgoing public (which
expects such guarantees of romance in movies), but it denies the expectations of many Austen devotees who, like the bankrupt Sir Walter, would
prefer to cling to the memory of what used to be. No one in Austen's world,
went the complaint, would ever engage in such public displays of affection.

Austen herself seems to have endeavored, in the parallel scene from the
novel, to wrest her lovers away from their immediate context in order for
them to realize their happiness:

> [They turned] their direction toward the comparatively quiet and retired
> gravel-walk, where the power of conversation would make *the present hour* a
> blessing indeed: and prepare it for the immortality which the happiest recol-
> lections of *their own future lives* could bestow. . . . There *they returned again
> into the past*, more exquisitely happy, perhaps, in their union, than *when it
> had first been projected*, more tender, more tried, more fixed. (240; emphasis
> added)

The present is appreciated only through imagining a future from which it
can be recollected; the past is reentered when it has been made something
more "than when it had first been projected." The confusion of tenses, the
sheer anachronism of the moment, opens up another world, perfectly suited to the movements of film.

As Anne Elliot and Frederick Wentworth kiss on-screen, a traveling circus slowly intrudes upon the Bath street, its music providing accompaniment for the embrace. In the outlandish procession of stilt-walkers, flame-
eaters, and clowns, we are given not an escape from the world so much as its
transformation. I believe we are meant to see this marvelous intrusion as the
film's message that the kiss, the realization of the impossible yet "even more"
love, is a sort of fantastic spectacle. And if the lovers' kiss on a busy Bath
street is impossible (impossible in the context of Austen's world), it is nevertheless a wonderful show, a performance of the suggestion that things
"should have been happier" had the past been different. The circus thus encourages us to transport Anne Elliot and Captain Wentworth into the
realm of performers—those whose work it is to present us with a changed
world—and thereby remind us of the work involved in acting (the circus
performers being the last instance of *Persuasion*'s repeated interest in showing

people at work). At the same time, the kiss of reunited lovers spreads its sense of fulfillment over the passing circus troupe: they act out the impossible, transforming the world as we know it (or have inherited it) so that it can accommodate gestures of long-lost love.

In keeping with the impossible union represented by their showy kiss, the film in its finale puts Anne Elliot and Captain Wentworth aboard ship together, at once transforming their world and the novel.[24] This world beyond is not so much the navy (though the ship is its vehicle) as it is simultaneously the fulfillment of Anne's desires and the work of film, as I have been arguing. Anne finds satisfaction here: taking her cue from Sophy Croft's earlier description of her voyages, the heroine finishes the film as a world traveler. But her transport, in every sense of the word, cannot be divorced from the movements of film. With great self-consciousness, then, the ending shows Anne standing on the deck while Wentworth peers through a telescope in the direction of the camera. The telescope's lens brings distant objects or lands closer to view, reminding us (anachronistically) of the movie's work. That Anne does not handle the instrument, but rather stands alongside it, raises questions about the woman's role in bringing the novel to our view: she does not manage the machinery, but can we be sure that she is not providing direction? This may be the final truth of the camera's collaboration with Anne: while it has been projecting her, her wishes have been directing it. In any case, when the telescope turns in our direction, two worlds stand looking at each other from across a distance.

The next shot, the last of the film, pulls back to increase that distance. The ship moves out of the frame to the horizon's edge. I suppose we can argue whether that ship, which takes Anne Elliot away from the world of Regency England, is also taking her away from us, the audience of *Persuasion*. The sequence of shots suggests a departure as the ship and its inhabitants recede further from view. This moving away signals the film's project, its gesture of faith to Austen's work: that Anne Elliot, Frederick Wentworth, and the world they make for themselves will have a future beyond and *more than* our vision of them. It is an unknown world, its future rimmed by war. Out there death remains a possibility, but it is not the only ending.

Perhaps *Sense and Sensibility* ends in a graveyard not because the characters must die (in fact, they never were alive) but because the film, unlike the novel, must insist that they have passed away: their nonpresence and fixed distance from us secure their fetishistic allure, and deny the ways in which the film is a product of the 1990s, rather than the 1790s.[25] Yet that closing scene is also meant, perhaps, to demonstrate that Austen's creatures would have no life outside of the movie: their possibilities end here, with the visual. After all, the avid consumerism promoted by the film ultimately links life and pleasure with Elinor's viewing, not Marianne's reading.

Persuasion privileges viewing too, of course, but in its presentation of Austen's world and the world of the viewer, there is continual slippage: Anne Elliot slides into our point of view and we into hers. In the end, with our camera trained on them and their telescope trained on us, the film suggests an alignment between worlds. But only a momentary one, for the waters beneath them and us do not hold still. Both worlds, neither quite stable, roll on. Although this method of being true to Austen strikes me as more energetic and open to the future than the alternatives offered in *Sense and Sensibility*, it has its own dangers, not the least of which is the suggestion that going to war is the preferred method for moving beyond a mortifying environment. Death here is not determining, as it is for the makers of *Sense and Sensibility*, but it lurks on the horizon. An intimation of death thus seems to preside, one way or another, over both these late-twentieth-century versions of Austen's novels, marking the perceptual limits of viewers, readers, and creators. In this intimation we find acknowledged, or perhaps constructed, the inaccessibility of a living past as well as our own postmodern inability to conceive in any substantial way of immortality—even for Jane Austen.

Notes

I want to thank the members of my graduate seminar, "Jane Austen in the Nineties," who helped me think through some of the issues presented in this essay. In particular I want to thank Karen Felts, Mary Herrington-Perry, and Anna Meek, as well as Andrew Miller, Anne Fleche, and Carol Ockman.

1. Jane Austen, *The Novels of Jane Austen,* ed. R. W. Chapman, 3d ed., vol. 1, *Sense and Sensibility* (Oxford: Oxford University Press, 1953), 378.

2. Fredric Jameson, *Signatures of the Visible* (New York: Routledge, 1990), 192.

3. Susan Morgan, *Sisters in Time: Imagining Gender in Nineteenth-Century British Fiction* (Oxford: Oxford University Press, 1989), 17: "These heroines [of nineteenth-century British novels] represented the fictional transformation of religious values into secular values, . . . of eternity into history, of fixity into change. The novels argue that a sense of history is the precondition for any social or individu-

al progress. That sense of history, including the sense that character means character in process, self is self in time, celebrates qualities of connectedness the culture has traditionally undervalued and labeled as feminine."

4. James Edward Austen-Leigh claimed that his aunt was "as far as possible" from the "ugly" practices of her day. An excellent study of the ambivalence in his *Memoir* and in late-nineteenth-century English reception appears in Roger Sales, *Jane Austen and Representations of Regency England* (rpt. New York: Routledge: 1996), 3–27. See also Deidre Lynch, "At Home with Jane Austen," in *Cultural Institutions of the Novel,* ed. Deidre Lynch and William B. Warner (Durham, N.C.: Duke University Press, 1996), and Margaret Kirkham, "The Austen-Leighs and Jane Austen . . . ," in *Jane Austen: New Perspectives,* ed. Janet Todd (New York: Holmes and Meier Publishing, 1983).

5. David Lyons, "Passionate Precision: 'Sense and Sensibility,'" *Film Comment* 32.1 (1996): 37–38.

6. On the practice in the Romantic era of quoting Shakespeare, see Adela Pinch, *Strange Fits of Passion: Epistemologies of Emotion, Hume to Austen* (Stanford, Calif.: Stanford University Press, 1996), 164–79.

7. See Austen, 343, 378–79.

8. On Ang Lee's use of painters, see Lyons, "Passionate Precision," 41.

9. During her illness, the novel tells us, Marianne "talk[ed] wildly of mama . . . her ideas were still, at intervals, fixed incoherently on her mother" (306–7).

10. Emma Thompson, *The Sense and Sensibility Screenplay and Diaries* (New York: Newmarket Press, 1995), 182–83.

11. Diana Fuss, "Fashion and the Homospectatorial Look," *Critical Inquiry* 18.6 (summer 1992): 713–37.

12. Fredric Jameson, *Postmodernism, or, the Cultural Logic of Late Capitalism* (Durham, N.C.: Duke University Press, 1991), 279–96.

13. Compare this expenditure with the emotional hoarding of Austen's novel, exemplified by Elinor: "Marianne restored to life . . . was an idea to fill her heart with sensations of exquisite comfort, and expand it in fervent gratitude—but it led to no outward demonstrations of joy, no words, no smiles. All within Elinor's breast was satisfaction, silent and strong" (275).

14. The penultimate sentence of the novel indicates that "the dread of a future war was all that could dim [Anne's] sunshine" (Jane Austen, *The Novels of Jane Austen,* ed. R. W. Chapman, vol. 5, *Persuasion* [London: Oxford University Press 1969], 252). Chapman explains that *Persuasion* is the most meticulously dated of Austen's novels; the action here takes place primarily between September 1814 and February 1815.

15. Stanley Cavell, *The World Viewed,* enlarged edition (Cambridge: Harvard University Press, 1979), 37.

16. Scenes at Uppercross especially show Anne not solely as furniture, but also as silent witness to a mode of being from which she remains apart: furniture made sentient.

17. The white screen presented to us by this gesture is also a reminder of the illusion of screening.

18. According to the *Oxford Concise Dictionary*, to amortize is to "gradually extinguish (a debt) ⸱ . . gradually write off the initial cost (of assets)."

19. A similar movement recurs later. While Anne sits on a stile during an outing, the camera leaves her and follows, at a distance, Wentworth and Louisa. Again, at Lyme, as Anne and her sister walk along the pier, the camera leaps ahead of them, tracking a running boy until his path intersects with that of Captain Wentworth and Louisa, walking in the opposite direction. By such movements of the camera, at these moments and others, we understand Anne's unspoken desire to be with Wentworth.

20. The movie omits any reference to young Dick Musgrove, who, according to the novel, died at sea under Captain Wentworth's command. In this way the movie shields Louisa and her family from any experience of death. It also leaves the idea of death in war open, not fixed on one particular body.

21. "You'd think everybody would have that trick in his bag by now: for a fast touch of lyricism, throw in a slow-motion shot of a body in free-fall" (Cavell, 133). Lyricism in this passage refers not simply to film technique, but also to the literary characteristics of the lyric: emotional self-expression, unleashed desire, and individual striving for transcendence.

22. Harvey Greenburg, in his review of *The Piano* (*Film Quarterly* 47.3 [spring 1994]: 46–50) dwells on this image: "One is left with a ruling image of her [Adelaide] eerily suspended in mid-ocean like some tenebrous, funereal blossom, before her 'will' chooses a tamer Eros over the Thanatos which may well be the ultimate desire prefigured by her muteness" (50). Adelaide is a woman who refuses to speak, preferring, like Anne Elliott, to play the piano.

23. Campion makes explicit her indebtedness to *Wuthering Heights* in this work. See Caryn James's review of *The Piano* and other neo-gothic movies in the *New York Times*, 18 November 1993, sec. 2, 13.

24. This collapsing of the distance between the separate spheres of (feminine) home and (masculine) work can be read as a tribute to Austen herself, whose published work was written amid domestic routine. Our entrance to the ship in fact begins with a scene of Anne writing belowdecks.

25. Austen wrote the first version of this novel in the 1790s, then revised it later for publication in 1811.

A Twentieth-Century *Portrait*
Jane Campion's American Girl

Susan Lurie

In describing her writing of *The Piano,* Jane Campion has stated that her representation of nineteenth-century characters "means that I can look at a side of the relationship that [nineteenth-century authors] could not develop. My exploration can be a lot more sexual, a lot more investigative of the power of eroticism."[1] Yet, if contemporary mores allow a greater freedom in erotic representation, Campion also claims that twentieth-century "rules and ways of handling" courtship have meant the loss of "the pure sexual erotic impulse" available to inhabitants of the previous century (138). For Campion, then, the nineteenth-century is the site both of a Victorian censorship of sexuality that her films can redress and of possibilities for erotic experience that have been lost in the twentieth century.

Both these ideas of the nineteenth century are present in Campion's *Portrait of a Lady,* a movie whose prime revisionary agenda is the eroticization of Henry James's frequently feminist but always desexualized heroine. On the one hand, Campion sees in the novel a particular variation on a Victorian reluctance to explore and validate female eroticism: a desexualization of women bound up specifically with their feminist resistance to patriarchal heterosexuality. Moreover, I will argue, for Campion James's asexual heroine registers an emergent instance of a feminist retreat from sexuality that survives into the present. On the other hand, the filmmaker also finds emergent instances of liberatory sexual practices in James's text. The first of these is the novel's inscription of a homoerotic resistance to compulsory heterosexuality; the second is a powerful heterosexual eroticism, lost in Campion's view to contemporary women, and linked for her to nineteenth-century women writers' notions of gothic romance.

In this essay, I will argue that the movie looks to the liberatory sexual practices that Campion discerns in James's novel, along with certain twentieth-century erotics, not only to redress the novel's desexualization of its feminist heroine but also to expand what she sees as the limits of late-twentieth-century feminist erotics. However, even as Campion privileges the returning of eroticism to desexualized feminisms in both centuries, she is prompted by the novel's insights to bring her own countererotics into question for their possible dominant effects. In the course of its dialogic encounter with the novel's themes, I will argue, the movie shifts from what is recognizable as a "pro-sex," postmodern feminism that uncritically and ahistorically embraces eroticizing discourses to a postmodern feminist analysis of how power can turn feminists against their own best interests. Because the latter trains attention on how dominant ideology profits when subjects mistake regulatory for resisting practices, Campion's movie begins to bring her own feminist countererotics under scrutiny.[2]

This questioning of the patriarchal implications of her countererotic lexicon, however, is figured forth in the movie only as visual repetitions and juxtapositions that fall short of recognizing how this lexicon has particular dominant affiliations. More specific insights, I argue, might have emerged had Campion discerned, through attention to historical context, the uncanny intersection between the discourses with which James desexualizes and she eroticizes the feminist Isabel; for, I will argue, just as James fortifies his homosocial/erotic challenge to sexual convention with an appeal to nineteenth-century xenophobic, nationalist ideologies that seek to control autonomous female desire, so does Campion seek to eroticize Isabel by invoking twentieth-century sexualizations of immigrants and women of color that dovetail with patriarchal, nationalist ideologies. Because Campion neglects historical contexts for the relation between feminist representation and discourses on female sexuality in both the novel and the movie, she not only affiliates her feminist erotics with discourses that are hostile to feminist sexual autonomy; she also limits what she can discover in the course of her other postmodern feminist agenda: the movie's eventual interest in entanglements between modes of feminist representation and patriarchal aims.[3]

Nonetheless, the scope of this interest in the movie is significant for its construction of a bridge between two notoriously antagonistic modes of postmodern feminism: the (often uncritical) pro-sex celebration, as a re-sponse to feminisms that retreat from sexuality, of discourses that eroticize women; and the analysis of how female and feminist erotics can be under-mined by their (witting or unwitting) affiliation with dominant ideologies. In building this postmodern bridge, Campion draws on two different Vic-torian legacies: the Victorian text as the site of emergent moments both for the desexualizing of feminism and for erotic ruptures in conventional sexu-ality; and the Victorian text as a site for emergent ideological processes that regulate subjects by making domination indistinguishable from agency. If the first of these Victorian legacies inspires Campion to valorize erotics per se in the interests of eroticizing desexualized feminisms, it is the second that inspires her to rethink feminist erotics and to predicate their efficacy on a wariness about their entanglements with the dominant ideologies that re-quire oppressive controls on female sexuality.

Victorian Asexual Feminism and Twentieth-Century Feminist Erotics

Despite the fact that the novel's Isabel is a feminist incarnation of the nineteenth-century, self-reliant American, the feminist eroticization of Isabel Archer requires a substantial intervention in James's portrait of the "American girl." Certainly, Isabel is the mouthpiece for an Emersonian per-sonal liberty and self-reliance that fuels a resistance to conventional femi-ninity, specifically the refusal of marriages proposed by adoring but dis-concertingly powerful men.[4] Yet to the extent that Isabel's resistance to patriarchal marriage paves the way for alternative modes of sexuality, such alternatives have nothing to do with her. Instead, the novel links her femi-nist resistance to the preservation for Ralph Touchett of the homosocial/ homoerotic world that initiates the novel. Given free reign by inherited wealth precisely because it is a "requirement" of Ralph's imagination,[5] Isabel's independent spirit becomes the catalyst for maintaining and enlarg-ing Ralph's homosocial world. Most important, the rejected Warburton sticks close to Ralph over the years, but even Caspar Goodwood, the American suitor, becomes one of Ralph's attendants at Isabel's behest. Isabel's feminist autonomy opens up space for an alternative male erotics while closing down her own eroticism almost entirely.

These dynamics emerge quite clearly in the novel's initial scene of homo-social bonding, where we are introduced to a congenial group of men taking tea on the grounds of Gardencourt, the Touchett estate. Almost immediately

James feminizes the group; Ralph Touchett, his banker father, and their aristocratic neighbor, Lord Warburton, we are told, "were not of the sex who are supposed to furnish the regular votaries of the ceremony" (59). But if they are prone to feminine rituals, one sort of involvement with the feminine does not appeal to Ralph and his father. When their discussion comes around to the possibility of Lord Warburton's marrying, James notes that Mr. Touchett's "own experiment had not been a happy one" (66), and the scene ends with Ralph, who has announced the imminent arrival of Isabel, promising to introduce his cousin to Warburton "on the condition . . . that you don't fall in love with her!" Ralph's reasons are multiple and contradictory; he thinks the nobleman "too good" for his cousin, who he hopes has not come like other American girls to find a husband; then again Isabel may be engaged; and further, he doubts that Warburton would make a "remarkable husband" (68). Whatever the reason, however, it is clear that Ralph does not want Warburton to marry. Indeed, when Isabel arrives and breaks in on the group of men, Ralph's first response is to complain, albeit in a jocular way, that Isabel has won over his little dog who only a moment ago had belonged to him. Breaking up the homosocial group, Isabel threatens to take possession of a companion that Ralph covets for himself (a threat, of course, soon assuaged by Isabel's feminist refusal of Warburton).

Echoing the opening of the novel, Campion's *Portrait* also begins with a homosocial group. But the movie ingeniously rewrites as it appropriates the countererotics of James's opening scene in terms of late-twentieth-century feminisms that put the vitalization, rather than the elimination, of female eroticism at the center of *female* homosocial/erotic and autoerotic refusals of patriarchal heterosexuality. In these discourses, heterosexuality is often seen as an intrusion into such homoerotic and autoerotic relations.[6] Emphatically cinematic, this intervention is posed as a twentieth-century revision that exposes how both James's feminism and his countererotics eliminate female sexuality in the interest of male desire.

Shot in black and white, the sequence begins with just the sound of women's voices over the credits, speaking in an Australian-accented English about their sexuality and relationships. What they deem pleasurable will return later as elements of the movie's eroticization of Isabel: being the passive recipient of a kiss, the special power of the very first kiss, and lastly, finding in a lover "a mirror, the clearest mirror, the most loyal mirror, so when I love that person I know that they're going to shine that back to me." When the voices stop, the camera cuts to an outside, wooded scene, filled with twentieth-century women who lie down together in a circle, bodies touching end to end, but each lost in what seem to be autoerotic reveries. From here Campion cuts to a succession of women, posed and perched among stark tree trunks, some singly, some in affectionate/homoerotic groupings. The women, who are racially diverse, frequently pose self-consciously for the camera, emphasizing both the cinematic aspect of this portrait of ladies and their ability to expose and return the controlling "gaze" of the camera; some dance and romp, while others stare into the camera assertively or melancholically.[7] Opening her *Portrait* as James opens his, with a homosocial, homoerotic alternative to compulsory heterosexuality, Campion locates feminist eroticism not as a threat to but as an integral part of such alternatives.

Campion's revision of the novel's initial scene emerges even more explicitly when the opening sequence culminates in a cut to a close-up of Isabel, seated alone in a wooded bower. Initiating the movie's representation of the novel's events, this cut also visually links Isabel to the opening sequence of twentieth-century women pictured in natural surroundings. Having established Isabel as the culminating subject in the parade of cinematic portraits of ladies, the movie goes on to deliberately repeat the novel's opening focus on a heterosexual intrusion into a homosocial scene. Here, however, this intrusion is perpetrated not by a heterosexual woman but by the patriarchal Warburton's invasion of Isabel's natural bower. Heralded quite pointedly by the march of his disembodied, phallic legs, seen through openings in the trees, Warburton's approach with his proposal of marriage is presented as threatening to an eroticized female/feminist world that Campion's Isabel now represents.

Although it begins the movie's representation of the novel, Warburton's proposal, of course, actually occurs some 160 pages into the book. By making her rewriting of James's opening homoerotic scene the beginning of the *movie,* and by making Isabel's resistance to Warburton's proposal the beginning of the movie's representation of the novel itself, Campion combines James's initial scene of homosocial/erotic resistance to heterosexuality with his most feminist moment, Isabel's refusal of the patriarchal Warburton. In doing so, Campion both eroticizes Isabel's refusal in twentieth-century feminist terms and points up a crucial shortcoming in James's feminism: his denying to Isabel the resisting sexuality that the novel's feminism supports for male homoeroticism.

Campion's representation of Isabel's subsequent refusal of Caspar Good-wood is likewise eroticized by linking it to the initial sequence's lexicon of feminist erotics. After ordering Caspar to leave the London hotel where she is staying, Isabel begins to caress herself; lying down, she imagines all her suitors lying with her on the bed, encircling her in ways that recall the circle of women in the opening scene, and making love to her. What the scene seems to register is Isabel's desire for a (perhaps nonmonogamous) hetero-sexuality that is modeled rather than violently intrudes on the pleasures of autoeroticism and erotic relations between women, the pleasures registered in the first sequence. It is a fantasy of translating an autoerotic pleasure asso-ciated with same-sex "worlds" and desire into a heterosexual desire under Isabel's control.

However, even as Campion redresses the feminist desexualization of Isabel that supports the homoerotics of the novel, she does not discern the more mainstream ideologies that inform the novel's linking of feminist au-tonomy to sexual retreat. Isabel's idiosyncratic feminism, I submit, marks her as a version of the "American girl" that James sought to construct in the interests of U.S. nationalist and patriarchal ideologies of race, gender, and class. Although the reserved Isabel may seem to be the virtual antithesis to the flirtatious Daisy Miller, her autonomous sexual choices are presented as posing the same dangers to the reproduction of elite U.S. ideologies and bloodlines that James attributes to his most well known "American girl."

As Lynn Wardley has compellingly argued, when the nouveau-riche, un-chaperoned, and untrained Daisy "picks up" swarthy foreigners in Italy, themselves linked to her picking up of a deadly Roman disease, she registers a peculiarly late-nineteenth-century American fear of the contagion that might result from the autonomous exercise of female sexual desire: the fear of miscegenistic liaisons between white, U.S.-born women and non-Anglo immigrants.[8] To this I would add that Daisy as a badly educated, self-made merchant's daughter poses a threat from another direction as well: she al-most seduces Winterbourne, the elite Anglo-American protagonist of the story. Anglo, white, and Protestant, yet hostile to the requirements of elite, patriarchal culture, the nouveau-riche American flirt threatens Anglo-American culture and bloodlines from two directions.

In contrast to Daisy, but on similar terms of female autonomy, Isabel re-fuses to exercise her sexual power over men of superior class and lineage. Despite her retreat from sexuality, however, the novel keeps the question of

Isabel's pursuit of personal liberty tellingly fixed on the question that is so crucial to "Daisy Miller": What is the relation between the American girl's autonomy and her capacity to marry across social boundaries? Importantly, it is a question that survives its unhappy but class-appropriate resolution for Isabel herself. After she marries Osmond, fully half of the novel displaces this question onto how Isabel's feminist independence of spirit will influence the capacity of her social-climbing, expatriate, American husband to marry his Italian, Catholic daughter into the English nobility. As with the question of Isabel's own possibilities for this kind of liaison, here her feminist resistance to patriarchal controls coincides with resisting the American girl's capacity to marry up.

I am suggesting, that is, that *Portrait,* like "Daisy Miller," plays out James's concerns about the American girl's pivotal role in reproducing U.S. citizens and U.S. culture in an age both of immigration and of the class rise through commerce of lower- and merchant-class Americans. Whereas Daisy Miller's main threat is in her capacity to choose swarthy foreigners, Isabel's autonomy threatens to empower the white but social-climbing American girl whose sexual powers over men of higher classes endangers the reproduction of elite culture more than white bloodlines. For James this figure seems to pose much the same danger as the white immigrant American girl who may prove attractive to the Anglo-American male (as Daisy intrigues Winterbourne). Capable of attracting her "superiors" in class and (in James's view) national culture, Isabel is repeatedly described as a "foreigner" in both U.S. and British contexts, one whose immigration to England rids America of its "superfluous population" (97). Indeed, Isabel's entrance into England with her arrival at Gardencourt is heralded as the coming of an American social climber (like the "plain little Annie Climber" we will hear about anon), looking for a noble husband in a land where, as Mr. Touchett remarks, "American young ladies" are liked very much (109). It is not surprising, then, that James has this "immigrant American girl" assert her autonomy by choosing another immigrant from the United States for a mate, a choice that both keeps Isabel within her class and nation of origin and positions her to help derail (again, precisely through her feminist resistance to an imperious man) the liaison of a dark Italian girl with an English lord.

But what does James's xenophobic and patriarchal appropriation of feminism have to do with *Portrait,* the movie? Certainly, Campion does not register an awareness of these thematics; yet this very lack of awareness may well have contributed to the movie's unwitting affiliation of its own feminist erotics with dangerous bedfellows; for, in her efforts to endow Isabel with the feminist sexuality that James withholds from her, Campion brings into play not only recent feminist erotics but also late-twentieth-century discourses whose eroticization of immigrant American girls serves similar nationalist, racist, and patriarchal agendas as those that inform James's desexualization of Isabel. In doing so, of course, Campion makes her feminist erotics the handmaiden of the dominant ideologies that regulate, rather than liberate, female sexuality.

As Lauren Berlant has argued, the pro-immigrant discourses of the late twentieth-century valorize both the talented immigrant who brings skills to U.S. culture and technology and an eroticized female immigrant who is often also a woman of color. In the latter case, as the eroticized object of a controlling U.S. nationalist, racist, and male heterosexual desire, the immigrant woman is made the reproductive agent of a continual incorporation of "others" into U.S. whiteness and the national ideologies this whiteness represents.[9] Campion's opening sequence resonates with both aspects of such pro-immigrant discourses. That the portraits of women in the opening sequence are emphatically cinematic ones, that they are Campion's inventive addition to the novel, and that they represent Australian women all advertise Campion the noted filmmaker as the foreigner who brings desirable talents to the United States (where the movie seeks its main audience). At the same time, when the sequence culminates in the portrait of Isabel/Nicole Kidman, it functions to affiliate the talented immigrant (both filmmaker and famous actress) with the incorporation of eroticized, racially diverse, and/or immigrant American girls into the white, Americanized immigrant as the representative American girl.

We will recall that the sound of Australian-accented women's voices over the opening credits, discussing what the women find sexually exciting, begins the movie. When the voices stop, the movie cuts to the black-and-white series of racially diverse women; and this series culminates in a color close-up of Isabel, played by the Australian-American superstar, Nicole Kidman, whose own Australian accent gives way in this movie to the U.S. English of the American girl. Such a culmination of images of eroticized racially and nationally different women in the close-up of the Americanized Nicole Kidman echoes the kind of incorporating, whitening effect that Berlant identifies in other recent visualizations of U.S. immigrants. Thus, in availing herself of the pro-immigrant but racist representations that valorize the eroticism of female immigrants, Campion uncannily appropriates for the eroticization of Isabel the discourses that in the late twentieth century pursue precisely the same ends as James's fearful desexualization of Isabel does in the nineteenth century: the regulation of female sexuality in the interests of homogenizing U.S. culture and bloodlines. In her "pro-sex" revision of the novel's antifeminism, Campion undermines her project by bringing into play a visual rhetoric that has profoundly antifeminist associations.[10]

The Power of Victorian Eroticism and the Critique of Feminist Erotics

Campion's problematic linking of feminist sexuality to discourses that eroticize people of color and the exotic immigrant is not new with her *Portrait*. Ada's sexual awakening in *The Piano* is indebted explicitly to her lover's affiliation with the native population, who are themselves represented as sexually uninhibited and close to nature. George, Ada's inspiring lover, marks his affinity to the Maori by his facial tattoos, and when the couple return to Scotland in the movie's final minutes, those native markings become the sign of Ada's access to an improved heterosexuality, made possible by the erotic but ameliorated masculinity that the nativized Anglo immigrant brings back with him from New Zealand. That is, Campion constructs feminist heterosexuality in the earlier film as enabled by the incorporation of native immigrant qualities into Anglo culture, the twentieth-century discourse that, as I have argued, serves patriarchal/nationalist agendas and informs the opening sequence of *Portrait* as well.[11]

As in *Portrait*, in *The Piano* Campion seems oblivious to the racist and imperialist discourses she invokes to enfranchise feminist sexuality, ones that also function to undermine her feminist aims. However, *The Piano* can be seen as an extended critique of how influential twentieth-century *feminist* erotics, ones that in Campion's view retreat from intense modes of heterosexuality, are vulnerable to patriarchal recuperation. In *The Piano* the mute Ada's presymbolic, autoerotic, and maternalized homoerotic feminist sexuality, all reminiscent of the feminist psychoanalysis of the 1970s and 1980s, is represented as too easily manipulated by her father and the unloved, tyrannical husband.[12] As a result, Ada's mute erotics give way to what the movie represents as a better feminist (hetero)sexuality. This is made possible when George's exotic appeal, inextricable from a sexy, ameliorated masculinity, is enhanced by what Campion has described as "the kind of romance that Emily Brontë portrays in 'Wuthering Heights' . . . [a] very harsh and extreme, a gothic exploration of the romantic impulse."[13] Accordingly, it is this nineteenth-century "gothic" impulse that shifts Ada from a maternal, autoerotic sexuality to a (more desirable, on the movie's terms) feminist heterosexuality.

As regards Campion's *Portrait,* of course, it is Ada's early feminist mode of resisting sexuality that resonates with the countererotics of the opening sequence. Nonetheless, here too Campion registers her critique of what she sees as the limits of those erotics. When she locates Osmond's triumph over the other suitors in his willingness to force a kiss (albeit a tender and sensuous one) that propels Isabel's autoeroticism into heterosexual choice, Campion constructs for Isabel the same kind of shift in eroticism that she constructs for Ada. Following out her desire "to respond to [Brontë's] ideas in [her] own century" (Bilborough, 140), Campion recruits an insistent male desire, as she has in *The Piano,* to redress what she sees as the limits of the feminist discourses that have sponsored the eroticization of Isabel's earlier refusals. Osmond's kiss that easily wins over the marriage-refusing Isabel is entirely Campion's invention. Played to the same music that accompanies Isabel's autoerotic reveries on the occasion of refusing Caspar in the London hotel, Osmond's audacious kiss seems to represent both an extension of and an improvement on those reveries as it translates a fantasy linked to a retreat from intersubjective sexuality into an actual heterosexual experience. If certain twentieth-century feminisms underwrite Campion's ability to suggest that patriarchal heterosexuality is an invasive displacement of female (auto)homoeroticism, nineteenth-century "extremes" provide an antidote to the possible hermetic consequences of that critique—the retreat from (here hetero)sexuality into autoerotic reverie.

However, unlike *The Piano,* Campion's *Portrait* proceeds to interrogate the wisdom of embracing forceful male eroticism as a feminist solution. Even as she represents Osmond's kiss as a sexual catalyst for Isabel, whose feminism (Campion has claimed) involves a denial of the power of eroticism that is similar to that of twentieth-century feminists, Campion follows the novel in making Osmond a successful villain.[14] If he inspires a new level of passion in Isabel, he also manipulates this passion. Thus, although she wants to register the need for feminists to embrace a "power of eroticism" from which Campion thinks they too often retreat, the movie's investigation of that power, as it must in eroticizing the troubling relationship the novel presents, comes to focus on patriarchal manipulations of what has first been presented as emancipatory, feminist sexuality.

At the same time, this focus on how power can construct a confusion between resisting and oppressive sexuality, a focus that constitutes the movie's other postmodern feminist project, builds on the novel's own representation of Isabel's capacity to mistake patriarchal plots for eroticized feminist agency. James's representation of the bond between Isabel and Mme Merle identifies eroticized mother–daughter–type relations as a prime site for patriarchal manipulation, especially when maternal figures are dependent on patriarchal ones for their own and their daughters' welfare. If in Campion's *Portrait* Osmond wins Isabel because he excites her sexually, in the novel he does so because Isabel first has fallen for Mme Merle, who, in her own daughter's interests, orchestrates Osmond's seduction of Isabel. What is so appealing about Mme Merle, importantly, is the coincidence of her maternal solicitude for Isabel with the independent, feminist femininity that the older woman seems to represent.

Such an analysis, of course, resonates with Campion's own critique of feminist mother–daughter erotics in *The Piano*. Not surprisingly, then, Isabel's first attraction to Mme Merle becomes the occasion for Campion to cite her earlier movie. In a considerable extension of the novel's scene of Isabel's attraction to the piano playing, Campion has her take almost two minutes to make her way through the Touchett mansion to the music salon. As the piano music takes center stage, Isabel lingers for several seconds near a mirror that creates a doubled image of her on the screen. In thus recalling the voice-over in the opening sequence that yearns for a lover to be like "a mirror . . . the most loyal mirror" of her own love, the scene links Isabel's attraction to the piano music to the feminist autoeroticism and homoeroticism of that sequence. Accordingly, the movie deliberately creates a feminist identity between the two women; soon after meeting, they walk under identical umbrellas when bonding over feminist ideas at Gardencourt.

Moreover, the first encounter between the two women reproduces a portion of the novel's dialogue that Campion must have been delighted to discover; as Mme Merle worries that her music may have disturbed the dying Mr. Touchett, she holds up her fingers and claims that she had been careful to play "du bout des doigts"—only with her fingertips, or very lightly (125). In the context of the scene's deliberate intertextuality with *The*

Piano, this reference to disciplining female fingers so as to keep piano playing from disturbing the household's patriarch brings to mind both the severing of Ada's finger by her husband and the way her prosthetic finger comes to register that her music and the resisting, maternalized erotics with which it has been affiliated are vulnerable to patriarchal regulation. As that is precisely the point James goes on to make about both Isabel's attraction to Mme Merle and the latter's efforts on behalf of her daughter,[15] the novel emerges as a precursor for the critique of feminist erotics that Campion has made in *The Piano.*

However, in contrast to *The Piano,* the novel emphatically makes seductive, forceful, "gothic" male sexuality inextricable from, rather than the remedy for, the ways that patriarchal power can regulate a feminist investment in eroticized mother–daughter relations. If Campion initially rewrites James's Osmond as inspiring a positive erotic leap for Isabel (as in *The Piano*), the movie very quickly shifts to representing his influence as, like Warburton's, invasive and appropriative of Isabel's autoerotic reveries. Indeed, the inventive sequence that represents Isabel's world travels by inserting Nicole Kidman in what looks like an anachronistic mix of flickering Nickelodeon images, "home movies," and early travel clips is dedicated to documenting this appropriation. Here Mme Merle's companionship emerges immediately as dangerous: the second frame of the sequence presents her as a menacing rather than an attractive double, mirroring Isabel as she keeps a controlling eye on her from behind. And this image paves the way for Osmond's declaration of love ("I'm absolutely in love with you") to inhabit the voice-over first as Isabel recalls his kiss, then as the voice of everything (she sees his speaking lips in lima beans), and finally as her own voice repeating these words to herself. With her repetition of Osmond's words, her articulation of love for Osmond ("I'm absolutely in love") amounts to his ventriloquization of her desire. Rather than being urged by forceful male eroticism toward intersubjective sexuality, here autoerotic reverie is infiltrated and regulated by such male desire.

Inspired by James's linking of the insistent patriarchal seduction that Campion has celebrated to Isabel's mistaking as feminist autonomy the doomed attraction to Mme Merle, Campion here puts her own previous representation of "powerful," feminist countererotics into question. Most important for my argument, however, it is in this context of reevaluating Osmond's "power of eroticism" that Campion also reevaluates the movie's early sequence, now not only for the limits of its feminist erotics but also for its possible participation in patriarchal modes of eroticism. As Alan Nadel has observed, the unusual travel sequence alludes to the opening one in its being presented as emphatically cinematic and shot in black and white.[16] This allusion would seem to underscore the sequence's role in the feminist revisions of the novel linked at the outset to the foregrounding of cinematic representation. However, Campion's feminist revision here links autoerotic reverie not to the resistance to invasive male desire but to Osmond's invasive regulation of such reverie; that is, now feminist representation as foregrounded cinematic revision interrogates modes of regulation that are implicated in the movie's own feminist representation in the opening sequence.

In this vein as well, the travel sequence represents Isabel both as the Anglo traveler exploring exotic lands (Egypt, among others) and as the exotic female other. At one point the tourist Isabel dons a veil as she rides a camel, as if Osmond's infiltration of her sexual reveries shifts her from the autonomous feminist traveler to the female foreigner eroticized for Anglo male interests. Indeed, it is the veiled Isabel in Egypt who hears Osmond's voice and comes to repeat his words in her own voice, even as she imagines herself to be the naked object of his desire. In representing Isabel both as privileged tourist and exoticized female other in a sequence that rethinks the patriarchal uses of feminist countererotics, Campion here seems to intuit connections that could illuminate the most troubling aspects of the opening sequence: connections between the regulation of female sexuality, the eroticization of exotic female foreigners, and the privileged foreigner's self-destructive seduction by such erotics.

In a subsequent scene in which Campion eroticizes what in the novel is simply Isabel's sense of obligation to Osmond, the filmmaker again makes her critique of Isabel's response to Osmond's "power of eroticism" the occasion to return to her own lexicon of countererotics with a critical eye. First, Campion emphasizes Osmond's sadism by adding a startling series of sadistic slaps to his verbal reprimand of Isabel for failing to secure Pansy's engagement to Warburton. In an even more surprising move, Campion has Isabel become aroused in response to Osmond's cruelty. However, Osmond is not interested in Isabel's masochism; and his refusal to respond to her marks the transformation of the forceful male impulse that fortunately initiates Isabel's heterosexuality into an expression of abusive strength that has nothing to do with her (even masochistic) desire.

What Campion leaves her with, instead, is a sexuality that harkens back to the initial sequence. Cutting from the scene of Osmond's abuse to Isabel alone, outdoors, among trees and caressingly running her hands first over her slapped face and then over her body, the movie again invokes its opening lexicon of feminist erotics. With this return, Campion seems for a second time to bring that lexicon under scrutiny for its possible imbrication with patriarchal power. Like the sequence of Isabel's travels, here that lexicon seems to be questioned for its possible affinity with modes of female sexuality that are bound rather than resistant to patriarchal power. Registering an autoeroticism that is generated by Isabel's masochistic response to Osmond's abuse and not by her retreat from imperious men, this image seems to acknowledge the possibility of confusing resisting with dominant modes of female eroticism.

Significantly, Campion constructs Isabel's masochism as one response to her "feminist" resistance to Osmond's noble aspirations for his dark, American-Italian daughter. An awareness of how James's xenophobia propels this resistance could have made Campion's critique of the erotics she adds to this struggle with Osmond a critique of the relation between a female passion that depends on sexist power and a feminism that is appropriated for patriarchal agendas through its participation in xenophobic ones. Such a connection, along with the important rendering of this powerful but self-destructive sexuality in the same visual terms of the opening sequence, could have made it possible to consider how those initial images similarly entangle feminist representation with twentieth-century U.S. nationalist and racist rhetorics.

But if Campion's critical but underhistoricized return to the opening sequence does not include such a consideration, what she does succeed in doing is to shift her own revisionary project from an uncritical, "pro-sex" eroticizing of desexualized feminisms in both centuries to questioning powerful erotics for their possible complicity with patriarchal agendas. Indeed, Campion ends her movie with revisions of the novel whose eroticization of Isabel's feminism is inextricable from stressing the need to distinguish a desirable female sexuality from the patriarchal erotics that can frame it. The movie's rendition of Caspar's forced kiss on the grounds of Gardencourt both follows James in presenting Caspar's desire as insistently possessive and patronizing (he tries to convince Isabel that he is her indispensable savior) and extricates Isabel's resistance to him from the sexual disgust ("she felt each thing in his hard manhood that had least pleased her" [636]) that is so important to James. Campion's Isabel is excited by the kiss, returns it with fervor, *and* runs from possessive male desire. Registering her enjoyment of sexual passion at the same time that Isabel flees the forceful male who has aroused it, this revision gestures toward a pro-sex feminism that is wary of achieving its aims in patriarchal terms.

The trajectory from Caspar's kiss to the movie's end leads to a final revision of the novel that seems entirely dedicated to emphasizing the importance of such a wariness. Significantly, the final scene plays in reverse the movie's ingenious revisions of the novel at the movie's outset, but with crucial differences. Whereas the initial sequence moves from Campion's feminist countererotics to Isabel's rejection of Warburton, here Isabel's rejection of the similarly invasive Caspar ("You frightened me," says Isabel as he, as Warburton has done, accosts her outdoors) leads directly to her taking a place in the movie's lexicon of feminist erotics. Fleeing Caspar, Isabel arrives at the door of the Touchetts' mansion; but whereas in the novel this is the moment when Isabel resolves on "the straight path" back to Osmond (636), in the movie it is an emphatic moment of irresolution. Upon reaching the door, Isabel turns back, and the camera freezes her in this movement, emphasizing the cinematic nature of this portrait, outdoors and turning toward the camera, like the twentieth-century women in the opening sequence. If, in her first portrait, Isabel refuses Warburton's invasion of an (auto)homoerotic world of feminist erotics, in her last portrait she flees from Caspar's forceful desire to the movie's visual space of feminist erotics.

Yet the image that finally occupies this space is not so neatly posed against patriarchal regulation and erotics as are those in the opening sequence. Arresting Isabel in movement between two patriarchal figures, the possessive Caspar and the sadistic Osmond, the space occupied by feminist erotics is now represented as one that can be framed by and lead directly to the patriarchal appropriation of female sexuality. A movie that takes as its project the feminist sexualization of Isabel Archer seems to end by gesturing toward the need to interrogate the discourses that eroticize females and feminists, the need to stop in the course of what seem to be feminist trajectories and to hold such discourses up to scrutiny for their capacity to take feminism to dominant discursive destinations.

Ultimately, then, Campion's revision of the Victorian novel produces an important and logical connection between two postmodern feminist narratives that are more often locked in tenacious conflict. The first of these seeks to redress what it sees as the desexualization of feminist resistance to patriarchal heterosexuality, and the second productively predicates pro-sex feminism on keeping in view the ease with which certain authorizing erotics can recuperate feminist aims. Campion's participation in the former discourse here is in dialogue with what she perceives as a Victorian emergence of both desexualized feminism and ruptures in erotic conventions. It is a dialogue, I have argued, that produces both a brilliant feminist appropriation of Victorian ruptures for the feminism that the novel insistently desexualizes and an uncritical appropriation of erotic discourses that are hostile to feminist aims.

The movie's ultimate critical engagement with its own countererotics, Campion's participation in the second of the postmodern feminist narratives, registers the wisdom of looking to Victorian texts not only for emergent moments in gender and sexuality, but also for the emergence of a subject understood as vulnerable to embracing its own oppression, especially as that subject mistakes regulation for the exercise of autonomy. Indeed, that Campion's *Portrait* locates important insights about the regulation of feminist subjectivity in James's novel, ones that prompt her to extend the scope of her own previous inquiries to include the powerful modes of eroticism she has previously posed against such regulation, points to a Victorian legacy for postmodern feminism that ultimately may prove as productive as a Victorian legacy of erotic constraints and erotic ruptures.

Notes

1. Miro Bilborough, "The Making of *The Piano*," in Jane Campion, *The Piano* (London: Bloomsbury Publishing, 1993), 140.

2. For a discussion of how Campion also links female sexual awakening in *The Piano* to images of female victimization, see Barbara Johnson, "Muteness Envy," in *The Feminist Difference: Literature, Psychoanalysis, Race, and Gender* (Cambridge: Harvard University Press, 1998). Johnson shows how the feminist debates about this film articulate impasses between a "pro-sex feminism" that celebrates women's ability to find pleasure within sexualities structured by male power and a feminism that points out the dangers in the film's "romanticiz[ing] the borderline between coercion and pleasure" (146–48). Johnson persuasively elaborates the latter position by stressing that culture is "invest[ed] in not being able to tell the difference between female victimization and female pleasure" (151). I argue that in *Portrait* Campion's revisions of the novel chart a trajectory from the uncritical "pro-sex" position to a critique of that position.

3. In the introduction to my *Unsettled Subjects: Restoring Feminist Politics to*

Poststructuralist Critique (Durham, N.C.: Duke University Press, 1997), I elaborate both how patriarchal hegemony counts on such feminist mistakes and the difficulty feminist theorists have encountered in diagnosing how feminists' appeal to dominant discourses undermines feminist politics.

4. Critics have also pointed out that Isabel's love of personal freedom is meant to invoke the revolutionary ideals associated with the Centennial of 1876, the only date actually mentioned in the novel. See Alfred Habegger, *Henry James and the "Woman Business"* (New York: Cambridge University Press, 1989), 180; Debra MacComb, "Divorce of a Nation; or, Can Isabel Archer Resist History?" *Henry James Review* 17.2 (1996): 130–31; and Adeline Tintner, "The Centennial of 1876 and *The Portrait of a Lady*," *Markham Review* 10 (1980–81): 27–29. Whereas these critics situate what they see as James's sympathy to Isabel's peculiarly U.S. brand of feminism in historical context, I argue that James's complex fears of feminist autonomy lead him to appropriate Isabel's feminism in the interests both of an oppositional male homoeroticism and a nationalist regulation of women's marriage choices.

5. Henry James, *The Portrait of a Lady*, [1908] (New York: Penguin, 1996), 238.

6. In her revision of the novel's initial scene of resistance to compulsory heterosexuality, Campion invokes the psychoanalytic feminism of the late 1970s and early 1980s, which privileged autoeroticism, mother–daughter erotics, and homoerotic relations between women as sites for resistance to patriarchal heterosexuality. For U.S. feminist object relations theory, see Nancy Chodorow, *The Reproduction of Mothering* (Berkeley: University of California Press, 1978), and Adrienne Rich, "Compulsory Heterosexuality and Lesbian Existence," in *The Signs Reader*, ed. Elizabeth Abel and Emily Abel (Chicago: University of Chicago Press, 1983), 139–68. For 1980s French feminism that, revising Lacan, valorizes mother–daughter relations as a site of resistance to a not yet assumed patriarchal symbolic, see Luce Irigaray, *This Sex Which Is Not One*, trans. Catherine Porter with Carolyn Burke (Ithaca, N.Y.: Cornell University Press, 1985); and Julia Kristeva, *Revolution in Poetic Language*, trans. Margaret Walker (New York: Columbia University Press, 1984).

7. Other critics have also read this opening sequence as articulating a specifically twentieth-century and emphatically feminist portrait of ladies. In her "'Conscious Observation of a Lovely Woman': Jane Campion's *Portrait* in Film," *Henry James Review* 18.2 (1997), Nancy Bentley locates the feminist import of the sequence in its commentary on the women's relation to the traditional cinematic gaze (175). Virginia Wexman points out Campion's attribution of sensuous bodily awareness to these women; see her "The Portrait of a Body," *Henry James Review* 18.2 (1997): 185.

8. Lynn Wardley, "Reassembling Daisy Miller," *American Literary History* 3.2 (1991): 232–54.

9. Lauren Berlant, *The Queen of America Goes to Washington City: Essays on Sex and Citizenship* (Durham, N.C.: Duke University Press, 1997), 200–208. Berlant describes this whitening effect in a discussion of a 1993 issue of *Time*, whose cover displays "a new face of America" as an interracial female one that whitens as it combines images of women of color. It is, Berlant claims, a fantasy of "mixed race but still

white-enough children" that responds to the racializing of whites in a new national order (207).

10. In an essay decidedly unfriendly to Campion's project of eroticizing Isabel, Marc Bousquet similarly notes that the opening sequence plugs into dominant representations of multiracial, eroticized women; see his "I Don't Like Isabel Archer," *Henry James Review* 18.2 (1997): 198. For a more positive reading of how the sequence's shift from the multiracial Australian women to the Americanized Nicole Kidman engages with dominant nationalist ideologies, see Priscilla L. Walton, "Jane and James Go to the Movies: Post Colonial Portraits of a Lady," *Henry James Review* 18.2 (1997): 188.

11. Indeed, *Portrait*'s opening sequence is reminiscent of the earlier movie's affiliation of natural, forested scenes with feminist sexual awakenings.

12. See Johnson, "Muteness Envy," for a similar reading of Ada's muteness as a feminist "form of resistance and subjecthood" that the movie represents as "confus[ing] women's oppression and women's desire" (143).

13. Bilborough, "The Making of *The Piano*," 140.

14. Rachel Abramowitz, "Interview with Jane Campion," *Premiere* Web site: www.premieremag.com/archive/WIH_96/campion/index.html.

15. Nonetheless, James's insightful analysis of how Isabel mistakes a "mother-daughter" relationship controlled by patriarchal design for an expression of independent, resisting femininity and female desire in no way mitigates his own patriarchal designs on Isabel's (lack of) sexuality; that is, he registers a sympathetic understanding of how patriarchal power can make use of certain "feminist" choices even as he appropriates Isabel's feminism for his own agendas. James's denunciation of Osmond's patriarchal control is entirely compatible with his desire to have Isabel's feminist resistance to Osmond assuage his racist and classist fears of the American girl's capacity to contaminate elite culture and bloodlines.

16. Alan Nadel, "The Search for Cinematic Identity and a Good Man: Jane Campion's Appropriation of James's *Portrait*," *Henry James Review* 18.2 (1997): 180–81.

Display Cases

Judith Roof

In its quotation and appropriation of Victorian display tactics, computer interface technology deploys the familiar Victorian graphic style associated with capitalist zeal, consumer appeal, and imperial zeal while repressing its specifically Victorian character.[1] Both Victorian exhibition techniques and contemporary computer interfaces employ icons, images, letters, multiple fonts, varying scale, and decorative partitions, often nested behind glass, to draw the eye, organize information, display curiosities, and invite their contemplation by onlookers. The similarities in the strategies and style of the Victorian exhibit and the modern computer are not only superficial; the coincidence of the same tactics in two very different contexts reflects a complex correlation between their purposes and logics. On the one hand, the computer's appropriation of Victorian style is an effective marketing strategy used to deflect anxieties about technology; Victoriana links new technology to an older tradition, making it seem safe and familiar. On the other hand, the reappearance of Victorian style signals a sustained practice of representing knowledge spatially that underpins forms of capitalism and national power by appearing to organize, master, and make all forms of information the object of consumer access and choice.[2]

Computer interface's subtle citation of Victorian display tactics signals, perhaps insidiously, both a new kind of imperialism—an imperialism of the mind—and a new sense of subjugation as computer display tactics reshape the ways we think about information, commodities, and ourselves as modern subjects. There are many ways that this reshaping occurs; the computer alters spatiotemporal relations, changes the relation between individuals and the group and notions of the group itself, shifts from a metaphorical to a metonymical organization of information, and dislocates identifiable sites of power.[3] Despite all of this change, as surface style might indicate, digital information systems are still quite Victorian with similar anxieties and means of allaying them and similar agendas and means of accomplishing them. One contemporary Web example strikes me as particularly symptomatic of the computer's more substantial connection to Victorian worldview: the Principia Cybernetica Project's (PCP) theory of Metasystem Transition, a postmodern "theory" of evolution that looks uncannily like Darwin recursively reinscribed in cybernetic terms.[4] If computer interface technology appropriates most of Victorian display's panoptical tactics of mastery as a way to lure us away from the strategies of control now resident in software, then Metasystem Transition, like the concept of evolution, appears to return control over the machine to the human in the form of knowledge—in the form of understanding and organizing the dynamics of digital systems. But unlike the theory of evolution with its complex and unlocatable selective forces, Metasystem Transition suggests that humans can shape and operate the evolution of systemic changes. What is instructive here is not postmodern cybernetics as some cutting-edge cyberphilosophy linked to postmodernism and hypertext, but its conservative Darwinism—the rehabilitated Victorian worldview imported to rescue us from a Cameronesque vision of a world governed by machines or, worse, a Gatesesque vision of an epistemology dominated by Windows.

On Display

The graphic similarities between Victorian museum and exhibit display and computer interface strategies (the use of boxes, frames, icons, and multiple fonts) as well as their more subtle structural affinities (spatial arrangement, organization by taxonomic hierarchy, the sense of spectacle) suggest a complex interrelation that extends well beneath the surface of the display function itself. The tactics of display developed in the nineteenth century built on the crucial seventeenth- and eighteenth-century advent of the complete separability of display strategy from the object displayed.[5] In working out the modes of exhibition in the eighteenth and nineteenth centuries, display technologies became the apposite to what they displayed, the augmenting complement, the prosthesis by which the information represented by the specimen might be more surely and pointedly communicated and savored just as the artifact was increasingly removed from any immediate contact with its original context, with other artifacts, or with the mode of display itself. A feathered headdress, for example, became a synecdoche for a colonized people rather than retaining any sense of its role in the rituals of the culture from which it came. Animal species represented the wonders of nature and the ascendancy of the human, while objects of historical significance such as souvenirs from Napoleon's army reflected the wise perspective of the ultimate victors as well as the lesson of excessive ambition.

Exhibitions, museums, and print advertisements organized objects with symbolic or representative (metaphorical) significance in a spatial arrangement where the contiguity of objects to one another as well as to the larger area related to organizing taxonomic schemes such as anatomy, geography, ethnography, evolution, nation, industry, or history. Thus, species or morphologies, or any other organizing principle (such as, for example, curiosities and freaks) could be conveyed through the arrangement of objects in space in relation to one another. In cordoning off, setting forth, and protecting, display technologies not only signaled an artifact's value and fragility, but also confirmed its dislocation from its natural or cultural context, enabled its neat resignification within a Victorian Anglocentric worldview, producing their meaning as they organized and situated the trophies of exploration and the innovations of science and industry.

That many kinds of objects might in less sophisticated exhibits be displayed in the same room attests both to the scene of imperial accumulation and wealth of knowledge and to the multiple categories within which artifacts might be classed—generally as curiosities, but within that as subcategories (animal, vegetable, mineral) whose clear taxonomic distinctions maintained the vestiges of a spatial discipline despite odd spatial associations (a suit of armor, for example, beside a palm tree). Bullock's "Egyptian eclectic" building, for example, housed geographically arranged animal and bird species (tropicals with the tropical even if the species never inhabited the region together), a "Roman Gallery" room for art objects, a "magnificent decorations" room for items considered to be such, and a "Mexican Room" for things Mexican.[6] Objects were made "art" of "magnificent decoration" by their location in these rooms and the exhibit itself gained an organizational mastery over disparate materials. Bullock's geographical *rum* categorical organization was analogous to the comparative anatomy schemes of Kahn's

Museum and Reimer's Anatomical and Ethnological Museums as well as to the various exhibits of mechanical marvels in the Polytechnic and the Adelaide.[7] These latter exhibits were less nationally organized than the Crystal Palace "Exhibition of the Works of Industry of all Nations," but all in their eclecticism reflected the basic theme of human (and British) ascendancy over the material world.

In many exhibits, the presence of glass, used as a basic protective element from the late seventeenth century on, rarefies, amplifies, and arrests these artifacts in time. Victorian museum display separated artifacts twice: once from their context and once from the consumer, producing in the museum or exhibit a contiguous or metonymic relation between the display and the artifacts, among artifacts, and between artifact and viewer. Although the arrangement of glass and label is designed presumably to protect the artifact with as little visual interference as possible while providing information, glass itself, as it later functioned in shop windows, became an element that both invited and restricted the viewer. As Georg Hirth suggested, "viewers were restrained by the invisible wall of crystal, if not by the burnished metal guard, you can look but you cannot touch, desire but not possess. Making goods look 'better than they really are,' windows simultaneously confer upon them an aura of shining accessibility."[8]

What is evident in the two-century transition from private cabinet to the public exhibit of Victorian England is the development of a technology of display designed to attract visitors to a vision of mastery and national wealth; exhibits' educational functions were only part of their allure in a culture where virtuous enjoyment meant a dose of didacticism. They also provided the occasion for the objectivized spectacle of scientific mastery, exotic commodities, and the products of industry that were testimony to British intellect, power, and the might of capital.[9] The fundamental technology of display, however, had also come to be a technology of allure. While the mastery endowed by the viewing relation reproduced the conjoined dynamics of Anglocentric perspective, imperialism, and the illusion of consumer choice, it also set exhibits apart, making them paradoxically both example and exception. The mastery presumably endowed by the viewing relation was continually delayed; if the objects on display were something to see, like rare species, bizarre anomaly, industrial marvel, or imperial booty, the view was frustrated by glass and arrangement, the very technologies designed to bring them into safe and informative view in the first place.

The Panopticon and the Lure

The discourses of display developed in nineteenth-century display consist of two broad strategies: the panopticon, which joined power to viewing through the construction of seemingly unilateral display techniques, and the lure, which allied desire to viewing through the simultaneous production of opportunities for viewing and their frustration. Both of these tactics were tied to burgeoning capitalism as evidence of its success, its benefits, and its emerging strategies for attracting customers. Museum items gained a symbolic value not only by means of their presence in a museum, but also by means of their arrangement, which in Victorian exhibits, as Tony Bennett points out, was concerned with producing an ordered vision over which the populace seemed to have control.[10] Showing how nineteenth-century exhibitions perform another aspect of Foucault's disciplinary panopticon, Bennett demonstrates how the "exhibitionary complex" places the people "on this side of power, both as its subject and its beneficiary" (80). This power is "a force created and channelled by society's ruling groups but for the good of all—a power made manifest not in its ability to inflict pain but by its ability to organize and coordinate an order of things and to produce a place for the people in relation to that order" (ibid.). Bennett's interest is in showing how the "exhibitionary complex" incorporates and extends the principles of the panopticon so that "together, with the panorama," both form "a technology of vision which served not to atomize and disperse the crowd but to regulate it, and to do so by rendering it visible to itself, by making the crowd itself the ultimate spectacle" (81). Evolving display technologies also enacted a new relation between display and object that not only related to the politics of power represented by the panopticon, but also marked a shift in technology in specific relation to the needs of a nascent and discerning commodity culture. This effect was produced not only by the arrangement of artifacts, their labeling, their denaturalization, and their dislocation, but also by the very presence of display technologies themselves, by the rearrangement of spatial relations between viewers and physical specimens and the presence of glass. To produce a subject/object dynamic between the viewer and the artifact was to reproduce a particular power arrangement between active and passive, between a subject with will and the possibility of movement and an object frozen in space. This subtended exhibits' panopticon quality with a dynamic of voyeurism which, in its mechanism of "reversal of affect," produced not only some of the spectator's pleasure in viewing, but also the wish to be viewed—to be the object of the imperial gaze.[11]

The artifacts' frozen entrapment in exhibition space was just as much a form of control over the natural and the alien as was their reclassification within the various schemata of a Eurocentric worldview. Artifacts in glass-covered boxes exhibited an evolving logic of contiguity, nonaccess, and indirection that characterized not only the paradox of display as that which makes it difficult to see, but also as that which produces desire as a product of thwarted contact. Frustrating the view and thwarting contact are both the effects of the operation of the lure that becomes increasingly prominent as exhibitions become overdetermined sites of capitalist might. A structural dynamic that entices without ever providing a clear view, the lure is enabled by the separability of display from artifact, and it operates quite visibly both in the print culture appended to exhibitions and in the exhibits' deployment of frames and glass. Printed handbills, catalogs, notices, and advertisements all augmented exhibits by marking their presence and pointing to them, by describing and even enumerating them. Clearly, the purpose of such advertising was to prime the exhibits' capitalist pump, to begin a flow of visitors who would attract other visitors by word of mouth and general acclaim.[12] The lurid connection between print's synecdochal relation to displays and its advertising function marks the intersection of display strategies as separable tactics and capital as a movable asset. The detachability of print media meant that it could be applied selectively and opportunely and withdrawn at will.

The micrologic of the printed handbills and posters plays out the complex relations of synecdoche and contiguity that constituted the lure as it operated in Victorian display technologies. Victorian letterpress printing achieved emphasis by using different point type; printers added variation and interest through the use of different typefaces, and organized information through the deployment of words on a page and the use of decorative lines, boxes, and woodcut icons and images.[13] But the most effective strategy was the placement of information on the page, which not only had to draw the eye in competition with many other handbills and advertisements, but also convey immediately the character of the information it displayed. For example, the notice for a lecture about the Great Exhibition is a letterpress poster using various print sizes and fonts (see figure 1). This notice deploys both word size and position to draw attention to the main exhibit, which is in this case a lecture about the Great Exhibition. The words *Exhibition* and

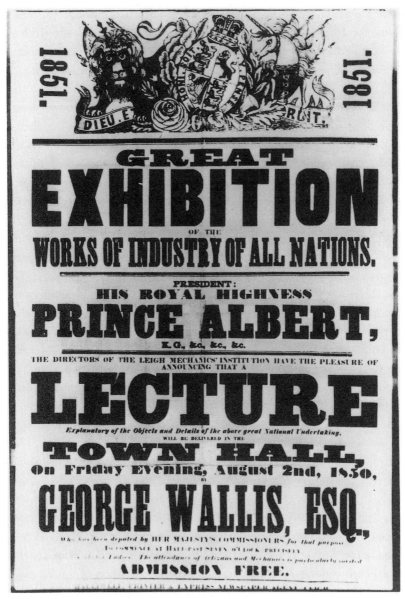

Figure 1. A notice of a lecture about the Great Exhibition of 1851. Leigh, 1850, printed by Halliwell, Leigh. Reprinted by permission of the Reading University Library, England.

Lecture are cast in the same-size print, but in different typefaces. Reading the two largest words produces the message "Exhibition Lecture." The information that the Great Exhibition is presided over by Prince Albert is separated from the rest of the notice by two decorative lines; the words are separated from the poster's crowning icon by another, more definitive line. Thus en-framed and separated, the three kinds of information provided—image, lec-ture, and Prince Albert—coexist in the same space, contiguous, lending cre-dence and authority to one another, but remaining graphically separate.

"Prince Albert"'s position in the middle of the poster connects to the icon at the top, an elaborate, cartooned version of the royal coat of arms, used often in relation to the Crystal Palace exhibition because of Albert's sponsorship. The coat of arms icon is a synecdoche, quite literally for Prince Albert, more figuratively for the official, even national, character of the 1851 Exhibition. On the notice it works as an efficient shortcut, a way to convey a large amount of information and complex associations by recourse to a single image. Its purpose is to attract; its information is framed, separated, arranged so that each item can be consumed, but also so that the elements work together for maximum efficiency. But while the poster informs, its at-traction occurs mainly in the form of a lure, of a representation that appears to exhibit its exhibit, which is a lecture about the Exhibit, by simply em-ploying the Exhibit's primary signifiers, "Exhibit" and "Prince Albert." But in enframing Prince Albert and then using Prince Albert's coat of arms to enframe the entire message, the poster plays through a series of enframe-ments that never in fact exhibit the Exhibit itself, but instead lead one to (and through) a lecture about the Exhibit that is itself another enframement of the Exhibit. The lure here is the Exhibit, which, signified multiple times across the notice, never actually appears itself, but is evoked only through its contiguous signifiers—Prince Albert, lecture, and the word *Exhibit*. This tactic of multiple enframement is more economically accomplished in an advertisement from 1889 that relies even more on the power of the icon. Included on a page full of advertisements, the ham draws attention through its graphic simplicity (see figure 2). In comparison to the Exhibition Lecture poster, the ham advertisement is simple, exemplifying the other end of a display continuum that ranged from the overcrowded conditions of the eighteenth-century Leverian Museum and the explosion of information conveyed by print advertisements and catalogs to the simple use of an icon or coat of arms. This advertisement combines one word, "USE," presented in large block print, with the two images of packed hams. Each image of a ham frames the words "our trademark ham," making the image of the ham simultaneously the company's trademark or coat of arms, which announces itself as a trademark by including the word *trademark* just as the Exhibit

Figure 2. An advertisement from the inside cover of *Chatterbox*, Boston. Estes and Lauriat, 1887.

exhibited itself as exhibit by using the word *Exhibit.* The ham enframes the trademark which is the ham which is in turn framed by the advertisement's border, producing a self-cycling economy where the enframing leads inexorably to what seems to be product which turns out to be a trademark which refers to the product. The ham, thus, becomes the lure that in this case both appears and disappears, oscillating between image and trademark. This points to perhaps the most clever of display technologies where the artifact or commodity seems to speak for itself, but can only do so because it has been made into a lure that speaks from the field implied by the advertisement, but that is never actually present in it.

This playing with the lure is no longer the kind of unitary universe-embodying display practice as that of the reliquary, but is rather a dynamic practice by which desire is produced through graphic and spatial arrangements. The lure, which, inauthentic, rivets our look as if it were the real thing, is the inauthentic thing that inevitably refers to the authentic it mimics. The lure captivates and provokes desire through displacement and by being not the thing we thought it was that arrested our attention. Wax models and taxidermal specimens are a species of lure, because they mimic the living, because they stand in for the real thing, while being its simulacrum. Oddities in bottles, which can claim the virtue of authenticity, look nothing like the real thing that they are because of preservation techniques that alter color, squeeze specimens into jar-shaped spaces, and produce a series of winding bowel-like curiosities that only barely resemble what is claimed for them. Reposing in death, the two-headed fetus and the giant squid look all too similar to one another. The enframement in these cases, which seems to be about the authentic view of that which we rarely see, is actually an abject lure that refers to death; these specimens signify less the unusual than the unusual presence of the corpse.[14]

Both the museum and print advertisements take advantage of multiple enframings and conjunctions of frames within boxes within rooms to connote the complex and multileveled significance (universal, national, evolutionary, and/or economical) of the objects they display, while printed handbills, more limited in their deictic scope, deploy frames, juxtapositions, icons, and distribution to point to the exhibit or to exhibits about exhibits, another kind of enframing that reveals that tactic's essential function as a lure. All of this reflects not only the mechanical character of Victorian industrial technology and the link between desire and capital, but also a habit of control via enframing, of protected curiosity, of spectacularized social relations as display becomes a way to define a culture's relation to the world. The spatial arrangement of objects was the beginning of a technology of access premised on a relation between location and system that underlies the operation of digital computers.

Windows Display

Like the Victorian exhibit, the modern computer attests to the technological superiority of the national cultures that developed and deployed it (though it masks its actual transnational origins). It has increasingly become a marketplace for the sale of goods and information and has, like the exhibit, become an ostensible site for sightseeing that also works as a panopticon—the opportunity to be seen and accounted for within the larger exercises of power that shape systems of information. Web sites keep track of user "hits"; it is difficult to be anonymous on the Internet, where each message is marked with date, time, and origin. The similarity in the cultural roles of exhibits and computers is reflected in the computer's appropriation of Victorian display tactics.

Computer display's deployment of Victorian techniques hints at a superficial relation between the old and the new, producing a veneer whose psychological profit exists in allaying fears and providing marketing strategies, but whose less obvious similarities in structure and motive point to the perpetuation of issues of control and human ascendancy over the machine that not only survive the introduction of the computer, but define the character of human/machine interface. While their similarities in purpose function at the level of product—the organization of and access to information, the display of might and wealth, the connection between product and panoptic power—the computer's borrowings actually function to make consumable systems of knowledge that have gone from the Victorian's metaphorical organizations to the digital's entirely metonymic and hence less accessible systems. Derived from attempts to produce mechanical calculating devices, the digital computer transforms gears into circuits, routing power through series of interconnected pathways that appear as binary choices (yes or no) in a series of enchained frames. The logic that drives the choice of circuit, pathway, and product incorporates metonymy not only in its constitution as a binary system where any choice is always contiguous to the other, but also in its pathways, which are literally linked to one another as circuits on microchips. If Victorian exhibits imposed a strategic metonymy on the display and arrangement of artifacts, specimens, exotica, and industrial marvels, the computer's very operation is constituted by such a metonymy.[15]

The Victorians' systemization of knowledge and their classificatory schemes are the computer's conceptual forebears in the connection of facts to a sequence that can be accessed by identifying a location. But whereas in a Victorian exhibit this access was physical—and metaphorical—in that museum-goers walked through galleries or rooms whose arrangement depicted a knowledge system via the association of one artifact to another, the computer employs metonymy within the machine itself and not as a tactic of display. This represents not so much a shift in epistemology as a shift in the scale of operation in which the computer incorporates the metonymic logic of the Victorian display as the basis for its operation. The difficulty in using a digital machine, however, is rendering visible and intelligible invisible microchip processes so that users might control them. In an apparent reversal of the Victorian's metonymic display of metaphorical artifacts, metonymic digital processes need to be rendered metaphorically. This is not so much an opposition, however, as it is an alteration in the location of human interface with information; the computer's visible site is an analogical matrix (the screen arrangement) that exists only on the scale of Victorian ideologies (panopticism, imperialism, capitalism). In other words, because the Victorian exhibit's arrangement of logics (metaphor, metonymy) has been reduced in size to the very workings of the computer, the computer's analogical interface makes visible the panoptical power through which the Victorian exhibit, already like the computer, attempted to systematize and wield information itself as the essence of capital and commodity.

This panoptical power manifests itself in the computer's increasingly analogical interfaces, which provide more concentrated power and control through fewer and fewer operations.[16] If Victorian display reflected a systematized worldview, computer display produces a view into a system defined more by its dramatization of panoptical effect. For some years now, computers (by fiat and otherwise) almost all employ a WIMP system that deploys icons arranged on a metaphorical "desktop" image to denote available functions and programs. Windows, following its innovative competitor, the Macintosh, cast access to information as an analogical activity. Windows renders a digital numerical location and set of operations into an icon that represents, poetically, the end result of a computer program as a simile— "deleting data is like throwing it into a trash can"—and displays this iconized function within a spatial representation of an office surface. Users "point" to the function they wish to select by means of a "mouse" whose movements on a pad beside the computer translate analogically into the movements of an arrow or pointing finger on the screen. The "mouse," the "desktop," even the Macintosh "trash can" are metaphors that transform all vestiges of metonymic computer logic, operating system language, and information location into trite, vaguely humorous, familiar metaphors, both announcing and masking the various computer programs that operate within a different logic through a cartoon version of empowerment.[17]

Instead of typing in lists of commands, one need only point to have one's will done, to locate information within a system over which one has the illusion of complete control. When one uses a computer, one seems to be operating the very system through which all Victorian display and knowledge was constituted. In aligning the consumer with the apparent locus of panoptical power, the computer captures the consumer even more completely as the knowledge base of the computer turns out to have had the consumer in mind all along; the computer and its various networked systems are both virtual museum and market that, in seducing through the lure of power, invite the computer user to consume all the more.[18]

The contemporary computer's use of Victoriana betrays the connections between the information systems of the computer and the systematized information in Victorian exhibits. Even more, it signals the continuation of a particular alignment of panoptical power and commodity culture as that is resituated along an apparent axis of control located within the commodity itself and managed by means of the very same strategies that finally mask the shift from one site to another. Its lure is not only information mastery (set within multiple frames or windows), but also the sense that such systematized knowledge offers a whole world, a parallel universe that is in fact the same universe organized for cybercontrol. Using a Victorian museum psychology, the Web contains the world (in both senses of the word).

In both Windows and Victorian display technologies, the object of interest—the program, the performance—is always receding, out of reach, hiding behind its cover of glass, its lettering, its graphics, its neighbor on a chain of representations that never ends. Yet the computer window has one capability Victorian enframing could only anticipate: the ability to leap from operation to operation through a logic of contiguity based paradoxically on the analogical movements of the mouse as it makes intelligible links in hidden series. The mouse is the metaphorical gloss that Victorian display technologies lacked; through the mouse, metaphor becomes again the actor through which meaning is produced and control retained. Only the human spectator of the Victorian exhibit could make the connections the mouse makes; the spectator could only do so by moving physically through exhibit space, taking shortcuts, and to do so meaningfully such a human would need to already know the connections between one artifact and another. The metaphorical control of the mouse function is even more evident in World Wide Web display strategies that work through a perpetual series of fields, connected by associative "links," indicated by the Victorian pointing finger, selected via the mouse, and attended by the iconic hourglass that connotes and masks processing time. Although World Wide Web graphics tend to be much more sophisticated than personal computer displays (photography as opposed to woodcut), their deployment on the screen still imitates Victorian poster display, with decorative bars, differing fonts and print sizes, and the use of icons.

This additional form of computer control does not, however, demonstrate the computer's necessary advance from the purposes of nineteenth-century exhibits, but rather illustrates its debt to them not only in the appropriation of specific display tactics, but also in its continuation of the motives of control resident in the arrangement and display of information. As display in its various forms becomes an overt tactic of a commodity culture and comes to depend on video and computer simulacra instead of the physical displays of artifacts, it still, even in its crassest commercial guise, does not lose its function as panopticon nor its strategies of allure. Via computers, contemporary commercial endeavors keep rigorous account of consumer patterns; credit card companies record every purchase and grocery stores track every item of food each customer buys. Computer display's history reveals not only a stylistic debt to the Victorians, but also a tradition of control sold through the apparent provision of information and mastery. The display that offered scientific information, opportunities for national pride, and marvel at industrial advancement is still also the display that engages its spectators in complex relations of power and capitalist manipulation disguised as entertainment and convenience.

The specific choice made by computer interface designers to employ a Victorianate iconic interface with its connotations of a more primitive technology is thus more a symptom of a deep and abiding legacy than a mark of imitation, pointing to anxieties about control that continue in the micro-technologies of contemporary information systems. Although we might see data or information as "raw material," what is worrisome is how our access to the information is already shaped, monitored, and delimited by the software conventions—such as Windows—that predefine our relation to any data and not only control us, but implant a particular ideology of value and a specific commodity epistemology in all our dealings with the machines that have become the tools by which ideas are crafted and disseminated. Although mice and joysticks and screen setting and software "choice" appear to make us the operators of these tools, they are the lures that enable the tools to employ us.

Evolution in Display

The imbalance between the machine's capacity and human capacity to employ the machine is what the PCP's reconstruction of Darwin addresses. The term "Metasystem Transition" refers, according to the PCP, to "the process by which control emerges in evolutionary Systems," and "evolution," according to the PCP, is "based on the trial-and-error process of variation and natural selection of systems at all levels of complexity." Their approach to evolution is cybernetic; that is, based on a "'bootstrapping' principle: the expression of the theory affects its content and meaning, and vice versa." Building on a cyberontological model, the group organizes concepts into what it calls a "semantic network," organized at an even higher level in relation to "the fundamental principles of cybernetics" (Principia Cybernetica Web). Basically, what PCP is suggesting is a cybernetic model of evolution to higher planes of complexity, to more complex organizations of knowledge, just as Darwin's idea of evolution was itself already to some degree cybernetic. Evolution serves PCP as an analogy, not only for the process of selection, but also for the underlying organization of levels and taxonomic species by which knowledge and epistemology are to be apprehended. What is important here is the reiteration of a hierarchical taxonomic model premised on levels of increasing complexity—and that sounds familiar, so familiar that the reappearance of evolution in a cybernetic context seems more a symptom of what the relation might be between the Victorian and the postmodern.

Although Darwin's theories seemed to fly in the face of a Victorian worldview, their reliance on taxonomies as well as on a centered human epistemology made them in some ways the objective correlative of the exhibition and vice versa. Presuming the notion of a visually identifiable species defined by the scientifically enlightened observation from the top of the chain, Darwin's notions of natural selection and evolution certainly relied on the same kinds of specular organization as the exhibit and with the same panoptical impetus of regulating, disciplining, and in turn becoming the objects of such ordered study. But the panoptical aspect most central and yet most veiled by the idea of the panopticon itself is its focus on the control of the uncontrollable. Just as the Victorian exhibit seemed to bring the untidy vestiges of empire into controllable proximity and the unpredictable masses into commercial compliance, so Darwin's theories, while admitting the uncontrollability of natural selection, produced control at the site of species organization—at the site of epistemology and theory itself. In this sense, Darwin was already a cyberneticist in that by proposing a notion of authorless change, he produced a site for the control of that change, not on the epochal level of species evolution, but on the level of philosophy. Although that philosophy does not alter the processes it organizes, the very fact of its existence does change the relation of the human to nature. Humanity is both a part of the process and the describer of it. The ability to describe and characterize inevitably suggests the ability to monitor and control the conditions by which natural selection might be accomplished, not only around other species (which humanity fairly systematically eliminates), but around the evolution of humanity itself.

This notion of control at the heart of the exhibition and evolution reappears as the central tenet of PCP's cyberevolution, where information rather than nature has become the field that must be organized. PCP's focus on control is a way of enlarging the framework of evolution to include information systems—and computers themselves. Defining control as a feedback relation between a controller and the controlled, PCP locates the controller and its perceptions as the soul of the system, organizing, on a metalevel at least, the operation of information systems that generally seem beyond our control. In other words, like Darwin, and using the same move, PCP takes a large set of phenomena—the informational universe—and organizes it within sets of simple operations and principles, the effect of which is to locate the human at the heart of the controlling center, again not as the agent who controls natural selection, but as the agent who sees the organization of the system and who can potentially shape its development.

Because computers are machines, we tend to believe that somehow somewhere someone—like Bill Gates—actually controls it all, and if that is the case, then we are controlled by it, becoming will-less subjects to a system that encompasses us. But if we return to Darwin and remember that all we need to do is *(a)* organize and *(b)* discern the basic operations of change, we too can regain control of a field that has evolved beyond most of us in a brief three decades. If the PCP's manifestos are indeed postmodern (which is where the Web organizes them), then the Victorian is still the heart of that postmodern, not only in terms of its display devices, but also in terms of the epistemological strategies by which we relocate the world, both physical and virtual, as our object. We may no longer have legitimating metanarratives, but we still have metanarratives of legitimization and control.

Notes

1. This essay draws on the dominant graphic style of 1990s computer technology, including the World Wide Web, whose display tactics are usually more sophisticated than the personal computer display. Observations about museum and print display techniques from the eighteenth and nineteenth centuries will focus more on Victorian practices, though these techniques were developed over several centuries. My main sources of information about Victorian display are Richard D. Altick's encyclopedic *Shows of London* (Cambridge and London: The Belknap Press of Harvard University, 1978); Thomas Richards, *The Commodity Culture of Victorian England* (London: Verso, 1991); and Michael Twyman, *Printing 1770–1970* (London: Eyre and Spottiswoode, 1970).

2. As Thomas Richards points out in *The Commodity Culture of Victorian England*, the 1851 Exhibition not only aestheticized consumer objects; what it "did was also to synthesize and systematize these elements of spectacle by putting them all together under one roof in the service of manufactured objects" (21). At this point, according to Richards, commodity spectacle becomes a specifically capitalist mode of expression.

3. The computer's deployment of Victorian display tactics also masks a more subtle interplay between two different logics of representation—a metaphorical (or analogical) logic where the visual field is composed of iconic and symbolic renderings that stand in the place of something somewhere else and a metonymical (or digital) logic where the visual field is organized by discrete units that gain significance in association with one another. Victorians presented metaphorically significant objects by means of a detachable set of physical techniques ordered through spatial contiguity—metaphor by means of metonymy. The computer displays digital information by means of an analogical display—metonymy through metaphor. Reversing their relation to one another in their passage from glass case to glass screen, these logics represent a transition from machine to code, from industrial to postindustrial

culture, from symbol to pattern. They also demonstrate how the seeds of the computer already exist in the nineteenth century's strategic relations between information and display.

4. The Principia Cybernetica Project's Web-site page "Metasystem Transition Theory" is authored by C. Joslyn, F. Heylighen, and V. Turchin, located at *Principia Cybernetica Web* at *http://pespmcl.vub.ac.be/MSTT.html*, July 1997.

5. The physical strategies of display have, of course, continually evolved in relation to available technologies and shifting formations of the visual. Religious relics and Holy Land curiosities, which constituted one of the first classes of objects for exhibition, were displayed in reliquaries whose shape and decoration reflected in small the allegorical environment of the relic's significance; display denoted a belief system and was completely inseparable from its object. After the late seventeenth century, display became increasingly separable from the object displayed, becoming visible in itself as display. It shifted from organic allegory to the pragmatic tactics of classification manifested in the spatial arrangement of objects as seventeenth- and eighteenth-century private collectors, who were interested in the burgeoning systematization of knowledge, accumulated vast collections of New World artifacts, animals, insects, rocks and fossils, and curiosities of scientific interest. Collections gathered specifically for scientific purposes, such as Sir Hans Sloane's in the early eighteenth century, reflected an orderly taxonomic style of display. Sloane "took pains to classify, arrange, and protect his specimens as systematically as a collector blessed with scientific intelligence and adequate money could. . . . The insects were preserved in boxes, with wooden sides and glass top and bottom; the stuffed birds 'often stood fast on small bits of board as naturally as if they still lived'; the West Indian hummingbirds were set in their nests under glass as though they had been living" (Pehr Kalm qtd. in Altick 15). The collection functioned as a reflection of scientific thought and imperial mastery when its display marked some larger conceptual order—when the spatial arrangement of the display corresponded to discernible categories of information that the collection in turn reproduced and reinforced. Such order also reinscribed imperialist practices as knowledge-bearing enterprises that resulted in the concrete enlightenment of accumulation. Sloane's classifications, arrangements, naturalized taxidermy, and glass protection set the standard for displays in the didactic public museums that opened in the latter part of the eighteenth century.

While the Enlightenment spirit of Sloane's collection continued in the National Museum's educational imperative, the cabinets of other, less discriminating private collectors became the model for the more public and frankly capitalist practice of display that began in coffeehouses and taverns as a way to attract customers and amuse them while they were there. These public museums displayed curiosities as decoration, though sometimes they enumerated their displays in printed catalogs that fixed the significance of those artifacts whose value might not be so immediately obvious upon inspection (such as "Queen Elizabeth's strawberry dish" or "a starved cat found many years earlier between the walls of Westminster Abbey") (Altick 18).

Many coffeehouse owners/museum curators believed in more direct publicity, running advertisements in London newspapers. Print extended the effectiveness of collections as tactics to attract customers. Display—both of artifacts and in print—was a mode of enticement as well as a form of mastery over the arcane, the exotic, and systems of knowledge themselves.

In the late eighteenth and early seventeenth centuries, the passive display of the museum became active performance in the industrial exhibition. With the specific aims of education and marketing, the industrial exhibit brought together the long tradition of collections with the equally long tradition of shows of mechanical ingenuity, performing animals, and gifted freaks. The Adelaide Gallery, the Polytechnic Institution, and ultimately the Crystal Palace and the Royal Panopticon featured exhibits of working machinery that included steam engines, pin-making machines, diving bells, looms, an oxyhydrogen microscope, magic lanterns, battery-powered toys, and other mechanical marvels. These exhibits were held in large halls, the Adelaide and the Polytechnic both equipped with interior canals for the demonstration of aquatic machines. Partitioned and labeled, displays emerged from the glass boxes of the natural history collections at which visitors gazed to be framed by boxlike architectural galleries through which patrons moved. See generally Altick for a painstaking description of specific collections and exhibits.

6. Altick, 238–39.

7. Ibid., 340–41.

8. Quoted in Andrew Miller, *Novels behind Glass: Commodity Culture and Victorian Narrative* (Cambridge: Cambridge University Press, 1995), 4. Richards also notes that "The organizers of the Exhibition had done their best to bring people as close as possible to things without actually allowing them to touch what they saw; some barrier, a counter or a rope or a policeman, always intervened to assert the inviolability of the object" (32).

9. See Thomas Richards for an extended argument about the relation between capital and spectacle and Sharon MacDonald, "Exhibitions of Power and Powers of Exhibition: An Introduction to the Politics of Display," in *The Politics of Display: Museums, Science, Culture* (New York: Routledge, 1998).

10. Tony Bennett, "The Exhibitionary Complex," *New Formations* 4 (spring 1988): 73–102. See also his essay "Speaking to the Eyes: Museums, Legibility and the Social Order," in *The Politics of Display*, 25–35.

11. Sigmund Freud notes the relation between exhibitionism and voyeurism in "Instincts and Their Vicissitudes," *The Standard Edition of the Complete Psychological Works*, trans. James Strachey (London: Hogarth, 1958), vol. 21, 152–57. The reversal of affect is the idea that any impetus—voyeurism, exhibitionism, sadism, masochism—represents a covert desire for the opposite. Thus, voyeurs actually wish to be looked at and sadists actually wish to be punished.

12. Richards shows how the modes of Victorian exhibition are organized into a mode of commodity spectacle that is quintessentially capitalist in *The Commodity Culture of Victorian England.*

13. The letterpress was a device that applied pressure to paper laid over an inked form in a method called relief printing (as opposed to intaglio printing used with the more expensive copper engraving and metal etching). Forms were composed of metal type and woodcut images, inserted into frames and spaced by hand. Woodcuts were simpler than the images made possible by the more expensive processes of copper engraving and metal etching. As a mechanical technology, printing relied on the contiguity of form to paper, transferring ink from one to the other. Its graphic design, which constituted its tactic of display, was partly an effect of the restrictions of the letterpress, which limited image quality and gave printed material a particular emphatic appearance. See generally Twyman.

14. The allure of the lure is its mimicry, its being taken for something it imitates, but which it is not. Overt lures such as wax museums work just as well as the covert lures in natural history museums to attract crowds, but the basis of their allure is different. Overt lures demonstrate the mastery of humanity over appearances; they all refer ultimately not to the figure or scene they represent, but to the mechanical genius of its mimicry. Covert lures demonstrate the power of humanity over nature and history, as nature and the past are enframed within modern techniques of preservation and classification. Both refer to the human power that brought them to view and the desire to see them is ultimately a desire to share in that power, either as the connoisseur of mimicry or as the savant at the top of the evolutionary ladder. This is, of course, in addition to the basic appeal of the object itself, whose mode of allure is a much more psychologically complex version of the lure.

15. For a detailed and clear account of the workings of a digital computer, see Ron White, *How Computers Work*, 4th ed. (Indianapolis: Que, 1998).

16. In *Understanding Interfaces: A Handbook of Human-Computer Dialogue* (London: Academic Press, 1994), Mark Lansdale and Thomas Ormerod define an interface "as comprising the collection of objects, tools, languages and displays which lies between people and the machines that they intend to use" (4). Interfaces may be aural, but screen displays "are the principal medium through which machines communicate information to their users" (50). Technology favoring the visual is both more in line with familiar notions of display and technically simpler. In any case, the epistemology of information, as developed in the eighteenth and nineteenth centuries, is primarily visual.

17. Computer designers acknowledge the use of metaphor as a primary tactic in creating user-friendly interfaces. The WIMPs system (Windows, Icons, Menus, Pointers) uses a complex composite of metaphors to produce an interface analogous to an office.

18. Despite its embodiment of ideas of power, computer interface often inspires simple, operational thought. Computer specialists understand the dilemma of the display interface as the difference between "description," which takes the form of the display of digital information or raw data, and "depiction," "a graphic or analog form." Their concerns are focused on the microdyamics of user response; aware of the "fatigue or visual discomfort, inaccuracy, and lower comprehension

rates" that come from reading text on a screen, they research how best to control eye movement (Lansdale and Ormerod 53). Display design takes into account the observation that reading occurs through a series of fixations (short rapid movements followed by resting periods) and that the eyes jump from fixation point to fixation point. Because depiction methods of display (use of pictographs and icons) can more easily vary the spatial frequency of information through layout, they are more effective in capturing and organizing eye movement. In addition, information is passed more efficiently if users can discern from the display the structure of the information. "The process of visual search is based upon the ability to find reliable and discernable indicators of structure in the display. These include the use of boundaries, colour coding, and partitions" (ibid., 70). The display tactics of nineteenth-century printed poster display, thus, seem to have already understood and taken advantage of the psychology and physiological propensities of cognitive function. For a much more thorough discussion of display representations, see Martin Helander, ed., *Handbook of Human-Computer Interaction* (Amsterdam: North-Holland, 1990), 29. Computer display tactics are not, however, only a matter of the physiology of reading or the politics of proprioception; programmers do pay attention to the metaphorical relation between computer display and the organization of information. Mark Lansdale and Thomas Ormerod advise, "a rule of thumb is that if it is possible to infer an apparent structure from the layout of information on the screen, then the user will undoubtedly perceive it" (60). For this reason analogical displays are seen as being more effective; "by presenting a visual model of the world being acted upon, direct manipulation interfaces provide a concrete framework on which the user can operate" (Helander 30). This field involves the deliberate use of "interface metaphors" such as "desktops" in WIMP (Windows, Icons, Menus, Pointers) interface style. The use of such metaphors "exploits prior knowledge that users have of other domains" (ibid., 57). WIMP interfaces employ composite metaphors (the metaphor of the desktop with the metaphor of the mouse's analogical pointing action). As John Carroll, Robert Mack, and Wendy Kellogg phrase it, "The use of interface metaphors has dramatically impacted actual user interface design practice" (ibid., 67).

engagements

Found Drowned
The Irish Atlantic

Ian Baucom

The lake supports some kind of bathysphere,
an Arab dhow

And a fishing-boat
complete with languorous net.

Two caricature anglers
have fallen hook, line and sinker

for the goitred,
spiny fish-caricatures

With which the lake is stocked.
At any moment all this should connect.

Paul Muldoon, "Paul Klee: *They're Biting*"

On the morning of 30 May 1847 an English brig bound for Quebec set sail from the Irish coast. On board were a Cumberland captain and his wife, a crew of some twenty men, a gentleman passenger named Robert Whyte, and some 110 Irish emigrants, refugees from the Famine. For the first twelve days the voyage proved uneventful. Whyte, whose diary serves as the record for the voyage, had opportunities to sketch the vessel and its company, to fish, and to divert himself in his cabin by reading Shakespeare. On the thirteenth day, however, the Head of Committee reported two cases of fever.

125

A day later six more cases were discovered. That same day a number of the water casks reserved for the emigrants were found to contain not water but a "foul, muddy, bitter," and entirely undrinkable substance. The captain, responding to this intelligence, elected to cut the emigrants' drinking allowance and serve a laudanum-spiced porridge to the sick. The medicine did not take. On the twenty-fourth day, the mate reported that a young woman, one of the first to run a fever, was experiencing a violent swelling of the feet and that her limbs were covered with "black, putrid spots."[1] She was in intense pain. The next day she was dead, her body hastily surrendered to the sea.

Over the next five weeks this anonymous young woman was followed by scores of her fellows. Whyte never reveals the exact number of fatalities. At a certain point, once the number of sick has reached thirty, he ceases to count the dying and the dead, surrenders his unofficial duty as census taker of this coffin ship, and abandons himself to the horrors of sight, smell, and sound that accompanied this voyage to the Americas. Settled in his cabin each night, bending over his diary, he struggles to ink the page as his ears are assailed by the "cries and ravings" drifting up from the hold in which the emigrants are cooped. Separated from the emigrants by the walls of his cabin, the privileges of class, and the health of his body, he is nevertheless unable to prevent the echoes of their cries from invading his text, from marking his writing as a cryptonymy, from coding his narrative of the Irish Atlantic as a narrative of abject melancholy.

Whyte's diary, later augmented with surrounding chapters decrying the treatment of the Famine emigrants and published as *The Ocean Plague*, is only one of the countless mid-nineteenth-century texts that documented the horrors of an ecological disaster that in five short years killed one and a half million people and spurred a similar number to depart their homes, their lands, and their island. That the Famine was not simply an ecological disaster, that it was also either a criminally mismanaged civic crisis, an act of divine wrath, a spectacularly brutal demonstration of the ethical bankruptcy of free-market capitalism, or a convenient excuse for the British state to starve and ship three generations of "surplus labor" off the Irish land, were, of course, arguments central to many of these Victorian commentaries. As John Mitchel, the leader of an abortive uprising by Young Ireland in 1848, famously declared, "The Almighty, indeed, sent the potato blight but the English created the famine."[2] Given the almost apocalyptic dimensions of the suffering, death, and upheaval caused by the Famine and consequent emigration and the immediately ensuing struggle to define the Famine as primarily, but alternately, an ecological, a providential, a capital, or an imperial event, one would think that the Famine would have survived its terrible happening as a central, if contested, episode in the Irish knowledge of the past. But as Ireland marked the 150th anniversaries of the deathly harvests of 1845, 1846, and 1847 with the opening of a Famine museum, a radio documentary, the republication of Famine letters, diaries, and poems, and a spate of new histories, the dominant note of these commemorations was that this labor of remembrance was shamefully belated, that, for most of the twentieth century, memories of the Famine had not only been neglected but silenced. The nation's older generation of historians, in particular, found themselves singled out for their desire to treat the famine with what Christine Kinealy has called, at best, a "historiographic silence" and, at worst, the "language of denial" (Kinealy, 2). "The tragedy," Cormac O'Grada notes, "has attracted little serious academic research. In Ireland itself the neglect is striking. . . . Here is an instance, then, where Clio's Irish devotees have by and large heeded the axiom that 'Anglo-Irish history is for Englishmen to remember, for Irishmen to forget.'"[3]

But why forget? Why attempt to dismiss from memory so cataclysmic an event? Kinealy, O'Grada, and a number of like-minded historians offer at least one fairly simple explanation. The historians who wrote Ireland's history in the half century after independence, they suggest, avoided addressing the Famine as part of a programmatic effort to devalue events whose recollection could nourish an anti-imperial and nativist discourse of Irish nationalism, whether that discourse operated within the relatively pacific quarters of the Republic or in Ulster's more troubled alleyways. Since the late 1980s, much historical debate in Ireland has focused on these "revisionist" writings as a younger generation of historians has revolted against this way of producing an Irish knowledge of Ireland's past. Prompted by Brendan Bradshaw's 1989 essay "Nationalism and Historical Scholarship in Ireland" (an essay that established an intellectual genealogy of the "revisionist" historiography, identified it as a sort of covert apology for imperialism, and urged the island's historians to produce a more "empathetic" knowledge of the nation's past),[4] a number of Irish scholars have begun to rewrite the nation's history and its historiography in efforts that have ranged from attempts to address the impacts of "revisionist" methodologies on the Irish historical establishment (the most comprehensive of which is D. George Boyce and Alan O'Day's 1996 collection of essays *The Making of Modern Irish History: Revisionism and the Revisionist Controversy*) to decisions to revisit those moments of "suffering" heretofore forgotten or ignored.

The Famine is not the only event these contemporary historians have found to be underrepresented in the historical archive. But the undertreatment of the Famine has begun to inspire an unease un-occasioned by the relative professional neglect of such events as the rebellion of 1798 or the Easter 1916 uprising (neither of which, as S. J. Connolly notes, has been the subject of a "full-length academic monograph" in Ireland).[5] And that may be, as Kinealy further suggests, because the Famine has been forgotten for other than political or professional reasons. Its unspokenness, she indicates, is not only a matter of the antinationalist prejudices of prior generations of historians. It is also a matter of shame. Kinealy, alluding to "deep" psychological scars, does not use that word. But Terry Eagleton does:

> Just talking about the Famine is a significant act in Ireland, for it was a horror that stunned many into a kind of traumatic muteness. . . . [It] produced a kind of culture of shame, of which this academic silence seems in its way a part. At the time, men and women boarded themselves into their cabins so that they could die in decent anonymity. There were villages in Ireland after the Famine that could still speak Irish, but didn't—it was considered bad luck. Many of the survivors seem to have thrust the event deep into their collective unconscious, where it has continued to fester.[6]

Robert James Scally, whose superb study *The End of Hidden Ireland: Rebellion, Famine, and Emigration* is one of the finest and most eloquent of the recent Famine histories, makes a similar argument in the closing paragraphs of his book. Describing the last sight of Ireland afforded a group of emigrants as their ship put out into the Atlantic, he quietly and sorrowfully remarks that for the emigrants that parting sight, which is also his book's and our moment's backward-looking sight of famine-stricken Ireland, "was sometimes accompanied by shame."[7]

To gaze upon the dead; to feel that to see them thus is not only to see them in their shame but to take that shame upon yourself; to board that shame up within the cabins of memory; to pretend it is not there: there is a name for such a condition, and a language that accompanies it. Freud's name for the condition is melancholy. But if the Freudian melancholic is one who cannot complete the labor of mourning, one who cannot surrender a lost, and degraded, object of desire, then the language of melancholy is not simply a language of fixation but an abject language of secrecy and hiding. For Nicolas Abraham and Maria Torok, the cryptic discourse of the melancholic is a discourse that founds itself on the inability to introject the lost object of desire and a consequent incorporation of that object. Where introjection implies an acknowledgment of loss that allows the mourner to transform the self "in the face of interior and exterior changes in the psychological, emotional, relational, political, [and] professional landscape,"[8] incorporation "is the refusal to acknowledge the full import of the loss, a loss that, if recognized as such, would effectively transform us" (*The Shell and the Kernel*, 127). A form of disavowal, incorporation also implies a secret labor of compensation: "The words that cannot be uttered, the scenes that cannot be recalled, the tears that cannot be shed—everything will be swallowed along with the trauma that led to the loss. Swallowed and preserved. Inexpressible mourning erects a secret tomb inside the subject" (ibid., 130). Within that tomb, Abraham and Torok continue, within that cryptic vault of memory, the mourner hides the terrible, fascinating, strangely "exquisite" corpse of the lost, violated, beloved, and suffers its serial hauntings.

The place of psychoanalytic discourse within the discourses of the postcolonial is, of course, subject to dispute, if only because *the* subject of psychoanalysis is so radically dehistoricized a self. And if I make use of Abraham and Torok's suggestions here, it is with a sense of both caution and curiosity. In *Imperial Leather: Race, Gender, and Sexuality in the Colonial Contest,* Anne McClintock has urged scholars of the world's various postcolonial conditions to develop a "situated psychoanalysis,"[9] a psychoanalysis, that is, that does not ground itself on a universal, transhistorical self, but that limits itself to what, in a related context, Chandra Talpade Mohanty calls a set of "historically specific generalizations," "generated through local, contextual analyses."[10] If the problem with "theory," in its earliest poststructural manifestations, was that it was a sort of belated modernism, an eagerly totalizing mode of apprehending codes of identification and structures of representation, and the problem with much contemporary, self-avowedly, postmodern theory is that it is a sort of belated romanticism that, as Alan Liu and David Simpson have suggested, so fetishizes the particular, the local, and the detailed that nothing that is true of one thing is ever true of anything else, then the promise of a "situated psychoanalysis" and of the "specific generaliza-tion" is the promise of constructing narratives of interpretation that are neither triumphantly global nor defensively local but, as James Clifford has it, "global enough" to be true to the particular and the collective.[11] This is certainly appealing. But is the Famine, or more accurately, the Famine as memory-event, susceptible to such an analysis? Is its unspeakability a pecu-liarly "Irish" manifestation of the unspeakability of the cryptic? Is its "cul-ture of shame" a culturally generated, collectively reproduced, and sympto-matically "Irish" code of melancholy? And if it is, what does it mean that that code is now being rewritten, that the doors to that crypt are now being unlocked, that the dead, so long cabined within the hidden vaults of memo-ry, are now being exhumed? And, when they are exhumed, what language will these "exquisite corpses" speak? What will be their secret word?

In an essay on nineteenth- and twentieth-century Famine narratives, Chris Morash, who in recent years has been doing for the literature of the Famine what Kinealy, O'Grada, Scally, and others have done for its history, indicates that the Famine enters collective memory through precisely the sort of will-to-incorporation that Abraham and Torok indicate characterizes the melancholic's cryptic recovery of loss. "The literature of the Famine," he argues, "provokes something of the same response; when we read a Famine text, we too feel that we are a kind of 'survivor.' It may be that when we en-counter these shattered fragments of the past, we wish to complete them; and the only way we can do so is by internalizing them."[12] It is not just that Morash finds this desire resident in himself. The texts he considers, from William Carleton's 1847 novel *The Black Prophet* to John Banville's 1973 work *Birchwood*, recollect the Famine less by constructing coherent narra-tives of its causes, effects, and meanings than by gathering into themselves a fairly fixed series of images—images, generally, of iconographically gro-tesque death: a dead mother whose suckling child is trying to "eat" her breast; a woman driven to nourishing herself on seaweed; an unburied man whose mouth is stained with the green juices of the grass that was his last meal; a tangle of corpses that have become the food of dogs and rats. Over and over these same images appear, contracting the vastness of the Famine to a tight catalog of horrors serially deposited within a set of narratives whose most common response to the appearance of these images is to draw a curtain over them the moment they are displayed. Serially incorporated, but never introjected, the only ever-partial bodies of the Famine dead seem perpetually to inspire a "wish to complete them" (which is also a will-to-narrative) that remains forever unfulfilled.

Morash suggests that this has the formal effect of dislocating images of the Famine from a surrounding narrative context, of generating a highly stylized and reusable set of *tableaux vivants,* or, more accurately, though more terribly, *tableaux mordants,* which do not so much plot narratives of remembrance as morbidly decorate narratives in need of a little local color. Fragmentary images of fragmented bodies and lives, the transposable visions of the Famine are thus, he argues, "liable to appropriation by larger narratives. . . . Having no narrative of their own, but possessing a hard-edged clarity that has been refined through decades of repetition, these Famine icons are transmitted to us like something flashing from the windows of a moving coach—unforgettable glimpses of a narrative whose full development is always just beyond our line of vision" (115). If Morash here accurately defines the way in which the Famine is incorporated into texts such as Banville's *Birchwood,* a novel in which Famine scenes flit disconcertingly, almost hallucinatorily, in and out of view as the sort of background scenery of an Ireland that seems to be of both the middle nineteenth and twentieth centuries, then what he also seems to have grasped is the ease with which the detachability and portability of the Famine image renders the Famine appropriable not only for a frustrated discourse of melancholic remembrance but also for the practices of tourism. It is precisely this ease with which the image of the incomplete can generate not only the historical pain but also the touristic pleasure of incomplete identification that Patrick Kavanagh so bitterly satirizes in his poem "The Great Hunger," as he damns the "travellers [who] stop their cars to gape over the green banks into his [the peasant's] fields / . . . and feel renewed / when they grasp the steering wheels again."[13]

The recent histories of the Famine, both popular and professional, also repeatedly organize themselves around the figure of the incomplete, and they regularly attempt to complete the record by offering their readers, once more, a transposable set of images. When they come to consider the "American Wakes," those strange rites of departure that preceded the Famine emigrants' journey to America, Thomas Gallagher's *Paddy's Lament: Ireland 1846–1847* and Kerby Miller's *Emigrants and Exiles: Ireland and the Irish Exodus to North America* frequently offer exactly the same set of anecdotes, songs, and events. And when, in *The Great Irish Famine,* Cormac O'Grada indicates that most prior and contemporary histories of the Famine are inadequate because they omit detailed descriptions of the "gruesome" deaths of the starving, he offers to correct those accounts not by producing new scholarship but by recycling two passages from Cecil Woodham-Smith's "popular" 1962 history of the Famine, by cutting and pasting those passages from her work to his. And once again, with a horrifying predictability, the deaths we are given are not narratives of death but afterimages of the dead, images of corpses half consumed by dogs and rats, corpses whose very bodily incompletion is offered as evidence that this history, at least, is complete.

But what does it mean to be "complete"? What sort of completion do such works offer the dead? Or is the offer indeed made to the dead? The dead whose brutalized bodies can be hauled into view but whose suddenly interrupted lives can never be restored. The gift of completeness that such texts offer is indeed an ambiguous one; for to complete something is both to perfect it and to have done with it. Do we complete the dead only for the relief of finally being able to dismiss them, for the chance to inform them that the incomplete act of mourning that is melancholy is now, at last, over, for the opportunity to insist that we are no longer, in Joseph Roach's terms, the dead's surrogates, the living effigies who bear within ourself the terrible responsibility of completing the lives that can never be completed?[14] Why are the dead returned to view? Why must their perpetually unburied bodies be exhumed and exhumed and reexhumed?

O'Grada provides some answers to this question. Or, rather, the death scenes that he includes in his text do, as do the images of death in the oral histories of the Famine: for, like O'Grada's *The Great Irish Famine,* those histories are littered with accounts not only of gruesome deaths but of inadequate burials, of bodies that evoke shame not because of the ways in which they died but because of the ways in which they were buried. The collective memory of the Famine repeatedly approaches and draws back from images of corpses buried in canvas sacks rather than in coffins, of bodies left to rot in collapsing cabins, of bodies tumbled together in lime pits, of bodies left to rot along the roads, and, as the gathering figures for all these accounts of dead matter out of place, of bodies that either fester in the holds of the "coffin ships" that carried the Famine emigrants to the Americas or tumble from the decks of these vessels to the unplaceable deeps of the Atlantic Ocean. Indeed, it is this fundamental "placelessness" of the dead that seems to inspire their serial re-covery, this failure of the dead to have been adequately honored and housed, this failure of past generations to have submitted the dead to the complete authority of the grave's law of place, that demands their endless reincorporation. It is from a series of shameful crypts which take the form of the coffin ships and the burial waters of the Atlantic, and the cabins, fields, and lime pits of the island, that the dead must be disinterred, before the labor of remembering and mourning and reburying the Famine can be "complete."

Thomas Murphy's 1968 play *Famine* is a work that seems to be constructed around this understanding of the need to give the dead a proper and final burial.[15] The play, which includes the predictable, perhaps the inevitable, visions of a dead body whose mouth is "green from eating the grass" (17), of a child "eating its mother's breast" (17), of a woman buried "in a bag" (69), of corpses bundled together in a lime pit (60), and of an emigrant who, on the eve of his departure for Canada, dreams that he is about to be dispatched to "the bottom of the ocean" (73), opens a wake and stages another in its penultimate scene. In the opening scene, as John Connor approaches the corpse of his daughter, a child who has just become the first member of his family to die of starvation, Murphy's stage directions and his lines of dialogue concisely define the burden of remembrance the Famine dead have placed on Ireland's living: *"(He goes to the corpse)* We can't send them off mean. . . . She was regal. . . . And—we—won't—send—them off mean. In spite of—In spite of—Whatever!" (19–20). One of the tragedies of the Famine was, of course, that most of the dead were sent off mean, or not sent off at all, that their families and friends, too weak or poor to bury them, or dead themselves, were forced to abandon the dead where they lay, to rot in their fields, in their cabins, in the holds of the coffin ships, or at the bottom of the sea. If the living are constantly obliged to go to their corpses, it is perhaps because in the moment of their dying so many of the dead were sent off mean.

Scholars have long been aware of the rhetorical equivalence granted to African and Irish subjects in British imperial discourse.[16] More recently, critics have begun to reflect on some of the structural similarities between the Irish experiences of Famine and emigration and African experiences of slavery and the middle passage. In one of the most developed such critiques, Luke Gibbons has suggested that the "devastation" and "uprooting" of the Famine and consequent mass emigration caused the Irish, like the African and African-American subjects of the Black Atlantic, to undergo the "shock of modernity" "before [their] time."[17] Paul Gilroy's model of an early, indeed an original, black experience of the "dilemmas and difficulties" of modernity, an experience forced by the introduction of black subjects to the Atlantic world system, is one, Gibbons suggests, that applies equally to the Irish. That may well be true; indeed, as the title of this essay suggests, it is a notion whose truth I am interested in testing and exploring. But on this subject, it seems to me that if, in the nineteenth century, African and Irish experiences of entering a migrant Atlantic modernity were in some ways similar (though emigration, however forced, dangerous, and punishing is clearly not at all the same thing as enslavement), it is in the late twentieth century, as these experiences came to haunt the troubled reaches of postcolonial memory, that the currents of the Irish and the Black Atlantic diasporas most fully intersect.

Addressing what he identifies as the sometimes "necrophiliac" aesthetic of diasporic remembrance, Kobena Mercer suggests that Black Atlantic structures of memory, like the cryptic forms of memory that characterize contemporary recollections of the Famine, serially approach but fail to hold a deathly past that appears under the guise of a misplaced body:

> Because the past cannot pass into representation—its passage blocked by forgetting and denial—the violence keeps coming back . . . descendants of enslavers and enslaved alike share in a predicament arising from the unrepresentability of the past. While the former may be unreconciled with a history that has been wiped out of collective memory, the latter, it may be said, are haunted by *too much memory*: ghosted by the floating bodies of lost and unnamed ancestors buried beneath the sea, how can you be reconciled with a past that can never be fully known?[18]

The solution to this predicament, Mercer suggests, is an act of "consititutive repression" in which the living find some way to open the doors to the cryptic vaults of the past and accord the dead a proper funeral, thus freeing them from their incompleted passage into the past, and, at the same time, exorcising their ability to "haunt" the present. Or, as Mercer notes, the Cameroonian filmmaker Jean Marie Teno has more clearly put it: "Funerals are so important to us . . . If we don't bury a friend or a foe well, we are likely to see his ghost often until the day we unbury him and bury him again according to the tradition. We didn't bury colonialism very well, and we can see its ghost everywhere."[19]

Between Teno's statement and Murphy's "we can't send them off mean" (a phrase whose plural subject and object—"we"/"them"—reveals its interest in resolving a problem greater than that faced by John Connor as he struggles to find the right way to bury his daughter) there is an encyclopedia of historical differences, but a continuity of sentiment; for, like Teno's friend and foe, the Famine dead, it seems, must be unburied and then buried again, recovered from their walled-up cabins and submarine cemeteries and then replaced in memory before the past with which they haunt the island's present can be complete. But as works such as Murphy's *Famine,* which dedicates so much of its lyric energies to finding the right language of keening with which to "wake" and then surrender the dead, make this evident, the question of knowing why the dead must be exhumed becomes less vital, less predictably answerable, than the question of knowing what the reappearance of these bodies will allow their mourners to see.

According to Kinealy and others, those "revisionist" historians who preferred not to gaze upon the Famine dead refused to do so because they feared that in doing so they and their countrymen and -women would see the killing hand of empire and the beckoning specter of the vengeful nation, because they feared that the word the dead would speak to the living would be the outraged and unrefusable word of nationalism. The recent "postrevisionist" histories of the Famine indicate that that fear may be at least partially valid. Standing at the stern of a boat bound for the Americas, looking back at the vast cemetery their island has become, Robert Scally's emigrants, we recall, are granted in this "last view of Ireland," their "first view of themselves." Ireland, Scally seems to suggest, emerges into view as a unitary entity, as an imaginable and collectivizing phenomenon, in this exact moment, as women and men from numerous local communities see a common Ireland for the first time. On the decks of these ships, and on the shipping wharves where, over a period of two or three years, a million Irish emigrants saw the scattered townlands of the island gathered together around their common flight from death, Ireland was born. "It was," Scally insists, "their first truly 'national' experience. The sight of the exodus was concentrated and magnified in the few square miles of the waterfront where, in a sense, all of Ireland's townlands met for the first time and witnessed the commonality of their fate" (212). Their fate, however, was not simply to become Irish in this moment of escape but to lose Ireland in the very moment of their becoming Irish. But such, of course, is the fate and the allure of every nation: to occupy a lost place, to exist only in the landscapes of the past, to call out to the living to embark on a voyage of return to the homeland of the dead.

But there is another way to read Scally's parting words and that parting view. The self those emigrants see for the first time may be the Irish self left behind, but it may also be the Atlantic self that stands gazing back at the island. And again, from this perspective, it is not insignificant that this less grounded view of selfhood becomes available on the deck of a ship and in the pages of a book written by an Irish scholar whose place of residence is in the city of New York, a city on the far side of the Atlantic passage; for gazing back at Ireland and at the dead from either of these two places, from the place of passage or the place of writing, both emigrant and historian see an Ireland that in that very instant in which it passes into national memory also disseminates itself, Atlanticizes itself. As Scally notes elsewhere in his text, in taking to the coffin ships, the Famine emigrants did not merely become Irish, they became "a nation afloat" (220).

Although he acknowledges this second, secret, view of an extranational Atlantic Ireland, an emigrant Ireland that comes into being "as though born from the sea" (227), in scattered moments throughout his text, this is not the knowledge of Ireland, Famine, and emigration that Scally seems to desire. The fundamental argument of his text is that the narrative of the Famine is a narrative of migration from place to placelessness, that the accelerated experience of "modernization" that saw a million peasants turned into wage laborers, often within a matter of weeks, was above all else an experience of exchanging a hyperlocalized territory of identity and belonging for the deterritorializing flow-dynamic of the Atlantic world system, that the Famine emigrants migrated less from Ireland to the Americas than from the knowledge of belonging to a place to the confusion of occupying the placeless space of the Atlantic economy.

Scally plots this narrative of the loss of place as he follows one company of emigrants from Ballykilcline to the Americas. "As they took the first steps on the road out and in the preceding months of distressful waiting among the emptying cabins, the sensations of loss," Scally notes, "were of their only place of belonging" (160). On their first stop on that "road out," in a town called Strokestown that is now home to Ireland's national Famine museum, Scally's emigrants are again seen to experience the loss of place: "It was their first 'outside' and their first experience as aliens, exposed now without *a place* of refuge" (161; emphasis added). But it is not until they embark on a ferry for Liverpool, and thus enter "the outer fringes of a system far more powerful and complex, whose extent and workings were still further beyond their experience and understanding," that, Scally indicates, the emigrants truly moved from place to space as they approached a city that lay at the center of "a world maritime trade" (193), a city that "represented the most dynamic core of world capitalism. . . . [That] in the movement of ships and cargo . . . the immense traffick in goods and people that passed through its docks and warehouses . . . was an exemplar of modernity to the rest of the maritime world" (194).

It is in the heart of this exuberantly Atlantic city that the historian situates the final, tragic encounter between the now irretrievably displaced representatives of a dying "localized mentality" and the "masters" of a "world maritime trade":

> pouring through this spectacle of dynamism and innovation in their tens of thousands annually were the living artifacts of the agrarian past, a great many of them the last remaining peasants, graziers, and transhumans of the British Isles. . . . Like the ships and cargoes being moved according to the mechanical rhythms of the docks, these recruits from the hinterland also had to be disciplined to the port's complex system of movement and engineering. In the process, whether as day laborers or steerage passengers, individual identity had to be submerged. (Ibid.)

Torn from their only place of "refuge" and "belonging," the emigrants, Scally suggests, are forced to departicularize themselves, to abandon their unique identities, to submerge themselves within the disciplinary flow, the mechanical, inhuman, interchangeable rhythms of the Atlantic world system as they complete their passage from the local into the global.

If the aesthetic of this narrative is obviously tragic, then its logic is essentially Heideggerian. As Edward S. Casey has demonstrated, the spatial rhetoric that supplements, and to some extent organizes, the temporal poetic of Heidegger's *Being and Time* is one that opposes the ontic security of being-in-place to the uncanny anxiety occasioned by Dasein's encounter with a world space. As Casey has it, Heidegger's "analysis of the uncanny continues to explore the homeworld and its loss in the form of Dasein's ineluctable being 'not-at-home' (*un-heim-lich*) in the world. For the uncanny is not only *nothing* . . . but *nowhere*: it represents the radical absence of any place or region." Anxiety is an ontological, not psychological, state and hence "discloses primordially and directly the world as world. . . . The world is precisely that which makes us anxious if we face it *as world*—and all the more anxious if we experience it as the source of indefinite possibilities for our being-in-the-world."[20] Anxiety, here, is precisely that which comes to haunt the self dis*placed* from a surrounding, familiar, limited, and customary context of meanings, what Heidegger calls a "region" and Pierre Nora refers to as an "environment of memory," and replaced within—or indeed not re*placed* within but, more closely, cast into—the atopia of an undifferentiated space, an absolute space coterminous with the limitless possibilities of the world.

Anxiety is thus both the loss of *a* place and the loss of place itself, the terrorism of the global. As such, Homi Bhabha suggests, anxiety is the founding "ontopological" condition of colonial and postcolonial migration: "Anxiety is the mediatory moment between culture's sedimentation and its signifying displacement; its longing for place *and* its borderline existence, its 'objectlessness' that does not lack an objective, the tryst between territoriality and the memory of dissemination."[21] Migrancy, on this account, is less a moving from one territory to another than an experience of the death of place in an apocalypse of space, and of the death of the self as something ontologically grounded in the reassurance of a localizable place. In this respect, Scally's emigrants are not, in a looser sense of the word, migrants—subjects who depart one place for another—but, regardless of whether or not they survived their ocean passage, a band of Heideggerian suicides drowning themselves in the waters of an Atlantic world system whose dis*placing* economies of flow serve as a hydrodynamic model for a vision of the end of history apprehended as the triumph of space over place.

This reading of Famine and emigration helps to clarify what can be at stake in the work of Famine remembrance; for if to bury the unquiet dead is not simply to honor and have done with them but to "place" them, to inform the dead that their vocation is to stay in place, then the task of Famine remembrance, which is also the task of warding off the end of history, of restoring a knowledge of place to an increasingly placeless world, can only be complete if it can return these dead from space to place—a conviction that rests on the assumption that the Atlantic does not, and cannot, constitute a place within the geography of Irishness. That this conviction can inform not only a disavowal of the extranational but an identification of the nation as the solitary, if belated, guarantor of place (and, hence, of history) and a bitter defense of an emplaced, nativist discourse of Irish nationalism becomes violently evident in Jim Sheridan's film *The Field*, as Bull McCabe, beating to death an Irish-American "outsider" who has returned to Ireland and sought to buy the Bull's piece of land, roars out to his son, "See this fella here? See this Yank? His family lived around here, but when the going got tough they ran away to America. They ran away from the Famine—while we stayed. Do you understand? We stayed! We stayed!! We stayed!!!"[22]

That the emigrants, in setting foot on the coffin ships, might be sailing from the placeable "inside" of Irishness to a space of cultural death beyond the shores is by no means an idea exclusive to the twentieth century. Before the emigrants ever departed their localized townland communities, before they set foot on the coffin ships, their families and friends had expressed the same conviction, not only, as may have happened, informally, but in a ritualized ceremony of departure that became known as the American Wake. On the eve of their departures to the New World, the Famine emigrants were regularly invited to attend such ceremonies. By the time the Famine had run its course, such events had become perhaps the most common ritual of Irish life, turning Ireland, in the words of the *Irish People,* into "one vast American Wake."[23] Treated as living corpses at these doleful occasions, the emigrants, particularly the young, were frequently reproached for their willingness to abandon their homes, their families, and, most shamefully, their mothers. As the wails and keenings and reproaches of those left behind washed over them, the emigrants, it would seem, were baptized into the communion not simply of the displaced but of the unplaced, the placeless. And as these occasions entered into the collective memory of the Famine, they were increasingly understood to mark not only the emigrant's losses but the nation's. As the Irish-Irelander Robert Lynd remarked in 1909, for post-Famine generations of Irish subjects, the Wakes were less a ritual of personal and familial tragedy than a "signal of national doom,"[24] a signal, perhaps, of a nation whose authentic places of belonging had been destroyed by the Famine, the moaning signal of a nation whose true places were now resident only in the past or secreted within the shameful tombs of memory.

But although it seems possible to read the American Wakes as the originary events in a cryptic discourse of Famine remembrance and national consciousness; as mass rituals of melancholy incorporation in which those left behind began to encrypt the dead, the past, and the nation; as the tomblike doorposts to that "culture of shame" that Eagleton and others suggest continues to haunt Ireland, Abraham and Torok, at least, indicate that to read the Wakes so is to misread their psychic economies. On their account the Wake, like any feast or meal "eaten in the company of the deceased, may be seen as a protection against incorporation," as an act of "communion" that signifies to its participants that "instead of the deceased we are absorbing our mutual presence in the form of digestible food. We will bury the dead in the ground rather than in ourselves" (129). What is crucial to Abraham and Torok is that the Wake is a collective activity and a public act, an act of mourning that acknowledges loss and grief, rather than one that disavows loss and hides it away. The Wake is thus an act of introjection, a licit rather than a furtive rite of burial. As such, the American Wakes, those proleptic acts of mourning, may contain within themselves a secret knowledge that can teach the Famine's backward-glancing mourners to free their mourning from the sovereign authority of a melancholic nationalism. The American Wakes, that is, may be less the doorposts to an endocryptic nation of the dead than the gateposts to Ireland's Atlanticization, the entryways to Ireland's reinvention as an extranational territory of belonging.

And this, I believe, is exactly what the American Wakes mark, not only as generalized rituals of introjection, but as specific, historical practices of mourning *and* remembrance. By many accounts, the central event of an American Wake was the reading of a letter from a prior emigrant who had arrived safely in the Americas, the circulation of textual proof that the death celebrated in the Wake was not, in fact, absolute. Such letters, which became so numerous, as Scally acknowledges, that they came to constitute a sort of "American library" for the inhabitants of Ireland's rural townlands (134), were supplemented by additional "proofs" not simply of the survivability of emigration but, more important, I believe, of its circularity. Of the numerous ballads that were sung at the Wakes, many—some scholars suggest most—were composed in the Americas and returned to Ireland in the mail packages of eastward-bound vessels. Added to these letters and songs were funds, monies sent back to family members to enable them to eat and, almost as significantly, to enable them to host a Wake. Indeed, the entire financial structure of the American Wakes depended on the circulation of capital across the Atlantic. As bodies flowed west, currency flowed east, so that the Wakes held in Sligo, Cork, and Skibbereen were financed by monies earned in Boston, New York, and Quebec. Other items also regularly joined this transatlantic flow. Thomas Gallagher indicates that it was not uncommon for the female lovers of departing emigrants to stitch cuts of their pubic hair or swatches of cloth dyed with their menstrual fluids into the clothing of their beloveds as guardians of their ability to occupy their lovers' imagination on either side of the Atlantic. And, as a form of protection against drowning, emigrants were also often given a "caul" ("the fetal membrane that sometimes covers the head of an infant at birth" [Gallagher, 125]) to carry with them on board ship and then to send back to Ireland for subsequent reuse.

Collectively, these circulating letters, ballads, monies, swatches of cloth, and prophylactic talismans indicate that the American Wakes served to do far more than mark the death of Ireland, or, more exactly, the birth of Ireland as a nation of the dead and the birth of the nation as a community of melancholics. The emigrants who received these things and sent them back from the other side of the Atlantic were not exchanging the place of the nation for the placelessness of the extranational; they were marking, with no little degree of agony, their entry into an Irish place of belonging unbounded by the borders of the nation, a place of belonging that was less insular than circular, less rooted than routed, less national than Atlantic. What the American Wakes reveal is that place is not the prerogative of the nation, that the nation is not the sole bestower of a sense of collective identity, and that Irishness encompasses more than an island, more than a nation, more than a fatal past. To remember the Famine, the Wakes thus suggest, is not so much to encrypt the nation as it is to discover that Irishness may be less a matter of staying in place, or mourning a lost place, than it is a movement of bodies and songs and letters from one place to another, a circulating of lives and memories and desires across the passage routes of the Irish Atlantic.

What the American Wakes seem to ritualize, then, is less a knowledge of loss and of death (the very temporal structure of the Wakes, in which something is recalled in advance of its disappearance, in which remembrance precedes departure, implies that in these rituals the acts of remembrance and of re-presentation, and hence the promise of recovery and of return, trump the experience of loss) than a transatlantic form of memory performatively realized in the presence of those who presently and proleptically mark the Irish and the American antipodes of a transoceanic community of belonging. In his recent study, *Cities of the Dead: Circum-Atlantic Performance,* Joe Roach has theorized the ways in which such performative rites of memory have acted to sustain a cross-Atlantic imaginary that is, to his mind, one of the defining cultural and aesthetic features of the Black Atlantic world. In creating a series of critical genealogies of such rites of memory, Roach identifies three constitutive characteristics of those performative acts through which an "arc of memory . . . launched by sustained contact and exchange among the peoples of the Atlantic world" (29) links together the dispersed subjects of Old and New World communities. The Atlantic is bridged, he suggests, by acts of memory and imagination that are essentially "kinesthetic," which orient themselves around locatable "vortices" that "canalize specified needs, desires and habits . . . [in such places as] the grand boulevard, the marketplace, the theater district, the square, the burial ground" (28), and which reproduce a prior environment of memory by "displacing" it, by reinventing it in the moment of its transmission. Collectively, Roach argues, such characteristics pattern complex social performances (most frequently, in his work, those performances that structure the collective theater of public funerals) that restore the past to the present, the dead to the living, the "there" to the "here," not by obliging the contemporary, the living, and the present to flawlessly surrogate the antecedent, the dead, and the distant, but by gathering the living together in a common place in which, as they recognize and avow the history of movements that constitute their link to the past from which they have been sundered, these performers re-create the past as they remember it. In so doing, they join not only a reinvented past to an experienced present, a recollected there to an occupied here, but situate the very space that divides the past and the present, the here and the there, *within* a reimagined environment of memory. They mark themselves as the inhabitants of an expanded *place* of belonging that encompasses the place of departure, the place of arrival, and the *place* of transit.

As they gather together to enact such performances, in other words, the migrant subjects of the circum-Atlantic world do not mourn the loss of place attendant on a terrorizing voyage into the anxious possibilities of *being in the world* so much as they re*place* a featureless space, placing themselves within a shifting territory of memory and belonging that spans the Atlantic world. That the American Wakes constitute such a circum-Atlantic performance, a performance that, rather than mourning the death of Ireland, agonistically celebrates its transoceanic dissemination, seems evident. Gathered together at these ritual reinventions of an antecedent rite of Irish memory, those who left and those who stayed behind mark the moment in which Ireland takes its place within a transatlantic world, the moment in which Irishness comes to encompass not a lost place but a circulating, cross-Atlantic economy of memories, letters, songs, bodies, images, and desires.

In the concluding chapter of *The End of Hidden Ireland,* Scally insists that this is exactly not the case. He argues that the emigrants did not enter, or open Ireland to, an Atlantic world. But he argues so largely because in departing Ireland the Famine emigrants did not join a pool of laboring bodies flowing back and forth across the Atlantic Ocean. In making this claim, Scally ignores the possibility that the Atlantic might channel a circulating economy not simply of workers but of narratives, that it might embed a cultural poetics of flow of the sort mapped in Roach's work and in Paul Gilroy's *Black Atlantic.* It seems to me that Scally's own text provides the counterproof to his argument, that his history of the Famine is one of those countless pieces of writing, one of those many documents of memory, one of those emigrant's missives that have continued to crisscross an *Irish* Atlantic offering proof of the ongoing existence of a transatlantic rather than a reductively cis-Atlantic community of Irish belonging. Taking their generic cue from those letters shared at an American Wake, these documents testify not to the irre*place*ability of the nation but, in the words of James Joyce's *Wake,* to "the birth of an otion," the birth, that is, of a nation unable to disavow the notion that its places of belonging are serially postmarked by the narratives of identity circulating the Atlantic Ocean.[25] It is to one of those "letters," with a poetic missive that Paul Muldoon has dispatched to Ireland from the Americas, that I now wish to turn; for it is in Muldoon's verse, I believe, that a contemporary refashioning of the Wake's a-national, Atlantic cartography of Irishness can best be found.

Muldoon may strike some readers as an unlikely candidate for the role of lyric historian of the Irish Atlantic; for, whatever else has been said of Muldoon, his admiring, if puzzled, critics have rarely identified him as a historical poet. When history does surface in Muldoon's work it tends to surface as literary history or as a highly stylized act of confession. Only rarely does history of the rougher sort—the violent, public history that many readers seem to expect from Irish poets—nudge its snout above the waters of his verse before slinking, silkie-like, away. Actually, there are fewer silkies in Muldoon's poems than bathyspheres, submarines, and nautiluses—mechanical devices for the return of the repressed that, by their very failure to be identifiably Irish, appear to indicate the poet's disinterest in sounding the themes of an Irish political history his work sometimes seems engineered to forget. But if Muldoon's work is haunted by the need to forget, it is also educated by his continuing discovery of the impossibility of certain acts of forgetting. A melancholic poet, as Guinn Batten has argued, Muldoon is also an obsessive elegist.[26] And from his earliest poems through to his most recent collection of verse, Muldoon has associated his elegies with an act of looking at, or inhabiting, a body of water that, like the waters crossed by the emigrants' coffin ships, has become a cemetery space.

In "The Waking Father," Muldoon's triple pun on the hydrographic, funereal, and somatic meanings of the word *wake* permits him to construct a poetic persona absorbed in the curious work of revivifying, reburying, and drowning his father.

> . . . I wonder now if he is dead or sleeping
> For if he is dead I would have his grave
> Secret and safe,
> I would turn the river out of its course,
> Lay him in its bed, bring it round again.[27]

The uncertainty expressed by the son in the first line of this verse ("I wonder now if he is dead or sleeping") baptizes an idiom of ambiguity evident not only in the following lines but in much of Muldoon's succeeding work. Cupping the waters of the river in the palm of his poetic hand, Muldoon accords himself the right to perform his dead father's lustral rites. He arranges the corpse in the silty coffin of the riverbed and pours the water of his verse over it. The will to secrecy that animates this apparent act of tenderness indicates that the poet is motivated not only by sorrow but perhaps also by shame, by embarrassment at the sudden vulnerability of a father whom he wills to hide in the bed of his verse. Scooping out a burial vault for his father between the banks of his own writing, Muldoon seems here to be the very model of Abraham and Torok's cryptophoric melancholic whose self-appointed duty it is constantly to "bring" himself "around" to the perpetually incomplete and relentlessly secret labor of mourning. Unable to abandon the object of loss, haunted by some humiliation suffered by the lost, the melancholic described by Abraham and Torok returns over and over to the lost, degraded thing. He identifies with the embarrassment it has suffered, and hides the unabandoned but humiliated object within his own psychic space. Secreted within the flooded ditch of Muldoon's poem, however, the father's corpse winks back at his poet son as the poem, like the redoubling river it describes and imitates, brings itself "round" to its inaugural uncertainty: is he "dead or sleeping"?

If, in this poem, Muldoon finds in the self-swallowing river a metaphor for his poetry and for the cognitive loop-sequences of melancholy, he does not thereby manage to lay his father's corpse to rest. As the final line of the stanza predicts, and as the logic of melancholy demands, the river will shortly bring itself, and its secret sharer, round again. In "The Fox," a poem published in the 1987 volume *Meeting the British,* the poet, disturbed at night by an obscure sound, stands looking out of his window and finds that a male corpse has resurfaced from its watery grave:

> You lay
> three fields away
>
> in Collegelands
> graveyard, in ground
> so wet you weren't so much
> buried there as drowned.[28]

Like a fox drawn to the scent of a grave, Muldoon finds himself once again worrying over his father's corpse, pawing at the muddy ground in which a dead man—or was he merely sleeping?—experienced his burial as a drowning. As mourning here implies the possibility of murder, elegy ceases to be an act of bidding farewell and reconstructs itself as a practice of disinterral.

Although in this poem Muldoon, once again confronting himself at the scene of a drowning, discovers himself to be a poet condemned to nourish his art on the grisly, waterlogged, but oddly animate remains of a dead father, in another poem in this volume he revisits the melancholy shore where he meets not his father but his grandfather. Actually, though the poem is titled "My Grandfather's Wake," the grandfather is conspicuous by his absence. Instead of an encounter with ancestry we are offered some deliberately quixotic meditations on the aesthetic:

If the houses in Wyeth's Christina's dream
And Malick's *Days of Heaven*
are triremes, yes,
triremes riding the 'sea of grain',
then each has a little barge
in tow—a freshly-dug grave. (*Meeting the British,* 13)

Extending the unending work of mourning another generation into the past, Muldoon seems to have hit the limit of his ability to keep the dead in view. Allegory substitutes for reverie as the unsurrenderable dead, rather than gnawing at the poet's consciousness, build themselves a funereal navy and launch themselves to sea (the "trireme" Muldoon makes so much of is both a warship and a ship used to ferry the dead). We have not yet arrived at the moment in which Muldoon's coronary obsession will wed a genealogical to a historical melancholy, in which the submerged and resurfaced cadavers of his familial past will join ranks with the bodies tipped from the decks of the emigrants' coffin ships, but we are close. For if in this poem Muldoon's grandfather vanishes into the hold of a trireme, that funeral vessel—which is at once the vault in which another father has been secreted and an allegory of the cryptic, cryptlike poem—gestures beyond itself to a more abject flotilla, a navy of little barges that drag behind, like floating coffins roped to the timbers of this elegy.

Guinn Batten, to whom I am indebted for my understanding of Muldoon's work as a poet of melancholy, has observed that Muldoon "is attracted to corpses that will not stay buried."[29] And thus far—other than suggesting that Muldoon is attracted to corpses that will not stay *submerged*—I have said little that Batten has not said better in her work on Muldoon. Where I do wish to diverge from Batten is on what this attraction might signify. In her reading, Muldoon's fondness for his corpses betrays not simply the melancholic temperament of a son unable to dispatch his father's and mother's ghosts but, more productively, his willingness to explore a space in language uncontaminated by the Law of the Father. Refusing to surrender his father, Muldoon refuses the paradigmatic plot of Oedipal revolt and hence refuses the work of psychic differentiation fundamental to the construction of normalized subjectivity. In the abject space in which he paws, sniffs, and devours the dead, Batten's Muldoon discovers a cryptonymic language that allows him to situate himself on either side of a Lacanian divide, to "disorder" the boundaries of his self, to abandon the myth of a unified subjectivity and so—by substituting the question "Where am I?" for the more usual "Who am I?"—to discover his identity as a diaspora. This strikes me as convincing and valuable, particularly at those moments in which Batten is able to demonstrate that if Muldoon eventually arrives at the place in which all good postmodern subjects are supposed to arrive— the space from which the self is able to recognize its "disseminations"—he does so not simply to celebrate the diasporization of the subject but in order to "show us the effaced pain, loneliness, and poverty that speak from beneath such playful multiplicities, no matter how culturally powerful their performative potential may be" (195).

What I want to ask, however, is whether there is anything particularly Irish about Muldoon's melancholy piping of the anthems of the postmodern, whether the sort of psychoanalytic reading that Batten has produced can be historically "situated," and if it can, whether it can be situated within both Ireland's national history and its transatlantic history. Is Muldoon's abject predicament merely personal and familial? Or is it also a historical predicament? Interring his corpses, and the bodies of earlier poems, is Muldoon communing not only with his past but with an Irish past, allegorizing not only his "boundary disorders" but Ireland's diasporization? More specifically, are the unsubmergeable, serially resurfacing bodies that litter his poems at least in some respects historically necessary rather than imaginatively gratuitous? Is their emergence informed by, and does it also inform, a knowledge of both those bleak mid-nineteenth-century years in which, as Robert Scally has it, Ireland became "a nation afloat" and all those subsequent years in which Irish bodies, narratives, and desires have continued to crisscross the Atlantic? Quite obviously, I think that the answer to these questions is yes, and that the Irishness of Muldoon's melancholy art has something to do with the inescapability of those funeral waters in which he discovers the secret of his, and the nation's, dissemination. But if this answer is correct, it then implies a second set of questions.

The Muldoon I have sketched thus far is a poet whose imaginary is relentlessly necrophiliac, corpse-chewing, incorporative. His dead may be submerged rather than walled up in derelict cabins, devoured by rats, tumbled into lime pits, or abandoned by the side of the road, but they seem to inspire no less a desire to "complete" *and* to hide them, no milder a form of cryptic melancholy than that so frequently inspired by the canonical images of the Famine dead. Is there then anything that distinguishes Muldoon's memorialization of these bodies from the brooding, melancholic forms of remembrance that typically attend the recovery of those Joyce referred to as the "hungried thousands"? Is his poetics of memory one that confirms or denies my suggestion that such cryptic forms of remembrance do not define the only way of remembering the catastrophic past? If, as I wish to suggest, Muldoon's dead often float into his verse from out of the depths of the Irish Atlantic, can his inspection of these bodies free itself from a cryptic melancholy and produce an alternate understanding of the relation of the living to these water-coffined dead, a relation similar to that which I have argued the American Wakes celebrate as they replace the fatal memory of a lost, damaged, past with the difficult knowledge of Ireland's cross-Atlantic present? Again, my answer to these questions is yes, though not because Muldoon's early poems subtly act, somehow, to "undo" the sovereign reign of melancholy to which they so willingly submit, but because in his most recent collection of poems, *The Annals of Chile*, Muldoon brings himself round, once again, to the scene of his earlier wakes, to his drowned ancestors and his triremes, but does so in order to view their bodies from a now American place of writing, from the scene of his own round-the-world wandering, from whence he will send back to Ireland, and to an earlier incarnation of himself, the news that the narrative of emigration is not necessarily the story of life's end.

The Annals of Chile is a waterlogged text. The opening poem—a translation of Ovid's account of Leto's metamorphosis—contemplates a race of women and men who have been rendered amphibian ("now they love nothing more than / to play in water, giving themselves over to total / immersion . . .")[30] and then gives on to a sequence of hydrographic lyrics that collectively suggest that if, in his earlier work, Muldoon found himself compelled to dredge bodies from the reservoirs of his past, he has now given himself over to total immersion, abandoned himself to the morbid spaces of the submarine in the hope that he might find some object of play beneath the waters. The first of these succeeding poems, however, finds the poet not disporting himself but having his hair scrubbed by a less than happy mother, who, as she washes her son's hair, administers some lessons on sexual purity. Head dipped over the sink, Muldoon watches the water whirlpooling down the drain and suddenly finds himself gazing not at a porcelain bowl but at the waters of a transatlantic territory ("it must be somewhere on or near the equator / given how water / plunged headlong into water" [7]) in which an exiled band of Irishmen have set up shop. Two poems later the poet upbraids himself for confusing his now deceased mother with "a woman slinking from the fur of a sea otter" (10). In the following lyric, he recalls cutting "a manhole cover" (12) out of a sheet of water-covering ice. The manhole cover then becomes a lens for him to peer into the past, where he espies a childhood friend who has mastered the art of being in "two places at once" (12). In "Incantata" a deceased lover manages the neat trick of rising from her "barrow" not as a zombie but as a "nautilus" (13). "Yarrow"—the long, generically hybrid poem that concludes the volume—opens with intimations of a coming apocalypse, a flood in which "all would be swept away by the stream / that fanned across the land" (39).

I will refrain from going on. Suffice to say that the volume is littered with scenes of drowning or submersion, with watering troughs passing as coffins, and sinks that entomb the waters of the Atlantic. Fleets of ghost ships—the *Marie Celeste,* the *Fighting Temeraire,* the *Hispaniola,* the *Caledonia,* the *Golden Hind,* the *Pequod,* one of Popeye's vessels, and an "Athenian galley"— put in appearances, and over and over "a nautilus / of memory" (152) surfaces from the submarine depths of Muldoon's work. Like the nautilus in Jules Verne's *Twenty Thousand Leagues under the Sea,* Muldoon's nautilus collects within its hold a variegated cargo of poetic figures and devices. First visible as an emblem of a cancer-eaten corpse, it subsequently functions as the diving vessel of memory. Both an emblem of the remembered and the act of remembrance, the nautilus links the many water scenes in the volume by suggesting that for Muldoon memory is an act of plunging into the oceanic, and history a collection of sea-changed bodies.

Let me briefly note two more things about those bodies. The dead in *The Annals of Chile* are hungry, and they are diseased. The lover in "Incantata" is devoured by cancer. In "Yarrow," another lover, or the poet's mother—the ambiguity is deliberate—is consumed from within by ovarian cancer. Blighted in body, the dying and the dead suffer further because their foodstuffs are sickly. "Yarrow"—a poem that refers repeatedly to an unspecified year of pervasive hunger—is seeded with ruined kale and rotten tubers. The yarrow-rising lover of "Incantata" offers the poet "what looked like a cankered potato" (13). Hunger, diseased bodies, rotten staples, bodies tipped into the wash: Muldoon is far too oblique a poet to announce exactly what he is up to, what he is remembering by only partially forgetting, but there is little doubt that the abject landscape of *The Annals of Chile* is haunted by the melancholy specter of the Ireland, and the Irish Atlantic, of the late 1840s, or that Muldoon's Ireland is thus oceanic in the maritime and in the Freudian sense. It is, in other words, both a seagoing territory *and* a spectral terrain; an uncanny Ireland in which the topographies of the present are overlaid by the ghostly architectures of the past.

If *The Annals of Chile* is thus a narrative of Ireland's dualization, the nation's uncanny doubleness emerges here as not merely temporal, but spatial. Muldoon's childhood Ireland, which serves as the scene for much of the 150-page-long "Yarrow," is a territory simultaneously occupied by the quotidian features of a rural home world, "The bridge. The barn. The all-too-familiar terrain" (55), and by the landscapes of the American West, the South African veld lands, the ancient Mediterranean, the Mexican desert, and any number of other boyish fantasylands. Remembering an occasion on which he entered the all-too-familiar interior of his father's barn, Muldoon recalls that that was also "the time I hunkered with Wyatt Earp and Wild Bill Hickock / on the ramparts of Troy" (71). Riding a fence on the farm, he finds himself also crouched "in the apple-butt of the *Marie Celeste*" and then, suddenly, pitched into "Mexico, 1918" (60). There is, of course, nothing particularly original about a child's ability to enchant his native surrounding with the mythic features of a world made available to him by the cinema, the classics, or pulp fiction. But that, in some ways, seems to be Muldoon's point, as he recalls the entire unexceptionality of an Ireland whose most indigenous places have become the playground to the world. But if we are here visitors to a place in which one is always in the world while at home, and in which no one place is ever content to be a single locale but always seems to house a library of no-longer-distant lands, then in entering this text we have also entered a textual universe in which the endless possibilities of a childhood fantasy of autodissemination decline to a more determinate doubling of the locations of identity as Muldoon supplements his childhood memories with reflections on his adult decision to emigrate to America. For if Muldoon's boyish voice speaks from an Ireland that is always home to the world, then the adult persona of *The Annals of Chile* exchanges the infinite possibilities of this multilocal place for the particularities of a transatlantic, Irish and American, territory of belonging. And it is as he attempts to map the contours of this strangely more anxiety-producing realm, as he finds himself in need of discovering a mode of poetic discourse adequate to the specific demands of an Irish childhood and an American adulthood, and as he struggles to maintain at least one foot in either place, that Muldoon's verse seems to find some odd sustenance in the memories of Famine and emigration so constantly rising above the surface of his verse.

Muldoon opened his previous collection *Madoc: A Mystery* with a poetic "key" that pretended to unlock the enigmas of the book (dare I note that that "key" text contains the image of a man emerging "from his sound booth like a diver from a bathyscope"?).[31] In *The Annals of Chile* he gives us two such keys, one of which he withholds until the final lines of "Yarrow." The poem ends thus:

> there's something about the quail's 'Wet-my-foot'
> and the sink full of hart's-tongue, borage and common kedlock
>
> that I've either forgotten or disavowed
> it has something to do with a trireme, laden with ravensara
> that was lost with all hands between Ireland and Montevideo. (189)

Wetting his foot (and the metrical feet of his verse) as he steps into the waters of an Irish history he has spent much of the volume simultaneously invoking and disavowing, remembering by not quite managing to forget, Muldoon returns us to the scene of his grandfather's wake, to the image of a lost funeral boat, which he now apprehends as a vessel steaming from Ireland to the Americas. In plotting a route to the recovery of that trireme, both from the waters of the Atlantic and from the pages of his own earlier writings, Muldoon has quite carefully positioned this coffin ship in a complex relationship both to the America he now inhabits and to the "all-too-familiar terrain" of the Ireland from which he has emigrated. For the trireme that appears in these lines is not only a mortuary vessel and a ship whose interrupted itinerary implies the passage to the Americas that Muldoon has managed to complete, it is also a sort of delayed slant rhyme that, in providing the book with its closing image, simultaneously completes the volume's most frequently repeated and its most organizing refrain.

In the opening pages of "Yarrow," Muldoon, recalling the farm on which he was raised, rests his eye on "The bridge. The barn. The all-too-familiar terrain" (55). Several times thereafter he begins a stanza with the opening portions of that statement, thus identifying "The bridge . . . the barn" as an inevitable, an inescapable ground of memory. But if the bridge, the barn, that all-too-familiar terrain, cannot be slipped, it can be transformed; for on one of its reappearances, the refrain completes itself with a slant rhyme on terrain, as Muldoon now contemplates "The bridge. The barn. The all-too-familiar seal-flipper terrine / with the hint of seaweed" (103). The abject comedy of this terrine/terrain substitution is in part a function of the substitution of seal for quail (the primary ingredient of an "authentic" terrine), but is also a result of the bizarre familiarity, to the poet, of this unexpected substitution. It seems he has eaten seal-flipper terrine not only before, but often. By the final lines of the poem, however, a quail has reasserted itself as the first ingredient thrown into a sink full of odd foodstuffs (borage, kedlock), but this strange, forgotten, disavowed terrine of memory, which has now taken the place of the earlier abject terrine, which has in its turn substituted for the all-too-familiar terrain of childhood, is then summarily displaced by a trireme sailing from Ireland to the Americas. If the poetic path Muldoon lays from the all-too-familiar *terrain* of a native place of belonging, to a too-often consumed seal-flipper *terrine* (with its hint of seaweed), to the all-too-familiar *trireme* efficiently demonstrates the metamorphic but enigmatic brilliance of his craft, then it also plots a narrative of Famine and emigration in miniature.[32] Driven from the familiar terrain of their birth by a Famine so pervasive it led multitudes to attempt to nourish themselves on grass, seaweed, and other strange but soon all-too-familiar foodstuffs before surrendering themselves at last to the ships that for so many were to become no more than floating coffins, the Famine emigrants, no less than Muldoon's readers, have trudged this path from terrain to trireme.

But is this also the path that Muldoon understands himself to have walked in his passage from Ireland to America? Is his passage from Ireland to the Americas no more than a late-twentieth-century version of the Famine emigrants' passage from terrain to trireme? If it is, then he, like Robert Scally's emigrants, has also passed from place to placelessness, from the "inside" of Irishness to the fatal depths of an Atlantic Ocean that does not bridge the abyss between one place and the other but is only, ever, a placeless space between Ireland and the Americas. If this is Muldoon's oblique but conclusive answer to the painful, haunting riddle of hunger and emigration, then his trireme allegorizes an absolute sundering of the present from the past, and of the Americas from Ireland, as it frames the relationship of "here" and "there," "now" and "then," only in terms of death, and loss, and vanishing.

It is my sense that this is, in part, exactly what Muldoon intends, and that we would be ill-advised to ignore this knowledge of emigration cooped in the hold of his funeral ship. For however mournful that knowledge may be, it is not, I believe, a signal of his inability to think beyond the tropes of melancholy that haunt the cultural poetics of imperial suffering, colonial migrancy, and postcolonial remembrance, but a sign of his awareness that catastrophe cannot be summarily redeemed simply because we deem it better to live euphorically than dysphorically. It is a measure of his recognition of what Batten calls the "pain and loneliness" too often effaced from the celebratory discourses of cultural multiplicity. But though this is Muldoon's last word on what it is like to live "between" Ireland and the Americas, it is not his only word. Indeed, if it were his only word, the volume could not have been written, not because Muldoon would literally have failed to survive his westward passage but because the adult world the text maps is not an apocalyptically sundered terrain but one that Muldoon is able constantly to cross and recross; because as it moves from stanza to stanza, shuttling from the memories of childhood to the experience of adulthood to the recollections of adolescence once again, attending to the appeals of an American lover, the admonitions of an Irish mother, and the delights of a New York bedmate once more, the volume charts itself as nothing less than a continuous circular navigation of the transatlantic. *The Annals of Chile,* as I mentioned, contains two "keys." The trireme lost with all hands between Ireland and America is one. But it is with the second of those keys, though it comes earlier in the volume, that I wish to conclude, for it is in that piece of writing, in a short poem titled "Twice," that Muldoon reveals the secret that allows him thus to inhabit the crisscross territory of the Irish Atlantic.

In the poem, Muldoon directs his readers to a photograph that in many ways provides a counterallegory of the difficulties and pleasures of his own transatlantic existence. The photo is from his childhood, a conventional classroom shot of a triple row of school-age youths smiling or staring sullenly, at the lens of a camera. What distinguishes the photo, what makes it both instantly memorable and retrospectively symbolic of Muldoon's and Ireland's experience of migrancy, is the grinning delinquency of one of the students, a boy named Lefty Clery, who gazes out at us "from both ends of the school photograph, / having jooked behind the three / deep rest of us to meet the Kodak's / leisurely pan: 'Two places at once, was it, or one place twice?'" (12). Uncannily present on either side of the row of children, Lefty's body jokingly poses the question that this essay has, in many respects, attempted to answer. For if Lefty is a cunningly wicked little boy, he is also a child who hides an Irish secret beneath the surface of his English nickname. The Gaelic spelling of Lefty's name, as Guinn Batten notes, signifies not only left-handed but "havoc" or "destruction." And so it is not only a classroom joker who smiles out at us but a portable catastrophe. But what does it mean to gaze upon that wandering catastrophe? To indicate that Lefty's magic is to be in one place twice is to see in the doubling of catastrophe an essentially temporal and melancholy unfolding of the uncanny. It is to see a single, unitary, place, serially haunted by the same image of destruction, to see one place giving itself over, time after time, to the same havoc-ridden vision. To occupy one place twice is to occupy a territory whose present moment is always overlaid with the image of another, catastrophic, moment. If that catastrophe is the havoc and destruction of Famine, and that one place is Ireland, then to be in one place twice is to be unable to escape the brooding specter of that nineteenth-century past, to inhabit a nation of the dead. And however suspicious one might be of the consequences of this knowledge of place, this, undeniably, has been the knowledge of Irishness that has frequently attended the inspection of the nation's great nineteenth-century catastrophe.

But Lefty's body offers another knowledge of catastrophe and the uncanny, a knowledge whose doubleness is less temporal than spatial. To the immigrants at an American Wake who found themselves occupying their native places not once but twice, as both the living and the dead, and to a late-twentieth-century Ireland that finds the present places of the nation similarly ghosted by the fatal landscapes of the past, Lefty offers the knowledge that to be Irish is not only to suffer the melancholy bewilderments of inhabiting one place twice but to entertain the promise of belonging to a community that has learned to meet itself on either side of an impossible divide, that has unlocked the riddle of finding itself in, at least, "two places at once." Marveling over the dexterity of a young schoolboy who has managed to invent himself as his own doppelgänger, Muldoon determines to master the same art and to advise his countrymen that whether they recognize it or not they have already been enrolled in Lefty Clery's school of self-portraiture. For to speak of the Irish, he here suggests, is to speak no longer only of a body of subjects whose eternal vocation is to stay in place, but to speak of a community that has learned the migrant art of replacing itself, as he has learned to replace himself, on either side of a transatlantic territory of belonging. To be Irish, Muldoon indicates, is no longer only to dwell in the island, or to mourn its loss, but to nourish oneself on the traumas and promises of the Irish Atlantic.

To speak of promise, given the universe of suffering I have addressed, may seem, at best, brutally glib. And I can only imagine that it would come as the coldest of comforts to the emigrants trapped in the hold of Robert Whyte's coffin ship that their sufferings would be recuperated in the ways in which Muldoon's verse and this essay seek to recuperate them. But it is my sense, driven in part by the tendency of a number of the recent histories of the Famine to treat the emigrants as truly dead to Ireland the moment they set foot on their westward-bound vessels and to read their passage to the Americas as a passage out of Irish history, that the terrible sufferings of these emigrants need to be resituated within a cultural history of Irishness, not that they may be returned to view as yet another of the nation's companies of ghosts but that the circulating economy of memories, knowledges, and desires to which their lives were joined might find its place within that map of Irishness visible in *The Annals of Chile.*

Notes

1. Robert Whyte, *The Ocean Plague* (Boston: Coolidge and Wiley, 1848), 43.

2. Cited in Christine Kinealy, *A Death-Dealing Famine: The Great Hunger in Ireland* (London: Pluto Press, 1997), 6.

3. Cormac O'Grada, *The Great Irish Famine* (London: Macmillan, 1989), 10.

4. See Brendan Bradshaw, "Nationalism and Historical Scholarship in Ireland," *Irish Historical Studies* 26.104 (November 1989): 329–51.

5. S. J. Connolly, review of Donald Kerr, *"A Nation of Beggars"? Priests, People, and Politics in Famine Ireland: 1846–52, Victorian Studies* 39.2 (winter 1996): 206.

6. Terry Eagleton, "Indigestible Truths," *New Statesman and Society* 8.355 (June 1995): 24.

7. Robert James Scally, *The End of Hidden Ireland: Rebellion, Famine, and Emigration* (Oxford and New York: Oxford University Press, 1995), 236.

8. Nicholas T. Rand, "Editor's Note," in Nicolas Abraham and Maria Torok, *The Shell and the Kernel*, ed. and trans. Nicholas T. Rand (Chicago: University of Chicago Press, 1994), 101.

9. Anne McClintock, *Imperial Leather: Race, Gender and Sexuality in the Colonial Contest* (New York and London: Routledge, 1995), 72.

10. Chandra Talpade Mohanty, "Under Western Eyes: Feminist Scholarship and Colonial Discourse," in *Colonial Discourse and Postcolonial Theory*, ed. Patrick Williams and Laura Chrisman (New York: Columbia University Press, 1994), 211 and 210.

11. See David Simpson, *The Academic Postmodern: A Report on Half-Knowledge* (Chicago: University of Chicago Press, 1993), and Alan Liu, "Local Transcendence:

Cultural Criticism, Postmodernism, and the Romanticism of Detail," *Representations* 32 (1990): 75–113. Clifford's discussion of those forms of cultural analyses that are "global enough" came in a lecture titled "The Reinvention of Tradition Reconsidered: Maps/Histories of the Future," delivered at Duke University, 15 September 1997.

12. Chris Morash, "Literature, Memory, Atrocity," in *Fearful Realities: New Perspectives on the Famine* (Dublin: Irish Academic Press, 1996), 118.

13. Patrick Kavanagh, "The Great Hunger," in *The Faber Book of Contemporary Irish Poetry,* ed. Paul Muldoon (London and Boston: Faber and Faber, 1986), 50–51.

14. See Joseph Roach, *Cities of the Dead: Circum-Atlantic Performance* (New York: Columbia University Press, 1996), 1–5 and 36–42. I discuss Roach's work at some length later in this essay.

15. See Thomas Murphy, *Famine* (Dublin: Gallery Press, 1977).

16. For an insightful review of this tradition, see Vincent Cheng, *Joyce, Race, and Empire* (Cambridge and New York: Cambridge University Press, 1995), 15–57.

17. Luke Gibbons, *Transformations in Irish Culture* (Notre Dame: University of Notre Dame Press, 1996), 6.

18. Kobena Mercer, *Witness at the Crossroads: An Artist's Journey in Postcolonial Space* (London: Institute of International Visual Arts, 1997), 67–68; emphasis in the original.

19. Cited in ibid., 68.

20. Edward S. Casey, *The Fate of Place: A Philosophical History* (Berkeley: University of California Press, 1997), 254–55.

21. Homi Bhabha, "Day by Day . . . with Frantz Fanon," in *The Fact of Blackness: Frantz Fanon and Visual Representation,* ed. Alan Read (London: Institute of Contemporary Arts and Seattle: Bay Press, 1996), 192.

22. Cited in Morash, "Literature, Memory, Atrocity," 118.

23. *Irish People,* 15 June 1901, cited in Thomas Gallagher, *Paddy's Lament: Ireland 1846–1847* (New York and London: Harcourt Brace Jovanovich, 1982), 130.

24. Cited in Kerby Miller, *Emigrants and Exiles: Ireland and the Irish Exodus to North America* (Oxford and New York: Oxford University Press, 1985), 558.

25. James Joyce, *Finnegans Wake* (New York: Penguin Books, 1976), 309.

26. See Lawrence Norfolk's review of Muldoon's *The Annals of Chile*: "The Abundant Braes of Yarrow," *Times Literary Supplement,* 7 October 1994, 32.

27. Paul Muldoon, *Selected Poems 1968–1983* (London and Boston: Faber and Faber, 1986), 6.

28. Paul Muldoon, *Meeting the British* (Winston-Salem, N.C.: Wake Forest University Press, 1987), 31.

29. Guinn Batten, "'He Could Barely Tell One from the Other': The Borderline Disorders of Paul Muldoon's Poetry," *South Atlantic Quarterly* 95.1 (winter 1996): 179.

30. Paul Muldoon, *The Annals of Chile* (New York: Noonday Press, 1995), 5.

31. Paul Muldoon, *Madoc: A Mystery* (New York: Farrar, Straus, and Giroux, 1991), 3.

32. Batten also notes the "terrain," "terrine," "trireme" chain in her essay.

The Embarrassment of Victorianism
Colonial Subjects and the Lure of Englishness

Simon Gikandi

In my youth we lived according to the tenets of Matthew Arnold; we spread
sweetness and light, and we studied the best that there was in literature in
order to transmit it to the people—as we thought, the poor backward West
Indian people.

C. L. R. James, "Discovering Literature in Trinidad: The 1930s"

Introduction: Colonial Victorianism

In 1953, C. L. R. James, the great Afro-Caribbean writer and intellectual, was
arrested and asked to leave the United States. It was at the height of the
McCarthy era and James's close involvement with the small Trotskyist movement in the United States was enough to identify him as an undesirable alien
involved in distinctly "un-American activities."[1] James was beginning to develop doubts about Trotskyism at the time of his arrest, but, still, he had
struck up what appeared to be a close friendship with Trotsky during a trip
to Mexico in the 1930s, and his closest ideological ally in the contentious
politics of the American left was none other than Raya Dunayesvskya,
Trotsky's former secretary and a prominent scholar of European commu-
nism. For members of the McCarthy circle, then, James's long admiration of
what he called American civilization—and his defense of American culture
against European snobbery—did not make any difference to their strong
conviction that this tall wry black man from the British West Indies posed a

clear and present danger to American values. Soon after his arrest and im-prisonment at Ellis Island, James tried to challenge his deportation order by writing a book on Melville and the meaning of American civilization, but this was not enough to mitigate the official view that he was part of the spec-tacle that McCarthy and his allies were trying to exorcise from the American body politic.[2]

James's case was not helped by the fact that he was also a radical Pan-Africanist, the author of a major history of the Haitian Revolution, and the mentor of a generation of Caribbean and African nationalists involved in the struggle against British colonialism. If McCarthyism drew its "moral energies" from a perhaps regressive and perverted ideal of Victorian values, then James could have appeared as a visible threat to these values. And yet, deep down, James was a product of—and one of the strongest adherents to—what I will call colonial Victorianism.[3] He was perhaps the last product of a residual Victorian culture that was to survive long after the end of the British Empire. How could such a strong opponent of imperialism also be a visible adherent of Victorianism?[4]

This identification of James's Victorianism is more than claiming that he was a connoisseur of things Victorian, or that he was a product of Victorian institutions and norms. As he had gone out of his way to show in *Beyond a Boundary*, his childhood memoir and history of West Indian cricket, James was the product of three colonial institutions—the family, the public school, and sports—whose identity and determinative power were derived from the core beliefs of Victorian culture long after Victorianism had been declared dead in Britain.[5] James grew up in a family in which the high Puritanism of Victorian culture had been appropriated and established as a personal creed; he went to schools run according to the rules and beliefs that Thomas Arnold had made famous at Rugby; he came of age as a student of cricket, a game that was considered to be the essence of colonial Victorianism. James's inheritance from his family, he often asserted, was a strict moral upbringing, cricket, and early Victorian literature, most notably Dickens and Thackeray. And what linked all these key institutions of Victorian culture as experienced by a colonial subject, James was to note succinctly, was "Puritanism; more specifically, restraint, and restraint in a personal sense" (James, *Boundary*, 47).

His restraint, which has been seen as one of the defining characteristics of Victorian culture, was something more than a set of beliefs and practices imposed on the colonized through literary texts and what James called "the

pervading influence of the university men who taught me" (ibid.).[6] The authority of the Victorian moral code in the colonial sphere, James reckoned,
came from a certain congruency between the organization of social life in
his family and community and the books he read, books that can be said to
have provided the models on which a modern life could be lived: "I absorbed it from [Aunt] Judith and my mother—it was in essence the same
code—and I was learning it very early from my *Vanity Fair*" (ibid.). In his
reading and misreading of Thackeray—especially from "the things I did not
notice and took for granted" (ibid.)—James internalized the dominant ideologies and social practices of Victorian culture almost a hundred years
since they were deployed in Britain itself.

The subject of this essay is the appropriation, rehearsal, and reformula-
tion of a belated Victorianism by colonial subjects. I am interested in two
broad problems that James's work and life foreground vividly. The first
problem is theoretical: it concerns the authority and residuality of colonial
concepts and categories among the colonized, of their fate in places far removed from their site of conception.[7] Colonial subjects were perhaps the
furthest removed from the centers of Victorian culture, but they were heavi-
ly invested in Victorian values as much, if not more, than the Victorians
themselves. But, as I will be arguing, in rehearsing Victorianism and its core
values, the colonized were also transforming Victorian categories; they were
using the dominant forms of colonialism to express their own experiences.
There is hence no better illustration of the unifying theme of this book—
the invention of a post-Victorian culture in our contemporary postmodern
or postcolonial world—than the process by which the colonized imagined
themselves to be Victorian and the way they adopted the idiom of
Victorianism to understand and inscribe their cultural and moral universe.
In this sense, colonial subjects were perhaps the first post-Victorians.

The second problem is one that has been central to revisionist studies of
colonial culture: this is what the Comaroffs have described as the "bitter
contest of conscience and consciousness" in the colonial zone and the resulting dialectic that came to mediate the relationship between the colonizer and the colonized.[8] On one side of this dialectic was the alien culture of
European capitalism imposing its "particular way of seeing and being" on
the colonized, seeking "to colonize their consciousness with [its] signs and
practices, [its] axioms and aesthetics" (235). On the other side were the forms
and practices through which the colonized tried to "recast the intrusive

European forms in their own terms . . . in the effort to formulate an awareness of, and gain a measure of mastery over, their changing world" (ibid.). My concern here is the discursive mechanisms through which some of the central categories of Victorianism—notions of labor, moral character, respectability, and progress—were transformed in the encounter between the colonizer and the colonized to create what has come to be known as postcolonial culture.

But how does one recover a discourse of freedom—and hence postcoloniality—in a colonized consciousness? When this consciousness is defined as Victorian, the analyst's task is complicated by the "retrospective illusion" that seems to overshadow any discussion of the moral culture of colonialism in general and the nineteenth century in particular.[9] The Victorians are so close to us, notes Charles Taylor, that "we naturally think ourselves to have evolved away from them, beyond them"; and yet the basic grammar of our moral, cultural, and political discourse, "the very picture of history as moral progress . . . is very much a Victorian idea" (394).

For the colonized, in particular, the temptation for a retrospective illusion or collective forgetfulness has been great: the Victorian age represents such a powerful reminder of colonial domination and cultural alienation that it is hard to associate it with a discourse of freedom or moral progress. It is much easier to privilege the narrative of decolonization and to read it as the process by which African subjects overcame the colonization of their consciousness than to posit it as the source of the cultural grammar that enabled decolonization. But, as James was eager to remind his postcolonial readers, the vocabularies through which generations of Africans at home and abroad used to will a decolonized consciousness into being—to go beyond Victorian culture, as it were—came from a set of beliefs that originated from, and were embedded in, mainstream Victorianism. What did it mean to be Victorian in a colonial situation? How did the colonized transform the key categories of Victorian culture to account for their own identities in and outside colonialism? These are the questions that I want to explore in the rest of this essay.

Victorianism in Reverse

From the vantage point of political decolonization, nationalism, and postcolonial theory, it is fashionable to read James's works as an attempt to escape colonial Victorianism either through a careful articulation or disarticulation of Marxism or the invocation of Caribbean nationalism. James has given credence to this transcendental explanation of his own works by a powerful suggestion, in *Beyond a Boundary*, that the Victorian culture of his childhood constituted a prison house for colonial subjects like himself:

> Me and my clippings and magazines on W. G. Grace, Victor Trumper and Ranjitsinhji, and my *Vanity Fair* and my puritanical view of the world. I look back at the little eccentric and would like to have listened to him, nod affirmatively and pat him on the shoulder. A British intellectual long before I was ten, already an alien in my own environment among my own people, even my own family. Somehow from around me I had selected and fastened on to the things that made a whole. As will soon appear, to that little boy I owe a debt of gratitude. (James, *Boundary*, 28)

James would, in retrospect, find it strange that he had internalized Victorian ideas and ideals without questioning their origins or purpose even when they were at odds with his own environment, an archetypal colonial situation defined by political domination, cultural alienation, and a colonized consciousness. What was remarkable about this retrospective interpretation of colonial Victorianism, however, was that James could not conceive his sense of self and his cultural agency as a product of forces extraneous to the process of colonization and in particular the Victorian text: "We lived according to the tenets of Matthew Arnold, spreading sweetness and light and the best that had been thought and said in the world. . . . Intellectually I lived abroad, chiefly in England. What ultimately vitiated this was that it involved me with the people around me only in the most abstract way" (71).

Although some of the most significant arguments in James's book arose from his retrospective recognition of his own estrangement from his Caribbean situation and his false identification with colonial doctrines on culture, family, and class, he never questioned his basic assumption that Victorianism provided him with the conceptual tools for understanding himself as a colonial subject. Moreover, it was in the process of trying to understand his own alienation that James came to understand the value of Victorianism in the constitution of Caribbean identities. In March 1932, to cite a famous example in *Beyond a Boundary*, James arrived in England ready to "enter the arena where I was to play the role for which I had prepared myself. The British intellectual was going to Britain" (114). But, as he was quick to recognize, there was a fundamental contradiction between his notion of England— derived from books and colonial practices—and the complex realities of

English life, the realities of class society and imperial power. But even after he had been exposed to this life—and hence the internal contradictions of his own positions and arguments—and even after his nationalist sentiments had been aroused under the influence of Learie Constantine, the great West Indian cricketeer, James still found it impossible to function outside the horizon of expectations and the hermeneutical circle established by his Victorianism: "My sentiments were in the right place, but I was still enclosed within the mould of nineteenth-century intellectualism" (117).

It would be easy to argue that James's radical political practices and writings since the 1930s were deliberate attempts to overcome the baggage of the nineteenth century, but this kind of claim misses the essential questions here: How are we to explain the fact that underlying James's most radical works, such as *The Black Jacobins,* is a theory of history—built on notions of heroism and moral progress—that are simultaneously Marxist, Hegelian, and Victorian (or rather Carlylean)? What did James mean when he claimed that "Thackeray, not Marx, bears the heaviest responsibility for me" (47)? Why, indeed, did nineteenth-century ideas seem to have this kind of hold on a radical colonial subject long after Victorian culture had been renounced in Britain itself? What are we to make of this residualism of key Victorian ideas in the works of one of the high priests of decolonization?

I think it is fair to say, in regard to the first two questions, that when James acknowledged the unshakable influence of Victorian notions about the family, culture, and sports as constitutive of his world picture, it was not simply because this was the world he had lived in but also because there was, in his work and life, a self-willed identification with this world as a source of the core values that had made him a modern subject. We have become so used to associating Victorianism with traditional values that we have often forgotten how, for the colonized in particular, Victorian ideas and practices heralded the irruption of modernity onto the colonial sphere. I will return to this subject later in my essay.

For now, let me call attention to what might visibly appear to be the paradoxical denotation of James's Victorianism: it was strange that a colonial subject born in 1901, the very year Queen Victoria died and the English middle class was welcoming her death as a liberation from the old world, should have seized on his belated Victorianism as the source of the social energies and the intellectual ideas that animated his life and work. But this adoption of Victorianism only appears strange if we fail to recognize that

Victorian ideas and categories had undergone significant, if not radical, transformations in the hands of the colonized themselves. Indeed, colonized subjects in the late imperial period had inherited a body of Victorian categories and concepts that had already been transformed by two generations of African, West Indian, or Indian Victorianists. What James was meticulously rehearsing as Victorianism in the last three decades of empire was a body of Victorian categories and ideas that had been reformulated since the beginning of the Victorian age in localized situations (in Africa, the Caribbean, and India) far removed from the heart of empire.

But *Beyond a Boundary* is not a book on Victorian culture in the colonial contact zone. On the contrary, it is a mapping of the process by which colonial subjects appropriated instruments of colonial rule, such as sports and literature, in order to transcend the colonization of their consciousness. This transcendence, however, could not be complete; its goal was to reformulate and rewrite Victorian ideas and institutions, not to discard them, to claim them as their own, not to go beyond them. In this regard, the project of post-Victorianism was intended to deploy colonial means to nationalist ends. James's cultural task in his book, then, was to understand how he and his nation and region were liberated from colonial consciousness by deploying Victorian ideas and practices differently. The desire for a liberated consciousness arose, in turn, from the colonized subjects' awareness of their own inadequacy in regard to established dogma, an awareness of the gap between their public investment in Victorian ideals and social practices (which were a source of status and empowerment in colonial society) and their very private disenchantment with the way such ideals had been corrupted by racism and racialism.

As he went through the colonial school and later traveled in England in the 1930s, James had become, in what he called his "private mind," increasingly aware of large areas of human history and experience not covered by his previous education, but he did not know how to move from an "uncritical admiration of abstracts" about England to a proper understanding of the complexities of English life (James, *Boundary*, 115). James was coming of age in a world where the politics of nationalism was challenging the edifice of Victorianism, but he did not know how to balance these two forces: "My sentiments were in the right place, but I was still enclosed within the mould of nineteenth-century intellectualism" (117). What he was acutely aware of, however, was that his abstract notions about culture and society, notions derived from established Victorian intellectual doctrines or dogmas, were incapable of accounting for ordinary life. The vocabulary of Victorianism was at odds with social life in both the colonial Caribbean and in Britain. To account for this cognitive failure, James was impelled to rethink Victorianism itself. As he traced the decolonization of West Indian cricket from its Victorian roots in the nineteenth century to its apotheosis as the symbol of autonomy in the 1950s, James was also exploring the ways in which a post-Victorian identity had emerged through a rethinking and rewriting of what Victorian culture really represented for colonial subjects. His major claim was that an interpretation of Victorian culture from the perspective of the colonized would inevitably proffer a different history of the nineteenth century.

Indeed, James would begin his revisionist task in *Beyond a Boundary* by discrediting the dominant liberal and socialist histories of Victorian England for, among other things, excluding popular intellectuals, such as the cricketeer W. G. Grace, from the pantheon of English culture in the nineteenth century. In calling attention to the role these figures had played in the making of British culture in this period, James's goal was to show that the essence of Victorianism, or at least its most influential idioms and practices, could be found in popular activities, such as sports, rather than the tomes of the sages. Grace was indispensable to our understanding of Victorian society, James contended, not simply because his views on the relation between sports and the shaping of character and society were to have a lasting influence on colonial society, but also because, in contradistinction to the dominant narratives of Victorian culture, his work and ideas promoted an alternative vision of Victorianism. Defined through the idiom of popular culture, Victorianism could be seen not simply as the imposition of a set of practices by the upper classes on the masses, or by the colonizer on the colonized, but as something inscribed more deeply in the imagination of the British people "and all who have been brought into close relations with their branch of civilization" (James, *Boundary*, 157).

A history of Victorian culture written from the perspective of popular figures such as Grace (and to this James would add Dickens and Samuel Smiles) could compel readers to reconsider Victorianism in three fundamental ways: First, it would force them to question the common belief that Victorian culture emerged from a radical rupture from its antecedents, that it acquired its distinctive identity or exceptionalism from its self-conscious break with the past. James wanted to challenge the view, valorized by generations of Victorian intellectuals, that Victorianism marked a radical departure from the culture of the eighteenth century. He wanted to show that the real essence of Victorian culture lay in its subtle connection to the past the preeminent Victorians thought they had transcended. The agents and practitioners of Victorian popular, middle-class culture—figures such as Grace, Dickens, and Thackeray—were unique because of their remarkable sense of the historical continuity within the discontinuity that defined the Victorian worldview. The language used by these public intellectuals (as we would call them now) and the institutions they promoted (cricket or the novel) had their roots in a world that preceded the institutionalization of Victorianism. Unaware of its radical newness and embedded in the politics of everyday life rather than abstract notions, Grace's cricket, like Dickens's early novels, was built on essence rather than artifice, utilitarian preconceptions rather than theoretically induced epistemic breaks.

The second reason why James was attracted to a popular version of early Victorian culture, in spite of his own intellectualism, had to do with his urgent need to rethink the temporality of Victorianism. As a student of British society in the nineteenth century, James was aware of the extent to which the dominant view of Victorian culture presented it as a set of ideas and practices whose exceptionalism lay in its transcendental desires rather than its grappling with the politics of everyday life. The popular figures that James admired were, like many colonial subjects, located both inside and outside the dominant ideologies of Victorian culture. It was significant for James that popular intellectuals such as Grace and Dickens, who had been produced on the margins of the dominant culture, had come to provide some of the governing images of their age. In his subsequent claim that colonial subjects had come to transform imperial culture in areas such as cricket and literature, James could point to these Victorian figures as important models.

In both cases, the Victorian populist and the colonial subjects had, out of their own sense of association and dissociation from the dominant weltanschauung, been able to produce a dynamic culture in opposition to the reified abstractions of the dominant intellectuals of the age. Victorian popular intellectuals, and the lower middle class they represented, had "a surer eye for society as it was and not as it might be" (James, *Boundary,* 166) and were thus able to adopt a critical attitude toward the emerging bourgeois society. The greatest contribution of the Victorian middle class, James would conclude, was its ability to understand life in the raw without abstract mediating systems or a philosophy of culture. For this reason, James did not think that Matthew Arnold's mid-Victorian critique of middle-class philistinism was justified; this cataloging of the intellectual deficiencies of the middle class amounted to "pathological malice" because it failed to recognize the extent to which philistinism, as practiced outside the narrow confines of the liberal culture of Whitehall, had significant cultural value for the middle class. James was emphatic in his claim that the Victorian middle class had a vibrant culture—"The Victorian middle classes read Dickens, loved Dickens, worshipped Dickens" (159)—but this was a different culture from the one being espoused by the high priests of Victorianism. In defending the Victorian middle class, James was, of course, also defending the colonial elite and its own version of culture and civilization.

Indeed, the third way in which James would force his readers to reconsider the normativity of Victorian culture could be found in his definition of culture as something other than the sweetness and light he had learned from Matthew Arnold via the colonial school. In James's view, what ordinary Victorians wanted—and this too could be said of colonial subjects—was culture as "a way of life" (160). The idea of culture as a way of life was not to be found in the works of the Victorian sages (Matthew Arnold, Carlyle, and Ruskin) or the poets (Tennyson and Browning) but in the works of Thomas Arnold, Thomas Hughes, and W. G. Grace. And it is in delineating the values and qualities symbolized by these men—whom he clearly identified as the creators of true Victorianism—that James begun to point toward a different meaning for Victorian culture, one inflected by the experiences and perspectives of the colonized. His basic claim here was not simply that the institutions created by these three men—the ideology of the public school, the role of sports in the shaping of character, and the centrality of virtues and manners—were the ones that were easily and perspicuously transported to the colonial sphere. More than this influence, these men created a cultural grammar and a series of moral imperatives that were crucial to the social transformation of the colonial world: they presented the colonized with alternatives to "traditional" cosmologies.

From the colonized subject's perspective, then, what might have appeared to nineteenth-century observers as conservatism in the work and thought of Thomas Arnold could be deployed as an argument to challenge the old vocabularies of moral or social life associated with, let us say, pre-colonial African cultures while challenging colonial normativity. Indeed, what made Thomas Arnold appear so modern, in James's view, was the way he was able to institute a moral culture, through the public school system and its codes of conduct, that could be used to counter both the claims of old traditions and the forces of radical social change. Arnold at Rugby, James argued, was able to create a space in which manners and virtues would have precedence over both crude politics and utilitarianism; he taught discipline and self-reliance, order and civility; he preached the essence of "moral excellence and character training" (163).

But why would a colonial subject perceive moral values intended to consolidate the status quo as essential to the emergence of a new society outside Victorian imperialism? Indeed, why would James seem to associate Thomas Arnold's conservative values with a modern moral order? We can best understand James's attempt to excavate a liberatory discourse from within Victorian moral culture by recalling two points made by Charles Taylor in *Sources of the Self*. The first point is one already mentioned, that is, the unexpected association Taylor makes between Victorian values and our modern identity: he argues that the basic moral and political standards of our contemporary world—the standards "by which we congratulate ourselves" (394)—are essentially Victorian. The core values that have come to define our modern identity and moral culture—the idea of universal benevolence, the notion of a "free self-determining subject," and the "language of subjective rights"—have come to us from the nineteenth century. And, as I will show in some detail, this language was central to the colonial subjects' attempts to transcend imperial conquest and rule. The second point Taylor makes lies at the heart of my argument here and elsewhere: "Our history since 1800 has been the slow spreading outward and downward of the new modes of thought and sensibilities to new nations and classes, with the transfer in each case involving some kind of adapting transformation of the ideas themselves" (ibid.). Or, as James puts it more aptly, the "translators and emasculators of Arnold were the vanguard of a world-wide movement" (James, *Boundary*, 164). What I am calling the embarrassment of Victorianism emerges from the unanticipated fact that forces, values, and cultures intended to consolidate colonial conquest could so easily be transformed into the foundational narratives of black self-determination and rights.[10]

Black Victorianism

Long before James was born in the last year of Queen Victoria's reign, colonial subjects had been working hard to transform colonial Victorianism into a discourse of their own liberation from imperialism. For more than eighty years, in fact, leading intellectuals in Africa and its diaspora had been engaged in a generational project whose goal was nothing less than the institution of Victorian ideas as the basis of a modern black identity and its accompanying set of moral imperatives. In their garden parties, their newspapers, schools, and universities, the African elite in places as far apart as Cape Town and Lagos displayed their Victorian identity and frame of reference as a badge of honor and celebrated their Victorian world picture as a mark of their arrival into the modern world, the world of civility and civilization. Some of them may have been former slaves from the United States or Brazil, or African-American colonists, but, as Michael Echeruo has noted in *Victorian Lagos,* that members of this new elite were African by birth or ancestry was less important than the fact that they were "a new kind of African"; and what marked their newness was their visible Victorianism: "What gave a special character to these new Africans was the fact that they were in a profound, not a polemical sense, Africans of a Victorian persuasion."[11] On the surface, black Victorianism was indistinguishable from its metropolitan version: its vocabulary was that of paternal empire, its axioms were those of the civilizing mission, its evangelicalism was as legendary as that of colonial missionaries, and its patriotism was properly English.

Consider the case of Alexander Crummell. He had been born a free black in New York City at the beginning of the nineteenth century, the century of opportunity, but all his efforts at self-improvement had been stymied by racial prejudice in the United States. His ambition to enter the mainstream of the Episcopal church had been dashed at almost every stage of his life; not even his education in moral philosophy at Cambridge University would earn him the recognition he deserved as a quintessential nineteenth-century man of letters. As W. E. B. Du Bois was to note in a celebrated eulogy in *The Souls of Black Folk,* Crummell had to cross the "the Valley of Humiliation and the Valley of the shadow of death" before he could find his true self.[12] One would think that having been disappointed by the Anglo-Saxon world, Crummell would seek to renounce Victorianism. But when he moved to Africa as a missionary in Liberia in 1853 to escape racial discrimination in the United States, Crummell held on to his Victorian ideas and ideals as an act of faith and sought to make them the foundational narratives of his "colonial" project. His goal in Africa was simply to transplant the "pagan" beliefs of his ancestors and turn his adopted homeland into a showcase for nineteenth-century ideas on morality, commerce, and progress. Crummell's passionate commitment to Liberia, notes J. R. Oldfield, was generated by the hope "that in time it would become a Christian state, a sort of Victorian England."[13]

What, then, was the nature and meaning of the Victorian interest that was to animate black nationalist thought in the nineteenth century? Wasn't there a fundamental opposition between Crummell's struggle for black rights in Africa and the United States and his unabashed celebration of Victorian culture and values? Strange juxtapositions make such questions inescapable. For most of 1896 and 1897, for example, Crummell's energies were directed toward the formation of the American Negro Academy (ANA), a society committed to the vindication of African Americans through literary, historical, and philosophical scholarship. The ANA was to bring together the best minds in African-American culture at the end of the century and was to provide the intellectual base for some radical work by W. E. B. Du Bois, among others. And yet, soon after the inauguration of the ANA, Crummell arrived in England to attend Queen Victoria's Diamond Jubilee. The emotions expressed during this occasion are a perfect illustration of the embarrassment of Victorianism and its productive contradictions:

> I have been in England on four previous occasions, but just now I am almost over-powered with the impress of greatness, magnificence & power which comes upon me, at every turn! How wonderful is this great city of London in its immense population & vastness of area, its palatial residences & fine equipages, its grand Cathedrals & noble churches, its countless charities & its boundless beneficence, its marvellous sanitation & unparalleled order. And the glory of it all is the unequalled fact that all this earthly magnificence is more or less allied with moral responsibility & the sanctions of religion both with regard to authority at home & governmental control abroad.[14]

In this paragraph alone we can see what impressed Crummell most about Victorian England: the impressive display of imperial power, the architecture of industrial civilization, and the fusion of morality with governmentality. But my initial question still remains: why did Crummell, the son of a former slave, feel impelled to express his identity and his salvation—and that of his people—through the idiom of Victorianism?

There are two main responses to this question. There is, first, what one may call a determinative explanation for Crummell's attachment to Victorian values: he was the product of the nineteenth century and hence incapable of representing his world outside the dominant *Zeitanschauungen*.[15] The second explanation, provided by Henry Louis Gates Jr. and Anthony Appiah, sees Crummell as hopelessly imprisoned in a certain Eurocentric discourse on literacy and civilization, a discourse that accepted the Enlightenment's view that Africa was devoid of the capacity for literacy and by extension rationality and a moral culture.[16] Both explanations are valid but incomplete. Like many other Afro-Victorians of his generation, Crummell was certainly interpellated by Victorian culture; he clearly carried the baggage of post-Enlightenment Eurocentricism and racial thinking; but he also strove to go beyond his condition of possibility. In both his life and his work, Crummell rehearsed the key tropes of Victorianism, but in trying to adapt the moral culture of the nineteenth century to the histories and experiences of colonial subjects, he also gestured toward a post-Victorian frame of mind in significant, but not always visible, ways.

My contention is that although Crummell's practical philosophy appeared to mimic the dominant vocabularies of Victorian society, he was also aware of the tension between his desire to establish Victorianism in his adopted African home and the realities of colonial rule on the continent. Beneath the triumphant and empathetic celebration of Victorianism running through Crummell's essays and sermons, there lies an important—and perhaps subversive—subtext that subtly calls the attentive reader to the struggle between two narratives at odds with one another: an archetypal nineteenth-century story predicated on the idea of self-emancipation, the supremacy of a moral order, and communal progress, and a regressive narrative obsession with questions of enslavement and the captivity of the self. True, these narratives are to be found in the works of the dominant Victorian sages—Carlyle, Arnold, Ruskin—who were cognizant of the long shadow of the past on the modern world, but the politics of time in the works of these mainstream Victorian intellectuals was distinguished by a certain ascension to inevitable triumph of the progressive narrative over the regressive one. This is how mid-Victorian culture came to be defined by what Taylor, among others, has called historical exceptionalism.[17]

But although Crummell was, by temperament and education, a member of this generation, history and social circumstances had placed him in a temporal cauldron: he lived in a world and time in which the regressive and progressive narrative were contemporaneous in a real sense. As Du Bois was to observe in 1903, Crummell had been born in a world of "puzzling vistas" when the slave ship "still groaned across the Atlantic, faint cries burdened the Southern breeze, and the great black father whispered mad tales of cruelty into those young ears" (235). But this product of a slave culture, Du Bois hastened to add, came of age in a century defined as the age of freedom, human sympathy, universal freedom, and the rights of others—a century "when clodhoppers and peasants, and tramps and thieves, and millionaires and—sometimes—Negroes, became throbbing souls whose warm pulsing life touched us so nearly that we half gasped with surprise" (234). Unlike his white Victorian contemporaries, Crummell could not invoke the politics of time to privilege the progressive narrative over the regressive one because the two were intertwined in the realities of black life. Whereas a Victorian sage such as Carlyle could invoke the ordered life of the medieval world of Bury St. Edmunds in *Past and Present* to counter what he considered to be the anarchy of industrial culture, a colonial subject such as Crummell, though a strong admirer of Carlyleanism, could not construct his narrative of freedom through this kind of temporal differentiation. Indeed, what would come to define Crummell's politics of time was not the paradigmatic opposition between past and present common in his time, but the impossibility of any serious differentiating of the old world from the new. Living in a universe in which the past was always in the present, Crummell's subjectivity was engendered by what Du Bois aptly identified as the cauldron of time itself: "He [Crummell] was born with the Missouri Compromise and lay a-dying amid the echoes of Manila and El Caney: stirring times for living, times dark to look back upon, darker to look forward to" (ibid.). The essence of Crummell's work—and by extension of black Victorianism—needs to be located in his elaborate engagement with the problem of a temporality trapped between the dream of the future and the shadow of the past.

Africa and Anglo-Saxon Culture

But the narrative of freedom was still the driving force behind black Victorianism and no one knew how to perform this story of freedom as an Anglo-Saxon value better than Crummell. As one of the major intellectuals of the new nation of Liberia, a black republic set up by African Americans disenchanted with racism in the United States, Crummell was often asked to give orations on almost every anniversary of his adopted country's declaration of independence. His intellectual charge on such occasions was to diagnose the problems facing the new republic and to promulgate programs for the consolidation of its autonomous identity in the age of empire. Although its political institutions had been fashioned after the United States, the political legitimacy of Liberia would, in the eyes of its African-American ruling class, depend on the establishment of a moral culture that would stand out as an example of the African's capacity for civility and civilization. And because Victorianism epitomized the ideals of such a moral culture, it was attractive as a model of social construction in Liberia and other enclaves of "Western civilization" on the African continent. As a consummate Victorianist—an Episcopalian minister, a graduate of Cambridge University, and a committed Evangelical—Crummell's thoughts and words on such occasions were weighted with the moral authority of a sage and were fitted "to illustrate the responsibilities" of the African American's lot on the African continent and "to show forth the nature and seriousness of the duties which arise out of it."[18] Given Liberia's precariousness and the liminality of the African American in colonial Africa, Crummell's addresses had an important performative function: it was his duty, as a nineteenth-century sage, to invoke a future in which Africa could become civilized without the tutelage of empire and to convince the returned Africans that they had a providential role to play in their adopted homeland in spite of the difficulties they faced. The rhetoric of Crummell's commemorative addresses was hence built on a careful balancing of the language of black nationalism and Victorian moral idealism. In his writings and thought, the language of racial exceptionalism went hand in hand with a European discourse of virtues and manners.

Consider the following example. On 26 July 1860, Crummell was asked to make an address to the citizens of Maryland County in celebration of Liberia's seventh year of national independence. On this occasion, his subject was the English language in Liberia. As he often did on such occasions, Crummell began his address by rehearsing the paradoxical circumstance, or the "providential event," that had created the African American as a modern subject: he reminded his audience that their parents had been exiled from their African homes through the process of enslavement, but in their encounter with the West, they had found one "item of compensation, namely the possession of the Anglo-Saxon tongue" (Crummell, *Future,* 9). The Anglo-Saxon tongue and its culture, Crummell insisted, were a moral prerogative and imperative. In matters of "color, race, and origin," African Americans in Liberia were identical to "the masses of rude natives around them"; but what marked them as different—and superior—was the "cultivated English language" (which was the outward manifestation of Anglican "habits and manners") and their access to (and mastery of) a literary culture built on the canonical texts of Englishness (11–12).

Although critics of Crummell's work, most notably Anthony Appiah, have seen this affinity between language and the providential role of African Americans in the new world as a mark of Crummell's racial exclusiveness, one should not forget how this privileging of English went beyond the established nineteenth-century association between language and nation.[19] In the common lexicon of nineteenth-century nationalism, after all, there was an assumption that what gave each individual nation a distinctive identity was the concurrence of language and national territory. In opposition to this view, however, Crummell was making the general claim that African Americans had acquired the language of the other and turned it into the basis of their identity in exile, outside their nation. More particularly, Crummell's speech made it quite clear that what he had in mind was not merely the use of English in civilized life, but its function as an instrument of moral uplift. My interest here, then, is not so much what Appiah has called Crummell's "burdensome legacy" (5) of racialism and ethnocentrism, but how and why, among the alternatives available to him, the father of black nationalism spoke the language of Victorian culture and celebrated its institutions. What I want to show is that the question of language was important to Crummell not only because it was a conduit to the politics of race and nationalism, but because it enabled him to play out, in a colonial setting, the moral and historical exceptionalism of Victorian moral culture.

If an autonomous African nation was the goal of Crummell's cultural project, why was it important that this nation be built on Victorian moral ideals? What Crummell was celebrating in English was more than the phonology or morphology of the imperial language; he was trying to invoke what he considered to be its moral force and civil grammar. Compared to English, African languages (which Crummell considered to be mere dialects) were rough and barbaric, devoid of ideas and the capacity to convey "moral truth"; these languages did not have a vocabulary for moral qualities such as justice and law; they could not lead one to "supernatural truth" (Crummell, *Future,* 20, 30). In contrast, English was the language of force, power, freedom, liberty, and religious faith. It was the language of a literary canon that would be used to counter the excesses of industrialization. Against the "trash" literature read by the lower middle class, Crummell had no doubt that the great writers of the English language from Chaucer to Milton provided one with "a chaste and wholesome imagination" (41). In addition, the acquisition of the English language provided colonial subjects access to the great social values of the nineteenth century, namely, commerce, self-help, individualism, and family. English was the language of a modern civilization that was "moving further and further interiorwards . . . and sweeping abroad with a wider and wider circumference" (34).

There is no doubt, then, that what Crummell saw in the English language was the power of a triumphant imperium and aggressive masculinity; civilization was embodied in the language of manliness. True, he was concerned, as were other Afro-Victorians, with the status of women in the emerging national community, but this concern with the nature of the feminine was subordinated to the demands of "manliness." In his discourse on the English language in Africa, as in all his seminal essays, Crummell was troubled by what he called "the frivolousness" of the female mind caused by bad reading habits and the absence of mental discipline. But he did not blame women for this state of affairs. On the contrary, he considered women so central to the work of civilization (as the first line of defense against heathenish practices) that he urged his fellow settlers to strive to raise "our daughters and our sisters to become the true and equal companions of men, not their victims" (44). In his concern with the status of women, however, Crummell shared the general Victorian view that the tenderness and respect with which a society treated its women was, in Catherine Hall's words, "the great mark of superiority and civilization."[20] For Crummell, women were the custodians of a private space—defined by moral purity and family values— that offset the dangers of the precarious colonial public sphere. In matters of gender, too, Crummell was a consummate Victorian.

There is nothing startling in the claim that the Afro-Victorian's discourse was built around a familiar set of beliefs or assumptions that were circulating among Victorian intellectuals in the middle of the nineteenth century. What needs to be emphasized, however, is the extent to which the colonial elite in Africa and elsewhere saw Victorianism, on the one hand, as a duty and obligation, and, on the other hand, as the burden of civilization. Victorianism was a duty and obligation because it had marked them out as modern bourgeois subjects with unprecedented privileges within the culture of colonialism. It was a burden because colonial subjects could not claim an inherent Victorian identity or a civilized culture: the logic of imperialism demanded the exclusion of colonial subjects from culture and civilization. From the perspective of colonial subjects such as Crummell, Victorianism was not an inherent value but a set of ideas, beliefs, and practices that the colonized needed to fight for and rehearse consistently.

In a speech he gave in 1855 (again in commemoration of Liberia's independence), Crummell invoked the idea of Liberia as a country whose "newborn" nationality had given place "to care, to thought, to the consciousness of burdened duty" (58). Although such key words as *duty* and *obligation* were axiomatic in nineteenth-century discourse, Crummell felt that they needed to be "mentioned"—that is, be rehearsed—in order to be felt. It was in the process of their enunciation in a specific national context that such key words could be animated and be forced to carry their full universal weight. In other words, because Victorianism was an idea associated with England and Englishness, the colonized could only claim it for their own by reading a certain universality in its discourse. Crummell's discursive dilemma, then, was how to transform (English) national ideals (and prejudices) into universal categories and then turn them into the moral bedrock on which Liberian nationalism could be constructed. But here, again, paradoxical questions emerge from Crummell's project: Why did the Afro-Victorian consider a Victorian moral culture to be essential to black nationalism? How could a discourse that privileged national or racial particularism in one situation be transferred to another without carrying over its inherent prejudices? How, indeed, could the drama of nationalism be presented in the language of universalism?[21]

Crummell considered racial exceptionalism to be the essence of nationhood and Appiah has exhaustively explored the problematic of race and nation in his work and thought.[22] What has not been properly considered was the extent to which the language of race and nation was validated by moral universalism; for even as he insisted on the exceptionalism of the "black race," Crummell insisted that even the "simple details of a common culture" could not be contemplated outside a larger moral universe of duties and obligations; a nation needed to be conceived as "a section of the great commonwealth of humanity, a phrase of the common type of being, and no more" (Crummell, *Future*, 60). If the language of morals seems to dominate Crummell's Victorianism, it is because he saw morality as an instrument both of self-identification and of transcendence. In the first instance, the cultivation of a moral culture in Liberia would validate the status of the black as what Taylor would call a "free, self-determining subject" (395).

As Crummell was to note in his inaugural address to the American Negro Academy in March 1897, black subjects living under the shadow of slavery in the United States had been denied access to all the matrixes of civility and subjectivity—art, science, and philosophy. They had been reduced to cultural and moral orphans without the capacity for "the reflexive powers" that were considered crucial to the identity of the modern subject. Until African Americans attained "the role of civilization," they could not stand up and hold their place in the world.[23] Entrapped in the philistinism of industrial culture—what Crummell called "mere mechanism"—black subjects in the United States would not acquire the capacity for self-reflection, the power with which, to quote Taylor, to confer the subject with "different kinds of inwardness . . . the powers of disengaged reason, and the creative imagination" (395). The procurement of a moral culture was the first step toward reflexivity and autonomy: in the Victorian enclave of Liberia, as opposed to slave culture in the United States, the African American could find "evidence of moral, industrial, and intellectual progress" (Crummell, *Future*, 139).

But if Crummell perceived Liberia first and foremost as a moral entity, it was because he conceived morality as an instrument of transcending the limitations and difficulties of Victorianism, especially the imperial culture that made it very difficult for the black republic to live up to the promise of modernity. In this context, Crummell's Victorianism, like that of C. L. R. James after him, was more than a program of moral conduct inherited from the colonial masters. Victorianism was the Afro-Victorian's mode of imagining institutions of society beyond the harsh realities of imperialism. Aware that the politics of Liberia was as corrupt as that of the United States, and that its cultural and social life was as impoverished as the enclaves of slave society he had left behind, Crummell needed to hold on to Victorianism as a transcendental moral ideal that could be a point of reference for his imagined community. In this respect, I want to argue further, what now appears to be a blind celebration of things Victorian in Crummell's writings was also an elaborate attempt to transcend some Victorian policies and practices, especially racism, that had injurious effects on the colonized African.

In order to come to consciousness of themselves as free and self-reflexive subjects, the Afro-Victorians had to recognize their colonized consciousness but also hanker for a transcendental point beyond it. Transcendentalism itself was an attractive element of Victorianism because it allowed one to celebrate dominant values from the vantage point of their future fulfillment rather than actual effects. It was precisely because his Victorianism could not be founded on a celebrated past or present marked by equipoise that Crummell turned more and more to the futurist language of Christian eschatology. This eschatology, which is also to be found at work in the writings of major Afro-Victorians, including Edward Wilmot Blyden and Du Bois, can be found in three elements that constitute important revisions of the Victorian doxa: a rethinking of the notion of time itself, a sense of moral exceptionalism, and a prophetic discourse. Let me examine these elements in turn.

First, there was the question of time in the construction of an Afro-Victorian identity. Now, nineteenth-century culture was dominated by a certain crisis of temporality and the Victorian age in particular came to be defined by its self-awareness of the radical schism between past and present; in order to deal with a society that seemed to be in a constant state of flux and to manage the shock of the new, Victorian writers and intellectuals established the transitional as one of the key tropes for explaining their age. It was through the language of the transient that temporality entered the language of Victorianism; and it was in their discourses on the transitional that Victorians came to deal with the anxieties of time. One could deal with the anxieties generated by unprecedented change by either appealing to nostalgia or invoking the future.[24] In this regard, one would have expected the Afro-Victorians, as colonial subjects who had perhaps undergone more traumatic experiences than any others in the orbit of Victorian culture, to have used the transitional trope to come to terms with the radical changes that had taken place in their own societies. But anxieties about the present were conspicuously absent from the works of Crummell and his generation: they conceived time as a challenge and opportunity rather than a problem; the work of time did not simply involve the management of secular culture—"the conservation of men's lives, bodies and goods"—but was also prompted by "remote and ultimate ends, which pertain to Morals, Duty, Obligations, and Justice" (Crummell, *Future*, 65).

This kind of association between the work of reforming civil society and higher moral ends was, of course, quite common in mainstream Victorian discourse. What was unique in Crummell's temporality was its concern not with how the work of time could reconcile secular culture (the conservation of lives, bodies, and goods) and moral principles. But how could morality, in itself, provide the ultimate justification for secular culture? Secular culture acquired its value when the work of time transformed it into a moral creed. Thus, while Crummell's contemporaries, most notably Matthew Arnold, were eager to separate the value of culture from political economy, Crummell's social epistemology was driven by an urgent need to translate political economy into moral discourse: commerce, for example, was not to be feared as the enemy of culture, but as a life-giving, humanizing, and civilizing agent (ibid., 71–72).[25] What made a futurist eschatology central to Crummell's project here was the belief that the abject conditions in which the African Americans found themselves, both in Africa and the New World, could only be rationalized by the goodness it would bring about in the future. And because Crummell could not invoke the future by appealing to the past (as the mainstream Victorians were wont to do in their rarefied images of antiquity or the age of Elizabeth), he had to conjure up the history of African Americans not simply as one of triumph over adversity, but one in which the future was guaranteed by an implicit moral exceptionalism born out of this suffering.

The second aspect of Crummell's Christian eschatology—the moral exceptionalism of the formerly enslaved African—emerged from his desire to connect racial exclusiveness to the moral universalism discussed earlier. His claim here was simple: "Our nationality is to be carefully guarded and cherished as a most precious jewel; but the obligations which are connected with it are of equal worth, and demand equal interest, and earnest zeal, for their preservation" (73). Among these obligations was the compulsion "to contribute to the well-being and civilization of man" (64). In order to do good, a nation and the individuals within it, needed to transcend their narrow interests, desires, and perspectives to serve the universal whole. A major part of Crummell's project was thus concerned with rationalizing moral transcendence and exploring what he called "an investigation of God's disciplinary and retributive economy in races and nations; with the hope of arriving at some clear conclusions concerning the destiny of the Negro race" (Oldfield, 40). Suffering in the past endowed subjects with moral authority in the present: "we are members of a but rising race, whose greatness is yet to be achieved—a race which has been spoiled and degraded for centuries, and in consequence of which has been despised" (Crummell, *Future,* 167). Here, then, was the schema in which moral exceptionalism could be recognized and celebrated: the black race was defined by a history of degradation and it was located in a cultural and philosophical vacuum; its hope and promise lay in a future foretold and guaranteed if certain conditions were met.

In the name of the prophetic, Crummell would call on the "enlightened sons of Africa" in the New World to undertake what he called a "higher work," a work that transcended "mere civilization as the abiding interests of eternity outvie the transient concerns of time" (280). And it was on the sustained deployment of the prophetic trope borrowed from the Old Testament that the authority of Crummell's moral discourse ultimately depended. In his speeches, sermons, and lectures, Crummell's goal was to exhort the black Victorians to rise beyond their existential condition and look toward the city of the future. The task of rehearsing the future would come to depend on appropriating two hermeneutical apparatuses: one came from the prophetic language of the Old Testament, especially Isaiah, which often provided Crummell with the epigraphic confirmation of his basic belief in the promise of redemption after slavery. In speeches such as "The Destined Superiority of the Negro" (1877), Crummell could read Isaiah's text as clear evidence of a "retributive economy" in suffering—had "the long and continued servitude and suffering" of the Jews been compensated in time?— but also posit the story of the Jews as a "prefiguration of the narrative of the enslaved African on the path to redemption" (Oldfield, 44). God had marked black subjects for future greatness:

> He has brought this race through a wilderness of disasters; and at last put them in the large, open place of liberty; but not, you may be assured, for eventual decline and final ruin. You need not entertain the shadow of a doubt that the work which God has begun and is now carrying on, is for the elevation and success of the Negro. (Ibid., 53)

The second hermeneutical apparatus in Crummell's prophetic discourse came right from the discourse of Victorian Evangelicalism: it was based on the conviction that God had a providential or transcendental design that could, retrospectively, provide an explanation for difficult historical experiences. As early as 1862, in "The English Language in Africa," Crummell had begun to rewrite narratives of loss and marginalization as providential indicators of the destiny of the black race. His orations were often invitations to his readers to seek such indicators beyond the politics of everyday life. In the case of the African American's relation to the English language, for example, Crummell's major claim was that what appeared on the surface to be a sign of the ex-slave's alienation from Africa was indeed a blessing, the basis of an identity that transcended both "pagan" Africa and the slave-owning cultures of the Americas. The African Americans' alienation from Africa was most apparent in their language—"they all speak in accents alien from the utterance of their fathers. . . . Our Speech is indicative of sorrowful history" (Crummell, *Future*, 18)—but this "fact of humiliation" could, from the pedestal of a high Victorianism, be celebrated as the means by which certain Africans came to acquire culture and civilization. Humiliation in slavery was "the transitional step to a higher and nobler civilization" (ibid.). Here, as elsewhere, the authority and force of Crummell's rhetoric depended on his ability to convince his listeners and readers that the key negative integers of nineteenth-century culture—slavery, colonialism, and racism—could be superseded by the compensatory force of culture in a moral landscape informed by the efficacy of Victorian ideas.

Conclusion: Pilgrims' Progress

In this essay, I have tried to map the colonial subjects' complex engagement with Victorian culture from two perspectives: from the vantage point of decolonization embodied in the works of C. L. R. James, a perspective that enables us to read the Victorian colonial narrative both in terms of its promise and failure; and from the perspective of colonial subjects such as Crummell who sought to hallow a moral landscape from the dominant idiom of the nineteenth century. The implicit opposition here—between James's ironical reflection on his own indebtedness to the Victorian past and Crummell's attachment to the moral landscape and cultural vocabulary of Victorianism—is, nevertheless, deceptive. James's *Beyond a Boundary* implies a certain transgressive seductiveness; it presupposes a readerly position that is predicated on our ability to have overcome the colonized consciousness that was the writer's condition of possibility. And yet, at the very end of the book, James insists that his search for what might be described as the alternative horizons of Victorianism, most notably Pan-Africanism and Marxism, had not altered the core of his character or that of his family: "I watch my brother and his three children. In very different ways they are all Jameses; sometimes always present is the Puritan sense of discipline" (James, *Boundary*, 246).

It has not always been easy for students of colonial culture to recognize the Victorian moral stamp that James celebrated and critiqued in his own memoirs as constitutive of postcolonialism either because the rhetoric of nationalism in the age of decolonization needed to exorcise Victorianism in order to valorize narratives of national liberation, or, as I have argued in this essay, the colonized identified so powerfully with key categories of Victorian culture that they made them the basis of their own stories of time, work, and morality. In the first case, the ghost of Victorianism had to be repressed in order for decolonization to be thought—and be valorized—as a real alternative to colonial culture. In the second case, colonial subjects did not seem to detect any implicit contradiction between Victorian ideas on questions such as tradition, morality, and progress and their own program of liberation and self-identity.

The nature and function of Victorianism in the culture of the colonized were further complicated by the project of modernism, which, because it sought its identity through the repudiation of the moral economy of the nineteenth century, had little patience for the beliefs and institutional practices of the Afro-Victorians. In one famous case of such a repudiation of the Victorian past, Graham Greene, traveling in West Africa in 1935, was simply revolted by the what he considered to be the Victorian facade of Liberia and Sierra Leone. Greene regarded Freetown, the capital of Sierra Leone, to be "just an impression of heat and damp," its Anglican cathedral a sign of the Dark Ages ("a Norman church built in the nineteenth century"), its culture an emblem of "a seedy civilization."[26]

Greene was, of course, in Africa searching for a primitivism that he might use to counter the "seediness" of Victorianism; anything that reminded him of "home" was too closely associated with the trauma of childhood, a trauma that, he assumed, originated from Victorian culture. But for many colonial subjects, what Greene considered to be the seediness of Victorian culture was nothing less than a manifest representation of their modern identity. As Crummell described the work of civilization on the West Coast of Africa to an American audience in Salem, Massachusetts, in 1861, he had no doubt what the monument of black progress in Sierra Leone was: "In Freetown, the capital, is a cathedral, and all through the colony are numerous, capacious stone churches and chapels" (Crummell, *Future*, 115). If Graham Greene's interest in Africa was motivated by his need to inscribe the rupture between Victorianism and modernism, colonial subjects were more interested in establishing the continuity between nineteenth-century culture and their own age. They were thus more willing to acknowledge the circulation of Victorian ideas and icons in their own post-Victorian world.

I want to end with a remarkable example of the kind of continuity I have in mind here. One of the most popular texts of the Victorian era was John Bunyan's *Pilgrim's Progress*. It was a treasured text among the newly literate Victorian working class; it was also an icon of cultural mastery among the products of colonial Evangelical missions such as the Lovedale Institute in South Africa. Bunyan's text was often awarded to new Christian converts as a sign of their faith and conviction. But, as David Atwell has reminded us, such icons of Christianity and Victorian colonialism could sometimes appear in places and situations that negated the ideals they represented: "Early in 1878, in the aftermath of the last Frontier War, whilst troops from the Cape Colony were preparing a mass grave for seventeen of their Xhosa enemy, they found a copy of John Bunyan's *Pilgrim's Progress* on one of the bodies."[27]

C. L. R. James could have identified with the Xhosa warrior's trust in the magical powers of Bunyan and his text. In Ellis Island, in 1953, as he awaited his deportation from the United States, and as he worked on his book on Melville as proof of his admiration of American values, James realized that, far from moving away from Victorianism in his years of radical politics, his life had completed a circle:

> I discovered that I had not arbitrarily or by accident worshipped at the shrine of John Bunyan and Aunt Judith, of W. G. Grace and Matthew Bondman, of *The Throne of the House of David* and *Vanity Fair*. They were a trinity, three in one and one in three, the Gospel according to St. Matthew, Matthew being the son of Thomas, otherwise called Arnold of Rugby. (James, *Boundary*, 29)

My claim in this essay is that Victorianism was not a discourse or ideology that was simply imposed on the colonized; it was also a set of ideas and ideals that were deployed by colonial subjects as a means to a different end—their own freedom. The Victorian frame of reference was indispensable in the construction of what would later come to be known as postcolonial culture.

Notes

1. On the circumstances surrounding James's arrest and deportation from the United States, see Stuart Hall, "C. L. R. James: A Portrait," in *C. L. R. James's Caribbean,* ed. Paget Henry and Paul Buhle (Durham, N.C.: Duke University Press, 1992). All the essays in this collection contain important discussions of different aspects of James's complex life and work. See also *C. L. R. James: His Life and Work,* ed. Paul Buhle (London: Allison and Busby, 1986). An essential collection of James's major essays is *The C. L. R. James Reader,* ed. Anna Grimshaw (Oxford: Blackwell Publishers, 1992).

2. The book James wrote in Ellis Island is *Mariners, Renegades, and Castaways: The Story of Herman Melville and the World We Live In* (Detroit: Bewick/Ed, 1978).

3. What "Victorianism" really meant to either the people who lived through it or wrote about it in retrospect has always been a contentious issue. My understanding of the term is derived from Asa Briggs, *The Age of Improvement 1783–1867* (New York: David McKay, 1959), especially chapter 9; and Walter E. Houghton, *The Victorian Frame of Mind 1830–1870* (New Haven: Yale University Press, 1957). See also G. M. Young, *Portrait of an Age: Victorian England* (Oxford: Oxford University Press, [1936] 1960), and David Newsome, *The Victorian World Picture: Perceptions and Introspections in an Age of Change* (London: John Murray, 1997).

4. James considered this question to be so central to his work that he did not want his readers and interlocutors, especially in the nationalist wave of the 1960s and 1970s, to forget that his intellectual origins were European, not African: "I want to make it clear that the origins of my work and my thoughts are to be found in Western European literature, Western European history and Western European thought" (C. L. R. James, "Discovering Literature in Trinidad: The 1930s," in *Spheres of Existence: Selected Writings* [London: Allison and Busby, 1980], 237).

5. C. L. R. James, *Beyond a Boundary* (New York: Pantheon Books, [1963] 1983).

6. James makes the significant observation that the West Indian masses "did not care a damn" for the Victorian moral code, but "they knew the code as it applied to sport, they expected us, the educated, the college boys, to maintain it" (ibid., 48).

7. What I am calling colonial Victorianism is an example of what Raymond Williams describes as "the very complex interlock in politics and culture of dominant and residual forms, and the even more complex process, in relation to that interlock, of specific and still-forming modes of emergence" (Raymond Williams, "Forms of Fiction in 1848," in *Literature, Politics, and Theory: Papers from the Essex Conference, 1976–84,* ed. Francis Barker, Peter Hulme, Margaret Iversen, and Diana Loxley [London: Methuen, 1986], 2).

8. John Comaroff and Jean Comaroff, *Ethnography and the Historical Imagination* (Boulder, Colo.: Westview Press, 1992), 235.

9. My discussion here is indebted to Charles Taylor's examination of the moral discourse of Victorian culture in *Sources of the Self: The Making of the Modern Identity* (Cambridge: Harvard University Press, 1989), 394.

10. This is the argument I have made in *Maps of Englishness: Writing Identity in the Culture of Colonialism* (New York: Columbia University Press, 1996). My current

contribution is from *Rethinking African Subjects: Reason, Culture, and the Work of Art* (forthcoming).

11. Michael J. C. Echeruo, *Victorian Lagos: Aspects of Nineteenth Century Lagos Life* (London: Macmillan, 1997), 111.

12. W. E. B. Du Bois, *The Souls of Black Folk* (New York: New American Library, 1969), 233.

13. J. R. Oldfield, *Civilization and Progress: Selected Writings of Alexander Crummell on the South* (Charlottesville: University of Virginia Press, 1995), 9. For important background to Crummell's life and work, see George U. Rigsby, *Alexander Crummell: Pioneer in Nineteenth-Century Pan-African Thought* (New York: Greenwood Press, 1987), and Wilson Jeremiah Moses, *Alexander Crummell: A Study of Civilization and Discontent* (New York and Oxford: Oxford University Press, 1989).

14. Quoted in Oldfield, *Civilization and Progress*, 12.

15. This seems to be the position taken by Moses in his magnificent biography of Crummell cited in note 13.

16. See Henry Louis Gates Jr.'s introduction to his *"Race," Writing and Difference* (Chicago: University of Chicago Press, 1986); and Anthony Kwame Appiah's discussion of Crummell in *In My Father's House: Africa in the Philosophy of Culture* (New York and Oxford: Oxford University Press, 1992), 3–27.

17. See Taylor, *Sources of the Self*, 397.

18. Alexander Crummell, "The English Language in Liberia," in *The Future of Africa, Being Addresses, Sermons, Etc., Etc., Delivered in the Republic of Liberia* (New York: Negro University Press, [1862] 1969), 10.

19. See Appiah, *In My Father's House*, 5–6.

20. Catherine Hall, "Domestic Harmony, Public Virtue," in *The Making of Britain: The Age of Revolution*, ed. Lesley M. Smith (London: Macmillan, 1987), 78. For the role of women in the moral and political economy of Victorianism, see also Hall's "Private Persons versus Public Someones: Class, Gender and Politics in England, 1780–1850," in *Language, Gender and Childhood*, ed. Carolyn Steedman, Cathy Urwin, and Valerie Walkerdine (London: Routledge and Kegan Paul, 1985), 10–33.

21. For an excellent theoretical discussion of these questions, see Étienne Balibar's "Racism and Nationalism," in Étienne Balibar and Immanuel Wallerstein, *Race, Nation, Class: Ambiguous Identities* (London: Verso, 1991), 37–68.

22. See Appiah, *In My Father's House*, 3–27.

23. See Alexander Crummell, "Civilization as the Primal Need of the Race," in Oldfield, *Civilization and Progress*, 196.

24. For this aspect of mainstream Victorianism, see Houghton, *The Victorian Frame of Mind*, 1–4; and Newsome, *The Victorian World Picture*, 1–6.

25. Crummell's celebration of commerce as a moralizing force is in stark contrast to Arnold's famous separation of commerce from culture in *Culture and Anarchy* and his claim that the latter was a "salutary friend . . . bent on seeing things

as they are" (Thomas Arnold, "Sweetness and Light," in *Prose of the Victorian Period*, ed. William E. Buckler [Boston: Houghton Mifflin, 1958], 463).

26. Graham Greene, *Journey without Maps* (London: Penguin Books, [1936] 1961), 37–38.

27. David Atwell, "The Transculturation of English: The Exemplary Case of the Rev. Tiyo Soga, African Nationalist," in *Occasional Papers in English Studies: No. 1* (Pietermaritzburg: University of Natal, 1994), 1.

Hacking the Nineteenth Century

Jay Clayton

Midway through William Gibson and Bruce Sterling's *The Difference Engine* (1991), a historical science fiction set in mid-nineteenth-century England, an automaton startles the protagonist Edward Mallory by whirring to life in the parlor of a foreign-service operative. The figure is a carved Japanese doll, fashioned entirely of bamboo, horsehair, and whalebone. It is lifelike enough to be mistaken for a kneeling lady, although stereotypes of the submissive Asian woman contribute to the deception. The urbane secret agent appears at ease with such marvels, so Mallory, who is jealous of his reputation as a scientist, recovers his composure with a show of expertise: he places the automaton in the context of other mechanical figures, comparing it to "one of those Jacquet-Droz toys, or Vaucanson's famous duck" and observing that it moves with the precision of a "Maudsley lathe."[1] The habit of associating windup figures and clockwork dolls with the latest precision engineering from the workshops of Henry Maudsley and his successors is an accurate reflection of early nineteenth-century scientific culture. The automata of Jacquet-Droz and Vaucanson were only the most famous predecessors of countless mechanical toys that were displayed side by side with inventions such as Maudsley's lathe, Marc Brunel's block-making machinery, David Brewster's stereoscope, Charles Wheatstone's telegraph, Michael Faraday's electromagnetic apparatuses, and Charles Babbage's calculating machine, the Difference Engine.[2]

Most of these scientific men were themselves fascinated by automata.

Wheatstone wrote a paper on machines for generating artificial speech, which begins with the history of automata and discusses the notorious hoax of Wolfgang von Kempelen, whose "mechanical" chess player concealed a midget in its base.[3] Babbage delighted in inviting guests to see his own automaton, a twelve-inch figurine he named the Silver Lady, which "attitudinized in a most fascinating manner."[4] Brunel, Brewster, Wheatstone, and Faraday—as well as Ada Lovelace and Charles Dickens—all attended evenings at Babbage's house in which the Silver Lady was the featured entertainment and traps were sometimes laid for the unwary.

Games and tricks played a more prominent role in early nineteenth-century science than many realize. Lifelike mechanical figures were only one end of a continuum of scientific stunts and public shows that ranged from Wheatstone's display of an "Enchanted Lyre" and the transatlantic race of Brunel's Great Western, to more disreputable schemes and criminal deceptions.[5] The illicit end of the continuum was visible in 1836, when two bankers from Paris were caught manipulating the semaphore telegraph in order to send advanced information about shifts in the stock market to a confederate in Bordeaux.[6] This episode is an early instance of what is today called "hacking," the diversion of communications resources for sport or profit. Hacking, however, has many connotations, some extending well beyond the communications world to include "any scam or clever manipulation," any bravura display of technological expertise.[7] The practice of hacking has generated its own subculture, full of flamboyant personalities, trickery, rivalries, and factions. With this cultural parallel in mind, it is easy to see many nineteenth-century technological marvels as imbued with the spirit of hacking, particularly those that involve computers, artificial intelligence, or communications. The mechanical devices of the previous century troubled the human/machine interface, just as do today's electronic devices. The greater the potential for unsettling this boundary, as in automata displays, the more open the field for "hackers," broadly conceived. Gibson and Sterling's *The Difference Engine* provides a clue: this novel not only hacks into nineteenth-century history but also extrapolates from that era's fondness for scientific tricks of all kinds. In a culture that did not make a rigorous distinction between showmanship and science—that was only beginning to develop the institutions that validate serious research today—rogue pleasures played a role in the advancement of knowledge.

Babbage's automaton was one such rogue pleasure. As a child, Babbage had been fascinated by an exhibition of machinery in Hanover Square. When the exhibitor entices the young boy up to the attic to view "still more wonderful automata" (Babbage, 12), the scene takes on a hint of illicit eroticism, which frequently seems to creep into accounts of mechanical figures, from E. T. A. Hoffmann's "The Automaton" (1814) and "The Sandman" (1815) to Ray Bradbury's *Something Wicked This Way Comes* (1962) and Thomas Pynchon's *Mason & Dixon* (1997). In the attic the boy sees two naked "female figures of silver," whose "eyes were full of imagination, and irresistible" (ibid.). In Babbage's hands, the boyhood story swerves away from any hint of corruption and becomes a portent of his future scientific curiosity. But years later, in 1834, he chances upon the attitudinizing lady at an auction, and the excitement returns. He purchases the figure, repairs all the mechanisms with his own hands, and recruits female friends to design clothing and coiffure. The whiff of eroticism returns too, now blended with Orientalist attractions: Babbage dresses the Silver Lady in a turban, pink satin slippers with silver spangles, and a tightly wound robe of Chinese crepe. This exotic outfit provokes animated discussion among his friends and leads Babbage to make a sexual double entendre at the expense of a lady who thinks the figure too slightly clad.

In a final scene involving his automaton, Babbage contrasts a gay circle of English friends delighting over the graceful movements of the Silver Lady with two serious foreigners, studying the operation of the Difference Engine, which was on display in an adjacent room of his house. Babbage takes a grim satisfaction in this contrast as a parable of how the English neglect his great invention while foreigners appreciate its significance. Willy-nilly, the two mechanisms have become a test for unwary visitors, another common side effect of automata exhibitions. The result of this memorable evening is an ironic inversion that partakes of what Freud called the *unheimlich,* the uncanny sensation aroused when something foreign or strange changes places with something familiar and domestic. The irony lies in the fact that only foreigners recognize the importance of what is supposed to be the special province of the English—science, engineering, steam-driven machines—while "three or four of [Babbage's] most intimate friends," in the drawing room of his home, are captivated by pleasures that are not only exotically Orientalist but vaguely sexual to boot (320).

Dickens may have been thinking specifically of his friend Babbage when he satirized a scientific proposal for constructing "automaton figures" in the third of the "Mudfog Papers" he composed for *Bentley's Miscellany*.[8] Scholars agree that the reports on the "Mudfog Association for the Advancement of Everything" are parodies of the scientific society Babbage was instrumental in founding, the British Association for the Advancement of Science.[9] The proposal for constructing automata occurs in a section of the report titled "Display of Models and Mechanical Science," one of Babbage's areas of greatest expertise. Dickens irreverently suggests using the mechanical figures to establish an "automaton police" for the convenience of carousing young noblemen who liked to knock the block off of the occasional constable.[10] Dickens seems to find something grotesque in the very idea of automata. His satire dwells on the perverse fascination of the prosthetic, nicely rendered in George Cruikshank's illustration "Automaton Police Office," which emphasizes detachable limbs and heads. His satire also establishes a link between the mania for Mechanical Science and the concurrent effort to reorganize the production of knowledge along "scientific" lines. Both are artificial aids, prosthetic devices, that transform the human world in valuable, if sometimes coercive, ways. No surprise, then, that the first use Dickens imagines for such automata is the establishment of new forms of police.

The trick involving the Japanese doll in Gibson and Sterling's *The Difference Engine* captures the spirit of both Babbage's evening gatherings and Dickens's "automaton police." There is no reason to think that the novelists are alluding specifically to either source, but Mallory's encounter with Japanese ingenuity fuses the contrasting attitudes found in Babbage and Dickens. The sexual undercurrent, the sense of uncanniness, the Orientalism—explicit in Mallory's patronizing talk of English engineering and empire—even the link with new forms of police, pick up on motifs prominent in the two nineteenth-century accounts. The novel uses Japan rather than China as an emblem of the Oriental Other, an updating in line with the geopolitical priorities of the 1990s, but Japan did figure in Victorian culture, and playful anachronisms such as a reference to the post–World War II Japanese economic miracle seem appropriate to the novel's blend of social commentary and alternative history. One of the merits of *The Difference Engine* is that it tends to evoke such paradigmatic nineteenth-century scenes with skill.

Gibson and Sterling's exuberant hacking of nineteenth-century science finds a precedent in the era's own willingness to mix science and entertainment. Their novel reflects the spirit of an age when the boundary between science and the rest of culture was not so firmly established. The novel,

however, stops short of unsettling its own boundaries. In the decision to conform to the conventions of a science-fiction thriller, the authors limit the implications of their "hack." The novel ends up affirming the alliance between
technology and traditional Victorian assumptions about female sexuality, empire, and the police that its irreverence about other historical pieties would
seem to reject. The ideological confusion of the novel can be brought out by
comparisons with two other texts: an important nineteenth-century precursor, Benjamin Disraeli's *Sybil* (1845), and a play by Tom Stoppard, which
invokes many of the same nineteenth-century scientific ideas. Stoppard's
Arcadia (1993), a thoroughly postmodern production, extends the hacking
spirit to its own dramatic conventions. The result is a text that performs tricks
with contemporary as well as nineteenth-century assumptions about gender,
science, and literature.

What is the relationship between postmodernism and the nineteenth-
century culture of hacking? Do today's rogue intellectual pleasures spring
from the same impulses that motivated the transgressive shows in Babbage's
drawing room? If so, then perhaps hacking with history finds its rationale in
a history that often produced knowledge through hacking. This notion
would suggest a justification beyond those usually offered by contemporary
theorists—the loss of faith in scientific norms of objectivity, for example, or a
belief in the inherent fictiveness of all writing—for considering metafiction as
a mode of knowledge. Alternatively, should the tone of nineteenth-century
hacking give one pause? Does the uncanny eroticism, the alliance of engineering and empire, or the link to the police indicate possible areas of concern in contemporary styles of thought?

Gibson and Sterling's *The Difference Engine* starts with an intriguing idea: it
rewrites Benjamin Disraeli's *Sybil,* an industrial novel about the reconciliation of the classes, as a historical fantasy that traces the roots of today's information society back to Victorian England. The authors, best known as the
originators of cyberpunk fiction, take Babbage's invention of a computing
machine in 1822 as warrant for imagining the advent of the computer age a
century before its time. Their novel presents the Victorian era as a full-blown
information order, complete with massive databases on citizens, surveillance
apparatus, photo IDs, credit cards, rapid international data transmission via
telegraph, and scientific societies that serve as unofficial intelligence arms of
the military. Idiosyncratic as their historical conceit sounds, it participates in
a thriving subgenre of science fiction known as "steampunk," which in-

cludes Rudy Rucker's *The Hollow Earth* (1992), Neal Stephenson's *The Diamond Age* (1995), and George Foy's *The Shift* (1996).[11]

Gibson and Sterling's novel is fun—at least in places. It is amusing to read of John Keats, consumptive former medical student, as a pioneer of the silent cinema; of Reverend Wordsworth and Professor Coleridge, leaders of a successful pantisocratic community in America; of Lord Engels, the Manchester textile magnate; of Lord Byron, Prime Minister of England, and of his daughter, Lady Ada Byron, Queen of a loose confederacy of hackers, called "clackers," because of the sound made by the mechanical parts in their steam-driven computers. The variations on Disraeli's novel are clever as well. Sybil Gerard, the idealistic daughter of a Chartist agitator, does not marry her aristocratic suitor Charles Egremont but is seduced and abandoned by that ambitious politician; she becomes the lover of a minor character from Disraeli's novel, Mick Radley, who here is involved in international espionage and computer software theft. Events in Disraeli's novel, both large and small, are effectively transmogrified for the contemporary plot. The riot at Mowbray Castle in *Sybil,* for example, becomes a vast Luddite uprising in London in the later novel, and offhand references to horse racing in the first two chapters of Disraeli inspire a key episode at the races, this time of steam-powered gurneys. The latter incident provides Gibson and Sterling with a vivid way of introducing to the story Ada Byron's gambling and laudanum habits, which are based on historical sources.

The scientific developments in *The Difference Engine* are not so far-fetched as they might seem, either. All of the information technologies portrayed by Gibson and Sterling existed in some form or other during the reign of Queen Victoria. Babbage is credited by most historians of technology as having been the first person to conceive of a computer. In 1821, frustrated by the multitude of errors in standard mathematical tables of astronomical positions and tidal charts, which were laboriously calculated by hand, he exclaimed, "I wish to God these calculations had been executed by steam!" One year later, he had not only drawn detailed plans for a mechanical calculator, which he named the Difference Engine, but also constructed and exhibited a working model for a London show. The Royal Society awarded Babbage a gold medal for his efforts, and he embarked on a many-year project to build a full-scale version of his machine. The finished engine would have contained approximately twenty-five thousand moving parts, manufactured to such precision that the first task was inventing entirely new machine tools and lathes, a task undertaken by Joseph Clement, who had been trained in the workshop of Henry Maudsley. The project was supported by the Duke of Wellington and received generous but irregular funding from the government—perhaps qualifying as the first government research-and-development program—but it was plagued by numerous delays, including Babbage's commitment to other scientific endeavors and a protracted dispute between Babbage and Clement.[12] The technical difficulties of the engine were not insurmountable: for the bicentenary of Babbage's birth, engineers at the Science Museum in London successfully built a fully operational Difference Engine, using only tools and materials that were available in the 1830s.[13] By the time Babbage's project was abandoned in 1842, more than £17,000 of government funds and £20,000 of his own money had been expended. By contrast, the first steam locomotive was built in 1831 for less than £800. Babbage viewed the failure to complete the Difference Engine as the central tragedy of his life.

This failure did not prevent Babbage from designing an even more ambitious machine, the Analytical Engine, which is the true ancestor of today's computer. "If the Analytical Engine had been built," writes J. David Bolter, "it would indeed have been the first computer."[14] All the essential components of a digital computer were present in the 1833 design: punch cards for input of data, internal memory storage, a central processing unit (called, in Babbage's industrial-age vocabulary, the "mill"), and printed output. This second design is the one actually featured in Gibson and Sterling's novel, although they use the name of his earlier, more famous invention.

In the few years since its publication, *The Difference Engine* has garnered some remarkable praise from sources as diverse as Ridley Scott, director of *Blade Runner,* Stewart Brand, creator of *The Whole Earth Catalog,* and scholars writing in *Contemporary Litrature, ANQ,* and *Victorian Studies.* In this last journal, Herbert Sussman nicely illuminates the way in which the novel rewrites Disraeli's *Sybil* but strangely reads the book as an optimistic celebration of the coming of the personal computer, whose decentralizing impulse has the potential to disrupt the emerging panoptic disciplinary order of modernity.[15] This reading misses the way in which visual technologies of surveillance dominate the imagery, structure, and resolution of the narrative. For Brian McHale, *The Difference Engine's* value lies in its postmodernism: like other contemporary metafictions, it represents "a new way of writing historical fiction or, better, a *new way of 'doing' history in fiction.*"[16]

The effusive praise and serious critical attention that the novel has received largely gloss over the book's pervasive misogyny and its long middle section that glorifies the violent exploits of Mallory in what amounts to a conventional science-fiction shoot-'em-up.[17] The story follows the violent plot form of the technothriller, a genre that relegates women to sexual appendages of the hero or to threatened objects of technological stalkers and government conspiracies. The women in *The Difference Engine* play one or both roles, but do little else. Mallory recalls with a shudder "rutting" with a "rank" Cheyenne woman on his geological expedition to America (197); his encounter with a London prostitute emphasizes the "exquisite thrill of disgust" (237) and is full of demeaning references to the smells of her sweat, urine, and "cunt" (223). Elsewhere, the thought of contraceptive devices for women—nineteenth-century versions of the diaphragm and sponge—"made his gut lurch" because "Mallory could not avoid the dark imagining of coitus involving these queer objects" (303).

Sybil Gerard and Ada Byron, the only women with more extensive parts in the plot, occupy the other conventional role, that of threatened objects of stalkers and conspiracies. As in popular cinematic technothrillers such as *Terminator 2* (1991) or *The Net* (1995), Sybil's resourcefulness aids in her escape from the clutches of her pursuers; even so, her wheelchair-bound form is still under aerial surveillance, some fifty years later, by the cameras of the "trans-Channel airship *Lord Brunel*" (1). Ada Byron, despite her computer genius, depends on men throughout to rescue her from her excesses. Moreover, neither character escapes persistent sexual slurs: Sybil is a "fallen" woman and a "politician's tart" (228), while Ada Byron is characterized as "the greatest whore in all of London. . . . she fucks whoever she pleases, and none dare make a peep about what she does. She's had half the House of Lords, and they all tag at her skirts like little boys" (232). This revelation prompts another shudder of repulsion from Mallory: "He knew that Lady Ada had her gallants, but the thought that she let men have her, that there was shoving and spending, prick and cunt in the mathematical bed of the Queen of Engines. . . . Best not to think about it" (232; ellipsis in the original).

These episodes might be read as critiques of upper-class Victorian attitudes toward sex were they not also reminiscent of the treatment of women's sexuality in Gibson's *Neuromancer* (1984) and its cyberpunk sequels.[18] The historical record suggests that Ada Lovelace had several lovers, but the insistence on such imagery in relation to woman after woman seems excessive, a quality of the narrative voice more than an effort to characterize Mallory.

When sex is the subject, *The Difference Engine* loses all its knowing irony in relation to the prior century. Instead, it adopts uncritically some of the worst aspects of the futuristic action thriller. The congruence between this predominantly male genre and Victorian sexual norms reveals that, in regard to sexuality at least, this novel is appropriating rather than interrogating the past.

The more serious claim for the importance of *The Difference Engine* lies in its postmodern approach to history. Critics have rushed to assimilate this novel's ironic rewriting of the nineteenth century, often invoking the postmodern genre that Linda Hutcheon labels "historiographic metafiction."[19] Gibson and Sterling's fictional transformation of the past accords well with postmodern arguments about the constructed nature of all historical knowledge. For example, McHale's assertion that the novel represents a "new way of 'doing' history" implies the postmodern corollary that history itself is a form of fiction.

When assessing this novel's relation to history, however, its affinities with a second, indigenous strain of science fiction should not be overlooked. This popular tradition is sometimes called "alternative history" or "parallel worlds," and its most celebrated exemplar is Philip K. Dick's *The Man in the High Castle* (winner of the Hugo Award for 1962), which imagines what the United States would have been like had Germany and Japan won World War II. The tradition stretches further back, however, particularly when combined with the paradoxes of time travel. Perhaps the most influential of such tales is Murray Leinster's "Sidewise in Time" (1934), but other notable examples include Robert A. Heinlein's "By His Bootstraps" (1941) and "All You Zombies—" (1959), Ward Moore's *Bring the Jubilee* (1953), in which the South won the Civil War, Fritz Leiber's cold-war parable *The Big Time* (Hugo Award, 1958), Keith Laumer's *The Other Side of Time* (1965), Larry Niven's "All the Myriad Ways" (1968), Harry Harrison's *Tunnel through the Deeps* (1972), and, most recently, Michael Crichton's *Timeline* (1999).[20]

Attending to *The Difference Engine*'s roots in popular science fiction helps locate its historical assumptions more precisely. The notion of alternative history raises anachronism, in the literal sense of something out of its proper time, into a methodological principle. There is nothing wrong with such a procedure: it underwrites the intellectual paradoxes of parallel world fantasies, and it may be the vehicle for astute social commentary. It should be recognized, however, that anachronism is a fundamentally Romantic attitude toward history, as Jerome Christensen has demonstrated. Christensen argues that willful anachronism marks the revolutionary character of Romanticism as a social movement: "*committing* anachronism romantically exploits lack of accountability as unrecognized possibility."[21] Whether in the form of medievalism, nostalgia, prophecy, or apocalypse, English Romanticism explores the untimely as a visionary alternative to the existing world. Christensen emphasizes the political potential of this investment, calling anachronism a "politics of the future" (475). For both conservatives, such as Burke or the later Coleridge, and radicals such as Blake, Hazlitt, or Percy Shelley, the untimely did have a political edge. But escapism—Christensen's "lack of accountability"—has been the specter that haunts Romanticism's social projects even more than its literary visions. "Romantic" or "visionary" are epithets still used today to belittle ideas deemed noble but foolishly impracticable. The charge of escapism, of course, bedevils science fiction too: it is a criticism even the finest achievements of the genre have had trouble evading. For all its dangers, then, anachronism describes an approach to history common to both Romanticism and science fiction. Christensen might be discussing *The Difference Engine,* not the Romantic movement, when he concludes: "its historicity [is] the willful commission of anachronism after anachronism linked by bold analogy" (476).

Anachronism names the narrative consequences of hacking with history. To hack the nineteenth century in a literary work means altering the temporal order of events, deliberately creating anachronisms in a representational world. The problem of accountability raised by such hacking, however, needs to be assessed on two different levels: the mimetic and the proleptic. Parallel world science fiction invites scrutiny primarily in mimetic terms, despite the fact that the mimesis in such novels is of an alternative reality. No matter how wild the anachronisms, the mimetic success of a work in this genre is usually clear to the initiated—the SF fan—and with good reason. The conditions of *vraisemblance* are fairly strict. In keeping with the genre's emphasis on time travel, let me chart these mimetic conditions across four dimensions. Two of these dimensions concern the relationship of anachronism to what readers think they already know: the past and the present. To be interesting, anachronism must first establish a creative relationship with the received wisdom about a period. Variations, however ingenious, must have a logic or plausibility that stems from accepted features of the past. Second, anachronism should suggest intriguing perspectives on the contemporary world. Whether as cautionary fable, satire, or allegory, the anachronisms of alternative history implicitly comment on present conditions. The other two dimensions concern matters that may be largely unknown to the audience:

Third, alternative history often highlights obscure or suppressed historical actors—those on the losing side in wars, whether of ideas or of armies; women, minorities, the poor, the otherwise silenced; people considered mad in their day; the young, the old, the infirm; even animals and other nonhumans (consider the partnership between dogs and robots in Clifford D. Simak's *City* [1952], the dolphins and computers in Ted Mooney's *Easy Travel to Other Planets* [1981]). Fourth, there is the matter of internal consistency. Whatever its liberties with external events, an alternative world must appear credible according to its own terms.

Proleptic anachronisms raise a different set of concerns. Prolepsis comes from the Greek for "anticipation." In rhetoric it is a method for anticipating and thus answering a potential objection to one's argument. In everyday language, prolepsis is a form of hyperbole that anticipates a result before it has occurred, as when sportscasters proclaim after an apparently decisive play: "It's all over now but the cheering." In poetry, prolepsis is the use of an adjective to anticipate the result of a verb: "He fouls the sick air." None of these senses of prolepsis really raises the issue of *vraisemblance*. Instead, the emphasis on anticipation and answering, prediction and consequence, indicates an orientation toward the future, an action in the present designed to intervene at a later moment. Hence the problem of accountability for prolepsis is ethical and political—that of assessing the integrity of a desired outcome, not of producing a consistent mimesis. Prolepsis makes present a future state of affairs by hacking with time.

The charge of escapism only seems to arise when readers feel that mimetic consistency is the principal question at stake. By contrast, argument or agreement are the responses prolepsis tends to elicit. Failed prolepsis provokes ethical or political disagreement—often violent repudiation—but not the simple dismissal, the shrug of the shoulders, that accompanies escapism. Take, for example, Disraeli's *Sybil,* the book that serves as a departure point for *The Difference Engine.* Disraeli's novel has often been praised for its mimetic accuracy in depicting the "condition of England," a country divided into two nations, the rich and the poor. Critics, however, have just as often rejected its proleptic politics.[22] Disraeli first came to prominence in the 1840s as the advocate of a platform founded entirely on anachronism: the Young England movement. In *Sybil* Disraeli expounds his notion that the only way to revitalize the Conservative party is by returning to the principles that governed class relations in a (mythical) time when England was young. In the days of yore, the aristocracy of England were not tyrants but "the natural leaders of the People" (334). That day will come again, and soon, but only when England awakes from the delusive dreams of equality that have animated the past two hundred years of political debate and are fueling the Chartist movement of Disraeli's day. Hence Disraeli's anachronistic movement displaces a recent with a more distant past in order to conjure a desired future. Whig philosophy, he claims, masquerades as freedom, but it actually results in an "oligarchical system" (354), in which a coalition of newly rich industrialists and middle-class tradesmen dominate the country. True equality will come only when England restores the grandeur of its aristocracy. "The future principle of English politics will not be a levelling principle. . . . It will seek to ensure equality, not by levelling the Few but by elevating the Many" (ibid.). Disraeli's character Egremont claims to bask in the light of another time, a future that revives a vanished past: "You deem you are in darkness, and I see a dawn. The new generation of the aristocracy of England are not tyrants, not oppressors, Sybil, as you persist in believing. Their intelligence, better than that, their hearts are open to the responsibility of their position" (334).

The Difference Engine attempts to repudiate Disraeli's political vision, not least in its cynical account of class relations, summed up in the ugly way its version of Egremont treats Sybil. All the same, the novel's anachronistic politics presents difficulties too. One can learn much about the two novels by comparing the handling of the uprisings in the respective narratives. Disraeli is at pains to distinguish two kinds of subversive agents: *insurrectionaries,* such as the mob's drunken leader (mockingly called the Liberator after Daniel O'Connell), outside Chartist agitators, and the profiteer, Mick Radley; and *rioters,* who are members of the local community, driven to desperate means by penury and unendurable working conditions.[23] Disraeli's sympathies are with the latter, even though he thinks they are duped by their leaders, and he portrays their hardships with sociological accuracy as well as compassion. Gibson and Sterling's novel contains no equivalent group, no sympathetically portrayed workers or rioters motivated by unendurable injustice. The London uprising is led by a "Frenchified race-track dandy" (187), who has adopted the Luddite name of Captain Swing and fomented revolution as part of his personal plot to achieve world domination (a science-fiction convention that appears gratuitously during the climactic battle scene). His chief assistant is a vicious murderess, Florence Bartlett, whose "Medusa glare" (304) goads a deluded band of followers to ever more savage acts of violence.[24]

What is disturbing about this battle scene is the acquiescence to the rigid limits of an action genre. If the authors' unruly spirit had seemed to revive for postmodernism an early-nineteenth-century irreverence toward discursive boundaries, the embrace of technothriller conventions reestablishes the familiar modern subservience of values to science. Irony and rogue pleasures, witty tricks and traps for the unwary, are once again relegated to the domain of culture, and science reassumes its place as the partner of the modern technological state. Mallory and his allies crush the insurrectionaries with an awesome display of high-tech military might, including computer-guided artillery, automatic weaponry, and a prototype streamlined vehicle.[25] This triumphalist conclusion contradicts the novel's larger critique of society, in which state powers of surveillance increasingly invade all aspects of its citizens' lives. In a novel intent on hacking history, this celebration of technological warfare and secret police is disturbing. It is as if the hackers have become agents of the modern police.

The political message of this conclusion seems as anachronistic as any of the novel's technological marvels, but the politics points not to the future but to the past. If computer databases and streamlined cars come from our time, the political attitudes come straight from Babbage's drawing room. The novel's climax is a throwback to the days when English engineering and empire reigned supreme, when few challenged the marriage of technology and the police, and when masculine power and the erotics of vulnerable femininity were widely approved norms. The anachronism is mimetic of Victorian attitudes that the novel's postmodern stance would otherwise seem to have left behind. Its militaristic escapism makes a poor conclusion to the project of hacking the nineteenth century.

Do the partial failings of Gibson and Sterling's experiment, like those of Disraeli's, imply a more general inadequacy in anachronism as an approach to history? Not necessarily. Babbage's invention of the computer one hundred years before its time indicates the need for a conception of history that registers the untimely. Ways of responding to lost threads of the past, to forkings in history that seemed to have vanished with little trace, are crucial to the historical enterprise.

Ada Byron, only legitimate child of George Gordon Lord Byron, is a precocious woman of nineteen, full of aspirations for greatness in some field of science or mathematics (it hardly matters which), and protégée of Mary

Somerville, the most eminent female scientist of the day. One month before Ada Byron's marriage to William King, later Lord Lovelace, she receives an invitation to Babbage's house to view his Silver Lady. Babbage's flirtatious note dilates on the charms of his automaton, its turban and new dresses, but Ada Byron sees through the trap—Babbage's usual test for visitors—and saves her admiration for the Difference Engine in the next room. A friend records her reaction: "While other visitors gazed at the working of this beautiful instrument with the sort of expression, and I dare say the sort of feeling, that some savages are said to have shown on first seeing a looking-glass or hearing a gun . . . Miss Byron, young as she was, understood its working, and saw the great beauty of the invention."[26] The only automata this young woman cared about were mathematical; she dreamed of commanding regiments of numbers, "harmoniously disciplined troops;—consisting of vast numbers and marching in irresistible power to the sound of Music."[27]

Ada Lovelace, née Byron, is a more interesting figure than her portrayal in *The Difference Engine* would suggest. Her story graphically illustrates the many barriers women confronted in attempting to engage in scientific enterprises during the last century. Despite these barriers, she became a close associate of Babbage, Somerville, Wheatstone, Brewster, and Faraday, and she went on to write the most penetrating account of Babbage's Analytical Engine published during the nineteenth century. Fortunately, a raft of biographies and encomia have appeared in recent years (no less than four books, as well as shorter portraits in many studies of the computer revolution), which can counter the portrait drawn by Gibson and Sterling. Lovelace's reputation, however, is not of primary concern here.[28] What is more interesting in the current context is how one approaches figures whose "untimeliness" makes their very lives seem anachronisms.

Babbage's invention of the computer is an example of untimeliness that rarely fails to astound. Lovelace's life and writings present a more complex case. She has no original discovery to her credit, and recent claims that she wrote the first computer program depend on drawing an analogy between software code and her diagram of how the (unbuilt) Analytical Engine would go about calculating Bernoulli numbers. Yet there are elements of her story that seem oddly out of sync with her time. Daughter of Lord Byron and wife of the Earl of Lovelace, mathematically gifted and intensely ambitious, a bold and often fanciful writer, equally at home with renowned scientists and with literary figures such as Dickens, Harriet Martineau, and Anna

Jameson, wealthy yet embarrassed by gambling debts, talented musically, sexually independent, often hostile toward the duties of motherhood—her life crosses boundaries, confounds roles, mixes genres, fields, and interests in ways that seem almost postmodern in their gender-bending and anticipation of today's technoculture. Yet she was not a feminist in any modern sense of the term, not a bluestocking, not a crusader for philanthropic causes, not a sectarian, not an ideologue of any recognizable sort. She simply does not fit any of the customary categories—either of her age or of our own. If she contradicts the usual image of an upper-class Victorian woman, she equally fails to conform to the few roles we have imagined for women who were "ahead of their time."

History of science has no useful vocabulary for discussing untimely figures such as Babbage and Lovelace. They are not "pioneers" of the computer age (as has sometimes been claimed) because their contributions were forgotten or ignored, playing virtually no role in the (re)invention of the computer in the 1940s. The first digital computers strikingly resemble Babbage's sketches and Lovelace's account of the Analytical Engine, but twentieth-century researchers derived none of their ideas from this long-forgotten machine.[29] The Romantic vocabulary of "unrecognized genius" or "visionary" does not fit for the opposite reason. Babbage received enormous recognition in his own time, and Lovelace, too, successfully published in a scholarly journal and was accepted by her scientific peers. Melodramatic phrases such as "inspired madman," "idiot savant," or "born too early" are still less applicable. The only words that seem appropriate come not from history but from literary discourse. Babbage and Lovelace can be said to "foreshadow" or "anticipate" later scientific developments, even if their works had no causal role to play in the eventual discoveries, only if these words retain their figurative status. As pure prolepsis, such words capture the way Babbage and Lovelace realized a desired future in the past until the literal present of their time reasserted its dominance. Historians, of course, use words such as *foreshadow* and *anticipate* all the time. But they use them for local effect; they use them to underline the irony, pathos, or wonder of history. Unless a causal line can be traced, unless there is evidence of influence, anticipation is usually more of a curiosity than an object of serious inquiry.

The most intriguing attempt to deal with the untimely figure of Ada Lovelace comes not from computer historians (and certainly not from Gibson and Sterling) but from the playwright Tom Stoppard. In *Arcadia*

(1993) Stoppard draws extensively from the biography of Lovelace to fashion the character of Thomasina Coverly, a mathematically precocious girl of thirteen (sixteen at the conclusion of the play). The drama is set entirely in the drawing room of the Coverly estate, even though it juxtaposes events separated by more than 150 years. The first story, set in the early years of the nineteenth century, mixes a conventional Regency farce—involving the young poet Byron, adulterous trysts, a jealous husband, and two threatened duels—with poignant glimpses of Thomasina's brilliance and yearning. The second story, set in the present, might be called an academic farce; it concerns the descendants of the Coverly family, still in possession of their country house, and two rival scholars who have come to investigate the very events portrayed in the nineteenth-century scenes. The play raises many of the issues that have animated this discussion: it shows Thomasina discovering scientific concepts years ahead of their time and creates deliberate anachronisms onstage—a tortoise appears in both time periods, a character in 1809 eats an apple left on the table during the twentieth century, and a coffee mug and a laptop computer remain onstage during nineteenth-century scenes.[30]

Although the dates of the nineteenth-century events (1809 then 1812) correspond to the years when Ada Lovelace's mother, Lady Byron, was entertaining Lord Byron's marriage proposals, Thomasina's personality and her mathematical ideas clearly stem from Lovelace rather than her mother.[31] The correspondences with Lovelace are numerous. In the play Thomasina initiates a romantic affair with her tutor, Septimus Hodge, on the night before her seventeenth birthday; Ada Byron, as it happens, was caught in a romantic entanglement with her tutor around her seventeenth birthday.[32] Thomasina's governess bears the same name, Briggs, as the one Ada had during the period of her affair, and the girls share a talent for drawing and a love of waltzing, which both learn at sixteen. Thomasina is given to enthusiastic bursts of ambition, which echo passages in Lovelace's letters. When Thomasina says playfully to Septimus, "You will be famous for being my tutor when Lord Byron is dead and forgotten" (37), she repeats a boast of Lovelace, who wrote in a letter to Babbage: "I do not believe that my father was (or ever could have been) such a Poet as I shall be an Analyst" (Toole, 156–57). In another letter Lovelace muses about fame coming to her only after her death (ibid., 112), and Stoppard has one of his characters comment about Thomasina, "She was dead before she had time to be famous" (76).

The most significant parallels lie in the area of mathematics. Stoppard has his thirteen-year-old prodigy anticipate three important ideas: recursion, the second law of thermodynamics, and contemporary chaos theory, including fractal geometry.[33] In interviews, the playwright attests to having mined a number of recent popular science books, particularly James Gleick's *Chaos* (1987), and it is easy to track down the exact passages in Gleick and other contemporary works (notably Douglas R. Hofstadter's *Gödel, Escher, Bach* [1979] and Stephen Hawking's *A Brief History of Time* [1988]) from which Stoppard has adapted speeches. What has not been noticed, however, is that Stoppard's characters also repeatedly echo passages from Lovelace and Babbage in the course of explaining Thomasina's mathematical intuitions. Babbage's most famous line about his Analytical Engine concerns its ability to use the conclusion of one equation as the starting point of the next; his colorful description of this recursive operation is that the Analytical Engine "eats its own tail."[34] Thomasina uses much the same analogy when she tries to explain what an iterated algorithm is to her tutor: "It eats its own progeny" (77). In the twentieth-century scenes, Valentine Coverly is using his laptop computer to create an algorithm that would model the changes in the grouse population on the estate over the last one hundred years. His project, which depends on ideas only developed in recent decades when computer modeling made chaos theory conceivable, echoes Babbage too: "This thing works for any phenomenon which eats its own numbers . . . it's a natural phenomenon in itself. Spooky" (45–46).

Valentine's comment about recursion being a spooky natural phenomenon gestures toward the mathematics of cellular automata, prominent in contemporary artificial intelligence research (AI), in which recursive routines take on a life of their own. Lovelace's image of numbers as living entities— disciplined troops—certainly should not be taken as anticipating the idea of cellular automata, but it makes one wonder what mathematical vistas might have been opened by a functioning Analytical Engine. Without such a machine, calculating iterated algorithms was virtually insane, as Valentine explains to the responsible historian in the play, Hannah Jarvis:

HANNAH: Why? Because they didn't have calculators?

VALENTINE: No. Yes. Because there's an order things can't happen in. You can't open a door till there's a house.

HANNAH: I thought that's what genius was.

VALENTINE: Only for lunatics and poets. (79)

Even though Lovelace never had a computer, she did have the idea of the computer, and the idea was enough to prompt her to speculate about AI. In the "Notes" she published on the Analytical Engine she suggests that Babbage's invention opens up for the first time "the idea of a thinking or of a reasoning machine."[35] Its power would enable a mathematics that "*weaves algebraical patterns* just as the Jacquard-loom weaves flowers and leaves" (273; emphasis in the original). A leaf, it turns out, is the pattern Thomasina chooses to weave with her first iterated algorithm. "I will plot this leaf and deduce its equation," Thomasina tells her uncomprehending tutor (37). It will take Valentine, the twentieth-century chaos researcher, to explain what Thomasina (and Lovelace?) could have meant:

> If you knew the algorithm and fed it back say ten thousand times, each time there'd be a dot somewhere on the screen. You'd never know where to expect the next dot. But gradually you'd start to see this shape, because every dot will be inside the shape of this leaf. It wouldn't *be* a leaf, it would be a mathematical object. But yes. The unpredictable and the predetermined unfold together to make everything the way it is. It's how nature creates itself, on every scale, the snowflake and the snowstorm. (47)

Thomasina, like Lovelace, chooses a leaf because she is in the habit of seeing numbers as revealing the secrets of nature itself. In a parody of Fermat's Last Theorem, Thomasina writes in the margin of her mathematics primer: "I, Thomasina Coverly, have found a truly wonderful method whereby all the forms of nature must give up their numerical secrets and draw themselves through number alone. This margin being too mean for my purpose, the reader must look elsewhere for the New Geometry of Irregular Forms discovered by Thomasina Coverly" (43). Her faith that "nature is written in numbers" (37) echoes Lovelace's frequent assertion in her letters that numbers reveal the "hidden realities of nature" (Toole, 101), as well as her published declaration that mathematics alone "can adequately express the great facts of the natural world" (Lovelace, 272).

Stoppard's use of historical material about Lovelace occurs in a play that insistently raises questions of history and temporality. The play mocks the jealousy, pretension, and unscrupulous careerism of a historian who is shown misconstruing the very nineteenth-century scenes the audience witnesses, but it also emphasizes the pitfalls that await even the most empirical of researchers. False leads, misleading survivals, and lost evidence make the full recovery of these events impossible. What the play offers in place of an unbroken linear history is a fluid nonlinear vision of time. This segue from the topic of history to that of temporality is characteristic of literary approaches to the anachronistic; it is a formal constituent of most parallel world fictions, including *The Difference Engine,* which signals as much by naming its five major sections "Iterations." Stoppard signals his interest in temporality by numerous small touches such as the stage directions about anachronistic props, speeches about the nature of time (5, 50, 79), characters from different eras who "iterate" one another word for word, and a tortoise that evokes Zeno's paradox.[36] The most dramatic evidence of this interest, however, comes in the final scene, where the characters from the two different periods appear together. Here the farcical maneuvering over historical method is subsumed in scientific musings about synchronicity and the circularity of time.

As the play nears its end, Thomasina's tutor and the present-day chaos researcher bend over the same drawing, a diagram by Thomasina illustrating the second law of thermodynamics. The stage directions read: "Septimus *and* Valentine *study the diagram doubled by time*" (93). Voices double one another too, weaving a pattern of nineteenth- and twentieth-century dialogue that resonates equally well in either time. The meaning of the diagram is slowly dawning on Septimus and Valentine, but Thomasina thinks only of learning to waltz. It is the night before her seventeenth birthday, and the audience knows she is to die in a fire before morning. The adults in each century speak to one another of entropy, the slow movement of history toward an inevitable end. But Thomasina speaks of dancing and love. She is in a rush and cannot wait on history when she is consumed by such timeless urges.

HANNAH: What did [Thomasina] see?

VALENTINE: That you can't run the film backwards. Heat was the first thing that didn't work that way . . . with heat—friction—a ball breaking a window . . . it won't work backwards.

HANNAH: Who thought it did?

VALENTINE: She saw why. You can put back the bits of glass but you can't collect up the heat of the smash. It's gone.

SEPTIMUS: So the Improved Newtonian Universe must cease and grow cold. Dear me.

VALENTINE: The heat goes into the mix.

(He gestures to indicate the air in the room, in the universe.)

THOMASINA: Yes, we must hurry if we are going to dance.

VALENTINE: And everything is mixing the same way, all the time, irreversibly . . .

SEPTIMUS: Oh, we have time, I think.

VALENTINE: . . . till there's no time left. That's what time means.

SEPTIMUS: When we have found all the mysteries and lost all the meaning, we will be alone, on an empty shore.

THOMASINA: Then we will dance. Is this a waltz?

SEPTIMUS: It will serve. (93–94)

In traditional history, as in entropy, time means one thing, but in art, as in love, it means another. The arrow points only one way, Valentine would maintain, but *Arcadia* as a whole suggests otherwise. Events repeat themselves, even individual words return through time. Discoveries are made, lost, made again, and their real meaning lies in the process of discovery. "It's wanting to know that makes us matter," Hannah declares (75). This conclusion may be the only response consonant with a genuine interest in anachronism. The true historical oddity of untimely figures—of Thomasina/ Lovelace, of Babbage—is obscured if the only question becomes whether or not they led to something in the future.[37] No matter what answer one chooses, the question itself implies a seamless, linear conception of history in which anything that is not demonstrably tied to a later moment is eccentric, trivial, or freakish. Stoppard, by contrast, knows that a loose historical thread may have much to teach *because* of its being unwoven into the fabric of history, *because* of how forlornly its frayed end sticks out from the pattern. Arguing exclusively in terms of influence and development eliminates the possibility of messiness, nonlinear phenomena, incoherence, stubborn unreadability. It eliminates the rogue intellectual pleasures provided by a culture that blends science, literature, and hacking.

The form of the play conveys the same message. Through its elaborate self-reflexivity, the play strives to function as the literary equivalent of an iterated algorithm.[38] It eats its own tail, in Babbage's phrase. This recursive structure implicitly comments on the limitations of any conceptual framework, especially that of traditional history. But this self-reflexive structure also comments on the anachronism of a nineteenth-century woman who sees things before their time. Formal recursiveness is a way of making anachronism accountable, of transforming anachronism into a kind of knowledge, the knowledge of what a young woman's life might mean. This is the kind of knowledge that *Arcadia* offers in place of historical certainty. This is what recursive forms—literary works, alternative history, cultural studies—can reveal about untimely lives. It will serve.

Notes

I would like to thank Alison Booth, Christy Burns, Jerome Christensen, and Dianne F. Sadoff for their comments on an early draft of this chapter; Robert O'Malley, professor of applied mathematics at the University of Washington, for sending me his review of *Arcadia* and the account of Stoppard's appearance at the Mathematical Sciences Research Institute in Berkeley; Joseph Bizup for letting me read his unpublished manuscript on Babbage's aesthetic of machinery; and the John Simon Guggenheim Memorial Foundation for a fellowship, which supported part of the research for this chapter.

1. William Gibson and Bruce Sterling, *The Difference Engine* (New York: Bantam Books, 1991), 168. The authors spell "Jacquet" with an "o" and "Maudsley" with an "e," which may be errors, but the novel consistently rings changes on the lives of real nineteenth-century writers, politicians, and scientists.

2. For the origin of automata in mechanical clock making, see Otto Mayr's study *Authority, Liberty, and Automatic Machinery in Early Modern Europe* (Baltimore: Johns Hopkins University Press, 1986), 21. Accounts of the elder Jacquet-Droz's writing-boy and the younger Jacquet-Droz's pianoforte player, as well as Vaucanson's duck and his equally famous flute player, may be found in Anson Rabinbach, *The Human Motor: Energy, Fatigue, and the Origins of Modernity* (New York: Basic Books, 1990), 51–52, 57. Jean-Claude Beaune's "The Classical Age of Automata: An Impressionistic Survey from the Sixteenth to the Nineteenth Century" contains an illuminating typology of automata (433–34) in what otherwise is indeed an "impressionistic" survey (in *Fragments for a History of the Human Body*, part 1, ed. Michel Feher, trans. Ian Patterson [New York: Zone Books, 1989, 431–80]). For a mid-nineteenth-century scientific account of these machines, see Hermann von Helmholtz, "On the Interaction of the Natural Forces," in *Science and Culture: Popular and Philosophical Essays,* ed. David Cahan, trans. John Tyndall (1854; Chicago: University of Chicago Press, 1995), 18–45.

3. See Charles Wheatstone, "Review [of Reed Organ-Pipes, Speaking Machines, Etc.], On the Various Attempts Which Have Been Made to Imitate Human Speech," in *The Scientific Papers of Sir Charles Wheatstone* (London: Physical Society of London, 1879), 348–67.

4. Charles Babbage, *Passages from the Life of a Philosopher,* ed. Martin Campbell-Kelly (1864; New Brunswick, N.J.: Rutgers University Press, 1994), 12; see also 319–20.

5. Wheatstone began his scientific career with an innocent deception he called the "Enchanted Lyre," in which an instrument was hung from the ceiling by a thin cord and was made to play musical pieces without any apparent human intervention. This show turned out to be a serious demonstration of the ability of sound waves to travel more rapidly through solids than air, for the lyre was connected to the sounding board of a piano in a room above, and the sound was propagated down through the wire. For more on Wheatstone's research into sound and its relation to his invention of the telegraph, see Jay Clayton, "The Voice in the Machine: Hazlitt, Hardy, James," in *Language Machines: Technologies of Literary and Cultural Production,* ed. Jeffrey Masten, Peter Stallybrass, and Nancy J. Vickers (New York: Routledge, 1997), 209–32.

6. The bankers introduced a secret code of their own into the signals of the telegraph by means of a preplanned pattern of errors. This story is recounted in Gerard J. Holzmann and Björn Pehrson, *The Early History of Data Networks* (Los Alamitos, Calif.: IEEE Computer Society Press, 1995), 75–76.

7. See Tom Forester and Perry Morrison, *Computer Ethics: Cautionary Tales and Ethical Dilemmas in Computing,* 2d ed. (Cambridge: MIT Press, 1994), 77. The chapter titled "Hacking and Viruses" supplies an account of the "wide range of meanings" (77) that accrue to this term.

8. Charles Dickens, "Full Report of the Second Meeting of the Mudfog Association for the Advancement of Everything," in *Sketches by Boz Illustrative of Every-Day Life and Every-Day People* (London: Oxford University Press, 1957), 660.

9. See Anthony Hyman, *Charles Babbage: Pioneer of the Computer* (Princeton, N.J.: Princeton University Press, 1982), 152–54, for the many references to Babbage and the British Association for the Advancement of Science in Dickens's "Mudfog Papers." Hyman (193–95) also detects allusions to Babbage in the scientific reports of the Pickwick Club in *The Pickwick Papers* (1836–37) and in the portrait of Daniel Doyce in *Little Dorrit* (1855–57). Babbage was a tireless advocate for the creation of scientific societies. He was a founding member not only of the British Association but also of the Analytical Society, the Astronomical Society, the Cambridge Philosophical Society, the London Statistical Society, and more. For a discussion of Dickens's satire of the British Association for the Advancement of Science, see G. A. Chaudhry, "The Mudfog Papers," *The Dickensian* 70 (1974): 104–12.

10. Dickens, "Full Report of the Second Meeting of the Mudfog Association," 661.

11. Steffen Hantke defines the genre of steampunk, relates it to postmodern historiographic metafiction, and lists numerous other examples in "Difference Engines and Other Infernal Devices: History according to Steampunk," *Extrapolation* 40 (1999): 244–54.

12. A sophisticated analysis of Babbage's quarrel with Clement and its implications for modern reconceptualizations of labor appears in Simon Schaffer, "Babbage's

Intelligence: Calculating Engines and the Factory System," *Critical Inquiry* 21 (1994): 203–27.

13. The story of this contemporary undertaking may be found in Doron D. Swade, "Redeeming Charles Babbage's Mechanical Computer," *Scientific American* 268.2 (February 1993): 86–91. Other modern sources on Babbage's engines are Hyman, *Charles Babbage*; Velma R. Huskey and Harry D. Huskey, "Lady Lovelace and Charles Babbage," *Annals of the History of Computing* 2 (1980): 229–329; Allan G. Bromley, "Difference Engines and Analytical Engines," in *Computing before Computers,* ed. William F. Aspray (Ames: Iowa State University Press, 1990); and Bruce Collier, *The Little Engines That Could've: The Calculating Machines of Charles Babbage* (Harvard University Dissertation, 1970; rpt. New York: Garland, 1990).

14. J. David Bolter, *Turing's Man: Western Civilization in the Computer Age* (Chapel Hill: University of North Carolina Press, 1984), 33.

15. Herbert Sussman, "Cyberpunk Meets Charles Babbage: *The Difference Engine* as Alternative Victorian History," *Victorian Studies* 38 (1994): 12.

16. Brian McHale, "Difference Engines," *ANQ* 5 (1992): 222; (emphasis in the original).

17. Sussman's article is an exception. He points out that "an orgasmic pleasure in violence affirms masculine bonds as the only refuge in an anarchic world" and that "*The Difference Engine* dwells at length on the macho derring-do of Mallory and his band of male-bonded heroes, in using the new military technologies to vanquish the 'Luddites'" (10).

18. A number of critics have leveled similar charges against cyberpunk fiction generally and Gibson's early work in particular. See Istvan Csicsery-Ronay, "Cyberpunk and Neuromanticism," *Mississippi Review* 47/48 (1988): 266–78; Andrew Ross, *Strange Weather: Culture, Science, and Technology in the Age of Limits* (London: Verso, 1991); Claire Sponsler, "Cyberpunk and the Dilemmas of Postmodern Narrative: The Example of William Gibson," *Contemporary Literature* 33 (1992): 625–44; and Sharon Stockton, "'The Self Regained': Cyberpunk's Retreat to the Imperium," *Contemporary Literature* 36 (1995): 588–612. Tyler Stevens extends the critique of sexual attitudes in cyberpunk to include homophobia; see "'Sinister Fruitiness': *Neuromancer,* Internet Sexuality, and the Turing Test," *Studies in the Novel* 28 (1996): 414–33.

19. See Linda Hutcheon, *A Poetics of Postmodernism: History, Theory, Fiction* (New York: Routledge, 1988). In addition to McHale, "Difference Engines," see Nicholas Spencer, "Rethinking Ambivalence: Technopolitics and the Luddites in William Gibson and Bruce Sterling's *The Difference Engine,*" *Contemporary Literature* 40 (1999): 403–29, and Takayuki Tatsumi, "Comparative Metafiction: Somewhere between Ideology and Rhetoric," *Critique* 39 (1997): 2–17. This last article also discusses Gibson and Sterling's Orientalism.

20. Harrison's novel features as characters both Babbage and Isambard Brunel, the engineer who completed the first tunnel beneath the Thames in 1843.

21. Jerome Christensen, "The Romantic Movement at the End of History," *Critical Inquiry* 29 (1994): 455.

22. Thom Braun, a recent editor of the novel, charitably terms Disraeli's political interpretation of history "idiosyncratic." See "Appendix: Disraeli's View of History," in *Sybil; or, The Two Nations,* ed. Thom Braun (London: Penguin Books, 1980), 499.

23. Christensen notes the tendency during the earlier Romantic period to make the same kind of distinction between these two categories of social rebels (469–71).

24. For a different reading of Gibson and Sterling's portrayal of the Luddites, see Spencer, "Rethinking Ambivalence." Spencer argues that the novelists propose a "Luddite utopianism," which "is the primary revolutionary act that exposes all other political viewpoints as simulations" (416).

25. Sussman has a good analysis of this aspect of the novel (10–11).

26. Sophia Frend de Morgan, *Memoirs of Augustus de Morgan* (London, 1882), 89.

27. Ada Lovelace, letter to Lady Byron, 29 October 1851, in *Ada: The Enchantress of Numbers: Prophet of the Computer Age,* ed. Betty Alexandra Toole (Mills Valley, Calif.: Strawberry Press, 1998), 292.

28. There is a problem in deciding how to refer to a figure with as many names as Ada Augusta King, née Byron, Countess of Lovelace. Traditional usage would dictate "Lady Lovelace," which seems rather stiff. The great majority of biographers and critics have chosen to call her "Ada," a habit that seems as unacceptable as the old practice of calling Austen "Jane." I have chosen to use the name "Lovelace," on the model of the way people commonly denominate a lord by his title: hence, William King, Lord Lovelace is usually referred to as "Lovelace" and George Gordon, Lord Byron as "Byron."

29. N. Metropolis and J. Worlton ("A Trilogy on Errors in the History of Computing," *Annals of the History of Computing* 2 [1980]: 49–59) have determined that only two of the inventors of the modern computer—Vannevar Bush and Howard Aiken—had any awareness of Charles Babbage's work and that this awareness did not influence their research. The best assessment of this question in regard to Aiken is by the historian of science I. Bernard Cohen, who concludes that while Aiken's admiration for Babbage was great, his actual knowledge of the Analytical Engine was superficial. Cohen writes: "Aiken's first machine (the Mark I/ASCC) suffered a severe limitation which might have been avoided if Aiken had actually known Babbage's work more thoroughly" (I. Bernard Cohen, "Babbage and Aiken," *Annals of the History of Computing* 10 [1988]: 172).

30. See the stage directions in Tom Stoppard, *Arcadia* (London: Faber and Faber, 1993), 15, 35, 43, and 53.

31. Anne Barton first mentioned Ada Lovelace as a possible source for the character of Thomasina in "Twice around the Grounds: *Arcadia,*" *New York Review of Books* 42.10 (8 June 1995): 28–31. Robert E. O'Malley Jr. mentions this possibility again and gives a brief account of Lovelace's career in "*Arcadia*: Algorithms and Echoes of Ada," *SIAM (Society for Industrial and Applied Mathematics) News* 28.3 (1995): 7–8. In a roundtable discussion at the Mathematical Sciences Research Institute in Berkeley, Stoppard denied that he had Lovelace in mind when he conceived Thomasina, but he has often told interviewers that he read biographies of Byron

while preparing to write the play (Gail Corbett, "Math Program Plays to Packed House" *SIAM [Society for Industrial and Applied Mathematics] News* 32.3 [1999]:1). In view of the many parallels between the two figures detailed below, it seems reasonable to conclude that Stoppard absorbed information about Lovelace's life from Byron biographies, which subsequently came in handy when writing about a mathematically precocious young woman in the nineteenth century.

32. See Toole, 32–33, and Doris Langley Moore, *Ada Countess of Lovelace: Byron's Legitimate Daughter* (London: John Murray, 1977), 52.

33. Brief explanations of the play's use of the second law of thermodynamics and chaos theory may be found in Prapassaree and Jeffrey Kramer, "Stoppard's *Arcadia*: Research, Time Loss," *Modern Drama* 40 (1977): 1–10; of chaos theory and Fermat's last theorem in David Guaspari, "Stoppard's *Arcadia*," *Antioch Review* 54 (1996): 222–39. The most thorough treatment of chaos theory in the play occurs in William W. Demastes, *Theatre of Chaos: Beyond Absurdism, into Orderly Disorder* (Cambridge: Cambridge University Press, 1998), 85–103.

34. See Hyman, *Charles Babbage,* 164. Babbage's image is quoted in a multitude of popular science books on computing, chaos theory, and mathematics. For example, see Douglas R. Hofstadter (*Gödel, Escher, Bach: An Eternal Golden Braid* [New York: Basic Books, 1979], 25), who credits Babbage with understanding the concept of Strange Loops and relates this idea to Babbage's interest in mechanical automata and Lovelace's interest in artificial intelligence (AI).

35. Ada Lovelace, "Notes by the Translator," in L. F. Menabrea, "Sketch of the Analytical Engine Invented by Charles Babbage," *Scientific Memoirs* 3 (1843): 666–731; rpt. in *Science and Reform: Selected Works of Charles Babbage,* ed. Anthony Hyman (Cambridge: Cambridge University Press, 1989), 273.

36. Michele Valerie Ronnick examines Zeno's paradox, as well as other Arcadian themes, in "Tom Stoppard's *Arcadia*: Hermes' Tortoise and Apollo's Lyre," *Classical and Modern Literature* 16 (1996): 177–82. Douglas Hofstadter's *Gödel, Escher, Bach* contains chapters of imaginary dialogue in which Zeno, the Tortoise, and Achilles are frequent participants. For more on the Arcadian elements in Stoppard's play, see Peter W. Graham, "Et in *Arcadia* Nos," *Nineteeth-Century Contexts* 18 (1995): 311–19 .

37. A controversy rages at present about whether Lovelace is an unjustly neglected pioneer of the computer or, in Bruce Collier's words, "the most overrated figure in the history of computing" ("Preface to the Garland Edition," in *The Little Engines That Could've* (n.p.). The most thorough of the debunkers is Dorothy Stein, *Ada: A Life and a Legacy* (Cambridge: MIT Press, 1985). The most passionate of the defenders are Betty Alexandra Toole, *Ada,* Joan Baum, *The Calculating Passion of Ada Byron* (Hamden, Conn.: Archon Books, 1986), and Sadie Plant, *Zeros and Ones: Digital Women and the New Technoculture* (London: Fourth Estate, 1997).

38. Lucy Melbourne makes this point in "'Plotting the Apple of Knowledge': Tom Stoppard's *Arcadia* as Iterated Theatrical Algorithm," *Modern Drama* 41 (1998): 557–72.

Queen Victoria and Me

Laurie Langbauer

One thing feminist scholarship does, in literary studies as well as in the study of history, is recover the work and lives of women made invisible, women lost to time. However various, even at odds with itself, feminist criticism might be, that recovery—whether called gynocriticism or Anglo-American literary history—has remained an enduring element; the annals of feminism depend on it. "Show us the life of the average Elizabethan woman all but absent from history now!" Virginia Woolf exhorts the women scholars at Newnham and Girton in *A Room of One's Own*. Adrienne Rich, in *On Lies, Secrets, and Silence,* or Alice Walker, in *In Search of Our Mother's Gardens,* criticize *A Room of One's Own* soundly; they are troubled—they are dismayed—that Woolf could only define her audience as those women scholars, the elite and well-placed, the daughters of educated men. But, in spite of that, they share with Woolf the deep conviction that such "special women," as Rich calls them, calls us (literary scholars), have an obligation to make known to all women what Walker terms that "unknown thing": women themselves, women's art, overlooked and unrecognized as those things still remain.[1]

It is in this context that I want to consider the recent writing of a group of feminist scholars devoted to nineteenth-century Britain, engaged in bringing into view the literary and cultural significance of a key woman they see ignored or misrecognized: the excerpts from Margaret Homans's *Royal Representations: Queen Victoria and British Culture, 1837–1876* (1998) that appeared in journals in 1993 and 1994, Adrienne Munich's *Queen Victoria's*

211

Secrets (1996), and the work of the thirteen contributors to *Remaking Queen Victoria* (1997), edited by Homans and Munich.[2] I am especially interested in this pioneering work on Victoria, although, partly because of it, she is now being discussed by feminist scholars ranging from graduate students to Nancy Armstrong.[3] At first glance, such critics might seem hard at work applying the standard feminist methodology of recovery to the woman in all of time who would seem least to warrant it: Queen Victoria, absent from history? Such writing actually demonstrates, I think, the enormous, if not sometimes crushing, weight obstructing the project of recovery. Queen Victoria, these scholars write, has been "hidden in plain view for a hundred years."[4] She has been overlooked precisely because we think she has not. We just assume we know everything about her, as we may assume that—with the establishment of feminism in the academy, say—women's lives, women's art, no longer need to be recovered; women have already arrived ("By and large," even Simone de Beauvoir wanted to claim so innocently—and so mistakenly—in 1949, "we have won the game").[5] If Victoria, the very figure who gave her name to a historical period, remains in effect invisible within it up till now, especially as these scholars argue because she *is* a woman, then the cultural resistance to recognizing women's history, and literary history, is still very powerful indeed.

Despite, in fact *because of,* the innumerable biographies and countless references to Queen Victoria in official history, these scholars argue that the particular relation of this specific woman to "the ideological and cultural signifying systems of her age," especially to the representation of women, remains largely overlooked (Homans and Munich, 2). If literary scholars cannot see Queen Victoria, how will we be able to see the average women that Virginia Woolf asserts as the object of scholarly study, that Rich and Walker demand as a subject position necessary to extend women's studies beyond the boundaries of the academy? Yet the question might be asked: what help would the study of Queen Victoria be in that transformation anyway? Critics might worry that, even if scholars can provide us with a fuller and more detailed picture of Victoria's role as a woman, and her relation to the definition of women at the time, doesn't that simply continue a story of privilege that ultimately prevents the recovery of any other story, that precludes difference? Those critics might ask: why should we wish to recover exceptional women, women who signify and uphold a dominant, unequal, and unjust realm of power and way of thought? Why Queen Victoria?

In part, these recent scholars of Victoria suggest that studying her allows us to understand those injustices more clearly. In their desire to "put Victoria back into Victorian," the studies at hand *are* attentive to issues of class and race—issues they find as much overlooked as gender in previous studies of the period that ignore Victoria (Homans, "The Powers of Powerlessness," 258 n. 11). An attention to Victoria's particular presence actually enables these scholars to redress that balance. For them, Victoria exercised power by swaying popular opinion rather than wielding a scepter. That relocation of the political realm provides another answer to the question, why Victoria? For, within the popular imagination, it seems impossible to fix Victoria's identity as single, simple—simply conservative. Could her representational power have always operated only in that way? What these scholars offer instead is "the existence of many Victorias" (Homans and Munich, 2). Within her own era, they claim, "many conflicting ideas of her increasingly came to be used to model or to justify a wide variety of cultural practices and personal self-fashionings" (3). To see Victoria herself as exceptional and conservative is just one part of a contradictory picture. To see what the idea of Victoria allowed within Victorian culture is another part.

The use of Victoria's image is what my essay is about. I am still centrally interested in the question—why Victoria?—but I want to ask it somewhat differently. I am interested in the cultural work attention to Victoria is doing for feminist scholarship and literary studies right now. What contradictory formulations and paradoxical myths does it inspire for those writing about her (including, by extension, myself too)? What informs the climate in which women in the academy want to write and read about Victoria now? Not only Why are we interested in her? But Why are we interested in her in the particular ways that we are?

If, as Adrienne Munich claims, Victoria "held up magic mirrors to the Victorian age to reflect images in which it could believe" (5), what mirrors does she hold up to us now? For me, the important particulars of that question have to do with what Victoria tells us about feminist scholarship. Most important: what does the recovery of Queen Victoria reflect of the aspirations of women in the academy, concerned about the relation of their special placement to what they see as the larger needs of women?

I am writing this piece, then, because these two things in my field strike me as a generative confluence right now. At the same time as this lively, exciting, and long-overdue reclamation of Queen Victoria's history by a group of Anglo-American critics, I have noticed what I would like to argue is a re-lated focus on history in feminist theory—its own. (Some of the critics writing on Queen Victoria—Mary Loeffelholz, for one—actually also write about academic feminism.)[6] Academic feminism's attention to its own his-tory, especially the various legends of its establishment within the academy, seems everywhere once you begin to look for it; I could argue it character-ized feminist critical writing in the 1990s. Such histories generally involve statements (like my own) that describe the present moment, and they do so in terms of its uneasy successes: what does it mean that feminism has found a place within an institution that to some degree is a site for cultural and ideological power? What are the costs of being inside structures of power?

What I find especially interesting is the *way* feminist scholarship asks it-self such questions; at the same time that it worries about its institutional history, it moves to a form—the personal essay—that supposedly (or so it argues, so it hopes?) has no secure place within the academy's structures of study, yet (beginning with *Lingua Franca*'s February 1991 headline "True Confessions: Feminist Scholars in the First Person") that form also seems to me to be everywhere these days too. Some critics have in fact argued that academic feminism's success and the personal essay go hand in hand: auto-biography and personal confession are possible to such an extent within feminist scholarship right now because a whole generation of women schol-ars have achieved the economic security and professional recognition within the academy that give them the protection to explore such forms, even though they may not acknowledge that standing, even though they cast auto-biography only as risk and not as privilege.[7]

In the context of feminist studies' concerns about its own appropria-tions within institutional power, Victoria seems almost an inevitable figure to whom to turn. Inevitable perhaps because her own autobiographical writing demonstrates the highly problematic ground of autobiography and identity to begin with. The royal "we," after all, is popularly associated with Victoria: is it even possible to conceive of a particular, singular self when it comes to Victoria? The Prince of Wales was reportedly "indignant and dis-gusted" that his mother could think to put her personal life—and the royal family—on display when she published her journals, *Leaves from the Journal of Our Life in the Highlands* (1868) and *More Leaves* (1884).[8] Yet it is hard to know what might have bothered the prince. When it comes to a public fig-ure like Victoria, any definition of the personal becomes strained. Despite their vague emphasis of the domestic—she travels and views Scotland in the midst of her family—Victoria's published journals contain nothing that readers can easily pick out as personal or private as we commonly know them, even when they give us the details of one of her daughter's engagements, say; instead, we get what Margaret Homans calls a "spectacle of royal domestic privacy," a "privacy . . . deliberately exposed" (Homans, "'To the Queen's Private Apartments,'" 4, 20). Only personal in the abstract, her journals institute a kind of state domesticity.

The recent scholars of Victoria also argue that any emphasis on the personal and domestic (no matter what else it might be) was a carefully orchestrated public move, the strategy of a female sovereign to rule indirectly by manipulating the cultural vocabulary of a woman's role current at the time. Victoria, after all, was given her first diary at thirteen by her mother in order that her mother could monitor through it her growth toward the throne.[9] The private was never fully private for Victoria; as Cynthia Huff suggests, how else could she view the world but to conceive of "the personal publicly and the public personally" (46)? Could it ever be possible to identify a Victoria outside her role as sovereign?

The almost necessary indirection of Victoria's relation to herself *as* a self already provides a model for the indirect identification I am implying that current feminist scholars have to her now. Yet I do not mean to argue that the complications of that form of identity in any way make it somehow essentially destabilizing. The Prince of Wales could not have been shocked at anything in particular his mother had to reveal in her journals, but at the stance of personal revelation she adopts. The scandal was that Victoria could gesture at having a personal identity at all. Karen Chase and Michael Levinson argue that "Victoria was seen at once to symbolize and to embody a mythology of private experience . . . even as she was held, and held herself, to the exacting standards of impersonality."[10] Her construction of a private identity at the same time reveals that it is empty—or, at any rate, that the personal cannot be thought outside the public for Victoria. Victoria provides a way to formulate what critics of the personal form argue that feminists have not yet fully realized—to think through whether, and how, the construction of the personal can "registe[r] its complicity with the institutions that structure its representation" (Bernstein, 140).

The imagination of something outside seems to me the most important commonality between the study of Victoria and the discussion within feminist studies of its relation to institutional power. While both focus directly on institutional sites of power, whether monarchy or academy, both also look beyond them to emphasize people—something, anything—outside such institutions. The study of Victoria, of course, places her in a context that addresses people and circumstances supposedly well beyond the throne as seat of power; it considers not only her own ambiguous construction of a private self (the attempt to split off some kind of self from queen) but also the cultural fantasies of an entire nation, empire, and world projected onto her during her reign (the attempt to separate populace and ruler).

Yet the enormous popular attention to Victoria in her time suggests that, however separate Victoria was from her subjects in terms of privilege and opportunity, she remained crucial to their subject formation: rather than just occupying separate (and unjustly unequal) stations, "Victoria" and "the people" are connected too (as she was always quick to claim, although perhaps not exactly connected in the ways she thought).[11] They are connected through the notion and formation of their very selves. All subjects constructed within systems of power help to constitute them, no matter how far removed they may seem from their benefits. But what if selfhood too was one of those benefits, although not commonly understood as such? Seen that way, Victoria's is not so much an exceptional identity as the most relentlessly average and conforming one, the denominator toward which all others tend.

I recognize that making the claim that the study of Victoria parallels questions of feminist identity—whether conceived personally or collectively—pushes the representational status of Victoria farther than I myself always find comfortable. I do not want to argue that feminist scholars study Victoria because they themselves personally identify with her. That statement might be a lot less problematic if we define "identify" itself as a problematic relationship that involves critique and rejection, rather than just unthinking bonding. This is the more complicated definition adopted by Evelyn Fox Keller and Helene Moglen when discussing the misunderstandings between supposedly established, senior feminists and their academic juniors (they do so in "Competition and Feminism: Conflicts for Academic Women," an early and often-quoted article about the problems for feminism imposed by its academic successes).[12] But, even so, the idea that feminist scholars personally identify with Queen Victoria (what would the personal mean here?) sounds literally mad (the Victorians incarcerated madwomen who believed themselves to be Victoria).[13] Even at best, in its figurative sense, it still sounds like the kind of bald statement that indicates the worst, most unsubtle, form of "symptomatic" reading.[14]

Rather than reading other feminists symptomatically in this essay, however, I would rather do just the opposite: use the criticism on Queen Victoria to query Freud's notion of the symptom, especially as he discusses the figure of the queen in *The Interpretation of Dreams*; he defines queens as one of those "symbols which bear a single meaning almost universally: thus the Emperor and Empress (or the King and Queen) stand for the parents."[15] This schematic notion—that a symbol can be univocal, universal, and, hence, easily deciphered—is almost immediately exploded within Freud's work, yet still held to fast within a cultural imagination that unites the academy and its supposed beyond. It would not be wrong to point to Freud to support a contention that the renewed attention to Queen Victoria, often in her time depicted or depicting herself as a maternal figure—"The Great White Mother . . . The Grandmother of Europe"[16]—makes sense now in a feminist climate that quite explicitly outlines problems in the academy as generational conflicts between senior and junior feminists seen as mothers and daughters.[17] Such a reading is plausible, but Queen Victoria is interesting to me as a figure precisely because what we might call her symbolic prominence requires that we ask something more.

Whether the representational status of Victoria can be universal, whether there are different opportunities, stakes, and likelihoods in even the attempt to identify with her, is, in fact, the subject of the African-American writer Adrienne Kennedy's play *Funnyhouse of a Negro* (1962), and of the scholars of Queen Victoria who take that play as their starting point.[18] Kennedy's heroine, Negro-Sarah, talks to a statue of Queen Victoria kept in her room and dominating her thoughts, but can ultimately take up no other relation to it than to commit suicide, hanging herself in front of it. All the recent scholarship on Victoria attests to the power of her image, but explores its manifold power, both to enable and to destroy. This is the notion of symptomatic that Freud actually employs, the sense that a figure's seeming obviousness (even in the argument of his own writing) carries with it a multitude of meanings, less recognized but still operative, that must to some degree work against those arguments. This definition of the symptom actually implies that the more obvious a symbol seems, the more strongly denied, and perhaps firmly entrenched, are its competing meanings. The multifariousness, contradictions, and ambiguities within Victoria's image, then, seem to me to make it an extremely useful one for considering the relation of feminist scholarship to ideological power.

An interest in Victoria captures our split and divided relations as subjects to ideology, the ways we occupy and can never wholly shed it, no matter how much we might wish (as feminists inside the academy, say) to imagine an outside to power. That notion of ideology complicates, as an interest in Queen Victoria complicates, any easy split between the academy and the arenas outside it as well; it helps to explore commonalities as well as differences between these realms too, as we try to account for the shared impulses and stories that keep such a figure alive in our imaginations.

To take Victoria as a powerful emblem for identity—specifically women's identity—is nothing new. The recent scholarship on Queen Victoria makes clear that this was a crucial function of her symbolic resonance in her own time. The introduction to Homans and Munich's *Remaking Queen Victoria* asserts that "Victoria is a model for middle-class women" (6); Victoria indeed, Alison Booth argues, performed "the function of codifying Victorian femininity."[19] Booth examines the many didactic collections of biographical sketches in the nineteenth century—intended for women readers, girls especially—that took Victoria as one of their patterns. Booth calls this genre "collective female biography or role model anthology" (60–61)—collective because it not only gives a model of woman through various pictures of women, but because it links a variety of women as well. In this form, "Victoria is used . . . to encourage aspiration," Booth claims (76), whether her role as sovereign sanctions the achievements of the other notable women who surround her in the pages of these collections, or the ambitions of the (often) female editors and writers putting them together, or—and Booth sees this as key—the aspirations of their readers. Victoria provides an image of women's importance at odds with their usual disparagement or disregard in standard European men's history. In this way, Booth argues, "collective, even collaborative, biographical history . . . has been one strategy for empowering . . . women" (76–77); Victoria's cultural power extends in however muted a way to those outside it, to the women "who could obtain but not get *in* such books" (77).

The queen as an image of women's power, inspiring other women who read or write about her—such a notion of Victoria's efficacy within role model anthologies might be applied to *Remaking Queen Victoria* itself. The richness and diversity of the various essays within it perform in our own time what Adrienne Munich claims for Victoria in hers: "Her uniqueness enabled those of differing interests and needs to create the Victoria of their particular dreams" (13). The dreams of women that strike feminists now, however (pace Freud again), are those that strike Booth—their dreams of aspiration, ambition, their dreams of power. Nancy Miller, exemplary writer of feminist personal criticism in the 1990s, pointed this out in her earlier influential essay "Emphasis Added: Plots and Plausibilities in Women's Fiction" (which first appeared in 1981).[20] In discussing Freud's claim that "in young women erotic wishes dominate the phantasies almost exclusively . . . ; in young men egoistic and ambitious phantasies assert themselves plainly" (32), Miller argued compellingly (especially at the time) that the repressed content of women's stories could actually be "not erotic impulses but an impulse to power: a fantasy of power that would revise the social grammar" (35). Yet these days Miller, as much as other feminists, wonders through her own autobiography if that innocent fantasy of power—now (only partially) realized—has become a bad dream.[21] By occupying traditionally male positions—and prestige—within the academy to the degree that they do, have academic feminists revised anything?

Hence the attraction of what Homans calls "the paradoxes of her power" (Homans and Munich, 5), which makes Victoria in particular so interesting to academic women, writers and readers, right now. On the one hand, recent studies allude to those contemporaries of Victoria's who saw her effect as coming as much from her structural role as from her own beliefs or choices. Munich quotes W. T. Stead, who wrote: "no one of her subjects could honestly repeat the old rubbish about the natural incapacity of women. What the Queen's own views are upon the subject of Women's Suffrage is comparatively immaterial. . . . The Queen has vindicated the capacity of her sex to perform political and social duties" (218). Maria Jerinic rearticulates this position for modern feminism, arguing in *Remaking Queen Victoria* that "any ruling woman disturbs a perceived natural order and upsets ideas, particularly Victorian ones, of normalcy."[22] Such views suggest that women's identity within institutions is of paramount significance, that women's institutional placement can even be transformative in and of itself. This account implies that it does not matter as much what views Queen Victoria (or Margaret Thatcher or Benazir Bhutto) holds; their cultural effect comes from their mere existence as woman rulers.

On the other hand, another description of Victoria's power insists that it resides expressly in her own agency. The status of the queen's own ideas is especially vexed, however, because—especially when it comes to women—they seem so orthodox. About women and power, Victoria could write (in 1852): "I am every day more convinced that *we women,* if we are to be good women, *feminine* and *amiable* and *domestic,* are not *fitted to reign.*"[23] Yet Homans insists that just because Victoria's ideas are orthodox need not mean they are not strategic. She asks us to consider how models such as Victoria still "construct their own versions of female authority . . . by means of the ideology of female submission" ("The Powers of Powerlessness," 245); after all, Victoria had been ruling for fifteen years when she questioned women's capacity to do so, and would go on ruling (in the face of requests to abdicate to her son) for almost fifty more. The effectiveness of Victoria's particular self-representation as subordinate and self-denying woman—as ideal nineteenth-century middle-class wife, mother, and widow—made it seem, like all her displays, a consummate performance to the foremost theater critic of the time: George Bernard Shaw felt "that it is a pity that so able an artist should be wasted on a throne."[24] However we ultimately regard Victoria's rule, this description of it seems to retain the notion of Victoria's agency as ruler.

This *undecidability* about agency seems to me to characterize recent discussions of Victoria's power. Such may be the particular questions raised by any sovereign—and women sovereigns in particular—when it comes to modern notions of identity. In the 1980s, another British queen represented similar issues for a new critical approach codifying its place in the academy—not feminism then, but New Historicism. Louis Montrose argued that we should be interested in an Elizabethan woman—the queen, Elizabeth I (not the average woman Woolf had demanded)—but precisely in order to understand the parameters of ordinary subjectivity. For Montrose, Elizabeth I epitomized the determination of the self and the revision of the concept of agency that was (via Foucault) arguably New Historicism's most salient contribution to literary scholarship—the sense of *all* selves as nodes of power that I have been working from in this essay. Building on the work of other New Historians such as Stephen Greenblatt, Montrose emphasized that however much Elizabeth was "the creature of her image as she was its creator . . . her power to shape her own strategies was itself shaped by her society and constrained within the horizon of its cultural assumptions."[25]

Homans specifically turns to Montrose's work as a precedent for exploring questions of agency: "What Montrose writes about Queen Elizabeth I in this regard could also be said of Victoria" ("'To the Queen's Private Apartments,'" 6). For Homans "the degree to which Victoria's own agency was involved in constructing [her bid for power through womanly submission], and the degree to which it was created for her by social forces operating independently of her, can of course never be established" (ibid.). In Homans's account, these queens keep the possibility and the degree of agency open.

For both Montrose and Homans, it is specifically Elizabeth's and Victoria's identities *as* women that complicate questions of agency. They assume as their starting point "Nancy Armstrong's contention 'that the modern individual was first and foremost a woman'" (Homans, "'To the Queen's Private Apartments,'" 2). Given this assumption, Homans writes:

> Victoria could have been said to have been herself such a woman, with no more than any other woman's share of power, a conduit for the sort of power a Foucauldian reading attributes to all—great, perhaps, but unrelated to individual empowerment or agency. On the other hand, she was unique, a woman whose life was related to ordinary female domesticity only by analogy and masterful tricks of representation, with powers that included her having—if any individual could be said to have it—individual agency. (5)

Such contentions about Victoria push the limits of the kind of reading based in the determination of identity made current in the academy by New Historicism: if there is *any* room for agency at all, Victoria as queen represents one of those liminal sites in which we might hope to find it.

The symbolic meaning of these queens seems to me to be different, then, for Montrose and Homans. The status of the queen resonates differently at different moments for the historical self-constructions of New Historicism and feminism. Montrose's treatment of Elizabeth I is ultimately not concerned with the position of Elizabeth herself as the head of English male society, except in those self-fashionings in which she represents herself *as* male, with "the heart and stomach of a King." Montrose focuses instead on the men—Philip Sidney, Walter Raleigh, William Shakespeare—who are contained under her rule. His sympathies (however understandably) lie in his sustained attention to her male courtiers, negotiating the contradictions and anxieties her female sovereignty poses for *them,* not for her. No matter his stated argument, Elizabeth is not so much a subject within power for Montrose, as she comes to stand in for power itself.[26] Homans, on the contrary, is specifically interested in what Victoria tells us about what it means to be a *woman* experiencing power *as* a subject in it. She argues that Victoria's different gender emphasis reflects a historical shift of the time ("Elizabeth served as the kind of ruler for which the paradigm could then only be masculine—prince or king. Two centuries and a half later, the monarchy required a symbolic ruler, for which the paradigm might well be a woman" ["'To the Queen's Private Apartments,'" 4]). But I want to argue that this history is more recent as well. Women scholars turn to Victoria to tell them something about the contradictions and anxieties of their own positions too—in an academy to which they are supposedly co-opted at the same time that they must still and repeatedly remind their brother scholars in it that women also have a subjectivity and point of view, no matter how we define them.

Questions remain about just how we might define that subjectivity and how relate it to power. Those are the questions occupying feminist criticism right now as it worries about the establishment of feminism within the academy and the move by some women into more clearly marked positions of power within it. The more notorious recent attacks on academic feminism by other women—Daphne Patai's and Noretta Koetge's *Professing Women: Cautionary Tales from the Strange World of Women's Studies* (1993), or Rene Denfeld's *The New Victorians: A Young Woman's Challenge to the Old Feminist Order* (1995)—(like Camille Paglia before them) assume a feminism coterminous with power itself, blaming feminism for women's ills. But even feminism's proponents share to some extent with its attackers the assumption that, by moving into the academy, feminism has moved into the very seat of power. Denfeld's book, by denouncing feminists as New Victorians, suggests that a notion of Victorianism still provides a compelling plot with which to code that history.[27]

Denfeld's excited indictment of the connection between current feminism and Victorianism actually builds on (often by misconstruing) the more careful work of academic feminist scholars. She relies on Judith Walkowitz, Gayle Rubin, and Katha Pollit, among others, for offering an understanding of recent feminist work through its identification with some picture of the Victorian it also creates (240–41). In Denfeld's all-or-nothing logic, however, such imagined links can only be bad. They have a lot to do for her with the questions that I have been suggesting engage scholars of Victoria too: the relation of "influence" to power (206–7, 221) and threats of diminished agency. Denfeld's book is predicated on the assumption that women, young women especially, already exercise individual choice unproblematically; anyone who might question how such choices—or even the illusion of choice itself—are socially determined in the first place is in her view responsible for attempting to deny choices to women (see her denunciation of university policies banning sexual relations between faculty and students, for example [239–40]). Denfeld circularly relies on statistics and arguments from academic feminist scholarship to buttress her wholesale rejection of academic feminism, which she sees as out of touch with real women's lives: "the movement that once stood for equality for all women has come to stand instead for extremist and often irrelevant academic theories and the patronizing views held by an elitist group of largely privileged women" (216–17). Yet this too provides a connection between her and the very academic feminism she rejects, because it is also worried about its own irrelevance and elitism.

By and large, the history recent academic feminism constructs for itself parallels this scenario of capitulation and loss. As Keller and Moglen outline it, "those of us who were engaged in the development of feminist scholarship in the early to mid-seventies experienced ourselves as radical innovators, operating outside conventional structures. . . . Over the last few years, all that has changed. Feminist scholarship has moved into the conventional reward system" of the academy (503). Debbie Epstein and Deborah Lynn Steinberg agree: "the world doesn't change just because we move up in it. Rather than feminism having purchase of the centre, what we have here is feminism repossessed."[28] In all the various maps of feminism's "legitimation," "professionalization," "appropriation," or "domestication"—to list just a few of the words applied to its movement "from the margins of the academy to its interior"[29]—what academic feminism seems to its historians to have lost is any direct connection to women who remain marginal, ordinary women, women without power.

Radical innovators do operate outside conventional structures. Keller and Moglen are not alone in suggesting that feminism's history placed it originally outside any taint of power; "as the doors to the ivory tower have swung open," they write, "as positions of influence and power have become available to women, we have lost both innocence and purity" (494). Taking the academy as site and figure for power assumes that power's institutional sites are public, discreet, easily localizable—structures outside, rather than at the same time part of the self; doing so assumes that selves can be both pure and innocent of power. The academy as type of power provides a story of such current fascination that almost all other problems can be laid at its door. For Jane Gallop, something as seemingly central in itself as tensions over racial differences within feminism is actually one effect of feminism's academization: "I would contend that one reason [race] is such a heated topic now is that it is also a debate about the institutional status of feminist criticism, an anxious non-encounter with the fact of our specific location as insiders" (6). Locating problems within the academy seems to shift them away from individuals—racial tensions become primarily a function of academic pressures (easier to locate and, perhaps, rectify) and not the racist internalizations that produce modern selves (much more entrenched).

This would seem, on the surface, to jibe with the imperative to move away from an unproblematic sense of self to a sense of our multiple and institutional determinations. And, on the surface, this history of academic feminism I am tracing here renounces a sense of self conceived in terms of simple individual agency. It blames the desire for agency—such as Denfeld's—in fact for the decline in feminism's history. Probably the most quoted of these indictments is Madelon Sprengnether's warning about

> the phenomenon of what I will call "careerist feminism," the version of academic feminism that focuses on individual achievement as its primary goal, disavowing the very value of collectivity in its definition of feminism. . . . ["Careerist feminists"] not only benefit from the struggles of us older feminists, who created the fields and markets that allow their work to flourish, but they also underestimate the levels of resistance that remain and are actually on the rise. (206)

Rejecting individual agency, this history has recourse to the spectacle of the personal nonetheless, with its picture of a battle between powerful mothers and ungrateful daughters. The agency denounced in current academic feminism is unwittingly retained for a prior generation supposedly once outside academic appropriations, one that had the power to "create" fields and markets, rather than one that (in an alternative explanation) might have found itself within the academy because large-scale demographic forces brought such markets into existence (and brought women into the academy as a field for those markets) in the first place. In an atmosphere in which academic feminism is felt both to flourish and to remain under constant threat, such a discontinuous notion of agency makes perfect sense; the political step missing here, I think, is to make that discontinuity explicit and theorized.

Yet, for me and for others, including many of these feminists too, the issue is whether such investments can *ever* be avoided. Keller and Moglen conclude that "it is neither possible nor advantageous for women to avoid the dilemmas of power" (510). Gallop cites Meaghan Morris's recognition that "institutionalization is not another name for doom. . . . It's an opportunity, and in many instances, a necessary condition, for serious politics"(5). Susan Stanford Friedman confirms: "Success within the system one is trying to change inevitably contains the possibility of co-optation. . . . I prefer to live and work within this contradiction, in a constant state of vigilance."[30] In order to realize this position, however, we would need to extend the meaning of institution beyond the academy per se—and sites like it—to such categories as identity, gender, race. Institutionalization therefore becomes inescapable; it is what allows us to be and do. That recognition transforms the understanding of power. The question becomes no longer so much Who's got it? as How to handle our implication in it to address its inequities? Since the assault on academic feminism in the 1980s by women of color and lesbians who felt left out of its accounts, academic feminism has been trying to ask this question in order to register its greater connectedness to others constructed in the network in power.[31] Ironically, admitting one's possession of relative authority becomes necessary to the very possibility of relation to women placed differently in the matrix of identity.

This understanding of power actually seems to me to motivate recent attention to Victoria; we can see in the mirror we make of her realizations that are harder to grasp than those we apply to ourselves. In this way, scholarship on Victoria remains symptomatic, but in the sense of revealing the indirection and displacement that identity seems to find necessary in order to explore its most poignantly vulnerable, its deepest, mainsprings—to confront and to try to change them. The parallels between Victoria's status and the self-questioning by recent academic feminism are various: just as Victoria's rule seems to recent scholars a manipulation of stereotypes of women that remains ambiguously intentional, Gallop writes of feminism's history: "the mainstream of academic feminist criticism implicitly defined its enterprise in a way that fit the literary academy. Cooptation or strategy? We may not be able simply to decide what motivated this split" (243). Whether senior academic women had, or have now, any power they can personally use, whether they figure even to other academic women as "either irrelevant in their impotence or anomalous in their strength" (Keller and Moglen, 496), echoes the questions scholars ask of Victoria's representational status too. Such parallels are not uncanny or in any way really surprising; they suggest that this is the frame of thought right now, these the terms of debate.

I have been arguing that Victoria acts as symbol especially of the breakdown of the category of identity for academic feminism right now—its own. The tension she personifies between a private self impossible to realize and the public persona required by institutional needs parallels tensions within academic feminism: between the deconstruction of the self and the need for a fiction of woman. All the essays on recent feminist history I have cited, no matter how they differ as to the particulars of that history, share a common form. They are all excursions into "personal criticism," as Nancy Miller calls it; some of these critics (Jane Gallop, for instance) have, like Miller, helped to establish this form within the academy. Of course, one of the rhetorical options within feminist discourse has always been the creation of a speaker located within specific space and time—a contingent construction meant to rebut a masculinist stance of universality and objectivity. Woolf, Rich, and Walker all adopt this writing persona. Academic feminism's recent imitation of this form certainly reflects its desire to heed those writers' call and reach out beyond its own limits—reach out to the audiences Rich and Walker themselves address but reprove the academy for ignoring.

Elizabeth Hirsh argues, however, that it also demonstrates "the extent that self-dramatization remains the prerogative of celebrities and senior faculty" (712). The very gesture of reaching outside boundaries paradoxically reinforces an inner circle. Susan Bernstein suggests that such disavowals get in the way of the impulse prompting critics to the personal form in the first place. Rather than provide connections beyond what some feminists conceive as their circumscribed place in the academy, personal criticism begins to substitute for such action. Simply by inserting an illusion of individual self in excess of—and often at odds with—their jobs, by asserting through their form their desire to reach out to others not directly concerned with traditional scholarship, such writers hope to "vindicat[e] academic feminist theory as some species of political activism" (123). For Bernstein, an assumption of commonality that does not explicitly engage differences means that such gestures are, at best, deluded, at worst, cynical. For me, it is actually an expression of those differences that could lead to any connections.

But this would involve redefining the academy as just one site of power, and not such a special one—for don't claims of its elitism and privilege also artfully carry with them implications of the academy's purity and innocence? Academic feminists need not lose these qualities after all if the definition of the academy as narrow and circumscribed, as ivory tower, also somehow exempts it from the pressures supposedly affecting only the masses outside it. The mea culpas of academic feminist criticism ironically allow no place for an understanding of the permeability of its own borders. They seem still to assume that academic feminism is special because it at any rate really *has* won the game.

For Bernstein, what is wrong with a lot of personal criticism is that this form often assumes a "teleological 'I'" whose personal disclosures somehow delineate the truth of 'myself as a person'" (128)—a form of presentation that is sometimes subtly but nevertheless in contradiction with the very critical contentions it may present. Bernstein insists instead that effective personal criticism self-reflexively and explicitly explore the "constructions of subject positioning," the "double register of representation and self-representation" (123). This double register is at the heart of recent scholarly attention to Victoria: not just what it means to be a woman undeniably within systems of power, but how such women might represent (even by denying) their authority. And I would suggest it goes farther too: how does the recent construction of Victoria, a woman with whom it would be mad to identify, attest to the political importance of imagined connections, even those at odds with logic or conventional political wisdom, even those that come (as they must) at a great price?

Victoria's own self-presentation followed the pattern of denial and circumvention that critics such as Hirsh and Bernstein locate in recent personal criticism. Her stance of personal revelation within her journals was meant to make her more accessible to her subjects by making her somehow more like them (all private women together, subject to cares, subservient to their families, just the same). Her ongoing disavowals of her own placement in power were—publicly, discursively—emphatic when it came to her self-dramatizations of her personal life (she vowed to "obey" Albert, for instance, in her marriage ceremony). Such disavowals on Victoria's part perhaps ring more hollow than they could if made by anyone else. No matter how effective her gestures of similarity to her female subjects might have been (and Cynthia Huff argues that they *were* effective [46]), none of them could have believed her sovereign was really just like her. Yet, in Victoria's case, as in feminist academic criticism, the personal stance does have specific political effects, although these may not be the exemption from the sites of power that such personal posturing can seek to signal.

That Victoria's authority rested in her sovereignty ironically might be as much a point of connection to other women as the personal stance she adopted to reach them. Kathleen Jones argues that the notion of "sovereignty" is central to notions of authority, and central too to feminist criticism's debate about its place in the academy right now: about who gets to speak, who gets left out, whether the site is necessarily elitist and exclusionary.[32] Jones defines sovereignty as the kind of authority that lays hold of "the singular right to speak for another" (114). Jones argues that the personal turn in feminism today is an attempt on the surface to elude this kind of representational logic, to give up the authority to speak for others and try merely to speak for one's self. It is a response to assertions that "if you are not me/like me, you cannot speak for, or even about, me or those like me. I alone have the authority to do that" (105), which she sees result in "politically stultifying arguments about whose voice is controlling, whose voice is sovereign, whose voice must be heard" (109). Yet Jones suggests that although "we are warned away from giving authoritative readings of others' lives" (107), the model of authority we retain for speaking of our own often remains just the same, just as sovereign. The personal voice often relies on the assumption of a separate and noncontingent self that still annuls the very others it tries to avoid.

When assumptions of the sovereignty of the individual voice itself are not explored or theorized, the bid to sovereign authority cannot be expunged by recourse to the personal. "Our struggles with authority," Jones writes, "become struggles over *who* should practice authority in feminism rather than *what* authority should be" (109). What we get instead is "a veritable cacophony of voices" (108) that "otherwise leaves unchallenged the structure and practice of authority itself . . . [as] a form of liberal individualism . . . [that] treats the autonomous subject as a sovereign. . . . Perhaps the feminist demand for women's inclusion really amounts to nothing more than an effort to vindicate women as sovereigns" (110–11). Yet, as Adrienne Munich suggests about Victoria, "one queen does not make room for others: Queen Victoria did not necessarily ease the way for ordinary women to gain autonomy" (131). The impossibility of Victoria's attempt to maintain a single and sovereign voice when it came to personal disclosure, however, so carefully explored by her recent scholars, might prompt us to a different tack, it seems to me—away from the very model of (self-)sovereignty she seems to epitomize.

For Hirsh, Bernstein, and Jones, until women attempting the personal voice imagine a different way of constructing the self that can "represent divided interests" (Jones, 114)—divisions within her self but also divisions from her audience's (to and for whom she speaks)—that form will not change anything. It will continue to proffer only the imposition of the personified writer's sense of self upon a supposedly identifying reader: right now, "the confessional mode," Bernstein argues," often capitalizes on promiscuous identification, championing an uncomplicated resemblance that disguises a vexed non-resemblance" (123). As long as the private voice still offers "authoritative interpretations of female experiences" (Jones, 107), the connections and differences between academic feminists and women located in other places cannot be explored in all their particularity.

Yet, unlike Hirsh and Bernstein, I do not mean to indict the personal form in particular for problems that seem endemic to all discursive constructions of identity—especially the relation of the self articulated (its divisions *and* commonalities) to its audience. Although my own criticism, for instance, has yet to explore more than just vestigially the rhetorical invocation of a private self, I still feel my own writing to be highly autobiographical, symptomatic—always betraying the possibilities and limits of my imagined relations to others (that tricky "we" that takes on so many meanings over the course of an essay, and fails to live up to so many more).[33] I think writers—whether Victoria in the nineteenth century or academic feminists now—turn to the directly personal form as much for an expression of the insoluble problems of relation and identification as for an escape from and denial of them. And, as I have been arguing, part of that identification involves the recognition of similarities where we least expect to find them: if even Victoria, Queen of England, remained a partial agent, who had repeatedly to capitulate, to resort to indirection, no matter how effective (in order to *make* effective) her long reign, no wonder at our frustrations, dismay, and self-indictments as we shoulder even a fraction of her administrative authority as feminists within the academy. And if Victoria *as* queen turns out not to be a convenient scapegoat for the injustices of the systems of power within which we live, not a special case but the very model of identity that we have all inherited, that makes us who we are too, then our connections to her turn out to be disturbing indeed.

In *Funnyhouse of a Negro,* Victoria is deadly to Sarah in part *because* she is one of Sarah's many selves. An internalized image whom Sarah in her different particularity can never fully realize because of the brutal restrictions of culture, Sarah can exorcise Victoria only by killing herself, the two seem that interrelated. If we as critics emphasize just their differences, without admitting and exploring these interconnections, we risk closing off political alternatives that might someday provide another path of connection than (self-)murder between disparately placed women. It seems to me that a turn to personal criticism within the academy might actually provide a way of making connections generative rather than destructive, but that would involve seeing the academy not as a site from which we should apologize but one of a network of places in which we can help. Tania Modleski defines this as "a view of feminist criticism as symbolic exchange—between the critic and the woman to who[m] she talks and writes—[which] is, I would argue, more egalitarian than much . . . criticism which frequently condemns as elitist the very idea that the critic might have anything to give to anyone."[34] For Modleski, academic feminists have something to say to other women—but only when they also embrace their identities *as* women, admitting similarity, not apologizing for specialness. Critics turn to Victoria to help us to see how in part we got to be who we are. We can learn through the picture those critics give us which forms of identity and connection are available to us, and begin to search for those we have yet to imagine.

Notes

1. Virginia Woolf, *A Room of One's Own* (New York: Harcourt Brace Jovanovich, 1929); Adrienne Rich, "When We Dead Awaken: Writing as Re-vision," in *On Lies, Secrets, and Silences: Selected Prose, 1966–1978* (New York: Norton, 1979), 33–49; Alice Walker, "In Search of Our Mother's Gardens," in *In Search of Our Mother's Gardens* (New York: Harcourt Brace Jovanovich, 1983), 231–43.

2. Margaret Homans, *Royal Representations: Queen Victoria and British Culture, 1837–1876* (Chicago: University of Chicago Press, 1998); "'To the Queen's Private Apartments': Royal Family Portraiture and the Construction of Victoria's Sovereign Obedience," *Victorian Studies* 37 (1993): 1–41; "The Powers of Powerlessness: The Courtships of Elizabeth Barrett and Queen Victoria," in *Feminist Measures: Soundings in Poetry and Theory*, ed. Lynn Keller and Cristanne Miller (Ann Arbor: University of Michigan Press, 1994), 237–59; Adrienne Munich, *Queen Victoria's Secrets* (New York: Columbia University Press, 1996); *Remaking Queen Victoria*, ed. Margaret Homans and Adrienne Munich (New York: Cambridge University Press, 1997).

3. For Armstrong's work, see "The Victorian Clarissa," a talk she gave at the Eighteenth- and Nineteenth-Century British Women Writers Conference in Chapel Hill, North Carolina, in March, 1998; in *Fiction in the Age of Photography: The Legacy of British Realism* (Cambridge: Harvard University Press, 1999).

4. Homans and Munich, "Introduction," *Remaking Queen Victoria,* 1.

5. Simone de Beauvoir, *The Second Sex,* trans. H. M. Parshley (New York: Vintage Books, 1989), xxxiii.

6. See Mary Loeffelholz, "Crossing the Atlantic with Victoria: American Receptions, 1837–1901," in Homans and Munich, 33–56, and her "Review: Women's Studies on Trial," *College English* 58 (1996): 85–92.

7. Elizabeth Hirsh, "The Personal Turn: Of Senior Feminists, Silence, and the Pastness of the Present," *Contemporary Literature* 36 (1995): 708–17; Susan David Bernstein, "Confessing Feminist Theory: What's 'I' Got to Do With It?" *Hypatia* 7 (1992): 120–47.

8. Giles St. Aubyn, "Queen Victoria as an Author," *Essays by Divers Hands* 38 (1975): 127–42; 133.

9. Cynthia Huff, "Private Domains: Queen Victoria and Women's Diaries," *a/b Auto/Biography Studies* 4 (1988): 46–52; 47–48.

10. Karen Chase and Michael Levinson, "'I Never Saw a Man So Frightened': The Young Queen and the Parliamentary Bedchamber," in Homans and Munich, 200–218; 201.

11. For Victoria on "the people," see Huff, 50, and Homans and Munich, "Introduction," 1.

12. Evelyn Fox Keller and Helene Moglen, "Competition and Feminism: Conflicts for Academic Women," *Signs* 12 (1987): 493–511; for their discussion of "identification," see p. 500.

13. See, for example, the work of the Victorian Dr. Hugh Welch Diamond in identifying such disorders, as described in *The Face of Madness: Hugh W. Diamond and the Origin of Psychiatric Photography,* ed. Sander Gilman (New York: Brunner/Mazel, 1976).

14. Jane Gallop defines symptomatic reading as her own strategy in *Around 1981: Academic Feminist Literary Theory* (New York: Routledge, 1992), 7.

15. Sigmund Freud, *The Interpretation of Dreams (Second Part),* vol. 5 of *The Standard Edition of the Complete Psychological Works of Sigmund Freud,* ed. James Strachey (London: Hogarth Press, 1953), 683.

16. William Fredeman, "Introduction," *Victorian Poetry,* special issue: *Centennial of Queen Victoria's Golden Jubilee* 25 (1987): 1–8; 8.

17. Keller and Moglen discuss these associations (57–66), as does Gallop (206–39). For another expression of them, see Madelon Sprengnether, "Generational Differences: Reliving Mother-Daughter Conflicts," in *Changing Subjects: The Making of Feminist Literary Criticism,* ed. Gayle Greene and Coppelia Kahn (New York: Routledge, 1993), 201–8. See also Darlene Hantzis and Devoney Looser, "Of Safe(r) Spaces and 'Right' Speech: Feminist Histories, Loyalties, Theories, and the

Dangers of Critique," in *PC Wars: Politics and Theory in the Academy,* ed. Jeffrey Williams (New York: Routledge, 1995), 22–49.

18. See, for example, Janet Winston, "Queen Victoria in the *Funnyhouse*: Adrienne Kennedy and the Rituals of Colonial Possession," in Homans and Munich, 235–57.

19. Alison Booth, "Illustrious Company: Victoria among Other Women in Anglo-American Role Anthologies," in Homans and Munich, 59–78; 74.

20. Nancy Miller, "Emphasis Added: Plots and Plausibilities in Women's Fiction," in her *Subject to Change: Reading Feminist Writing* (New York: Columbia University Press, 1988), 25–46; originally published in *PMLA* 96 (1981): 36–48.

21. See Nancy Miller, "Criticizing Feminist Theory," in *Conflicts in Feminism,* ed. Marianne Hirsch and Evelyn Fox Keller (New York: Routledge, 1990), 349–69, and Miller's *Getting Personal: Feminist Occasions and Other Autobiographical Acts* (New York: Routledge, 1991).

22. Maria Jerinic, "How We Lost the Empire: Retelling the Stories of the Rani of Jhansi and Queen Victoria," in Homans and Munich, 123–39; 126.

23. Quoted in Munich, 190.

24. Quoted in Stanley Weintraub, "Exasperated Admiration: Bernard Shaw on Queen Victoria," *Victorian Poetry,* special issue: *Centennial of Queen Victoria's Golden Jubilee* 25 (1987): 115–32; 121.

25. Louis Montrose, "*A Midsummer's Night's Dream* and the Shaping Fantasies of Elizabethan Culture: Gender, Power, Form," in *Rewriting the Renaissance: The Discourses of Sexual Difference in Early Modern Europe,* ed. Margaret Ferguson, Maureen Quilligan, and Nancy Vickers (Chicago: University of Chicago Press, 1986), 65–87; 86; see also his "The Work of Gender in the Discourse of Discovery," *Representations* 33 (1991): 1–41.

26. Montrose, an excellent critic, remains explicitly and "uncomfortably aware that the trajectory of [his writing] courts the danger of reproducing what it purports to analyze: namely, the appropriation and effacement of the experience of both native Americans and women by the dominant discourse of European patriarchy" ("The Work of Gender," 3).

27. Rene Denfeld, *The New Victorians: A Young Woman's Challenge to the Old Feminist Order* (New York: Time Warner Books, 1995), especially 237–39.

28. Debbie Epstein and Deborah Lynn Steinberg, "No Fixed Abode: Feminism in the 1990's," *parallax* 3 (1996): 1–6; 3.

29. *Margin to interior* is from Marianne Hirsch and Evelyn Fox Keller, "Conclusion: Practicing Conflict in Feminist Theory," in Hirsch and Keller, 370–85; 379. *Legitimization* and *professionalization* come from Cora Kaplan, who finds singularly more capitulation within America than England: "One inevitable measure of the successful legitimation of feminist scholarship in American academia is that it has been subject to the intensive professionalization that has transformed higher education in the United States since the seventies" (Cora Kaplan, "The Professional Fix: Anglophone Feminist Criticism in National Contexts,"

Tulsa Studies in Women's Literature 12 (1993): 229–40; 233. *Appropriation* and *domestication* come from Margaret Ezell, who writes: "the question has already been raised as to what extent feminist literary theory has benefited from its growing reputation, from its appropriation and redirection of traditional literary criticism, and to what extent it has itself been appropriated and 'domesticated' to fit within existing modes of patriarchal, institutional academic thought" (Margaret Ezell, *Writing Women's Literary History* [Baltimore: Johns Hopkins University Press, 1993], 2).

30. Susan Stanford Friedman, "Relational Epistemology and the Question of Anglo-American Criticism," *Tulsa Studies in Women's Literature* 12 (1993): 247–61; 257.

31. See, for instance, Mary Poovey, "Cultural Criticism: Past and Present," *College English* 52 (1990): 615–25; 619–20.

32. Kathleen Jones, "The Trouble with Authority," *differences* 3 (1991): 104–27; all subsequent references to this essay will appear in the text.

33. This would be the place to make good on one promise of my title: Victoria and *Me*. For me, this is a story of broken promises, gifts not given, because my relation to scholarship on Victoria up till now has consisted of an inability to perform it. I had originally promised the editors of *Remaking Queen Victoria* an essay for their anthology, but the demands of living, both personal and professional—a new baby, a new job—kept me from writing it, until now. This is definitely not the essay I thought I would write (that was going to be on Dickens); in recording my debt to those scholars who have given me so much, in part by remaking Victoria, I have tried to do something better.

34. Tania Modleski, *Feminism without Women: Culture and Criticism in a "Postfeminist" Age* (New York: Routledge, 1991), 46.

Sorting, Morphing, and Mourning
A. S. Byatt Ghostwrites Victorian Fiction

Hilary M. Schor

For most contemporary readers, the Victorian novel matters because of its plot: whether old-fashioned, garden-variety readers (those who "love a good story") or costume-shop haunting, melodrama-adapting producers for the BBC, moderns who turn the novel backward are looking for the confidence of psychological realism and the faith that character will emerge from incident, fact from fiction, and conviction from clutter. In the realist novel, all will be fitting, all will be appropriately clothed, and all will be well. The unspoken rules of Victorian fiction promise moral unity and historical veracity and generate adaptations that (in that new periodization that makes Jane Austen and Thomas Hardy contemporaries) allow the present to patronize the past, and the past to congratulate the future on its good taste in memorialization.

For contemporary novelists, the Victorian novel has meant something else. For them, what we might think of as Victorian debates about realism—the relationship between mind and matter; between spirit and body; between a hypothesized past and an unrealized future; between questions of form and questions of morality—have a new life, and elicit, indeed, require, new solutions within the novel. For women writers in particular, including Margaret Drabble, Elizabeth Jane Howard, Andrea Barrett, and Pat Barker, long, serial novels, family romances, the "condition of England" question, and the debate over science and faith have opened new possibilities for discussion of the nature not only of fiction but of material reality. The Victorian past has come to uncanny life in contemporary fiction.

But that reincarnation is provisional, in pursuit of new visions of human relations and new questions about literary forms. The Victorians, we might theorize loosely, matter not for their answers but for their bewilderment. It is too easy to say that the "new" Victorian novel frames itself around doubt, not faith, for any careful reading of the fiction of the mid-nineteenth century reveals the same uncertainties posthumously, but somehow the contemporary weaving together of certainty and implausibility (all that makes up the rather uncertain "probabilities" of realism) has been accomplished differently. One last reviser of Victorian fictions, A. S. Byatt, who comes to her resurrection work from a career seemingly far from the comforts of realism, character, and plot with which I began, suggests the essential difficulty of the work of remembering the Victorian novel, and the productive labor of materialization (bringing memory to uneasy life) that the novel itself made possible.

Even the most cursory review of A. S. Byatt's professional history suggests that she has an extensive relationship to literary adaptation. In fact, she has had an extremely successful career since she began writing other people's novels. Her most extended incarnation as a Victorian, however, is somewhat different. Although from her earliest fiction she has been a highly mannered stylist, and certainly one dependent on forms, metaphors, even texts imported (or, if necessary, invented) from other disciplines or literary periods, in *Angels and Insects* she attempted something more complete: two novellas, of the Victorian period, written with no visible interruptions from the twentieth century. Writing as a Victorian does not mean an absolute seamlessness, for these novellas continue her modernist habit of internal disruption and interpolation: variously, pseudoscientific works, journals, bits of poetry, and fables of animal life dot the text, as do more palpable intrusions: séances; encrypted messages; and ghostly visitants. Byatt comes to the Victorians by way of interruptions and borrowings: the novellas further invoke a series of spectral Victorian predecessors, conjuring up variously Alfred Lord Tennyson, Charlotte Brontë, John Ruskin, and Charles Darwin, as if Byatt conceived of writing a novel by herself as altogether too lonely an activity, and hence invented imaginary friends to help her through.

But something more than literary companionship seems to be going on here, as indeed it has from the beginning of Byatt's career. From the first, she has been remarkably uninterested in much of the ordinary business of novel writing: her plots move painfully slowly, if at all, and in some novels (the recent *Babel Tower* most significantly) a period of very few years, and almost fewer events, is covered at great length. What has seemed to draw her on is a layering (what *Babel Tower* calls "laminations") of fictional levels, or, more accurately, of textual devices.[1] Her own set of serial novels, those following the heroine Frederica Potter, suggests the range of her borrowings: *The Virgin in the Garden* depended on an Elizabethan masque written in the 1950s to revive the verse drama (it fails to do so) and performed for the coronation of Elizabeth II; the author of that play, Alexander Wedderburn (a lovely name for a Victorian novelist—as it was the name of one of Ruskin's editors and biographers) reappears in the second novel, *Still Life*, and writes a play about Vincent van Gogh, whose meditations on light and pigment punctuate the drama of the novel; *Babel Tower* is interspersed with a fairy tale, the heroine's own scribblings and "cut-up" texts, and (most prominently) with a pornographic novel set during the French Revolution and involving an assortment of Sadeian theatricals and games—none of which, to my surprised disappointment, we get to read, because that novel goes on trial for obscenity but *our* novelist does not bother to finish it.[2] Byatt's mania for (literary) world making and text laminating reached its apogee in *Possession,* which invented two imaginary Victorian poets, wrote letters, diaries, and poems for them, and yet managed (somewhat skillfully) to mock the very readers it invoked, by placing at its heart a number of bad academic readers whom we were *not* to be. *Possession* carries out its own kind of property wars, finally claiming as its own not only its imaginary poets but the "real" figures of Browning, Barrett Browning, Rossetti, Tennyson, and Morris out of whom they are crafted—and reclaiming possession of these poets (and any fantasies about them) from bad feminists, nasty editors, and a series of textual ghouls who (most risibly) attempt to dig the dead poet up and read his embalmed text.[3] "How dare they!" the novel seems to be trumpeting—at the same time, of course, as it invents exactly the dead texts it wants for *its* dead poets, and rewards the good readers of poetry with happy marriages, blissful sexual adventures, and a choice of tenured positions—all of which are awarded to the decent, kindly, manly (unghoulish) hero.

Literature itself, then, seems to occupy some privileged site for Byatt, which criticism does not; literature constitutes the "real" property. But it is more difficult to determine just what Byatt thinks literature—and in particular fiction—really is. Since her first novel, *The Shadow of the Sun,* she has been obsessed with where fiction comes from, and in particular with what kind of novel people write who have no novelistic gift; a comparison with Margaret Drabble's *The Garrick Year,* a much smoother and more affecting novel published the same year, suggests that Byatt knows herself all too well.[4] Her continued interest in fiction suggests not the love of story making per se, but some sense that the novel is a kind of organizational structure, some way of knowing and naming material, some way of resurrecting interest, available nowhere else. It is as if for Byatt there were some problem, some question, some *vision* she could achieve only through the novel, even if it requires an almost entire violation of the novel's forms and the invocation of everything else; or rather, as if she thought (and this is an instinct much more akin to the Victorian than the postmodern novelist) that the novel's form was at its heart to invoke everything else. Byatt's fiction moves from the dictum of modernist fiction ("it is above all to make you see") and back toward the impulses of the Victorian novel: she invokes the desire to take the roof off the houses, as Dickens's Asmodean spirit will in *Dombey and Son,* but every house, including the grave, is to be opened. In *Angels and Insects,* the form of writing she invokes is ghostwriting, which she reads in a double sense: first, that of the "borrowings" ("writing like . . .") that seem to approach the postmodern forms of pastiche, and second, a ghostwriting that is speaking with the dead, not so much as writers but as moldering bodies, decaying forms. What Byatt is resurrecting is a concern with writing that she is identifying as peculiarly Victorian: forms of organizing matter that are linked not only to the novel but to other "ghost huntings," to Darwin's romancing of the evolutionary past, to Swedenborg's spirit investigations, to Dickens's (and others') memory texts. Byatt's own fiction (from "The Day E. M. Forster Died" to "July's Ghost," to which I will return) has always connected writing and death; in *Angels and Insects,* Byatt invents a contemporary version of realism that can reanimate the complicated literary genres of the past. For Byatt, the novel is not only a ghost story but a catalog organizing the material and immaterial world. It is a "literary" device for giving forms form.

Angels and Insects is (or pretends to be) two "Victorian" novellas. The first, *Morpho Eugenia,* opens with a Darwin-like figure at a dance in an English country house: his visions intercutting English mating rituals with Amazon rites punctuate the story of his courtship and marriage to the eldest daughter of the house, Eugenia, who (as he learns after the couple produce a swarm of small children) has been incestuously involved with her brother, Edgar, since childhood. By the novel's end, the hero has left the family estate with the overeducated, sharply intelligent governess-companion of the children, Matilda Crompton, who has encouraged him and joined him in the writing of a fabular book on ant culture; together, they sail to the Amazon to resume his scholarly explorations.[5] The captain of their vessel, Arturo Papagay, provides the only plot connection to the second novella, *The Conjugial Angel.* There, the captain's wife, Lilias, presumed a widow following her husband's disappearance at sea, is one of the spirit guides of an oddly mixed group of ghost hunters, who join in séances of a Swedenborgian nature, seeking (primarily) contact with Arthur Hallam, the dead fiancé of one of the séance attendees, Emily Jesse, sister to Alfred Tennyson, who appears (in one of the book's strangest scenes) hypnotizing himself with the mantra of his own name. The slight link between the tales is almost irrelevant to their telling: the presumed connection (are William and Matty lost in the same storm that drowned Captain Papagay?) goes unremarked upon, and, when the captain defeats the laws of nature and plot by returning, miraculously but materially, at the book's end, no mention is made of drowned companions; where Matty and William sailed off into romantic happiness, the captain returns home, Odysseus-like, to rejoin his wife and reverse the pattern of voyaging and dispersal.

In so blunt a summary, the paired novellas suggest other paired oppositions: body and spirit; social criticism and religious doctrine; science and faith; masculine investigation and female inspiration. But what they share is an obsession with the nature of matter itself, and the question of how to render matter: it is matter, as Byatt has Tennyson remark in *The Conjugial Angel,* that is truly mysterious.[6] The balance of a material world and one of mystery is not easy to effect; but it remains a goal (if an elliptical one) of the fiction. As a character thinks of a Morris sofa used for the company's séances, "Mr. Morris's sofa acknowledged both worlds; it could be sat on; it hinted at Paradise. Emily liked that" (204–5).

Byatt likes that, too, and thus, the precise nature and referentiality of any sofa, then, is never accidental. For Byatt, as I have suggested, fiction offers a space for a series of strategies for the deployment of *and the debate over* matter, what I am calling sorting, morphing, and mourning. These techniques make clearer the connection between the Victorian forms of scientific and spiritualist thinking that Byatt is both utilizing and commenting on, but they also draw our attention usefully to the current *technologies* of representation and replication available—not just a taxonomy of matter, or the moments of yearning for matter's former purity, but the fluidity of motion between one state of matter and the next: we can organize it (sort); we can regret its loss (mourn); but we can also watch as it changes form before us (morph)—a change that is a kind of death and rebirth, and that threatens the ultimate total dissolution of matter into mystery. On the one hand, Byatt is drawing on a particularly contemporary working out of Victorian forms of material life—not only readings of the fiction, but scholarly investigations that connect what we think of as nonfiction ways of reading (Darwin's revolutions in thought; Victorian death practices) to narrative forms. On the other, she is connecting these older fictional and fictionalizing forms to contemporary media, to our computer-generated fascination with morphing and transformation, to cinematic and other technological ways of drawing attention to form itself. And it is here that Byatt's own *formal* revolutions become part of her working out of the problem; rather than form's following function (think of the sofa), here the formalist qualities of the work threaten to take over, and the mere pleasures of parody (morphing and remorphing) hint at another level of literary, and material, desire: the desire to escape any single form whatsoever.

These anxieties (and pleasures) of form return us to the postmodernist questions with which I began: with the difference between formal innovation or renovation, and a purely (were there such a thing) nostalgic form. Despite the costumey quality of the film adaptation of *Angels and Insects,* the novel takes its investigation of material remains with a certain skepticism, mirroring its hero's return from the Amazon with a newly anthropological gaze, estranging the Victorians it (like he) looks upon, their manners and customs and dress all grist for a skeptical mill. This is no costume drama; rather, it is a mating game. But its elements of mixing and matching on a formal level, as I am suggesting, contain a similar skepticism, one we are prone loosely to call "postmodern," in the belief that to look back, as Fredric Jameson puts it, in a moment when we have "forgotten how to think historically," is also to look at the present—and to look at the present is to estrange it as well.[7] For Jameson, as I think for most literary critics, anxieties about the past are most easily transformed into formal anxieties, particularly an anxiety on the level of the sentence, the problem of parody or pastiche, of an echo (either satiric, in parody, or dead-on, affectless, in pastiche) of an earlier voice.[8] This gets to the heart of Byatt, who has affected a series of pastiches in *Angels and Insects* that listen uneasily to the past so as to stage the present moment. But Jameson has further directed us to this listening backwards, this quotation, as an act of resurrection: with the impossibility of new forms and new voices, he says, we find the "unforeseeable return of narrative as the narrative of the end of narratives, this return of history in the midst of the prognosis of the demise of historical telos" (xii). This is exactly what Byatt stages: the novel has returned; characters return; then she stages (renders self-conscious) the return. The "appeal to experience" that Jameson claimed died with the postmodern also returns—but here, the return to the real is staged as itself almost comic, mostly horrifying. As Jameson says of the return of the return-to-the-past, it "fuses its unlikely materials into a gleaming lump or lava surface" (xiii).

The brilliance of Byatt's staging of the return of the repressed (the "matter" of the novel) lies in her choice of Victorian realism, which itself repeatedly stages this return as a material problem, and worries about precisely the organization of forms equally at the heart of postmodernism. Byatt takes the uncanny nature of realism, which must always stage the return of matter as a deeper ("lumpier") form of material, as her subject. There is already something elegiac, nostalgic, and downright creepy about the novel; the act of writing is an act of mourning, but it is also a refusal to let nature take its course. The act of preservation at the heart of the novel is simply unnatural, its way of cataloging, transforming, and resurrecting matter an intervention in the world it pretends merely to "show"; what better form than the Victorian novel for gathering, for interrogating, for estranging the forms of representation themselves?

This essay, a bit like Byatt's novellas, must take for granted the Victorian anxieties about materiality (an index-card view of Tennyson, Dickens, and Darwin is all I can hope to present here) but it is enough to allow us to begin to focus on the primary job of any novelist/cataloger: how to sort the forms out? Sorting is linked, for Byatt, to both the realist and the romancer: her hero, William Adamson, finds himself "at once detached anthropologist and fairy-tale prince" (25). Sorting offers both a quest narrative and a form of material investigation, but it is also a version of interiority, which for William is marked through the evolution of his journal, from "a daily examination of his conscience" (10), to journals of his collection, as he discovers "the Crucifers, the Umbellifers, the Labiates, the Rosacae, the Leguminosae, the Compositae, and with them the furious variety of forms which turned out to mask, to enhance the underlying and rigorous order of branching families, changing with site and climate." The journal becomes "alive with a purposeful happiness," as he begins to collect insects, "a mass of mess moved by an ordering principle" (11), and "the journals began to intermingle a rapt, visionary note with detailed practical sums for outfitting, for specimen boxes, with useful addresses" (12). The journals return with him, "much stained," with

> scribbled descriptions of everything: the devouring hordes of army ants, the cries of frogs and alligators, the murderous designs of his crew, the monotonous sinister cries of the howler monkeys, the languages of various tribes he had stayed with, the variable markings of butterflies, the plague of biting flies, the unbalancing of his own soul in this green world of vast waste, murderous growth, and lazily aimless mere existence. (113)

Other forms of writing in the novella follow this quality of "descriptions of everything." The book William and Matilda write is similarly wide-ranging: she says it would be "very interesting to a very general public, and yet of scientific value. You could bring your very great knowledge to bear on the particular lives of these creatures—make comparisons—bring in their Amazonian relatives—but told in a *popular* way with anecdotes, and folklore, and stories of how the observations were made—" (108). Interestingly, he is not to "set out again on another foreign journey to collect more information"; he is to sort what is in front of him, an enterprise Matilda, at least, connects with a female (almost domestic) science: "My sphere is naturally more limited. I look naturally more close to hand" (108, 90).

All of these investigations, of course, are still framed by writing, but the more interesting versions of "sorting" in the novel are the nonliterary, more visibly taxonomical enterprises, the activities suggested in Miss Mead's telling of the story of Cupid, Psyche, and the sorting ants. Here, Byatt seems both to draw on and to mock slightly the works of such "naturalists" as Edmund O. Wilson: as William remarks, "We look in their [the ants'] societies for analogies to our own, for structures of command, and a language of communication" (127). But the more powerful critique is reserved for the anxious, Victorian forms of sorting: William has been brought to the manor to organize Harald Alabaster's collection, which is in a disused saddle room,

> half-full of . . . things Harald had purchased—apparently with no clear priority of interest—from all over the world. Here were monkey skins and delicate parrot skins, preserved lizards and monstrous snakes, box upon box of

dead beetles, brilliant green, iridescent purple, swarthy demons with monstrous horned heads. Here too were crates of geological specimens, and packs of varied mosses, fruits and flowers, from the Tropics and the ice-caps, bears' teeth and rhinoceros horns, the skeletons of sharks and clumps of coral. . . . William asked his benefactor on what principle he was required to proceed, and Harald told him, "Set it all in order, don't you know? Make sense of it, lay it all out in some order or other." William came to see that Harald had not carried out this task himself partly at least because he had no real idea of how to set about it. (28)

The same incoherence of purpose and principle informs Harald's own writing, his attempts to find a design of the creator in the multitudinous natural world, but his own writing circles around, finding only his own *desire* for form at its heart.

An in-joke about form and particularly about the repetition of forms is at the heart of the "morphological" impulse that offers another version of materialism for the novellas, and that similarly reflects back on the novel's own inscription. As William explains to Eugenia, when he shows her the butterfly that shares her name, "It means beautiful, you know. Shapely."

"Ah," said Eugenia, "The opposite of amorphous."

"Exactly. The primeval forest out there—the endless sameness of the greenery—the clouds of midges and mosquitoes—the struggling mass of creepers and undergrowth—often seemed to me the epitome of the amorphous. And then something perfect and beautifully formed would come into view and take the breath away. Morpho Eugenia did that, Miss Alabaster." (24)

The slight gender mockery implicit here (and made explicit, of course, by the revelation that Eugenia, far from perfect and beautifully formed, is in fact a monstrous and incestuous mess) does not entirely belie the desire for perfect form, one marked in part by the book's playing with the conventions of *Victorian* form. The novel's play with Amazonian mating ritual (a seemingly postmodern gesture toward contemporary skepticism about exploration and anthropology) masks an astonishingly conventional two-heroine plot, one in which William first loves the beautiful, golden, and shallow Eugenia, only to be freed from her to marry the dark, sallow, and perceptive Matilda—and less we miss the convention, Byatt has William and Eugenia the parents of twin daughters named Agnes and Dora. Again,

the Victorian novel comes back, but here in an even more directly incestuous version of itself, the twinned heroines twinned. Byatt "materializes" the
romance of the hero's choice by reinvoking what seems to be a dead form,
bringing it to weird (and rather comic) life.

The series of perfect forms Byatt mocks and emulates include not only
Dickens's coming-of-age novels but Brontë's (in particular *Jane Eyre,* invoked through the governess plot and Matilda's attic room, and *Villette,*
whose shipwreck metaphors inform *The Conjugial Angel,* only to be van-
quished by that novel's happy return of the hero from the sea); further, Byatt
"morphs" Ruskin's stories of crystals written for little girls (here, revised into
the stories of the ant fortresses Osborne and Red Fort), Darwin's journals
from *The Beagle,* and fragments of Paley's *Natural Theology.* Indeed, she
writes her own ant histories, acknowledging in her afterword the work of
Wilson and others; similarly, she not only borrows liberally from Tennyson
and makes him "her" character, but outdoes the poet laureate by writing answering portions of *In Memoriam* in dialogue with Arthur Hallam, and
rewriting the poem in séance form. These parts of the novel read almost like
a deconstruction, posing and counterposing key terms, returning to them in
uncanny fashion and making them speak to each other; but her readings of
the "parodied" and quoted texts come with a double set of quotation marks,
not only to the "original" author, but to critics who have resurrected them
and set them spinning. Byatt reads Victorian literature in the company of
scholars, as well as "primary" writers, and whereas *Possession* posed scholarship as "mere" (and repugnant) grave robbing, here the doubled reading becomes the stuff of fiction, again echoing fiction's uncanny mediation between forms and experience, between one form and another, as one writer
morphs (through the mediation both of fiction and criticism) into another.[9]

But if morphing has come, through computer and film nerds, to mean
not only "form" (as linguists use it, for pure structures) and "varieties of
deep structures" (as narratologists use it, for folk and fairy tales) but the
amazing process through which Arnold Schwarzenegger or Michael Jackson
can become anyone at all (a derivation of metamorphosis, presumably), it
suggests the absolute *lack* of form behind formalism of any sort: Byatt's
writing here is more neurotics than erotics; and certainly more borrowing
than inventing; but what erotics and invention there is goes into this other
writing, this disappearing author routine that becomes, precisely, as she
continues, routine. "Ah," we say, "there goes that author, disappearing again."
By the time we reach *The Conjugial Angel,* in which the version of writing

we get is automatic writing, where characters need assume no responsibility for their texts, Byatt's insistence on her own absence seems considerably less perverse than it did initially—if also, perhaps, less charming. Byatt's writing (and here we engage again questions that have come to us through post-modern debates) disenchants the absent author.

For Byatt's habit of lifting texts seems to be contagious: everyone gets to be an omniscient narrator; a dead character; an absent author. The ghosts as well as the ghostwriters in *The Conjugial Angel* write other people's books: Lilias Papagay's husband quotes his own erotic neologisms; when Hallam sends messages to Emily Tennyson Jesse, he quotes his own translations of Dante and his citations of Chaucer in letters he wrote decades earlier; when he appears later in the novel, he wants to hear Keats's poems read aloud. Mrs. Hearnshaw's dead children also send poetry and play word games, and even the odious Mr. Hawke quotes (or is it inhabits?) the meditations of Swedenborg.

All of this material (every author dead; no author dead) forces us to con-nect the novel's work of "collection" with something much more macabre, returning us to the problem of "mourning," the final of my Victorian bor-rowings for the organization of matter. To the extent that the realist novel is a collection of material things, it, I have been arguing, partakes of the macabre itself: it must bring things to life, keep them in life, arrest their decay. But it also studies decay: the novel is primarily an animist fantasy, of making the dead live, of making "mere" forms "matter." Like *In Memoriam*, with which it is obsessed, *Angels and Insects* worries considerably about whether or not it wants the dead to return: like Tennyson thinking that he might not want Arthur Hallam to watch his every move, the characters in *Angels and Insects* want their dead in their places, even if that place is un-comfortably lodged between two worlds. And, like another resurrection man, Sigmund Freud, the novel poses mourning, the constant return to the dead, as a testing ground for experience. For Freud, mourning is "work," and that work the "testing of reality," the making real of the absence of the beloved from the world. Mourning may be extraordinarily painful, but, he claims, this pain seems "natural to us": loss is consciousness, and the prob-ing of that loss the way we know the world and its (and our) limits.[10] When those limits fail—when what we experience is not the loss of another but the ego loss Freud associates with melancholia—the world becomes overly full and crowded and we ourselves become empty. We must reintegrate the self and the world; we must resurrect not the world but ourselves. If we do not, if we can only mourn, then what we can express, Freud says, is only "the conflict of ambivalence."

That form of ambivalence—where is the material reality, in the self or the world? how are we to inhabit a world overly crowded with living and dead, with matter and decaying forms?—is at the heart of both Byatt's project and the return of the repressed to which Jameson directed us. But in some ways, Byatt's answer is more productively ambivalent. We have full selves, but they are overly full with the words of others—and that is at once "natural" and "naturally unnatural," uncanny, "realistic" in the haunted sense of realism I have been insisting on. The realist novel's problem was always what to do with the macabre detritus of a "real" world, and it can organize that material (catalog, transform, wax elegiac) only by playing games with language. But Byatt does not assume that language is dead—or rather, that its death is permanent. The novellas point insistently to a different kind of postmortem inhabitation. The Swedenborgian's favorite speech, we are told, is to unravel "all the threads of connection between the Divine Human and local lumps of clay." Like the gleaming lump that Jameson imagines the return of past forms "fuses its unlikely material into," the "lumps" of this novel insist on resurrection. The incessant return of the dead in *The Conjugial Angel,* in the form of language as well as in the form of clay, seems to call out for the rematerialization of the dead. In Byatt's brilliant story "July's Ghost" a rather stiff young man finds himself the lodger of a reserved older woman, whose dead son he begins to see in the garden. The woman, herself always a skeptic, longs to see him only once; the young man, who sees him in spite of himself, cannot speak to the boy, can only intuit and try to enact the boy's desire, in this case, that the young man make love to his mother and (somehow) bring him to another form of life. That longing is a site of profound anxiety in *The Conjugial Angel,* where the stakes of materialization are rather different, and not exactly so loving. In the long passage recounting the aging Tennyson's double recollection of Hallam and the poetry of *In Memoriam,* he dwells lovingly on "the clay and the mould and the moulding" (313). For him,

> If the air was full of the ghostly voices of his ancestors, his poem let them sing out again, Dante and Theocritus, Milton and the lost Keats, whose language was their afterlife. . . . He saw it as a kind of world, a heavy globe, spinning onwards in space, studded with everything there was, mountains and dust, tides and trees, flies and grubs and dragons in slime, swallows and larks and

carrier-birds, raven-glossed darkness and summer air, men and cows and in-
fants and violets, all held together with threads of living language like strong
cables of silk, or light. The world was a terrible lump of which his poem was
a shining simulacrum. (312)

This lump, this bit of earth, poses the problem of matter at its darkest: the
"common clay ta'en from the common earth / Moulded by God, and tempered with the tears / Of angels to the perfect shape of man," as Tennyson
quotes himself within the novella. And "now there was Darwin," as he goes
on to say, "grubbing away at the life of the earthworm, throwing up mold
and humus all over the place." Hallam himself appears to Sophy Sheekhy
not as a gleaming angel, but as a "terrible face, with its flaring lights, and its
smoke and its bone-pits"; as "a dead cold weight" with "disintegrating fingers," and finally, "he was being unmade, undone, and she could not, lying
there, hold him together with her arms, or hear his voice any more in her
ears, he had no more face, or fingers, only clay-cold, airless, stinking mass,
plastering her face and nostrils" (313–18). When the dead return, it seems,
they do *not* promise, as Tennyson fears, that "the spirit does but mean the
breath"; more ominously, it would seem that matter lives on only and more
terrifyingly as itself, as pure matter, pure lumps, pure clay.

All the progress of the novella leads us to expect its climax to be the inspiration of the dead: the moment when the clay re-forms, revives, is revitalized; the equivalent of the literary afterlife Tennyson here imagines and
Byatt is practicing. But the return of the dead is more material, and more
matter-of-fact than that: rather than the ghastly Arthur Hallam, the last page
of the novel resurrects Captain Papagay, who presided over the happy ending of *Morpho Eugenia,* and reunites him with his loving wife. Not an elegy,
then, or a threnody, but an epithalamium—or rather, a *re*-epithalamium;
not the mourning verse, but the marriage plot. Byatt offers not the grave, or
even gravity, but, at the end, the comic spirit—an astonishing resurrection,
we might think, not only of domestic realism (hearth winning over horror)
but of a Dickensian pious fraud, a trick played on the reader to startle us out
of our own cynicism, our faith in the decay of matter *and* spirit.[11] Like a
benevolent fairy, for Byatt, the final materialist strategy is the triumph of
love over death; or (speaking more literarily) of living memory over the
deadly stratagems of history, a memory here made flesh.

These strategies (of text as well as of materialism) both are and are not
Victorian: in their adherence to a Wordsworthian sense of "spots of time,"

they give a hint of metaphysical realism: the sense that in every household object, paradise peeps through; that grace abounds in the beetles and the bread knives.[12] But, as I suggested earlier, they also share a more postmodernist state, the "laminations" Byatt has invented in *Babel Tower,* that take their name from the tracings on the snail's shell, but need no reasoned order or meaning. This seems to locate Byatt's experiments less within a Victorian reversion, and more powerfully within her own oeuvre, and in particular within her attempt to rewrite the "connections" of E. M. Forster and D. H. Lawrence through the notebooks (and particularly *The Golden Notebook*) of novelists such as Doris Lessing, but what I am also trying to trace here is the way in which it is marked less as "postmodernist" than as "postrealist"— that is, with a still persistent and terrifying clarity about realism *as* ghost-writing. Nobody really thinks A. S. Byatt is George Eliot—and indeed, the almost total silence of her narrator suggests she is making no such claims. But she has claimed as her own that quest for a larger vision, one that encompasses a range of voices much like Eliot's—and goes farther, for Byatt, like any brave New Historicist, is trying to talk with the dead.

It cannot be accidental that the book ends with the raising of the dead, because for Byatt, the image of resurrection runs deep: the possibility of endless return, of the boy playing in the garden, of the child rising from the foam, of (to use one of her favorite images) Persephone rising from dark to light, informs most of her fiction, and makes the whole of *Angels and Insects* into (to borrow the subtitle of *Possession*) a "romance." But the image of Dickens's resurrection men also hangs over this text: what is it, we might wonder, that allows Darwin to give way to grace, insects to angels, except the immersion of all matter in the grave? And here, of course, we are back to the grave-robbing image of *Possession,* in which literary property is clearly theft, publication a violation of the dead, and (as *Angels and Insects* would have it) our power to speak through the voice of the dead, most ominously, its exact opposite: their threatening power to speak *for* us. This again is a huge site of ambivalence for Byatt: her own relationship to the canon, which she pillages with such enthusiasm, seems unambivalent, but the inability of people to see the world without seeing a world of texts at times seems a dismaying prospect. So, similarly, Frederica Potter, in *Babel Tower,* "a woman whose life appears to be flying apart into fragments," sits at her desk and "re-arranges scraps of languages" including "legal letters, letters about the Initial Teaching Alphabet from Leo's school; Leo's first written words, which are BUS and MAN; the literary texts and the quite other texts that dissect these texts; her reviews, her readers' reports"—texts piled on texts piled on texts, we might note, until she concludes: "Language rustles around her with many voices, none of them hers, all of them hers" (*Babel Tower,* 381).

But the language of *The Conjugial Angel* suggests one last rustle of language, one last act of uncanny life—that of mating with the dead, of an angelic connubial visitation, of not speaking with but sleeping with the dead. Again, to marry Freud and Jameson, however uneasily, is to bring us to a sense of the erotics of the past, the erotics of resurrection, and the uncanny birth of the self that ritual repetitions of seemingly dead material bring forth: for Freud, remember, mourning is both work and production; for Jameson, to estrange the world is to make the unnatural as natural as anything else, to make the unnatural again "our" (however acculturated) "nature." What does this do to the unnatural act of re-membering literature? I can offer one other, powerful image, one common to both Byatt and Margaret Drabble: the image of a woman in childbirth reading, or, in the case of Drabble's heroine, screaming out the lines of Wordsworth.[13] If the Eliot narrator is dead, Byatt seems to be saying, that does not mean she cannot still be giving birth; for Byatt, despite the intensity of her own labors, her own earnest sortings, morphings, and mournings, the literature she (and in this volume, clearly I mean we) loves still has a life, and more powerfully, a death of its own. Out of that death comes an eerie, but strangely satisfying, new form of vision, one that resides (if a tad uncomfortably) in *both* worlds—theirs and ours; dead and living; resurrected, if still a tad moldy. That world, unlike Mr. Morris's sofa, may not always be that comfortable to sit on, but it may still, nonetheless, give off its own hints of paradise. So, we may suggest, Byatt returns us to our uneasy perch on the Victorian novel: realism may not be comfortable, but that discomfort may be the source of our most generative imaginings.

Notes

1. A. S. Byatt, *Babel Tower* (New York: Vintage International, 1996), 314; 360; 385; all subsequent references are given in the text. The laminations themselves are bits of texts (by the heroine and by others) that she cuts up and rearranges in a "laminated" notebook; Frederica begins using them as a vision of "being able to be

all the things she was: language, sex, friendship, thought, just as long as these were kept scrupulously separate, *laminated,* like geological strata, not seeping and flowing into each other like organic cells. . . . Things juxtaposed but divided, not yearning for fusion" (314–15). Later, she "has the first vague premonition of an art form of fragments, juxtaposed, not interwoven, not 'organically' spiralling up like a tree or a shell, but constructed brick by brick, layer by layer, like the Post Office tower" (360).

2. Byatt's use of the pornography trials offers an interesting microcosm of her technique: she is echoing not only the *Lady Chatterley's Lover* trials, though Lawrence remains a touchstone in all her novels and is so in this one, but the trial over *Last Exit to Brooklyn,* which, like the verdict on her imaginary *Babbletower: A Tale for the Children of Our Time,* is reversed on appeal (Byatt notes this in her "Note for American Readers," ix). *Last Exit,* of course, is a novel of gritty and aggressive social realism; the novel that Byatt puts on trial is abstract, historical, and highly literary, a Sadeian pavane as opposed to the violent underworld of *Last Exit.* The suggestion remains: when Byatt rewrites history, she not only cleans it up, but dresses it up to go out.

3. Her male poet, Randolph Henry Ash, has elements of Robert Browning in his excessive physicality and the linguistic play of his works, as well as his slightly heretical views (and his occasional long-windedness); her female poet, Christabel LaMotte, borrows Elizabeth Barrett Browning's reclusiveness, allusiveness, and coyness. But her letters seem to owe more to Christina Rossetti and Emily Dickinson; her poetry seems more clearly tied to Rossetti's (and of course Coleridge's, as *Christabel* is a recurrent motif in the novel), and she has acquired Christina Rossetti's habit of writing fairy tales and short stories. In turn, Ash has acquired William Morris's Norse epics and Dante Rossetti's translations; the scene of their first meeting at "Crabb Robinson" (a parody, it seems to me, of the breakfasts of Victorian almost-laureate Samuel Rogers) is reminiscent of the scene of self-pronouncement ("I am Christina Rossetti") that is at the heart of Virginia Woolf's powerful essay on Rossetti in *The Common Reader.* The scene Woolf depicts took place at a tea party given by Mrs. Virtue Tebbs; if this woman had not existed, A. S. Byatt would have had to invent her (Woolf, *The Second Common Reader* [New York: Harcourt, Brace and Company, 1932], 261).

4. Byatt's own rather difficult novel, *The Game,* takes up exactly this problem of two sisters writing books, the one difficult works of criticism, the other more popular (and more vulgar) novels of romantic life. Typically, the novel undoes some of its own binaries by the end: the "cheap" sister writes a good novel, one unfortunately taken in part from her conflicts with her "serious" sister, and the serious sister kills herself, but it is not entirely clear that the more serious sister is not herself at fault for her own death and for her inability to create anything more lasting. Interestingly, Drabble's most recent novel, *The Witch of Exmoor,* has returned to the image of a childhood, Brontë-like magic game, which is the central motif of Byatt's earlier novel; it also features two rivalrous sisters who quarrel over one man—in hers, the older sister is the more manipulative and (interestingly again) also finally suicidal.

5. William is living at the estate because his own scientific discoveries, his collection, and all his belongings were destroyed in a fire on board ship while he returned from the Amazon; such an accident had indeed happened to Alfred Wallace, and William notes that he did not fear such an accident for exactly that reason. This same detail (Wallace's accident, the hope of protection, and the loss of an entire South American collection) occurs in Andrea Barrett's wonderful story "Bird with No Feet" in *Ship Fever* (New York: Norton, 1996), where the scientist, a young American, is unable to resume his collecting, but meditates similarly on the nature of collecting and of science itself.

6. A. S. Byatt, *Angels and Insects* (New York: Vintage International, 1992), 306. All subsequent references are given in the text.

7. Fredric Jameson, "Introduction," *Postmodernism, or, the Cultural Logic of Late Capitalism* (Durham, N.C.: Duke University Press, 1991), ix–xii. All subsequent references are given in the text.

8. I am drawing here on Jameson's earlier work in "Postmodernism and Consumer Society" in *The Anti-Aesthetic: Essays on Postmodern Culture,* ed. Hal Foster (Port Townsend, Wash.: Bay Press, 1983), 111–26, which draws on the difference between the pointed, satiric quotations of "parody" and the affectless, emptied-out quotations of "pastiche," which no longer hold the possibility of a stable meaning, but echo the past for its own sake.

9. The dependence on Tennyson should by now be clear; although Byatt cites Michael Chinery's *Collins Guide to the Insects of Britain and Western Europe* and Derek Wragge Morley's *The Evolution of an Insect Society,* there are also clear echoes of Edmund O. Wilson's *Naturalist* (New York: Warner Books, 1994) and (with Bert Holldober) *Journey to the Ants: A Story of Scientific Exploration* (Cambridge: The Belknap Press of Harvard University, 1994). Byatt's debt to Gillian Beer is more general, but see in particular the connections between the sense of "evolutionary plot" and Victorian social relations (particularly familial relations) in *Darwin's Plots: Evolutionary Narrative in Darwin, George Eliot and Nineteenth-Century Fiction* (London: ARK Paperbacks, Routledge and Kegan Paul, 1983). My reading here is indebted to Louise Yelin's fine essay, "Cultural Cartography: A. S. Byatt's *Possession* and the Politics of Victorian Studies," *Victorian Newsletter* 81 (1992): 38–41, which argues that Byatt makes "an implicit claim to possess Victorian secrets known or knowable by no one else," particularly by scholars and critics (40). The reconciliation of the Victorian (Arnoldian) imagination carried out by a culture at once androgynous and feminine, benevolently financed by a "sanitized," Thatcherite merchant (industrial) class, is, as Yelin describes it, far creepier than any of the moldering corpses of *Angels and Insects*—but for the later resurrection, it would seem, you need to have the critics on your side.

10. Sigmund Freud, "Mourning and Melancholia," in *General Psychological Theory,* ed. Philip Rieff, trans. Joan Rivière (New York: Collier Books, 1963), 165, 166, 172. I have selected this translation both for its closeness to the German and its relation to the language of literary realism.

11. My reading of this resurrection is influenced by Edwin Eigner's discussion of *Our Mutual Friend* and the "pious fraud," in "Shakespeare, Milton, Dickens and the Morality of the Pious Fraud," *Dickens Studies Annual* 21 (1992): 1–5.

12. This discussion draws on Edwin Eigner's *The Metaphysical Novel in England and America* (Berkeley: University of California Press, 1978). For a more extended treatment of these issues in Victorian fiction, see my "The Stupidest Novel in London: Thomas Carlyle and the Sickness of Victorian Fiction," *Carlyle Studies Annual* 16 (1996): 117–34.

13. The Byatt heroine is Stephanie in *Still Life*; Margaret Drabble's is Frances Wingate in *The Realms of Gold*.

Asking Alice
Victorian and Other Alices in
Contemporary Culture

Kali Israel

Carol Mavor's *Pleasures Taken: Performances of Sexuality and Loss in Victorian Photographs* begins with a description of a revision. Mavor used to perform, she tells us, as a "portmanteau" figure who combined the Alice of *Alice's Adventures in Wonderland* and *Through the Looking Glass, and What Alice Found There* with "the real Alice" (Alice Liddell [Hargreaves]) and with the figure of Lewis Carroll. In these stagings, she says, she called into question who is an author, who a character, and who a muse, while "insist[ing]" on the "sexuality" of children.[1] Mavor's first chapter, on Carroll's photographs, in turn begins with an allusion to Nabokov's *Lolita,* immediately followed by a claim: "Very few critics have been willing to touch the little girls Carroll photographed" (7).[2] Mavor's choice of names here (the photographer is Carroll, not Dodgson—the fictionalist, not the don) announces that her chapter will follow the precedent of her enactments in moving across histories and stories, while her phrasing extends the suggestion that *she,* unlike most, will dare to touch. Mavor thus begins by evoking stages—the stages of her past performances and the "stages" of child development—and by implicitly staging her own text's daring. The conjunction of these themes—the uses of fictional and "real" characters and names, claims about children and sex, and claims to be breaking taboos—with the name of Alice will recur throughout this essay; I begin with Mavor's beginnings because her text brings them into play so rapidly and usably. I also begin with Mavor, however, because of the simultaneous rightness and wrongness of her claim that others have not dared to touch *those* photographs.

Mavor is, within the strict phrasing of her sentence, correct: she cites Helmut Gernsheim's and Morton Cohen's disavowals of anything troubling in Carroll's photographs. For Gernsheim, Carroll's liking little girls was "strange" but "innocent," and Cohen attributes only "natural" and reverent feelings to Carroll and explicitly dismisses the possibility that he had "anything in common with . . . Humbert Humbert."[3] These texts, however, bring into view that which they wish to dispute. Other texts too display tactics that do not work by the simple repression of erotic possibilities. In several cases, displacement is more notable than a blanket erasure of sexuality. Colin Ford, director of the National Museum of Wales and curator of the 1998 exhibition of Dodgson's photographs, *Lewis Carroll: Through the Viewfinder,* at the National Portrait Gallery in London, recognizes but denies the legitimacy of "the question of pedophilia." That question "overshadowed everything this year," by contrast to a 1974 show of the photographs when, he says, "no one asked me about pedophilia."[4] According to Alan Riding in the *New York Times,* "Ford believes that any sexuality seen in Dodgson's photographs is a product of our age, which has made 'Carroll's always innocent nude children . . . dangerous and threatening.'" While Ford at one level simply denies sexuality in those photographs, he also both displaces perversity onto contemporary viewers and syntactically locates danger and threat on/in the depicted children rather than in Carroll/Dodgson.[5]

A more complex form of displacement utilizes a display of "knowledge" about class. Morton Cohen's essay, "Are You Kissable?" for the catalog of a Grolier Club exhibit and the text that accompanies Carroll's photograph *Alice Liddell as a Beggar-child* in the Pierpont Morgan Library's 1998 Carroll exhibit both briefly and coyly invoke the question of sexuality only to place it elsewhere.[6] Edward Rothstein's *New York Times* essay on the Morgan exhibit calls the seven-year-old Alice a "seductive" "Lolita"—locating sexual agency in the depicted child—and assumes that the normal reaction to the sight of a child in rags, whether a truly impoverished child or a middle-class child in costume, is to feel sexual desire.[7] The Morgan and Cohen texts are scarcely less offensive. The Morgan caption explains: "Beggars were a common sight in both London and Oxford as mid-Victorian culture struggled with the problems of child prostitution, for poor parents would sometimes sell their daughters to the streets. However, in this photograph, Dodgson seems to aim at the image of an alert personality despite her rags." The caption confounds the questions Carroll's photograph might raise about masquerades of class with questions viewers are presumed to have about sexuality, and it conflates poverty with prostitution and street children with sexualized children. It too assigns agency: child prostitution is the result of the decisions of working-class parents.[8] Despite its displacements, however, the Morgan caption retains middle-class agency: an "alert personality" in a poor child, even in a middle-class child pretending to be poor, is an "image" created by the photographer. Cohen's Grolier essay similarly moves quickly from the question of Carroll's desire to an invocation of child prostitution in its second paragraph. Cohen's essay works to separate that which it has itself pulled together while preserving middle-class agency, rapidly explaining that "Polite Society" idealized and worshiped children and was tormented by social misery. In short, sex is something that may happen to children but only to working-class children, principally because of the failure of their immiserated families.[9] As Judith Walkowitz has taught us, stories about Victorian child prostitution can be extremely useful.[10] Despite their different allocations of agency, the Rothstein and the Morgan/Grolier texts are mirror images; in all these texts, the invocation of class allows both the raising and the quick banishment of questions. For Rothstein, class and age disparities are naturally erotic, whereas for Morgan and Cohen, desire for children disappears into pseudosociology. All these texts shift attention away from Charles Dodgson.

I will return to the uses of knowingness about class in stories about children and sex. But if my quick reading of these exhibition texts suggests that Mavor's statement about unease and avoidance as dominant tropes in discussions of the Carroll photographs can be both sustained and revised, her claim about the undaringness of other critics may evoke a response of uneasy laughter. If "few *critics*" have "touched" those photographs, that has not stopped anyone else. If we look around, we find a proliferation of Alices. This is not in itself new. Carolyn Sigler has compiled and commented on the rich tradition of Alice-revisions, and there is, besides the substantial Carroll industry in literary criticism, a lively world of nonacademic buffs and an undiminished trade in Alice tchotchkes like those that filled the display tables and cases of the Morgan Library's giftshop.[11] Despite the Alice trade's affiliations with other branches of marketing the cutely Victorian, Juliet Dusinberre has explored connections between the *Alice* books and literary modernism, and Alice's attractions also seem strong for those overtly locating themselves in postmodernity.[12] "Cyberfiction" writers Jeff Noon and Jonathan Lethem make use of Alice more or less overtly: Noon's *Automated Alice* plunges Carroll's character into a dystopian fantastic 1998 Manchester of chaos theory, human/machine and human/animal hybrids, and blurrings between the real, virtual, and automated, while Lethem's *As She Climbed across the Table* offers jokes about deconstruction and a central character named Alice Coombs whose rabbit hole is a wormhole named Lack, created in a university particle-physics lab.[13] Both books mark Carroll's compatibility with postmodern thematics of fragmentation, deconstruction and reconstruction, inversion, hybridity, logic and language games, reflexivity, jokiness, and punning.[14] But the point is not simply to claim in a register of (slightly exasperated) hyperbole that no one can keep their hands off Alice; my argument is not just that Alices are ubiquitous. I also want to dispute and complicate the status of "denial" as a ruling term in writing about Alice and Carroll. Just as the Morgan, Cohen, Rothstein, and Gernsheim texts invoke even as they deny or displace, a wide array of texts that evoke the Alice books are haunted by the "problem" of those pictures, by possible stories about Charles Dodgson, Alice Liddell, and other little girls.

This essay explores a constellation of Alices, most of whom have been removed from the Victorian era and only some of whom are "little girls." My questions are part, however, of a larger interest in the uses of little girls, especially historicized "Victorian" and "Edwardian" little girls, in contemporary culture. Carolyn Steedman's account of the place of girl-children in stories about human interiority and Judith Walkowitz's analysis of W. T. Stead's "Maiden Tribute" have taught us to pay attention to the political and cultural uses of little girls in the nineteenth century.[15] But Victorian girl-children have also been deployed in more recent fictions, often as emblematic figures of resilience and courage, as in films such as *The Secret Garden* and *A Little Princess* and novels such as Neil Stephenson's cyber-Dickensian *The Diamond Age.*[16] My interest is not in judging such works for adherence to "true" Victorian history but in noticing how fiction and scholarly writing participate in large ongoing cultural arguments about agency and victimhood, survival and damage. More pointedly: the wholehearted reclamation of Victorian and other little girls into stories of survival, courage, and high-spirited triumph may be not only exhilarating but wishful. Celebrations, including scholarly versions, of the endlessly undaunted girl-child who is triumphant despite her vulnerabilities are deeply appealing. This is especially true when such stories are presented as revisionary, when they are marked and marketed as alternatives to narratives of feminine passivity or helplessness.[17] Despite the fillip of daring that may attend them, however, stories of resilient children intersect with a cultural truism, a reassuring knowledge that "children are resilient," a knowledge that can easily slide into comfortable knowingness. Stories of resilience also risk inadvertent collusion with backlash politics in which speaking of victimization is demonized and liberal autonomy is refetishized. However appealing, the proliferation of stories of agency and survival may overshadow other, bleaker, possible narratives. In what follows, I consider several texts that move between "real" and "fictional" characters, including both kinds of Alice, and yet an important intertext for my larger argument is not an Alice text. Geoff Ryman's brilliant *Was* is about an invented "real" Dorothy Gael, the "real" Judy Garland, and "real" L. Frank Baum, and their figures in *The Wizard of Oz*, Hollywood, and the imagination of a young gay man with AIDS; it is a novel about stories and secrets.[18] In Ryman's novel, figures of strong, resilient, courageous girls hide as well as tell stories. We are reminded that the gorgeous, moving circulation of figures does not annul other histories, and that writing lives is not the same as saving them.[19] We also know that Ryman's text is fiction too.

If the production of resilient children is a wider theme, the reiteration of Alices suggests that the possibility of dark stories or irrecuperable losses creates a particular anxiety around that figure. Rothstein's *Times* article is an excellent example of a widespread familiarity with the possibility of sexualized readings of Carroll's photographs of little girls, an instance in a larger pattern of knowingnesses about the perversions of "those Victorians."[20] Such knowingness includes a familiar sniggering but also can range from gleeful appropriation to more worried and even panicked manifestations. At the appropriative pole, at least one pedophile magazine and an Internet child-pornography site have used the title *Wonderland*, while—in the register of panic—an Oklahoma City "family values" activist sought to have *Alice in Wonderland* itself banned from libraries not only because it allegedly promotes drug use but because it was written by a "suspected pedophile."[21] Knowing about the Carroll photographs is both productive and anxious. Productively, the photographs themselves draw attention to the smallness and fragility as well as the beauty of children; they suggest many stories about little girls, many pleasures of fantasized and not necessarily pedophilic intimacy.[22] Anxiously, these stories include the possibility of danger and damage, and not only to long-dead children. Those photographs, that is, may not only suggest dark narratives about past and present, but may threaten our pleasure in narratives we already have. Possible but unknowable stories may impinge on the *Alice* books' ability to offer an angry, active, lively little girl, obstreperous and uncowed—a resilient heroine.

Against this possibility, Rothstein's essay chooses knowingness about seductive girls as its resolution.[23] Others, as we have seen, choose knowingness about class to direct our attention elsewhere: Alice's stories are managed by knowingness about "Victorians." Others yet, such as Mavor and Nina Auerbach, find in the photographs evidence of strength or anger or confidence or traces of "resistance"—that is, they read the photographs for narratives of resilient girls.[24] Reading Alice as a desiring figure is presented as preservative of her autonomy; it also preserves her allure to us. Mavor and Auerbach, in arguing for and about the sexuality of children, echo and intersect long-running tensions inside and outside the academy about agency. An important branch of that larger argument has moved within and around feminism: how do we represent both sexual danger and sexual pleasure, both oppression and agency?[25] In what circumstances must we? Texts about little girls can proffer sexuality as if it were *the* alternative to hapless objectification, but Rothstein's crude naming of Alice Liddell as a seductive Lolita highlights how easily a claim for children's subjectivities can slide into troubling attributions of full sexual agency to children. Moreover, we will see that the allocation of natural and authentic sexuality to girls is often secured through contrasts to repressed or repressive adult women, especially mothers. More broadly, the ascription of sexuality risks becoming an easy knowingness; the knowledge that "children 'have' sexuality," a deeply orthodox position routinely presented with a fanfare about one's sophistication, can be not daring but comforting, not unsettling but gratifying. Like other knowingnesses—for example, about Victorian prostitution—knowingness about children and sexuality displaces and contains the wonderings unleashed by cryptic photographs and untouchable bodies.

I have already set in play some themes that move through the Alice texts I read. My concern is *not* to make claims about the Carroll photographs themselves, Charles Dodgson or Alice Liddell, Victorian children and ideas of childhood, or child sexuality.[26] My interest is in how modern Alice-invoking works by novelists and filmmakers are repeatedly crossed by questions about knowledge and sexuality. The texts I read grapple with the tensions of knowing about and wondering about Alice; they thematize stories as much as sex. Like Mignon in Carolyn Steedman's study of another little girl's circulation through texts and across stages, Alice is a "word for little girls you fancy," but also a name for the "thing you want," and while "wanting" includes sexual desire, it covers many other possibilities, including wanting stories (*Strange Dislocations,* 38–39, 2–3, 5, 173–74). We recall stories of Alice Liddell's requests that Charles Dodgson tell and write stories for her. Alice is a name for wanting stories to have, stories to keep, and stories to continue.[27]

To return to the ubiquity of Alice and the pervasiveness in Alice works of questions of sexuality and boundaries: I can only allude to some recent works that use the Carroll books (see also Sigler, introduction and bibliography). Christopher Hampton's stage version of the Alice novels moves between the world of the books and the life of Dodgson, and cannot avoid wondering about those photographs.[28] Pat Barker's *The Ghost Road,* the culmination of her extraordinary World War I trilogy, includes W. H. R. Rivers's and his sister Katharine's memories of Charles Dodgson.[29] Barker's Rivers painfully and even ironically muses about Dodgson/Carroll, memory and trauma, inadmissible desires, the uncertainty of stories, and the evocativeness of pictures. Barker's novel even raises the issue of the cultural value of little girls: Rivers recalls—in the context of a war in which men's lives are endlessly and meaninglessly expended—Dodgson's contempt for boys. Less obvious Alice texts include Blanche McCrary Boyd's lesbian-feminist odyssey, *Terminal Velocity,* which begins with a Wonderland costume party/play before telling its tale of shifting rules and changing languages, and "Nicci French" (Nicci Gerrard and Sean French)'s murder mystery, *The Memory Game,* which evokes Alice and (a conjunction to which we will return) Dennis Potter for its plot about children, sexual violence, and the knowability of the past.[30] Emma Tennant's novel *Alice Fell* and the Australian Dorothy Hewett's long biographical poem-sequence, "Alice in Wormland," center on female sexuality, families, storytelling, and escape, and they include overt allusions to the Carroll texts.[31] Philip Pullman's children's trilogy, *His Dark Materials,* may draw its title from Milton, but its first volume, *The Golden Compass,* crosses the Alice books.[32] In its early chapters, the heroine, Lyra, inhabits an alternative Oxford that is simultaneously Victorian and futuristic, in a world of mysterious technologies (including forms of photography) and communicating animals. In a moment of danger, Lyra gives Alice as a false name, but immediately afterward declines to enter the "Chthonic Railway" and risk "being trapped underground" (89). While offering intrepid child characters, Pullman's plot impressively and ruthlessly explores the dangers of adult theories of sexuality, including stories about children's sexlessness; betrayal and narcissistic self-justification by adults, including parents; and the violences to children, beyond murder, that class can authorize.

Given these instances of Alice, it is impossible to be surprised when in *As If,* a study of the child murderers of the toddler James Bulger and the fantasies and furies they evoke, Blake Morrison's rhapsodic account of the intense sensory pleasure of dressing and caring for his young daughter concludes with his wife entering the room to read her *Alice in Wonderland. Alice* appears between Morrison's description of his love of the physicality of his daughter and the (notorious) passage in which he tells us that he has experienced an erection with a child on his lap.[33] The ubiquity of Alice's associations with children and danger—sexual or otherwise perverse and mortal—is marked by her range from the quality-press writings of a literary author such as Morrison to contemporary U.S. television. "Paper Hearts," a 1996 episode of *The X-Files,* features a serial murderer of little girls who stores his "trophies"—cloth hearts cut from his strangled victims' pajamas—in a hidden volume of *Alice in Wonderland.*[34] The episode is shot through with Alice/Carroll references, including hearts, number games, and the incessant repetition of the word and theme of dreams. The episode's title—*paper* hearts—evokes books and writing, even though the hearts in the plot are cloth; the murderer is called a Mad Hatter; and the denouement takes place on "Alice Road." The episode's place in the series's larger story-arc both offers the enticements of endlessly elaborating stories and underlines unknowability, as it reiterates the theme of irretrievability that motivates and haunts other Alice tales: Special Agent Fox Mulder may "never find out what happened" to a particular little girl.

Not every Alice in contemporary film and fiction leads us directly back to Oxford, not least because of the name's resonances. Teresa de Lauretis's *Alice Doesn't* tells us that her cryptic title should suggest both the "unqualified opposition of feminism to existing social relations" and the multiplicity of signification, summoning thoughts of "Alice in Wonderland or Radio Alice in Bologna . . . Alice B. Toklas, who 'wrote' an autobiography as well as other things; or . . . Alice James, who produced an illness while her brothers did the writing; or Alice Sheldon, who writes science fiction but with a male pseudonym; or of any other Alice."[35] The ambiguity of Alice's name is explored in Susan Sontag's play *Alice in Bed,* whose book jacket combines an 1891 photograph of Alice James, ill in bed, with a reproduction of the Tenniel drawing of Alice too big for the house that contains and constrains her.[36] Sontag's Alice James wishes and worries about holes to fall down and muses on the problems of bigness and littleness (the stage sets for scene 6 place her in an oversized chair that makes her child-sized in her world), and the play includes a fantastic tea party in which the making of stories about women is discussed. Sontag's epilogue is explicit about her movement between Alices (see 25, 42–80). Sontag's play and her epilogue are deeply concerned with names; "Perhaps nothing about a person is more potent, and also more arbitrary, than the person's name," and both Alices, Liddell and James, were members of famous clans, female bearers of the names of powerful fathers (114). Sontag's own title illustrates the circulation and doubling of names; the play bears, but for its subtitle, the same name as Catherine Schine's 1983 novel, *Alice in Bed.*[37]

Sontag's Alice play illustrates the importance of taking the naming of Alice seriously but not allowing it to constitute a limit. Noon's *Automated Alice* and Alison Habens's *Dreamhouse* underline the mutability of names by a Carrollian device: Noon offers an automated/cyborgian double for Alice named Celia and (*Ali*son) Habens's Alice tale's heroine is also Celia—an anagram of Alice.[38] More important, Alice is only one name, if a ubiquitous one, in stories and histories that evoke her. Like Steedman's Mignon and Ryman's Dorothy, whose names change and who conjure other figures, Alice texts often allude to other much-narrated female figures. We have already seen several authors—Cohen, Mavor, and Rothstein—establish even if by disavowing a relationship between Alice and Nabokov's Lolita; we shall see it again.[39] Sontag's epilogue cites Virginia Woolf's story of Shakespeare's sister, but her Alice is a figure of the nineteenth century. Sontag's play's tea party brings her Alice together with two "real" women—Emily Dickinson and Margaret Fuller—as well as with two "fictional" (and theatrical) women, Kundry from *Parsifal* and Myrtha, Queen of the Wilis, from *Giselle.* In a collection of contemporary fantasy short stories, *Fantastic Alices,* two other authors associate their Alices with Emily Dickinson; Dickinson's fabled "smallness," imagination, and wordplay seem to make her if not a mirror image at least an associate of Alice for some authors.[40]

Sontag's play, moving beween Carroll's Alice and Alice James, also repeats the theme of class. Sontag's play and its epilogue contend, directly and indirectly, that material histories matter and that the class limits of Alice James's imagination should shape the uses of her story, including how we make her story emblematic of women's lives in the past or present.[41] In this critical awareness, Sontag's play is not only a sharp contrast to texts such as the Morgan caption and Cohen's essay, but to another fiction about historical figures, David Slavitt's 1984 novel, *Alice at Eighty.* In Slavitt's text, class and pseudohistoricity are harnessed to very problematic claims about sexuality and gender.

Slavitt's novel works through a series of fictional encounters in the 1920s and 1930s between Alice Liddell Hargreaves, her husband Reginald ("Regi"), their son Caryl, Isa Bowman (an actress who had been among Dodgson/Carroll's "child-friends," who played Alice on the stage and to whom *Sylvie and Bruno* is dedicated), and Glenda Fenwick, a (fictional) London madam who had known Carroll/Dodgson as a child at Eastbourne.[42] In Slavitt's text, there is no ambiguity about the sexual dimensions of Carroll/Dodgson's relations with children; he is a "paedophile," a "poor sad pervert" who masturbates beneath his photographer's drape while taking pictures and who holds little girls onto his erections (79–80, 208). But Slavitt's novel "acknowledges" (and thematizes the acknowledgment) of sexuality only to deny any possible damage except that caused by "repression."[43] Slavitt's novel engages in two moves. First, Slavitt's Glenda and Isa are unharmed by Dodgson because they understand and embrace sexual desire; more, they are indebted to the good sense of their sexually savvy mothers. Isa's mother presents her to Dodgson as younger than she really is and shaves the hair from her daughter's vulva in order to support Dodgson's desire; Glenda's mother manipulates Dodgson and teaches her daughter the skills of prostitution, including auctioning her virginity to the highest bidder. Isa and Glenda expound theories about the "power" of sexualized children, as well as sexually liberated women, over men, although Isa also explains that all "females" secretly want to be seduced and controlled by more powerful men.[44] Both tell stories in which Dodgson's sexual desires, along with their mothers' enlightened attitudes, are gifts that endow them with happy lives. In contrast, Alice Hargreaves is sexually "cold," but not because she was damaged in any way by Dodgson (49). She and Regi have chosen to accept repression, whose most powerful embodiment was the converse of Isa and Glenda's enabling mothers, the puritanical and limited Mrs. Liddell. However—and here is Slavitt's second move—Alice has her own dark and guilty secret that has nothing to do with sex. Alice and her younger sister Edith had been rivals for Dodgson and that relationship caused Alice lasting shame and guilt; that is, the violent emotions of children, and the inadequacies of middle-class, unimaginative Victorian mothers, are dangerous, *not* the sexual actions or emotions of adults.

Slavitt's novel, in short, resolves the questions of those photographs—banishing any uncertainty about the question of Dodgson's sexuality or the sexual agency of children—while rendering them safe largely through the construction of stories about class. Working-class or class-marginal people, especially women, are cheerfully realistic and free, even if occasionally endangered. Middle-class men like Regi and Caryl, however, are victims of sexual hypocrisy, and middle-class women like Mrs. Liddell and Alice Hargreaves are sexually repressive or repressed. Although Slavitt's Isa (like Cohen and the Morgan exhibit) tells us en passant that it is common for the poor to sell their daughters into prostitution, prostitution is also presented as predominantly a space of female power, a picture that owes less, one suspects, to historical analyses of the complexities of Victorian prostitution than to old fantasies about brothels as red-flock-wallpapered free zones in a "prudish" Victorian society.[45] In sharp contrast to Sontag's emphasis on materiality and the power of culture, Slavitt makes sex the key to history and class, sexual knowingness the key to happiness, and gender a self-chosen burden that women can refuse or reshape at will.

In Sontag's Alice play and its epilogue, the powers of stories are stressed. In the play's final scene, Alice James asks for a story, "without the unhappy ending," and Sontag associates fallenness with being captured into a narrative: Alice recalls that she "used to be a real person" but now "I feel as if I fell" (109–10). Sontag's epilogue ends with an insistence on the dangerous limits of stories, including those told by historians. Jean Strouse's biography of Alice James is, in a sense, a story of survival: it culminates in a chapter titled "A Voice of Her Own" and concludes with one in which Alice James crafts "a legacy of her own"—the preservation of her (literary and other) remains—and the achievement of "peace."[46] Sontag, however, concludes: "the victories of the imagination are not enough" (117). For Sontag, stories are powerful in several ways. In contrast, Slavitt's characters are symptomatically contemptuous of stories. The "liberated" characters—Isa and Glenda—depict the *Alice* books as saccharine, bland, and escapist, "charming [but] irrelevant," "neat [but] unsatisfying" (84, 187–88).[47] Their, and Slavitt's, stories seem to require banishing anything scary, angry, or even complex or engaging from Carroll's work. If, as I suggested earlier, some possible stories threaten readerly pleasure in *Alice* and Sontag warns of the costs of such pleasures, Slavitt's characters deny that any grown-up should have or want such pleasures anyway.

Another contemporary "Victorian" Alice text, the 1985 film *Dreamchild,* written by Dennis Potter and directed by Gavin Millar, oddly shares Slavitt's immediate point of departure but offers a far more complex account of the multiple powers of stories.[48] Slavitt and Potter begin with the same story: Alice Liddell Hargreaves's 1932 trip to New York to receive an honorary degree from Columbia University. But *Dreamchild* makes very different use of Carroll's texts. The film is about possible stories around those photographs, possible relations between men and little girls, and about the nineteenth century, but *Dreamchild,* like Sontag's *Alice in Bed,* is also about storymaking.

Dreamchild is visually imaginative in depicting pleasure and menace in its "own" stories and in Carroll's. The film opens on a strange, uncanny, and frightening shore where the Gryphon and Mock Turtle confront the seventy-nine-year-old Alice Hargreaves. Here and in later scenes with the Mad Hatter and March Hare, Carroll's characters are scary and grotesque; the stories with which Alice Liddell is associated, in which Alice Hargreaves sometimes feels trapped, are given dark power. In both *Dreamchild* and in *Labyrinth,* an Alice-inflected 1986 film, storybook creatures are animated by Jim Henson's workshop to be genuinely unnerving; they are ugly, have prominent teeth or talons, and leer close to the camera.[49] In the story the film tells of Alice Liddell and Charles Dodgson as well, Alice is unsure if Dodgson is in some way dangerous; when he tells her, "I like you exactly the way you are. . . . I wouldn't change one hair of your head," she seems to hear both love and threat. Dodgson has Alice dressed up in Chinese costume for a photograph at the time; the film hints that he likes her just as he has made her and as he wants to keep her. Nonetheless, *Dreamchild*'s Alice enjoys Dodgson's love and feels affection for him. Potter and Millar's film neither denies Alice's emotions nor makes them symmetrical with Dodgson's.[50] Elsewhere, too, Potter emphasized the complexity of children's emotional lives even in circumstances of clear-cut abuse. Speaking of his own experience of sexual assault by an uncle at age ten, Potter stressed that such deeply damaging experiences can generate many kinds of stories, many kinds of containments, and representations that should not be reduced to their traumatic origins.[51] Children are not free of power for Potter—in *Blue Remembered Hills* and in interviews, he argued that children's imaginations may contain and reiterate the violence or sinfulness of the adult world—but *Dreamchild* is very different from Slavitt's novel when it depicts children's power over adults. Throughout the film, we see that Alice can hurt Dodgson—thoughtlessly, in half-understood self-defense, or in petty but cruel malice—but even to her cruellest action, Dodgson responds with restraint, his face suggesting forgiveness and comprehension that her actions may be responses to the pressures of his emotions. *Dreamchild* does not render adults and children equals in responsibility.

Dreamchild values a kind of Victorian restraint as morally and psychologically complex, not just a denigrated Victorian "repression." In the film's very moving story, Charles Dodgson is stoic in his desire and sincere in his love, accepting that what he loves most in Alice Liddell—her childness— makes her unable to mirror his love. The film's final scene returns to that strange shore. Dodgson has his face buried in his hands, as if weeping, but to Alice Liddell's question, "what is his sorrow?" the Gryphon replies, "Ah, it's all his fancy, that; he has nae got any sorrow." Dodgson raises his smiling face; he was only pretending to cry; he and Alice join hands and laugh. Nonetheless, we *are* back on that strange shore, the Gryphon and Mock Turtle are still dark and ugly, and we have had our attention drawn to the powers of pretense. We may conclude that Alice—Liddell or Hargreaves— need not have been frightened and that Dodgson and his stories were never dangerous, but we are not surprised that she was. The film has taught us that even "untrue" or incomplete stories have power—to limit, to scare, to mark, as well as to yield pleasure, profit, and adventure. In these double scenes on the fantastic shore, Potter's screenplay and Henson's creatures thematize the problem of those photographs—the simultaneous existence of playful and deeply scary possible meanings—and they give real scariness to the scary possibilities, even while they offer a generous resolution for their Alice.

Dreamchild is visually and verbally dense; every line, including—characteristically for Potter—the lines of the songs, resonates with possible double meaning. Doubleness is the film's method—as in the opening and closing scenes—and one of its central themes. Alice Liddell and Alice Hargreaves shift between and within scenes, and throughout the film, double names are highlighted. Mrs. Hargreaves sharply corrects those who call her Alice or refer to Mr. Dodgson as Lewis Carroll; she draws attention to the presumptions of familiarity and knowledge that naming may signify. These concerns are linked to a repudiation of others' claims to own her story. She argues with a New York reporter, Jack Dolan:

JACK: We all want you to be the little girl you once were.

MRS. HARGREAVES: The little girl Mr. Dodgson made me out to be, you mean.

JACK: Yes, yes! Lewis Carroll's Alice.

MRS. HARGREAVES: . . . [it would be] utterly impossible to be what I never was.

JACK: . . . can't you just . . . play the part?

Like Sontag's Alice, Alice Hargreaves worries about being caught in a story. However, Potter's Mrs. Hargreaves learns to use the cultural industries that initially try to use her—advertising, radio, and Hollywood—and to make use of her image. That plot, as well as the romantic subplot between her companion, Lucy, and Jack, are given happy endings. Nonetheless, each repeats the questions about duplicity, seduction, and exploitation that haunt Mrs. Hargreaves's memory of Charles Dodgson.

Dreamchild shares another theme with Slavitt's novel and other Alice texts: a concern with mothers. Christopher Hampton's Alice play, like Slavitt's novel, makes middle-class Oxford women the enforcers of painful repression on Charles Dodgson's emotional expressivity. But *Dreamchild* is more complicated. Mrs. Liddell appears suspicious of Dodgson from the first scene in which she appears, and Alice explains to Dodgson, "You know how very tiresome mothers can be." Later, Mrs. Liddell tells her daughters, "sitting still is good for little girls," and again regards Dodgson's attention to Alice with concern and an expression of recognition. But Potter's screenplay does not simply use Mrs. Liddell as an emblem of repression. Alice Hargreaves, in conversation with the Caterpillar, worries, ". . . like my mother . . . my mother tore up his letters to me . . . why should she want to do that unless there was something wrong, something I can't bear to think about," but we also repeatedly see Alice Liddell both enjoying and being puzzled by Dodgson's attention. Mrs. Liddell is partly a stand-in for, not simply a source of, Alice's own fears.[52] Mrs. Hargreaves even catches herself becoming a double of her mother, badgering and castigating Lucy, "If I'd behaved like that, my mother would've . . . my mother would've. . . ." Lucy's orphaned state underlines the hint that mothers are not the only source of fear; Lucy is "frightened of everyone and everything, frightened of the world." If Potter's Alice's mother is irritating and repressive, she is not simply opposed to victimized or liberated daughters. She is troubled, and her troubledness is usable by her daughter. That usability, indeed, slyly hints at the usability of the Victorian-mother figure in texts such as Slavitt's and Hampton's and in the wider set of stories in which Victorian middle-class mothers are the condensation of class-coded Victorian repressiveness.[53]

Sontag's, Slavitt's, and Potter's works quite differently use Victorian Alices to make claims about Victorian culture, Victorian mothers, and Victorian sexuality. Other writers have created more contemporary Alices that nonetheless circle around the same themes: stories, sex, and sometimes class, mothers, and photographs. Among these more recent Alice stories, Wim Wenders's 1974 film, *Alice in the Cities,* shares *Dreamchild*'s focus on the elusive, unspoken relations between an adult man and a young child.[54] Wenders's film, like *Dreamchild,* is a story of an awkward sad man and a stroppy but sometimes frightened little girl, wandering through strange lands. The protagonist, a German photographer and writer who has been traveling in the United States, meets and becomes responsible for Alice, aged nine, whose mother—not repressive but simply inexplicably detained— fails to turn up as expected; he travels with her to Amsterdam and in search of a home in Germany that she cannot remember clearly. Like some other Alices, Wenders's Alice is vulnerable, in need of help, and uncertain about some memories, but she is sure about food and stories and is willing to be uncooperative and rude as well as charming. She is decisive about words and referents and eager for reality; playing hangman on a plane, she fails to guess that the word is *Traum* (dream) and insists, "words like that don't count, only things that really exist." *Alice in the Cities* asks questions about vision, pictures, and stories that move across Wenders's oeuvre; his more recent *Until the End of the World, Lisbon Story,* and *The End of Violence* are also about the pleasures and dangers of images.[55] These questions nonetheless evoke Carroll's Alice. The characters in *Alice in the Cities* repeatedly worry about photographs, stories, and truth. The protagonist's work is rejected by an editor: "that's why you came here—for someone to listen to your stories—which are not really intended for you alone—but that's not enough in the long run." He himself is divided by anxieties about images, about "what really exists"; pictures "never really show what you've actually seen" but "taking photographs has something to do with proof." *Lisbon Story,* although not exactly an Alice tale (its presiding texts are by Pessoa, another writer of shifting names), has a protagonist with the same name as in *Alice in the Cities,* played in both films by Rüdiger Vogler, and it slyly includes a white rabbit and a Cheshire cat and is even more explicit in wondering about looking.[56] In short, *Alice in the Cities* is like other Wenders films in worrying about the invasiveness of images, but pictures also provide memory and preserve connection. Wenders's films, like *Dreamchild*, are aware of their own complicities in the dangers of pictures and yet emphasize the potential of photographic apparatuses to offer joy and relationship. In *Alice in the Cities*, Alice takes a picture of the protagonist in Amsterdam; their two faces reflect and combine in the photograph. Later, in a moment of sadness and jealousy, she comforts herself by looking at a photostrip of the two of them, mugging silily at the photobooth camera. *Lisbon Story* worries about the intrusiveness of vision but concludes with a comic coda that emphasizes the pleasure of pretense in a slapstick homage to early cinema. As in *Dreamchild*, stories are self-consciously thematized, and they can be both ended and left open. In the final sequence of *Alice in the Cities*, the protagonist is taking Alice to her mother in Munich. As he is reading a movie magazine, Alice asks what he will do next. "Finish off this story." "Your scribbling?" He nods and asks, "And you, what'll you do?" She is pensive, silent, then rises and the two lean out an open window over an unfolding panorama of river and land.

Alice in the Cities, like *Dreamchild*, offers an understated and ultimately gentle story of adult–child relations. Like *Dreamchild*, too, it raises the question of eros but comically banishes threat. Alice and the protagonist are lying in their underwear on the grass after swimming.

ALICE: I wonder if people think you're my father?

HIM: Me? No! Why? [pause] I don't know, why not? What else would they think?

Alice then announces that she will ask a woman sitting nearby; he protests; she leaps up and runs over. When Alice reports that the woman does not believe he is her father, he asks why not, to which she calls the reply "Too fat!"; they continue in a joking game of naming his faults. Soon after, the protagonist sleeps with the woman but silently understands Alice's temporary jealousy. In short, Wenders's film raises the question—what kind of relationship *might* there be between a man and a little girl?—and, like *Dreamchild*, tells a story in which a child desires adult attention and love, but those feelings are comprehended without transgression. In both films— Victorian or modern—the possibilities of dangerous relations between adults and little girls are acknowledged but contained. Both films can be read as haunted by those photographs—unable to tell Alice stories without wondering, without raising the question of the relations between adults and children—but both dispel, through silent recognitions as well as overt laughter, the possibility of Alice's story toppling into pathology.

A number of novels have, like Wenders's film, de-Victorianized Alices to tell stories set in modern worlds, but in stories in which pathology of various kinds is overtly present. Unlike Wenders's film, however, these modern stories are not about adults and children but are stories of young women, in late adolescence or their early twenties. Stephanie Grant's *The Passion of Alice*,[57] Catherine Schine's *Alice in Bed*, Alison Habens's *Dreamhouse* (in which multiple Alices appear, sometimes anagrammatically), and, perhaps, A. M. Homes's *The End of Alice*, all offer older Alices. These older Alices nonetheless evoke questions I raised earlier about the production of resilient heroines. In Grant's and Schine's novels, Alice is a young woman in a position of considerable constraint and even danger, who is nonetheless demanding, clever, recalcitrant, and intrepid. These Alices are ill: a young college student is hospitalized in bed with a mysterious, immobilizing ailment that causes intense pain, and a twenty-five-year-old young woman is in a clinic for anorexia. Sontag, too, told a story of an older invalid Alice subject to medical discipline, and Schine and Sontag share a multiplication of possible causations—psychic and medical, as well as familial and cultural—for their Alices' immobilizations. In all these tales, girls' and women's bodies are the sites of failure or success, are subject to investigation and constraint, flattery or condemnation. Marya Hornbacher's recent memoir, *Wasted*, like Grant's novel, invokes Carroll's Alice's struggles with bigness and littleness and the powers of looking glasses to tell a story of anorexia, bulimia, and the control of bodies.[58] In Grant's and Homes's fictions, Carroll's trope—"eat me"—is associated with eating disorders and with eucharistic passions; pleasures, not simply self-abnegating starvations, are evoked in intense, unsettling scenes that are not reducible to displaced sexual appetites.

These texts also share with other Alice tales the interconnected themes of proper femininity, class, and mothers. Grant and Schine—like Sontag and Potter—recognize that their Alices' imperiousness, even in bed, is indebted to class privilege, and the powers of middle-class mothers move through these novels as much as through Slavitt and Potter's works. In Grant's and Schine's stories, mothers are loving but inadequate; Homes's narrator tells us that his nameless female correspondent (like Schine's Alice, a college student from an upper-middle-class suburb) has an ineffective mother who attempts to cajole her into proper femininity, and his Alice— the twelve-year-old girl he murdered—was subject to her mother's ineffective attempts to control and protect. Habens's feminist *Dreamhouse* offers a more punitive and oppressive mother who shoves her daughter hard in the direction of a dismal marriage, and Pullman's fantastic *The Golden Compass* contains a scary mother who is seductively ultrafeminine and deadly. Across Alice-invoking texts, mothers' limits and their powers are associated with class. In some stories, they are dangerous queens, subjecting daughters to frightening games; more generally, they are enforcers, tantalizing examples, or sad reminders of the costs of respectable womanhood.

Schine's, Grant's, and Homes's novels overlap with other Alice texts as well in offering looking-glass worlds that their resilient heroines must negotiate. For Schine's Alice Brody and Grant's Alice Forrester, hospitals are looking-glass worlds of language games, rules, arbitrary decisions, and strange people, although Grant also offers a mall bridal salon as a seductive and dangerous mirror-world. In Homes's novel, the nameless male narrator, a convicted pedophile, is in prison.[59] These repeated fictions of institutionality allude both to Carroll's *Alice* books, and indirectly, even unconsciously, to the institutionality of Oxford, another world of strange, arbitrary rules and word games. In Homes's, Grant's, and Habens's novels, middle-class culture, especially in suburbia, can, like Alice Liddell's Oxford, be as weird, confusing, rule-bound, and illogical as any looking-glass world. *The End of Alice* and Schine's *Alice in Bed* also, like Slavitt's *Alice at Eighty,* comment on the strangeness of even recent histories; if Regi and Caryl highlight the repressiveness of Victorian society, Homes and Schine highlight the oppressive dailiness of, respectively, the 1950s or 1960s and the early 1970s in Westchester and Westport. But Homes's novel also offers a warning. Her narrator asserts that there is no, or little, difference between his prison and the outer world, and between him and "us," but his claims are an attempted seduction by a highly unreliable narrator; his knowingness about the secrets of suburbia and about "our" secret identifications are deeply self-serving and allow him to claim a kind of "innocence," which the very overtness of his crime "proves" (74–75, 109). More narrowly, it is worth remembering that Grant's and Schine's protagonists choose to reenter worlds more normal than the hospitals they inhabit.

Alice's attractions for stories about female adolescence and young womanhood—especially the themes of confusion, boundaries, parent–child relationships, the costs of adulthood, and the arbitrariness of various social worlds—thus run across these novels by Grant, Schine, Habens, and Homes. The appeal of Alice's name for exploring such themes is not limited to fiction, as Hornbacher's memoir and Mandy Sayers's autobiographical *Dreamtime Alice* illustrate.[60] These contemporary, un-Victorian, novels do more than simply borrow a name, invoke an image or moment from Carroll's texts, or take advantage of the suitability of Carroll for stories about youth and liminality. Their plots subtly or overtly present knowledge of those photographs and the stories sometimes told about them. Certainly, one could read the aging of Alice as a response not just to the ways in which photographs freeze moments of childhood but as a riposte to Charles Dodgson/Lewis Carroll's sadness about girls' growing up, the wish attributed to him (by biographies and by *Dreamchild*) to keep little girls just as they are forever. But these novels do not just reassert time. They are also stories about young people and erotic agency. These Alices must struggle to comprehend, respond to, or resist other people's imputations or refusals of sexuality. These stories are not about little girls but they are definitely about sex.

Grant's Alice's erotic struggle is to find a way to formulate her desire for another woman, to find a language that does not feel entrapping. Schine's Alice in bed is seduced by a creepy doctor who addresses her in diminutives and eroticizes her smallness and physical helplessness. The heroine of Habens's *Dreamhouse* finds that desire in women, and desire for women, is not a "fall" but a leap into heights (250). Grant's Alice and Habens's Celia both have (like Alice Liddell?) important friendships with sexually dissident/dissonant men; Grant's Alice's recovery includes a reconciliation with her black gay friend Ronald, a friendship that had been destroyed by sex and denial, and Habens's Celia grapples to understand her housemate, Dodge(son), a transgendered man with whom she argues about names and with whom others confuse her. Sexual labels and languages must be refused, reworked, and claimed in these books. Grant's *The Passion of Alice* suggests that sex and stories need to be disentangled. Like *Dreamchild*'s Alice Hargreaves, Grant's Alice comes to understand that she has been more afraid than necessary; sexuality can bring pain as well as pleasure but desire is "only a fact"; it "lacked agency" in itself and it did not determine what stories might be lived (256).

Schine's novel more overtly echoes questions about Carroll/Dodgson and the applicability of sexual labels. Alice wonders about her ludicrously Anglophilic father. He has abandoned his marriage and embarked on a new life, and he asks Alice to send him some of her childhood books, including one about a rabbit, in order, Alice suspects, to woo the child of his new girlfriend. Alice muses:

> her father loved nine-year-olds. He had been wonderful to Alice and Willie when they were nine. It seemed futile for him to start with another nine-year-old, though. . . . It was bound to become ten sooner or later, and then eleven, and then twelve [and then an adolescent with a sex life]. . . . Poor Daddy, she thought. This can only end in tears. (121)

Alice and her brother, talking about their father, jokingly wonder whether he's "entering his second childhood" or is "a pederast," but Alice sadly concludes that he simply cannot accept her maturation: "Alice looked at her father in his blue blazer and silk ascot and thought how difficult it must have been for him to watch her turn from a happy girl earnestly coaxing her spirited pony over a stone wall into a sullen teenager locking herself in her room to listen to loud rock and roll. A chair in the dollhouse that suddenly violated the decor. . . . And then of course I was sick as well as sullen. He must have found that a kind of obscenity" (217).

The aging of Alice into adolescence or young adulthood can both mark and deny the ways in which Alice texts are haunted by those photographs and the possible stories about them. If class offers some authors a way of suavely acknowledging while immediately displacing questions of the sexualization of children, the age shifting of Alice allows her to figure in stories that are sexual but not pedophilic while still being about youth and power. If those photographs cause us to wonder if we should wonder about the sexualization of little girls, the aging of Alice allows an open exploration of the erotic. Stories about not-little girls can freely be stories about sex. As in Schine, questions about pedophilic desires can even resurface jokily or indirectly. This is not to say that these novels are settled, let alone comforting, in the effects of this displacement. Schine's novel, for example, risks a troubling conclusion. Her Alice, virtually paralyzed, is seduced by an infantilizing doctor, and yet she is a lusting, voluntary participant who feels desire for him and other men.[61] If readers are meant to be startled out of the easy assumption that the disabled or the ill are sexless—that is, if Schine's text means to draw attention to and overturn a taboo—does it intend an analogy to be made to other taboos? If Schine is out to challenge us to imagine that (even) sick girls might like sex, even in situations of maddening constraint and pain, even when addressed in smarmy diminutives, does her placement of this quite reasonable claim under the sign of Alice invite analogies to other girls who have limited power and are conventionally seen as erotically inert? Are we meant to wonder if little girls like sex too? Schine's novel does not make such a clear claim but it risks such analogizing.

The shift of Alice's name to stories about Alices indisputably old enough to be erotic agents may both exhibit awareness about those photographs—and questions about sexuality and agency—and offer an easy out. Even Slavitt's *Alice at Eighty* may be marked by this anxiety; his tale insists that Isa Bowman, when first involved with Dodgson, wasn't *really* eleven, she was *really* thirteen, only pretending to be younger.[62] Of course, the question of Alice's age and Alice's agency overflows the category of Alice stories per se. To use a trite recent example, media and popular discussions about Monica Lewinsky highlighted the confusion and opportunism of allocations of sexual adulthood to female figures; Lewinsky, in her twenties, was cast in some accounts as the child victim of adult male lust; that is, the aging of Alice in some texts may not secure her erotic agency for some readers, given the volatility of ideas about gender and sexual agency in young people.

This incoherence is not new: Carolyn Steedman argues that the instability and sometimes unknowability of Mignon's age—she is sometimes a "little girl," sometimes "older than her years"—is central to that figure's repetition and usefulness in nineteenth-century plots (*Strange Dislocations,* 34, 36, 41). In our time, however, Lolita is the (unstable, covering, fetishized) name for female figures whose desirability depends on their youth but whose age itself and whose status as sexual agent are famously unstable. The instability of Lolita's age underlines questions about the repercussions of aging Alice. While Rothstein applied the name to a seven-year-old, Lolita is more often, like Schine's and Grant's Alices, older than her "original." Whatever the reasons—capitulation to "prudery," casting difficulties, or legal issues—the aging of "Lo" in both film versions, from Nabokov's twelve-year-old to fourteen or fifteen, has effects. Most obviously, it removes the necessity of thinking about Humbert's category of "nymphets" as including nine-year-olds. By enlisting our knowledge that "of course" teenage girls are sexual and can be flirtatious and aggressive, the Lolita films risk aligning themselves with Humbert at his most self-serving, speaking of his helplessness in the face of nymphetic actions, rather than Nabokov at his most complex.[63] James B. Harris, the producer of Stanley Kubrick's *Lolita,* claimed: "We wanted [Humbert] to be the only innocent person in the piece," and Adrian Lyne's *Lolita* as well aspires to be *Humbert's* tragedy.[64] The shifting of Dolores Haze's age helps "Lolita" to become the name for sexually aggressive minors, as in popular usages such as the "Long Island Lolita."[65]

Lolita is not just a parallel to Alice as an often-aged figure. We have seen that their names often appear together in critical texts—in Mavor, Cohen, and Rothstein—whether to claim or deny that "their" stories are the same.[66] A. M. Homes's *The End of Alice,* however, goes beyond a quick invocation to a more sustained bringing together of Nabokov and Alice while reiterating the questions that Alice's aging in other texts might raise. Homes's novel is a first-person narrative by a nameless, imprisoned pedophile and murderer who tells us about his correspondence with a nameless female college student who writes to him about her desire for and seduction of a twelve-year-old boy. *The End of Alice* is a Lolita text as much or more than it is an Alice text; Homes's novel is deeply, fundamentally Nabokovian. The narrator depicts himself as a Humbertish gentleman-aesthete, infinitely nuanced in his pleasures and pains; he is seductive and unbearable in his language games and jokiness, his lovingly detailed accounts of the degradations and pains he suffers and those he tells us about having inflicted or wishing to inflict. As in Nabokov, too, the disjunction between the narrator's account of his helplessness and the account of what he did to Alice that he finally repeats to us exposes his self-interest. Throughout the novel, we must wonder at even his "slips," the moments at which his text claims or seems to be out of control.

I will return to *The End of Alice*'s affiliations with Nabokov, but Homes's novel shares themes with other Alice texts: the trope of eating as transformative; an institutional setting and a depiction of "normal" middle-class society as a looking-glass world that is arbitrary, confusing, and scary. As in other Alice texts, mothers are dangerous: Homes's narrator depicts his mother as unstable, seductive, unpredictable, and sexually exploitative, and the mothers of his victim, his young woman correspondent, and the young boy that correspondent allegedly seduces as controlling but ineffective, unattractive stereotypes of suburban femininity. *The End of Alice* also sharpens some of the questions I have pursued through other Alice texts, questions about attribution and agency and the making of sexual stories. Homes's narrator, like other authors, freely attributes desires to others, including "us." We know nothing about "the girl" who writes him but what he claims are her words, and he repeatedly draws attention to how he has "translated" her inadequate accounts into detailed stories of her actions and desires; he tells us how much he hates it "when they believe they can think for themselves" (52). Homes's narrator's repeated and overt claims to know, and thus to be licensed to act upon, the "truth" of others' desires alerts us to the usefulness and the dangers of such claims. Victorianist James Kincaid's scholarly *Child-Loving* similarly claims to offer a brave knowledge that "we" are all child lovers and all share in pedophilic desires, but Carolyn Steedman has rightly noted how Kincaid occludes other possible deep subjective relationships to stories of child sex (*Strange Dislocations,* 166–68).

Homes's narrator tells us about his attractiveness to filmmakers, writers, and academics, who visit or write him, as well as the placement of his childhood belongings in a museum of crime, and Homes compounded this theme by publishing, alongside her novel, an art book of pictures of artifacts linked to the novel.[67] Homes's text(s), that is, highlight the desire to understand extreme acts and the belief that a careful enough scrutiny can yield comprehension. But her narrator also draws attention to the glamour and self-congratulating sophistication that can attend the desire to encounter, to know, to claim terrible things, to hear and tell horrifying stories, and she shows us how this glamour ratifies the narrator's story of himself as too good, rather than too bad, for "normal" life. Homes's novel, like other Alice texts, conjoins desires and knowledge with the power of stories. Homes's narrator tells many stories before and instead of the story of his murder of Alice. Throughout his accounts, the possibly fantasized status of his stories taunts that we are, after all, reading a novel, a fiction, while the narrator also tells us how powerful stories are. He quotes his young woman correspondent, who tells him that the stories of his murder of Alice, who lived on her street in *Scars*dale, shaped her life: "I live differently because of you, there is no such thing as safety" (164–69). But we have only his account of her words.

The End of Alice both thematizes and works by exciting the desire for stories. The narrator presents himself as desperate for the young woman's stories and willing to create them himself if necessary, but while telling many other stories, which may be fantasies, of other children and what he did to them, he withholds the story of his Alice, the child he killed. The sadistic suspense of his withholding, as much as the sadistic pleasure of his recounting, places the reader in the perverse position of wishing for the plot to move forward, if only to end the suspense—wishing for something to "happen" in a plot in which only terrible things happen. The stories he does tell—excruciating or nauseating for at least some readers—dare the reader to endure. Instead of the universals other authors offer—-we are "all" pedophiles or we "all" know about children, sex, or Victorians—Homes's novel implicates us by suggesting a different universal: we "all" want stories. Homes's novel can be read as responding to those photographs in a different register. *The End of Alice* suggests that we prefer stories over uncertainty and undecidability; we may even prefer scary stories, including those that use the language of brave exposition of sociological or psychological truth, because they confirm our own resilience.[68] In short, Homes's Alice tale speaks deeply to the problem of those photographs—not what they mean but how they incite desires to find and to use stories.

The End of Alice's extremely sophisticated relations to Nabokov complicates its conjunction with other Alices, however, especially in its ending. In her killer's (deeply unreliable) account, the denouement—that is, the murder—is in some sense caused by Alice's female biology. Alice becomes extremely, violently upset on getting her first period, for which she was unprepared; her hysterical fear and distress "make him" stab her to death and mutilate, dismember, decapitate, and rape her dead body (267–69). This plotline is related to the narrator's earlier story of his mother's body and his mother's blood, but the theme of female reproductive biology compounding female vulnerability both echoes *Lolita* and brings Homes's narrator's account oddly near Slavitt's *Alice at Eighty*. Homes's narrator insinuates, like Slavitt, that it is children's emotions that are dangerous. Adequate sexual knowledge might allow sexual engagement with adults to be untraumatic or at least not fatal. In her murderer's tale, which is the only tale we have, Alice's sexual ignorance and wild emotions lead to her end.

Homes's Alice's textual relations also oscillate between *Lolita* and other Alice tales in another regard. Like other modern Alices and like Dolores Haze, Homes's Alice is not a little girl. Indeed, the narrator sometimes conflates his child victim, Alice, who is twelve and a half, and his nameless female correspondent, who is nineteen or twenty. Moreover, although the narrator had earlier told of younger girl-victims, Alice—the girl he "loves" and kills— is pubescent and she is extremely sexually aggressive. The narrator surmises that her actions—masochistic as well as aggressive and taunting—may be the result of earlier sexual abuse, but they nonetheless allow him to tell a particular kind of story, of a man tormented by a seductive child/adolescent.[69] Alice is only partly a child and is in some respects, like Mignon, "old beyond her years." Homes is truer to *Lolita* than the films of that name, which age Dolores even further, and her novel does not, any more than Nabokov's, present Alice as deserving her fate. Yet by placing Alice on the cusp of adolescence, by foregrounding Alice's body's sexual maturation, Homes both raises and restricts the terms of questions about children, sexuality, and agency.

Homes ensconces Alice's story in Nabokov's. But if Homes's novel's relations to *Lolita* incite metaphors about halls of mirrors, this essay too has become a looking-glass world of texts that mirror or modify each other and speak to other stories. I end therefore by doubling back, to say more about an Alice text cited earlier, which is itself about moving, mutating figures. Alison Habens's *Dreamhouse* thoroughly uses Carroll's Alice novels while commenting on the uses of Carroll, Alice, and Charles Dodgson.

Habens's story of how Celia changed her mind combines Carroll's wordplays, reversals, and multiplication of figures—the anagrammatic Celia is but one of several Alices—with contemporary satire. *Dreamhouse* includes violence—an attempted rape and a murder—and sharp-edged allusions to sexual violence and threats to children, and it refuses to manage the question of those photographs by producing a contained story of sexual predation. Habens's Dodge(son), a housemate of her central character, Celia, is neither desireless nor a dangerous deviant; although sometimes unsure in his loyalties, he is not a villain and his desires are absurd, moving, and uncategorizable within simplistic schemata. He is sexually dissonant/dissident without being either Slavitt's harmless "poor sad pervert" or a dangerous heterosexual pedophile. Instead, *Dreamhouse* gives *Dreamchild*'s strategy of doubling an extra turn. Celia first thinks that Dodge is sexually interested in her but then realizes that his desires are more complicated. His room is a "mirror image" of hers and he pleads to borrow her Alice-blue frock: "Dodge doesn't want her. Dodge wants to *be* her" (140). In a mirroring conversation, Celia and Dodge argue about Alice and Victorian men; Celia tells him that in Tenniel's illustrations, "Alice looks like a boy. A boy with a wig on. Wearing a dress. Just like you." Dodge bristles, "A girl doesn't want to be told she looks like some Victorian queen's sexual fantasy. It's unnatural" (141). He defends his own masquerade's power but is also the only one who can recognize Celia through her costumes. Despite Habens's satirical take on Dodge's love of the stereotypical femininity by which Celia is endangered, he is a perceptive voice about sexual danger and a defender of Celia's choices. In Celia's dress, he is attacked by a Mad Hatter who thinks he is "Alice," and he learns, "No matter what I said, it would have been Alice talking. And you know that men don't listen to little girls. His 'Yes' was worth a hundred of my 'Nos,'" and in another context, he reiterates: "Celia said no. She said no, and she meant no. So we're just going to have to take no for an answer" (266, 324).

Dreamhouse reminds us that the demonization of some marginal men may divert attention from dangers inside families. But Habens avoids the countermove of Kincaid's *Child-Loving,* in which a critique of the demonization of the figure of the pedophile as utterly deviant Other is oddly purchased, as Carolyn Steedman notes, by a remarkable silence about incest and parafamilial abuse (*Strange Dislocations,* 167). Habens does not buy recognition of familial dangers by glibly eclipsing other dangers, as in the *The End of Alice*'s narrator's attempts to elide what he did—torture and murder—with all the hidden violences of suburbia. In *Dreamhouse,* danger is neither wholly outside nor wholly inside; Habens's text refuses that economy. After the murder, police attempt to break down the door of the house, but by ironic "luck," "the door is substantial; designed to have old-fashioned families raised behind it, designed to keep strangers out and secrets in" (326). Habens's Dodge draws attention both to continuities in forms of violence ("you know that men don't listen to little girls") *and* to the reality of non-familial assaults (266). Dodge (cross-dressed as Celia) and the novel's Alice are attacked, and those attacks make clear that sexual danger is not located only in individual strangers or in secretly pathological families. One attack is an attempted date rape by a man who feels entitled, while the Mad Hatter is both a rapist and a policeman. Habens also suggests that violence is not the only means by which some men secure power. Like *Dreamchild,* in which Alice Liddell sometimes finds Dodgson's adoring gaze oppressive, *Dreamhouse* notes that male pathos can be a weapon: Celia's father has always found the making of "sad doggy-eyes . . . his best weapon against women and socialists alike" (261). Conventional marriage is presented as a risk of starvation and mutilation, and some mothers are punitive enforcers of constraint on their daughters, but Habens does not simply repeat the trope of repressive mothers; a subplot involves intense, loving mourning by two daughters for their mother.

Habens's novel moves between the "real" and the "fantastic," and, like *Dreamchild,* argues that the two are not separable. When Celia protests that the Alice tales are "a bedtime story for children," her double, Alice, "drawls," "That's just what I used to think" and expounds the looking-glass realpolitik of Wonderland: "Wonderland is an institution like any other. Riddled with corruption and rotten with internal politics. It's back-stabbing all the way to the top" (91). One of Habens's Tweedledee/Tweedledum twins, Hebe, tells Celia: "It is always daylight in the depths of your unconscious mind. And it is a political unconscious. It's up on current affairs. It reads the papers. It knows what's going on," while Celia's mother learns from the Sheep that "something she thought was a figment of her own childhood imagination . . . is out on general release. How many hundreds of people must have the same dreams?" (228, 239–40). Habens's brilliant concluding sequence comments on Alice's mobility. Celia is mysteriously transformed; she becomes—like Disney's Alice?—a cartoon, a giant image, towering, transparent, luminescent, naked, singing. But this transfiguration is not a containment in yet another fantasy; she then becomes invisible. Her unlocatable voice explains:

> "Generations of girls have sat at that tea table and been told to shut up and listen," Celia's tones are terrible, "and all they hear are nonsense crimes, but the Hatter's word is the law. . . . We must get out of Wonderland. . . . Disillusioned? I know I am." (312–13)

Her friends think they glimpse her, through a tiny, unpassable door, in a mysterious garden, shimmering under a tree, but to Dodge's question—can she hear him?—she replies, "No." A cryptic, jubilant postcard later falls through the box of an empty house. Celia doesn't live here anymore.

Habens's novel pays paradoxical homage to the stories whose dangers she cites and evokes the complicity of stories with violence while seizing their plots of escape. Celia both escapes Alicehood—containment in stories about little girls—and claims that figure's powers, mutabilities, and elusiveness. *Dreamhouse* condenses, therefore, much of the work of this essay: Habens's novel knows that Alice is always on the move and endlessly usable, that Alice stories contend with the powers of gender and sex and the powers of stories to contain and deflect; that Alice is always being dressed up and unmasked, being attacked and idealized, being reiterated and disappearing. *Dreamhouse* knows that Alice's mutability is not unambiguous; it knows that Alice's name has been inscribed in misogynist and trite stories as well as feminist fantasies. *Dreamhouse* knows that there is no end of Alice.

To repeat my own earlier words, in a new context: *Dreamhouse's* multiplications—of Alices and stories—offers a microcosm of the wider, multiauthored profusion of Alices. But if no one can keep their hands off Alice, few can not wonder what it means to touch her. This doubleness—Alice's endless appeal, but the apparent necessity of containing the stories to be told about her, a necessity often shaped by a desire for stories of agency, resilience, autonomy, and durable selfhood—often generates plots in which wondering is central. Alice-writers do not only or always tell stories about desire—stories that explicitly inscribe or deny the sexual—but when they do, they often displace the stories they claim to tell. Some use class and prostitution to localize and displace the sexualization of children; others resort to the *Lolita*-film gambit, in which an age shift ensures that Alice is not just a sexual victim by ensuring that she is not a child. Wondering is also often banished by claims to knowledge—knowledge about sex, knowledge about children, knowledge about Victorians. Yet if some stories align us with a fantasied figure of Alice Liddell and her sisters—asking for more stories— the problem of those photographs is not just the stories they suggest but that they will never say enough, never move us from storymaking to knowledge. Thus, other authors, including me, tell stories that draw attention to Alice's revisions and perambulations, appearances and disappearances: stories about the making of stories. In mirror images of knowing-stories, Alice becomes a figure or a name for unknowability. Potter and Wenders, Homes and Habens, darkly or comically thematize not only the threat of sexual stories but the elusive power of stories more generally. More: in their tales, desire is a capacious, uncertain category, including but not reducible to sex. These authors remind us that stories, desire, and knowledge can appear in many sentences, in changing combinations and weights.

Indeed, the proliferation and mobility of Alice is not new—since her first appearance, she has been usable for many purposes. Her mobility is not distinctively postmodern, however appealing she has been for writers who position themselves as such. Nor is wondering about Charles Dodgson, or about relationships between children and adults, vision and possession, especially fin-de-siècle. Potter and Millar's film draws on a play written in the 1960s, and Wenders's Alice-invoking films—however they have been seen as distinctively postmodern—run from the 1970s through the 1990s. The trope of the repressive Victorian was also certainly far from unique to late-twentieth-century culture. Alice tales can easily form part of a story of continuities between postmodernism and modernism, as in her continued usability for those interested in children, language, and eros (Dusinberre). Nor need Alice remain where *I* have put her: in an unfinished and provisional story about the appeals and costs of the desire for stories of resilience and agency, and in a story about tensions between knowingness, wondering, and narrative. There are many more Alice stories than I have told, and there will be more to come, more that we may wish for, more than we may wish for. No one can keep their hands off Alice, but no one can hold on to her either.

Notes

I am grateful to Yopie Prins and Geoff Eley, who combined suggestions and improving comments with unfaltering enthusiasm for this essay; they not only made it better but made it a site of pleasure, friendship, and shared thinking. JP made it possible.

 1. Carol Mavor, *Pleasures Taken: Performances of Sexuality and Loss in Victorian Photographs* (Durham, N.C.: Duke University Press, 1995), 1; Lewis Carroll, *Alice's Adventures in Wonderland* (1865) and *Through the Looking-Glass, and What Alice Found There* (1871), in *The Annotated Alice,* ed. Martin Gardner (Harmondsworth, England: Meridian, 1960).

 2. Vladimir Nabokov, *Lolita* (New York: Fawcett, 1959).

 3. Helmut Gernsheim, *Lewis Carroll, Photographer* (New York: Dover, 1969), 18, and Morton Cohen, *Lewis Carroll, Photographer of Children: Four Nude Studies* (New York: Potter, 1978), 4, 30, both cited in Mavor, 8. For another argument about the presence or absence of pedophilia in a Victorian image of a little girl, see Laurel Bradley, "From Eden to Empire: John Everett Millais's *Cherry Ripe,*" *Victorian Studies* 34 (1991): 179–203; Pamela Tamarkin Reis, "Victorian Centerfold: Another Look at Millais's *Cherry Ripe,*" and Laurel Bradley, "Reply to Pamela Tamarkin Reis," *Victorian Studies* 35 (1992): 201–8.

 4. Colin Ford quoted in Alan Riding, "Lewis Carroll Revisited: In a Looking Glass, Darkly," *New York Times,* 20 August 1998.

 5. See some texts by Penelope Fitzgerald for another version of this displacement: in "Renewing the Struggle" (review of Geoffrey Palmer and Noel Lloyd, *Father of the Bensons: The Life of Edward White Benson, Sometime Archbishop of Canterbury*), *London Review of Books,* 18 June 1998, Fitzgerald simply announces that falling in love with, and proposing marriage to, an eleven-year-old was not "considered in any way strange in the 1850s," and her prizewinning novel, *The Blue*

Flower (New York: Houghton Mifflin, 1997), tells a historical story of a (young) man falling in love with a twelve-year-old girl. For Fitzgerald, it is only our century that finds falling erotically in love with (not just plotting marriage with) little girls unsettling; we are the perverse ones. Elsewhere, Fitzgerald—like others—reaches for *Lolita* to tell stories about latter-day prudishness; see *The Bookshop* (London: Duckworth, 1978), and note 22.

6. Morton N. Cohen, "Are You Kissable?" in catalog for Jon A. Lindseth collection, *Exhibition in Commemoration of the Hundredth Anniversary of the Death of Lewis Carroll* (New York: Grolier Club, 1998), 68–69; "a.k.a. Lewis Carroll," exhibition at the Pierpont Morgan Library, New York City, 22 May–30 August 1998.

7. Edward Rothstein, "The Man Who Turned Sense into Charmed Nonsense," *New York Times,* 22 June 1998. But see Seth Koven's important essay, "Dr. Barnardo's 'Artistic Fictions': Photography, Sexuality, and the Ragged Child in Victorian London," *Radical History Review* 69 (1997): 6–45, esp. 37; see also Mavor, 35–42.

8. This trope also appears in David Slavitt, *Alice at Eighty* (New York: Doubleday, 1984), 135: one of Slavitt's characters explains that there were "child brothels all over London," and that the selling of children by parents into prostitution "the way the Chinese sell their daughters. For rent or food, or more likely for gin" was "not uncommon." For working-class parents selling their daughters, see also Roberta Rogow's mystery novel, *The Problem of the Missing Miss* (New York: St. Martin's Press, 1998), 151. Rogow also tells stories of upper-class men, outwardly respectable but secretly corrupt, whose jaded sexual palates create the market for girl prostitutes, and of a French market for abducted virgins. The inadequacy, familiarity, and sometimes sheer wrongness of these stories of Victorian prostitution is too enormous to be discussed here, but see Judith Walkowitz, *Prostitution and Victorian Society: Women, Class, and the State* (New York: Cambridge University Press, 1982), chapter 1, and Walkowitz, *City of Dreadful Delight: Narratives of Sexual Danger in Late-Victorian London* (Chicago: University of Chicago Press, 1992), chapters 3 and 4.

9. For a more historical view, see Anna Davin, *Growing Up Poor: Home, School, and Street in London, 1870–1914* (London: Rivers Oram, 1996).

10. Walkowitz, *City,* chapters 3–4; see also Koven.

11. Carolyn Sigler, ed., *Alternative Alices: Visions and Revisions of Lewis Carroll's Alice Books* (Lexington: University of Kentucky Press, 1997).

12. Juliet Dusinberre, *Alice to the Lighthouse* (London: Macmillan, 1987).

13. Jeff Noon, *Automated Alice* (New York: Crown, 1996); Jonathan Lethem, *As She Climbed across the Table* (New York: Doubleday, 1997). Carroll's Alice can also be de-Victorianized in an explicitly multicultural and urban modernization; see Whoopi Goldberg, *Alice* (New York: Bantam Books, 1992).

14. For other science-/cyberfictions that allude to the Alice books, see, for example, Tim Powers, *Expiration Date* (New York: Tor Books, 1996); Astro Teller, *Exegesis* (New York: Vintage Books, 1997); and Melissa Scott, *Trouble and Her Friends* (New York: Tor Books, 1994), 16, 18, 336; for stories mostly in the subgenre of fantasy, see Margaret Weis, ed., *Fantastic Alice: New Stories from Wonderland*

(New York: Ace, 1995). Appropriately, Martin Gardner's *Annotated Alice* is available on CD-ROM; see *The Complete Annotated Alice* CD-ROM (San Francisco: Voyager). See also Robert Gilmore, *Alice in Quantumland: An Allegory of Quantum Physics* (New York: Copernicus, 1995), and an older science-fiction nod toward Alice in children's literature, Kirill Bulychev, *Alice: Some Incidents in the Life of a Little Girl of the Twenty-First Century, Recorded by Her Father on the Eve of Her First Day of School,* trans. Mirra Ginsburg, illus. Igor Galanin (1968; New York and London: Macmillan, 1977). Noon's novel shares a somewhat nostalgic attraction to "the Victorian" with other texts by cyberfiction authors; see Neil Stephenson, *The Diamond Age or, A Young Lady's Illustrated Primer* (New York: Bantam Books, 1995); William Gibson and Bruce Sterling, *The Difference Engine* (New York: Bantam Books, 1991); and Paul DiFilippo, "Victoria," in *The Steampunk Trilogy* (New York: Four Walls/Eight Windows, 1995). The issue of Alice, modernity, and nostalgia is perhaps relevant to another body of Alice works, the compositions of David Del Tredici: *An Alice Symphony* (1969; revised 1976); *Pot-Pourri* (1968); *Adventures Underground* (1971; revised 1977); *Vintage Alice* (1972); *Final Alice* (1976); *Child Alice* (1977–81; this includes *In Memory of a Summer Day* [1980], *Quaint Events, Happy Voices,* and *All in a Golden Afternoon*); *Virtuoso Alice* (1984); *Haddocks' Eyes* (1985); and *Dum Dee Tweedle* (1992); see K. Robert Schwarz, "A Composer Caught in Alice's Web," *New York Times,* 24 May 1998, Arts and Leisure 25, 29; the caption on the front page of the Arts and Leisure section ("K. Robert Schwarz on David Del Tredici and the End of Alice") invokes another Alice work I shall discuss later in this essay. See also Schwarz, liner notes on Del Tredici for Michael Boroskin, piano, *Works by George Perle, David Del Tredici, and Nicholas Thorne* (New World Records, 1989).

15. Carolyn Steedman, *Strange Dislocations: Childhood and the Idea of Human Interiority 1780–1930* (Cambridge: Harvard University Press, 1994); Walkowitz, *City of Dreadful Night*; see also Steedman, *Childhood, Culture, and Class in Britain: Margaret McMillan, 1860–1931* (New Brunswick, N.J.: Rutgers University Press, 1990); see also Deborah Gorham, "The 'Maiden Tribute' Re-examined: Child Prostitution and the Idea of Childhood in Late-Victorian England," *Victorian Studies* 21 (1978): 353–79. Jacqueline Rose's *The Case of Peter Pan, or The Impossibility of Children's Fiction* (1984; Philadelphia: University of Pennsylvania Press, 1992) is indispensable for thinking about the uses of stories about and "for" children. See also Valerie Walkerdine, *Daddy's Girl: Young Girls and Popular Culture* (Cambridge: Harvard University Press, 1997), and Annette Kuhn, *Family Secrets: Acts of Memory and Imagination* (London: Verso, 1995), for the uses of little girls in British culture since 1945; see also Lauren Berlant, "The Theory of Infantile Citizenship," in Lauren Berlant, *The Queen of America Goes to Washington City* (Durham, N.C.: Duke University Press, 1997).

16. *The Secret Garden* (1993; dir. Agnieszka Holland; screenplay Caroline Thompson*);* *A Little Princess* (1995; dir. Alfonso Cuarón; screenplay Richard LaGravenese and Elizabeth Chandler); both films are based on novels by Frances

Hodgson Burnett, and *The Secret Garden* film was preceded—and in a sense publicized—by a successful Broadway musical, whose book was by Marsha Norman.

17. The distribution of resilience along class lines in these works is an important issue that I cannot explore here other than to note its salience in, for example, Rogow (254–55) and in several of the modernized suburban Alice texts discussed later.

18. Geoff Ryman, *Was* (New York: Penguin Books, 1992). Ryman's *The Child Garden, or A Low Comedy* (1989; New York: Orb, 1994) also abuts some themes in this essay.

19. See also Leo Bersani, *The Culture of Redemption* (Cambridge: Harvard University Press, 1990).

20. For a worried knowingness earlier in the century, see Louise Brooks quoted in Tom Dardis, "What Lulu Wanted," *Vanity Fair,* April 1998, 176. For a muddle, see Rogow's "Victorian" *Problem of the Missing Miss.* Rogow unites Charles Dodgson with Arthur Conan Doyle in pursuit of an abducted little Alicia against a backdrop of the "Maiden Tribute" and the passage of the Criminal Law Amendment Act of 1885; her text displays tropes of class and sexual secrets I have noted elsewhere along with an extravagant and clunky knowledge about "Victorians."

21. Information on Oklahoma City's Bob Anderson from the Electronic Freedom Foundation conference on the WELL computer conferencing system, May 1994; I am grateful to several WELL EFF contributors for these citations, but such references have been made en passant over several years and I have synthesized them, with consequent risk of having misunderstood. The "Wonderland" Internet child-porn site was raided by British police, acting with international police cooperation and claims to have uncovered an international ring of practicing pedophiles; see http://online.guardian.co.uk for 18 September 1998 (report by Duncan Campbell).

22. See Mavor, 35ff. But see also Penelope Fitzgerald, "In the Golden Afternoon" (review of Morton Cohen, *Lewis Carroll,* and Jo Elwyn Hughes and J. Francis Gladstone, *The Red King's Dream*), *TLS,* 17 November 1995. For Fitzgerald, even Cohen's exculpating stories need containment: they are "ungainly speculations," and "[t]he biographer's task is not to *picture* wild scenes at the Deanery" (emphasis added).

23. See Kali Israel, *Names and Stories: Emilia Dilke and Victorian Culture* (New York: Oxford University Press, 1998), chapters 3 and 5, however, on the usefulness of preserving the ambiguity of rhetoric in Victorian relationships marked by disparities of age, gender, and power.

24. See, for example, Mavor, 11–20. Mavor modifies the more unqualified claims of Nina Auerbach's "Alice and Wonderland: A Curious Child" and "Falling Alice, Fallen Women, and Victorian Dream Children," in Nina Auerbach, *Romantic Imprisonment: Women and Other Glorified Outcasts* (New York: Columbia University Press, 1980).

25. The two most important collections in this argument at its height in the 1980s were Ann Snitow, Christine Stansell, and Sharon Thompson, eds., *Powers of*

Desire: The Politics of Sexuality (New York: Monthly Review Press, 1983), and Carole Vance, ed., *Pleasure and Danger: Exploring Female Sexuality* (Boston: Routledge and Kegan Paul, 1984). On the competition in and between narratives of sexual danger and sexual agency in Victorian society, including Victorian feminism, see Walkowitz, *City of Dreadful Delight*, and Israel, *Names and Stories*, chapter 6.

26. Among the texts I shall not engage at length are James Kincaid's *Child-Loving: The Erotic Child and Victorian Culture* (London and New York: Routledge, 1992), although I shall return to its use of the trope of "knowingness"; Kincaid has returned to his themes in *Erotic Innocence: The Culture of Child Molesting* (Durham, N.C.: Duke University Press, 1998). Nor shall I say more about the many literary critical studies of the Carroll Alice books or works on Carroll/Dodgson and Alice Liddell Hargreaves such as Morton Cohen, *Lewis Carroll: A Biography* (New York: Alfred A. Knopf, 1995); Stephanie Lovett Stoffel, *Lewis Carroll in Wonderland: The Life and Times of Alice and Her Creator* (New York: Harry N. Abrams, 1997); Colin Gordon, *Beyond the Looking Glass: Reflections of Alice and Her Family* (London: Hodder and Stoughton, 1994); Anne Clark, *The Real Alice* (London: Michael Joseph, 1981); and Jo Elwyn Hughes and J. Francis Gladstone, *Lewis Carroll: The Alice Companion* (London: Macmillan, 1998). See also Christina Bjork, *The Real Alice: The Story of Alice Liddell and Alice in Wonderland*, illus. Inga-Karin Eriksson, trans. Joan Sandin (Stockholm: Raben and Sjogren, 1993), a work for children. For the wider literature on Victorian children and childhood, see Steedman, *Strange Dislocations* and *Childhood, Culture, and Class*; and Dusinberre, *Alice to the Lighthouse*, chapter 1, and the excellent notes to those works.

27. See also Alex Owen, "'Borderland Forms': Arthur Conan Doyle, Albion's Daughters, and the Politics of the Cottingley Fairies," *History Workshop Journal* 38 (autumn 1994): 56–57. For the conjunction of Alice, fairy tales, photographs, and continued stories, see also John Crowley, *Little, Big* (New York: Bantam Books, 1981); my thanks to Isaac Land for directing me to Crowley.

28. Christopher Hampton, *Alice's Adventures Under Ground*, adapted from the writings of Lewis Carroll, in collaboration with Martha Clarke (London: Faber and Faber, 1995). Appropriately, Hampton stages Dodgson's denial of any impropriety through scenes involving a Mr. and Mrs. Mayhew (36–39); Mayhew is a loaded surname in the history of the representation of Victorian little girls; see Steedman, *Strange Dislocations*, 114–27, 171–74, and her *Landscape for a Good Woman: A Story of Two Lives* (New Brunswick, N.J.: Rutgers University Press, 1987), 128, 134–38.

29. Pat Barker, *The Ghost Road* (New York: Dutton, 1995), 18–19, 22–27, 32, 86–95. See also Katharine Rivers, "Memories of Lewis Carroll," intro. Richard Slobodkin, *McMaster University Library Research News* 3 (1976).

30. Blanche McCrary Boyd, *Terminal Velocity* (New York: Alfred A. Knopf, 1997); Nicci French, *The Memory Game* (London: Penguin Books, 1997), 58, 357; see also 335, 337.

31. Emma Tennant, *Alice Fell* (London: Jonathan Cape, 1980); Dorothy

Hewett, "Alice in Wormland" (1987), in *Collected Poems 1940–1995* (Fremantle, Australia: Fremantle Arts Centre Press, 1995), 211–306.

32. Philip Pullman, *The Golden Compass* (New York: Ballantine, 1995); the second volume of the trilogy, *The Subtle Knife* (New York: Alfred A. Knopf, 1997), includes, perhaps, a rabbit hole and certainly a continuation of Pullman's exploration of arguments about children, sexuality, and class. Pullman is also the author of several other children's books with Victorian settings; see his *Spring-Heeled Jack: A Story of Bravery and Evil*, illus. David Mostyn (New York: Alfred A. Knopf, 1989), and the Sally Lockhart trilogy: *The Ruby in the Smoke* (New York: Random House, 1985), *Shadow in the North* [British edition: *The Shadow on the Plate*] (New York: Alfred A. Knopf, 1986), *The Tiger in the Well* (New York: Alfred A. Knopf, 1990), and the linked novel, *The Tin Princess* (New York: Alfred A. Knopf, 1994).

33. Blake Morrison, *As If* (London: Granta, 1997), 151–53, 154.

34. "Paper Hearts," *The X-Files,* Fox television; episode directed by Rob Bowman; written by Vince Gilligan; series created by Chris Carter; first broadcast December 1996. The murderer John Lee Roche (Tom Noonan)'s motives are not specified; we do not learn if he sexually molested or "only" killed the known victims, perhaps to keep them from getting older. The episode has plot elements in common with A. M. Homes, *The End of Alice* (New York: Scribner's, 1996); discussed later in this essay.

35. Teresa de Lauretis, *Alice Doesn't: Feminism, Semiotics, Cinema* (Bloomington: Indiana University Press, 1984), vii; see also 36.

36. Susan Sontag, *Alice in Bed: A Play in Eight Scenes* (New York: Farrar, Straus and Giroux, 1993); first produced in Bonn, Germany, 1991.

37. Catherine Schine, *Alice in Bed* (New York: Plume/Penguin, 1983).

38. Alison Habens, *Dreamhouse* (New York: Picador, 1994).

39. Nabokov's translation of *Alice in Wonderland* has obviously licensed but does not exhaust this association; see Mavor, *Pleasures Taken,* 129 n. 1. See also John R. Cook, *Dennis Potter: A Life on Screen* (Manchester: Manchester University Press, 1995), 110: "is *Alice in Wonderland* the English equivalent of *Lolita*?"

40. Gary A. Braunbeck, "The Rabbit Within," 15, and Bruce Holland Rogers, "A Common Night," in Weis, ed., *Fantastic Alice,* esp. 15 and 63–70; both stories are, like Sontag's, about mortality and loss. On the trope of Dickinson as small and childlike, as well as the countertrope of Dickinson as—like Alice—angry, see Adrienne Rich's influential "Vesuvius at Home: The Power of Emily Dickinson" (1975) in Adrienne Rich, *On Lies, Secrets, and Silence: Selected Prose 1966–1978* (New York: Norton, 1979), 157–83, esp. 166.

41. Sontag, scene 7, and 116.

42. See also Stoffell, 120–21.

43. Slavitt, 49; see also 72, 235.

44. For the trope of children as powerful in sexual relationships with adults, see Kincaid, *Child-Loving,* 24–25, and, among his sources, Theo Sandfort, *The Sexual Aspect of Paedophile Relations: The Experience of Twenty-Five Boys* (Amsterdam:

Pan/Spartacus, 1982), and Tom O'Carroll, *Paedophilia: The Radical Case* (Boston: Alyson, 1982), 166–82. But see Steedman, *Strange Dislocations,* 166–68.

45. Slavitt, 135; see also DiFilippo, "Victoria," and, more disapprovingly, Rogow, 22–23, 45–46; cf. Israel, 200.

46. Jean Strouse, *Alice James: A Biography* (Boston: Houghton Mifflin, 1980), chapter 16 and 307, 314–17.

47. See also Rogow, 252.

48. *Dreamchild* (1985; dir. Gavin Millar; screenplay Dennis Potter). Mavor also comments on this film (*Pleasures Taken,* 42). Potter's 1965 "Wednesday Play," *Alice,* is in many details a rehearsal of *Dreamchild*; see Cook, *Dennis Potter,* 109–11.

49. *Labyrinth* (1986; dir. Jim Henson; screenplay Terry Jones) also concerns a strange, unstable world, rigged games of logic, and a young girl uncertain about losing or keeping her status as child.

50. Cf. A. N. Wilson, quoted in Rachelle Thackray, "Confused by Childhood," *Independent on Sunday,* 28 June 1998; Wilson says his novel, *Dream Children* (New York: Norton, 1998), was motivated by a perception that in discussions of pedophilia, the media present children as without feelings.

51. See Cook, 51–52. See also Humphrey Carpenter, *Dennis Potter: The Authorised Biography* (London: Faber, 1998); and Blake Morrison, review of Carpenter, *Independent on Sunday,* 20 August 1998.

52. See also Barker, 92.

53. I am grateful to Adela Pinch's essay "Rubber Bands and Old Ladies," in Nicolas B. Dirks, ed., *In Near Ruins: Cultural Theory at the End of the Century* (Minneapolis: University of Minnesota Press, 1998), 147–71.

54. *Alice in the Cities* [*Alice in den Städten*] (1974; dir. Wim Wenders; screenplay Wim Wenders and Veith von Furstenberg). For Wenders as postmodern, see Roger F. Cook and Gerd Gemunden, eds., *The Cinema of Wim Wenders: Image, Narrative, and the Postmodern Condition* (Detroit: Wayne State University Press, 1997).

55. *Until the End of the World* [*Bis ans Ende der Welt*] (1991; dir. Wim Wenders; screenplay Wim Wenders and Peter Carey); *Lisbon Story* (1995; dir. and screenplay Wim Wenders); *The End of Violence* (1996; dir. Wim Wenders; screenplay Nicholas Klein; story by Klein and Wenders).

56. It is not quite possible to say that *Alice in the Cities* and *Lisbon Story* have the *same* protagonist: in *Alice,* Philip Winter is a photographer, in *Lisbon,* a film soundman, and in an intervening Wenders film, the *Until the End of the World,* Vogler is again Philip Winter—as a kind of loopy Philip Marlowe, a detective who tracks missing persons. Yet the characters are not quite separate, either: *Lisbon Story* is about finding a missing person, and *Alice in the Cities* about finding a missing place. *Until the End of the World* underlines affinities between Wenders's films and Alice tales: themes of looking and violation, dreams, and movement across strange landscapes.

57. Stephanie Grant, *The Passion of Alice* (New York: Houghton Mifflin, 1995).

58. Marya Hornbacher, *Wasted: A Memoir of Anorexia and Bulimia* (London: Flamingo, 1998); cf. Grant, 57, 116–17, and 134–35.

59. Homes's *In a Country of Mothers* (New York: Vintage Books, 1993), like Grant, deals with the powers and languages of therapy.

60. Mandy Sayers, *Dreamtime Alice* (New York: Ballantine, 1998), esp. 74.

61. The jacket copy of the paperback version of Schine's novel, as well as excerpts from reviews reprinted before the title page, repeatedly hit the note of "sexiness"; Alice is a "sexy sickie" in a "highly compromising position."

62. Slavitt, 131–32.

63. See Richard Corliss, *Lolita* (London: British Film Institute, 1994), 25–26. The age-shift's status as an open secret allows a frisson of further knowingness; the much remarked upon "stylishness" of both films underlines such responses. On the films, see also Nick James, "Humbert's Humbert," *Sight and Sound* n.s. 8.5 (May 1998): 20–23.

64. Harris quoted in Corliss, 32; see also 87; James, 22.

65. "Long Island Lolita" was the tabloid name given to teenager Amy Fisher; see also Elizabeth Patnoe, "Lolita Misrepresented, Lolita Reclaimed: Disclosing the Doubles," *College Literature* 22 (1995): 81–104. See also Walkerdine, *Daddy's Girl,* chapters 5, 7, and 8; but Walkerdine's own analysis sometimes combines "little girls" and teenagers; see, for example, 155–56.

66. See also jacket copy for Wilson, *Dream Children* (note Carrollian title), which announces that it is a daring new "*Lolita* for our times."

67. A. M. Homes, *Appendix A: An Elaboration on the Novel The End of Alice* (New York: Artspace, 1996).

68. See Israel, chapter 3; Steedman, *Strange Dislocations,* 168–69.

69. See Homes, 223, 225–26.

Specters of the Novel
Dracula and the Cinematic Afterlife
of the Victorian Novel

Ronald R. Thomas

Sartre, a movie-goer since the age of three, tells us somewhere that the theory of contingency—the fundamental experience of *Nausea* and the cornerstone of Sartrean existentialism as such—was derived from the experience of film, and in particular from the mystery of the difference between the image and the world outside. . . . Did human nature change on or about December 28, 1895?

Fredric Jameson, *Signatures of the Visible*

"Here I am, sitting at a little oak table . . . and writing in my diary in shorthand all that has happened since I closed it last. It is nineteenth-century up-to-date with a vengeance. And yet, unless my senses deceive me, the old centuries had, and have, powers of their own which mere 'modernity' cannot kill."[1] So writes Bram Stoker's character Jonathan Harker while imprisoned in Dracula's Transylvanian castle, lost in an unmapped region of Eastern Europe while on a business trip selling London real estate to that strange foreign gentleman. Despite Harker's repeatedly expressed concern that he cannot pinpoint his location on any available map or in any book, his sense of disorientation is not principally geographical. He is as lost in time as he is in space, stranded uncomfortably in some uncharted territory between what he calls the "powers" of "the old centuries" and those of "modernity." The young solicitor's act of writing an "up-to-date with a vengeance" account of the bewildering events that transpire in this temporal and spatial

288

limbo impresses upon him the consciousness of a profound historical dislocation, placing him squarely on the threshold of what might justifiably be called the post-Victorian.

Harker penned his diary in the recently invented language of business shorthand in a notebook that would eventually be transcribed by his wife on her typewriter and collated with a number of other typewritten documents from other modern media—phonograph records, newspaper clippings, intercontinental telegraphic messages, personal letters, shipping records, railroad timetables, Kodak photographs—all of which together comprise the text of *Dracula*. Those documents, each of them written originally in the hand of Bram Stoker, of course, would eventually be typeset and then mass-produced for the modern readers that made this late-Victorian gothic sensation a best-selling novel in both the nineteenth and twentieth centuries. But Harker's diary and the novel that contained it would find another equally enduring medium and a still wider audience when *Dracula* was adapted for the screen. David Pirie has counted more than two hundred vampire movies produced in the period between 1955 and 1970 alone, in markets ranging from the United States to England, Spain, Mexico, France, and the Philippines.[2] The actual number of Dracula films in existence is ultimately incalculable because it is difficult to determine which of them qualify as actual adaptations of Stoker's novel and which are more properly regarded as mere parodies, pastiches, or allusions to it.[3] Regardless, unless, like Jonathan Harker, our senses deceive us, *Dracula* has been made into moving pictures "with a vengeance," more frequently than any other literary work—Victorian or otherwise.

We should not be surprised that Hollywood's obsession with making and remaking nineteenth-century novels into movies simply will not die, nor that "the movies" have become the principal medium through which the Victorian novel, and even Victorian culture, has maintained its ghostly afterlife in modern society. I will argue here that the reasons for this irrepressible haunting of contemporary "visual culture" by the specters of nineteenth-century "novel culture" are embedded in modernity's mixture of anxiety and nostalgia over these two deeply interrelated phenomena that are also at the heart of Bram Stoker's *Dracula*: the modern sense of having lost a nineteenth-century conception of the autonomous individual "character" (on the one hand) and (on the other) the modern belief that the forces of the past drain the life from the present even as they sustain it. I will explore how this combination of concerns is singularly embodied in the plot of this most frequently filmed Victorian novel and, more specifically, in the history of its myriad film adaptations. In both instances, the message about character and historical consciousness becomes inseparable from the medium in which that message is delivered, so much so that the media themselves transform the subject—and subjects—of the text beyond recognition or reclamation.

Dracula adaptations have by no means cornered the market of Victorian novels made into movies. In the last few years alone, not only has virtually the entire Jane Austen oeuvre been put on film, but classic nineteenth-century novels from almost every novelistic tradition continue to offer a potent source of material for the screen. Kenneth Branagh's 1994 version of *Frankenstein* was only one more in a seemingly endless stream of adaptations of Mary Shelley's story of perilous self-making, dating back to the first Edison studios' silent production of 1910. Recent film versions of Hardy's *Jude,* Brontë's *Jane Eyre,* James's *Portrait of a Lady,* and yet another *Great Expectations* (this updated variant set in modern-day Miami and New York City) make clear how deeply implicated the medium of film continues to be with core Victorian issues. These very different novels from the nineteenth century all deal in their distinct ways with the crucial concern of maintaining a stable and definable moral "character" who takes his or her place in the forward progression of history. Not accidentally, these are the very Victorian virtues so frequently longed for by contemporary politicians and pundits who vilify the decline of modern society and condemn the influence modern movies inflict upon it.

Stoker's novel, and its legion of film versions, make these same issues their central concern as well; but here they are staged as the problematic symptoms of fundamental conflicts between the past and the present in which the traditional conception of character is threatened by primitive forces from within and by modern forces from without. The modern compulsion to repeat and recapture a Victorian past symptomatizes an ambivalence in the relationship between now and then—a simultaneous desire to recover the lost sense of "character" the Victorians at least seem to have embodied and a simultaneous fear of being recaptured by that archaic formation. "The death of the novel," D. A. Miller has argued, "has really meant the explosion everywhere of the novelistic" into a modern mass culture, a phenomenon that treats the essentialized "liberal subject" at the heart of the Victorian novel as, at once, the lost paragon *and* the antitype of post-

Victorian persons.[4] The medium of film itself, especially when it lives off the Victorian novel as its source for scripts, captures this ambivalence in a particularly eloquent way.

Uncertainty about the status of persons and historical consciousness is absolutely central to the plot of *Dracula,* a story in which a spectral figure from the past literally threatens to extinguish the will and agency of Victorian *character* as they exist in a series of stock Victorian *characters* in the present: the young woman and the young man coming of age; the progressive physician at the vanguard of scientific theory; the effete aristocrat in decline; the lunatic confined in an asylum; the flirtatious "new woman"; the ambitious professional; and so on. That ghostly figure from the past lives by drawing its lifeblood from the present and transforming individual characters into zombie-like automata, essentially denying them their character and autonomous agency. Dracula does this by first inciting and then disciplining their suppressed erotic energies.[5] But this is not his only tactic. The vampire also manages to stimulate and then inhabit the same informational technologies with which his victims try to document his activities and resist his power. Considered in the light of its subsequent cinematic incarnations, the materials of Stoker's novel conspire with its screen history to offer a compelling metaphor for the way nineteenth-century texts and textuality, together with the sense of subjectivity they symbolize, haunt the modern cinema and even the modern sensibility.

This haunting effect is dictated first by the way Stoker's plot is presented to its reader: in the form of a series of written texts generated in more and more technologically sophisticated media, which themselves become mysteriously possessed by the mediumship of the same hallucinatory power they seek to master and destroy—the "undead" force from the past we call Dracula.[6] From the very first screen adaptation of the novel (F. W. Murnau's *Nosferatu* in 1922), modern filmmakers have extended that impulse by foregrounding the cinematic vampire's genealogy from the world of texts and the modern media's simultaneous enthrallment by and transcendence of all that is represented by the more primitive medium of textuality. Because the vampire's power (especially in these film adaptations) is expressed through his ability to access his victims through their eyes and to manipulate what they see and what they do not see, the cinema may be the teleological principle silently guiding the evolution of modern media technologies so elaborately documented in the novel. In this light, Mr. Harker would seem to have gotten it right in that diary entry. There are some powers of past centuries that the media of modernity cannot kill, and *Dracula* is foremost among them.

The force of that now prior time—Harker's "up-to-date nineteenth century"—seems to live on in our own time not in spite of but within the representational machinery of modernity: not just in the typewriter, the phonograph, and the telegraph, but (even more persistently) in the moving pictures of the cinema, where that spellbinding power of the past is ritually recalled and disposed of in the darkness of the local cineplex with each new incarnation of yet another vampire movie. The point is not simply that cinematic style began with the Victorian novel, as Sergei Eisenstein famously proclaimed in his classic essay on Dickens, Griffith, and the cinema.[7] Nor, as Marshall McLuhan put it in *Understanding Media,* that "even the film industry regards all of its greatest achievements as derived from novels" of the nineteenth century.[8] What we sometimes fail to remember is that the cinema itself is a nineteenth-century invention, one that came to life not only just in time to record Queen Victoria's Diamond Jubilee, but also to witness the publication of Bram Stoker's *Dracula* in the very same year. Through the magic of this reel-to-reel device, we make our own ceremonial return to Victorian culture each time we enter a movie theater and the house lights go dim, regardless of what title is listed on the marquee.

In the selection of Dracula films with which I will be concerned here (ranging from Murnau's silent 1922 German Expressionist *Nosferatu,* to Tod Browning's 1931 early "talkie" version of the book starring Bela Lugosi, to Francis Ford Coppola's 1992 postmodern treatment of the subject, *Bram Stoker's "Dracula"*) this ambivalence is expressed most elaborately in the increasingly sophisticated ways in which a dialectical relationship between text and image is played out on the screen. This dynamic, in turn, may be read as combining the historical confusion that inhabits Stoker's novel with an investigation of what is at stake in the transition between the self defined novelistically (as a substantial character with continuity, integrity, and agency) and the self portrayed cinematically (as an evanescent flickering of machine-made shadows that appear and vanish in time intermittently). Seen in this light, the common cliché of film criticism—that cinema is a medium incapable of portraying the complexity of human character and interiority—misses the crucial point.[9] Such observations, faithfully trotted out to dismiss the latest film adaptation of virtually any nineteenth-century novel, overlook the fact that the cinema is the medium of the modern subject, for whom the essential interiority of the individual is a Victorian myth that has been displaced by a congeries of impulses shaped by the mechanical forces of time and place, producing only the illusion of continuity, coherence, and self-control.[10] The story of this displacement is illustrated quite explicitly in each of the film versions of the novel to which I will allude here.

An analogous narrative of displacement, it should be noted, may be traced in the fundamental shift in film theory that occurred in the 1970s, when a dominant semiological framework for analyzing cinema was supplanted by a psychoanalytic one—a turn that directed emphasis away from the content of the cinematic sign to the effects the cinematic apparatus registered upon the spectator. Jean-Louis Baudry and others drew the analogy between the experience of film and that of the Freudian dream work, arguing that both function as devices by which the subject constituted itself through images. According to Baudry, dream and cinema alike are expressions of the primitive desire "to construct a simulation machine capable of offering the subject perceptions which are really representations mistaken for perceptions."[11] Central to this analogy between dream and film, however, is a crucial distinction between the "hallucinations" of the film spectator and those of the dreamer—a distinction based in what Baudry called the essentially "*artificial* character of the cine-subject." "It is precisely this artificiality," he argued, "which differentiates it [the cinema] from dream or hallucinations" and which problematizes the "subject effect" of the film spectator in a peculiar way (706–7). This distinction, which underscores the evidently artificial nature of the cine-subject, may also be seen to illuminate the fundamentally different conception of the self that is cultivated in the private act of reading a book from that which is constructed in the process of watching the mechanical apparatus that projects a movie, a point that is quite explicitly illustrated in the history of film adaptations of Bram Stoker's *Dracula*.

In Stoker's novel, Harker is particularly impressed by the "vast number of English books" and "bound volumes of magazines and newspapers" he finds on the shelves of Dracula's library when he arrives in Transylvania (19). Though the books represent widely divergent fields—history, geography, law, politics, political economy, botany, geology to name a few—Harker notes that they are all out of date and that they all deal with "English life and customs and manners" (ibid.). It is as if the anachronistic character of English life and manners is bound up with their status as written texts. At the same time, Dracula characterizes these books as his "good friends," who have offered him "many hours of pleasure": "Through them I have come to know your great England; and to know her is to love her," he confides to Harker (20). All that this ancient figure knows about the character of the modern person, that is, is a product of these outdated English texts, which together he has humanized and subjugated to his desire and will. And it is through whatever he has absorbed in these texts that the primal and subversive force he represents takes the artificial form of a strange "modern" character when he enters the world of London and takes up his parasitic residence at Carfax Abbey.[12]

Fittingly, therefore, one of the first demonstrations of Dracula's ascendant power over the character of Jonathan Harker takes place when the vampire forces his unwilling guest to compose yet another text by writing a letter to his fiancée, Mina. The monstrous host dictates the content of that text to the young law clerk, a letter that specifies the length of his planned stay in Transylvania and the state of his mind. As the vampire inhabits Jonathan's writing here and gradually transforms his character, so will he occupy and work through all of the elaborate array of written texts (and writers) that comprise the novel. "Here is the book," Jonathan eventually says to Mina when they are reunited in marriage, presenting her with the diary of his secret ordeal with the vampire and his consorts, "Take it and keep it, read it if you will" (104). In the form of this book, Jonathan not only ritually offers himself to Mina and reveals what he has become, he exposes her character to Dracula's invasive influence as well. (Dracula seems to similarly take up occupancy in Dr. Seward's diary, the newspaper accounts of his activities, the ship's log recounting his journey, and the telegraph messages of Van Helsing.)

At the same time that the vampire derives his power from these media, however, he also takes control over them and cancels their authority, as he does quite literally back in London when he burns the very manuscripts and melts the phonograph cylinders that had so carefully documented his existence there. By the end of the novel, therefore, Harker is forced to admit that "in all the mass of material of which the record is composed, there is hardly one authentic document" (378). If the goal toward which the narrative strives is to invoke and then destroy the vampire that has transformed these Victorian characters into the modern persons they have become, that objective can only be achieved by producing and then destroying the very written media which that hallucination vampirically occupies and usurps.[13]

The Dracula films identify this transformation of character with the transformation of the novel from page to screen. As in Stoker's story, Murnau's *Nosferatu* introduces the vampire to the viewer through an elaborate series of texts that practically structure the film—a real estate contract, the "Book of the Vampires," a ship's log, newspaper articles, and even a piece of needle-point made by the Mina character that spells out (in German) "I Love You." In each case, the appearance of the vampire is preceded by the appearance on the screen of a passage from one of these texts, as if the text were an intertitle sequence providing a portion of dialogue or narrative transition between scenes (as silent films frequently deploy for such purposes). In *Nosferatu*, however, these projected passages of text play a more complex role: they are detail shots of objects in the mise-en-scène; they are intertitles advancing and explaining the film's narrative; and they are indices connoting the medium's origins in and departure from the world of textuality.

Jonathan Harker's first encounter with the vampire in the film, for example, is preceded by his reading about such creatures in a mysterious "Book of the Vampires" he discovers in his hotel room on the night he arrives in Transylvania. Before he goes to sleep, close-up images of Jonathan reading this book are intercut with extreme close-ups of the words written on the pages of text he is reading before he goes to sleep. After Harker journeys to the vampire's castle the following morning, a parallel montage is presented at the entrance to Nosferatu's castle. A medium shot shows a pair of massive doors opening mechanically like the parting curtains of a movie screen (or the covers of a massive book). That shot is intercut with a medium shot of a dark passage within the castle, now seen from Jonathan's point of view, in which the strange white figure of Nosferatu gradually appears— as if a fade-in seen through the viewfinder of a movie camera. In the logic of this pair of parallel sequences (like many that follow it) the *book* of vampires is effectively transformed before our eyes into the starkly framed *image* of Nosferatu, as first we and then Jonathan move from the subject position of readers to the subject position of spectators.[14]

In a later sequence back home in Bremen clearly intended to echo this one, Nina gets her first view of Nosferatu only after she reads the same "Book of the Vampires" Jonathan had been reading in Transylvania (Murnau's script moves the London setting to Bremen and changes Mina's name to Nina). After secretly reading from this text that her husband has forbidden her to read, Nina rises out of her sleep in a trance, approaches the open window of her room, and gazes outward. The camera cuts from a shot of Nina with her back to the camera, looking out the window, to a shot (from her point of view) of the ghostly visage of Nosferatu, appearing like a hallucination framed in another window that fills the screen directly opposite. It is as if Nosferatu now exists as a two-dimensional figure projected on a screen before her, just as he does for the spectator. Reinforcing the analogy between Nina viewing the vampire and the spectator viewing the film, the pallid face in the window begins to move offscreen to the left, beyond the camera frame, until the figure disappears. Then, in a subsequent sequence, Nosferatu enters Nina's room in the form of an oversized shadow projected upon her sleeping body, a transformation warranted, we might argue, by the fact that this is the vampire as cinematic effect, as specter, no longer as the mere subject of a text. Here the shadow and silhouette of Nosferatu, backlit and framed by the lighted window, seem to deliberately call to mind cinematic images projected upon the flat, screenlike field of the window. Accordingly, those images vanish in a puff of smoke once the sun dawns through that same window to disperse the cinematic illusion the vampire symbolizes. Once more, the sequence of shots depicts the words of a book about vampires being turned into a powerful play of light and shadow that fundamentally transforms the subject gazing upon them from one kind of person to another.[15]

Subsequent Dracula films reference their predecessors continuously, each one seeming to function as an homage to those that came before. This is nowhere more apparent than in the way these films repeatedly commit sequences to acknowledging the emergence of the cinematic vampire from the world of texts and his subsequent superseding of those texts. In Tod Browning's *Dracula* (1931), for example, Lucy's deadly encounter with Dracula is also intercut with shots of her reading a book, an action that once again offers itself as a metaphor for her unconscious act of opening the window of her bedroom for Dracula's entry. As his shadow merges with her dreaming figure in the darkness at the end of the sequence, the scene dissolves to an overhead shot of a surgical theater in which Lucy's dead body is now being gazed upon by a group of doctors whose studied gazes replace Dracula's. Lucy is, in fact, not dead but undead, fully transformed from the reader she had been to a disembodied object of the gaze.

In a later sequence, Browning again presents Dracula's hallucinatory, spectral power as a product of and an alternative to the private world of textuality and individual autonomy. During a climactic confrontation with

Figure 1. From *Nosferatu, A Symphony of Horror* (1922), directed by F. W. Murnau. Typical of the *Dracula* adaptations, Murnau represents the vampire as emerging from the world of textuality—in a play of light and shadow—to haunt the human world. The vampire thus appears as a cinematic effect, as specter. The Museum of Modern Art, Film Stills Archive.

Figure 2. The shadow and silhouette of Nosferatu, backlit and framed by the lighted window, again call to mind cinematic images projected on a flat, screenlike field. Here, at the end of the film (just as the house lights go up), those images begin to vanish once the sun disperses the cinematic illusion the vampire symbolizes. The Museum of Modern Art, Film Stills Archive.

Dracula that takes place in a library where the walls are lined from ceiling to floor with books, Dr. Van Helsing first notices that Dracula's image is not visible in a mirror's reflection. When the doctor accidentally observes the scene before him reflected in a mirrored cigarette box, the count's image is strangely absent from the room. Browning then presents an elaborate montage on the screen in which a medium shot of Dracula speaking with the mesmerized Mina is intercut with two others: a close-up of the mirror reflecting the same scene with Dracula vanished from view, and a third shot of Van Helsing and Jonathan alternating their gaze between the mirrored reflection and the scene of Dracula and Mina taking place before them. In this complex shot sequence, the mirrored surface seems to function like a cinematic device that reveals to the viewer (here in the library) that the vampire is, on the one hand, a real threat and, on the other, that his threat is that he is not real—that he is but a phantom, an artificial image with no substance, present and yet not present.

Like its successors, this film version of *Dracula* stages the vampiric transformation taking place in the characters in the form of a ritual interchange between the acts of reading, dreaming, and viewing. In the movies, the appearance of the vampire as transformative visual spectacle consistently emerges out of these other acts of imagination (reading and dreaming) performed by the subject/spectator. In this, and in his own invisibility in the mirror (both in Stoker's novel and in most film versions), the vampire calls to mind Christian Metz's comparison of the act of watching a film with the imaginary stage of subject development as theorized in psychoanalysis. Although the film is like a mirror, Metz argues, in which we as spectators view the images by which we constitute ourselves, "it differs from the primordial mirror in one essential point."[16] Unlike the mirror stage, where the subject sees its own image undifferentiated from those of other objects, "there is one thing and only one thing that is never reflected in it [the film]: the spectator's own body" (44–45). The film spectator, then, constitutes itself not as a discrete object (or character) as seen in the mirror, but as a pure act of perception, as what Metz calls "a transcendental subject" that sees but is not seen (49). With film, the spectator is present only as perceptual act, and not as discrete object. In the mirror scene of the Browning film, for example—a stock scene in Dracula films—the spectators' shocked recognition that Dracula's reflection does not appear in the mirror confronts them with the truth of their own transformation from personal essences to perceptive events. Different kinds of cinematic apparatuses, shots, and techniques, then, produce different kinds of spectators—voyeuristic, sadistic, masochistic, fetishistic, masculine, feminine—as many film theorists have argued.[17]

In this context, Coppola's *Bram Stoker's "Dracula"*—titled, provocatively, to bring attention to the novelistic source of the film—offers itself as a tour de force of the transformation of textuality into spectrality, alluding prolifically to its host of cinematic predecessors and foregrounding dramatically Stoker's preoccupation with turn-of-the-century media and textuality. Through a series of complex dissolves and superimpositions, Coppola brilliantly weaves montages of handwriting, typewriting, and phonograph recording with the shifting settings and dramatic action of the narrative throughout the film. In Jonathan's first encounter with Dracula, the conflict between text and photographic image is emphasized as the young solicitor negotiates with his client over the "little oak desk" where they do business, a surface littered with texts of various kinds. When Dracula discovers Mina's photographic miniature lost among these written documents, a stream of spilled ink creeps significantly across the image of Mina's face, and the count picks up the portrait to caress it desiringly.

That drama of ink and photograph, text and image, is then projected as a kind of film-within-the-film directly behind Harker and Dracula, where a giant map of London has been mounted on the wall. As if in a turn-of-the-century cinematic exhibition, Dracula casts an eerie and threatening shadow across the map and the dense jumble of type that fills it; but this shadow is weirdly out of sync with his body, moving with unsettling delays and inconsistencies—perhaps evoking the crude technology with which early films produced the special effect of shadows on the screen. But then, inexplicably, this disjunction is exaggerated, as the vampire's shadow begins to act entirely independently of his body, performing a dumb show on the map behind the two figures. Combining techniques of front and rear projection, Dracula's shadow reaches out to strangle that of young Jonathan against the map's printed surface, while in front of it their bodies calmly discuss the details of their business transaction, surrounded by the necessary documents. The essential artificiality of the cinematic subject and the transformative power of the shift from text to image could not be more effectively visualized than it is in this scene.

This interpretation of the way Dracula seems to represent the vampiric power of the cinema in these films over against a different set of powers invested in texts is indebted to two influential essays—one dealing with Stoker's novel, the other dealing with films of Victorian novels. The first is

Jennifer Wicke's "Vampiric Typewriting," which demonstrates how Dracula himself may be regarded as an articulation of and a figuration for, mass culture, that he "supervenes" the media of mass culture, and that his "individual powers all have their analogue in the field of the mass cultural."[18] In other words, those same "technologies of social control relied upon to defend against the encroachments of Dracula" in the novel (the telegraph, the typewriter, the phonograph) "are the source of the vampiric powers of the mass cultural with which Dracula . . . is allied" (477). My second point of reference is Garrett Stewart's essay, "Film's Victorian Retrofit," which shows how movies made since the 1950s about the Victorian period commonly use photography as a metaphor for their nostalgia about a period perceived to be more authentic than our own.[19] Stewart explores how the photographically based narrativity of film adaptations reflects upon cinema's descent from the still photograph and film's superiority to that more primitive medium. "In the age of the digitalized generation rather than the chemical registration of images, there is a growing nostalgia for the real itself," as he puts it, "and for the way the real once gave itself up to film, first to photography and then to cinema" (184). Coppola's *Dracula* provides Stewart with one of his most compelling examples of how "cinema promotes its own representational agenda by recovering the naive ruptures that greeted its arrival on the scene of mere photography," and thereby suggests to the audience that the moving picture is a more vital and authentic form of representation than the photograph that freezes its subject in a corpse-like and motionless silence (194).

I would like to draw from both of these essays, and to suck a little life of my own from the novelistic host to argue something a bit more specific about *Dracula*'s peculiar involvement with the media. First, with respect to Wicke's point about *Dracula*'s collusion with mass media, I want to shift the focus somewhat to the way this Victorian novel's general fascination with the media corresponds in important ways with the origins of the particular medium neither Wicke nor the novel deals with directly, but with which the text is so thoroughly saturated—the cinema. The fact that cinema effectively represents the transition from a Victorian past to a modern present—for those late Victorians and for us moderns alike—is substantiated not only by the record of the novel's continual adaptations into film but also by the increasingly explicit self-referentiality of these films as they relate to Dracula as a visual phenomenon and as a text. Second, with respect to Stewart's analysis of the way modern film uses the Victorian photograph by transcending it in order to inspire nostalgia for the real, I want to emphasize that the nostalgia expressed in Stoker's novel is *not just* for a sense of the real, but specifically for a sense of the real "self" or character that is threatened by Dracula's archaic "self"-consuming, mesmerizing power. This point is stressed in the film adaptations by their self-reflexive identification of Dracula's threat to persons with the medium of cinema itself. In his protean, evanescent appearances as shadow or mist on the one hand, and his apparently substantial existence as human form on the other, Dracula presents himself in the novel and in the films as the incarnation of what Metz has defined as cinema's representational mode: the projection of a "lost object" that is desirable because it is presented only "in effigy, inaccessible from the outset, in a primordial *elsewhere*."[20]

Fittingly, *Dracula*'s appearance in 1897 came less than a year after London's Empire Theater began attracting capacity crowds to its sensational new diversion—Lumière's spectacular Cinematograph, the first public projection of moving pictures in England. In that same year, the English optical instrument-maker Robert William Paul would invent a new film projector, the Theatregraph, and produce the first British fiction film (or "made-up" movie), *The Soldier's Courtship*. A month after Lumière began his popular reign in the Empire, Paul commenced his own two-year run to equally large and enthusiastic crowds in the Alhambra Theatre: "So animated and real," ran one Scottish press notice of these "animated picture shows," "that one sat spell-bound."[21] "The action represented was so realistic," marveled another (as if describing Mina Murray's encounter with that other spellbinding specter that looms suddenly out of the darkness), "that in several cases the audience could not restrain their wonder, and even startled with surprise at the events which were flashed before their eyes."[22] The year 1896 also saw the pioneer British filmmaker and producer George Smith invent a new movie camera and found (along with his partner James Williamson) the "Brighton School" of filmmaking, famous for its pioneering work in trick photography and optical illusions. Appropriately, these two men are credited with being (among other things) the first to use what was then called "spirit photography" (or, to us, superimposition), creating the special effect we have become so accustomed to seeing in movies where the projection of simultaneous images suggests the coexistence of parallel realities, or, by way of the "dissolve" transition, implies the ghostly persistence of the past in the present.[23] In 1896, in short, the history of British cinema began.

All these developments in the new mass medium of cinema took place

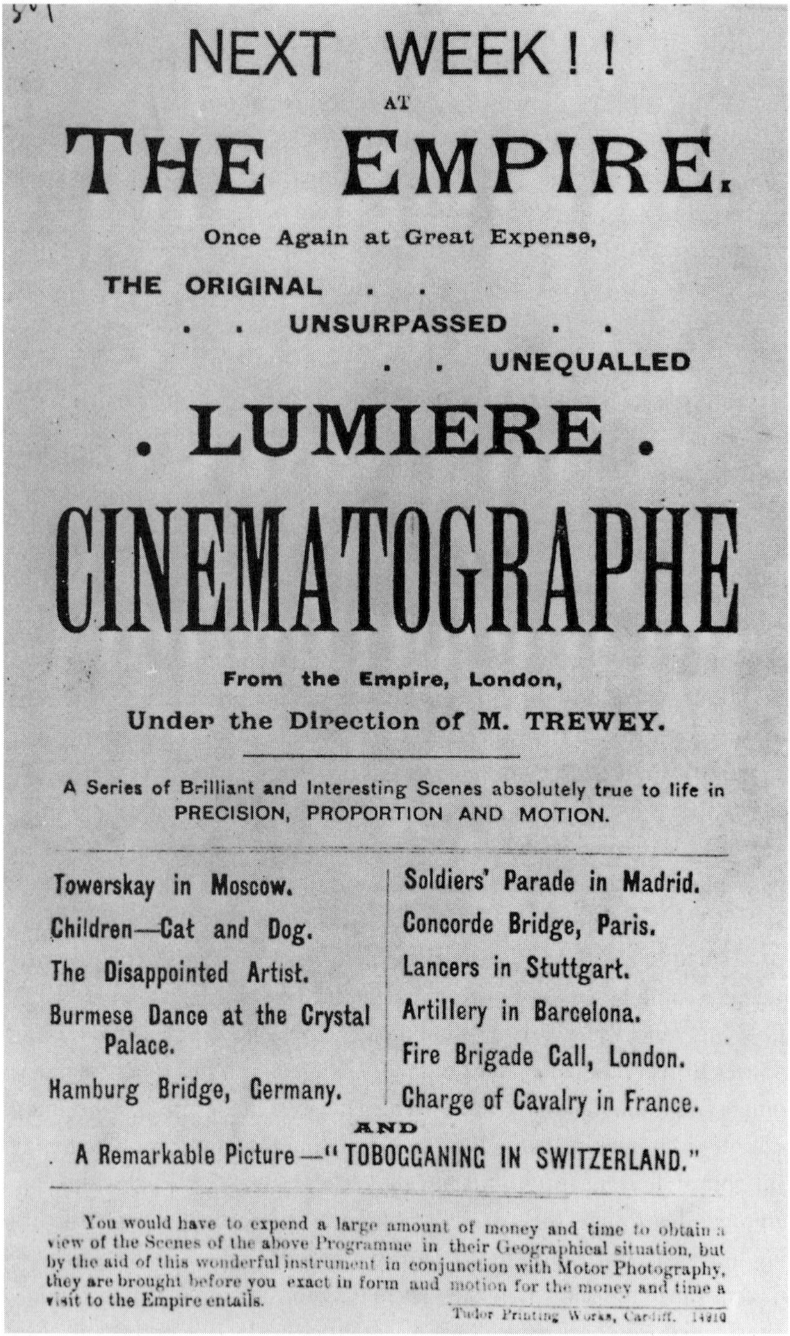

NEXT WEEK!!

AT

THE EMPIRE.

Once Again at Great Expense,

THE ORIGINAL . .

. . UNSURPASSED . .

. . UNEQUALLED

. LUMIERE .

CINEMATOGRAPHE

From the Empire, London,

Under the Direction of M. TREWEY.

A Series of Brilliant and Interesting Scenes absolutely true to life in
PRECISION, PROPORTION AND MOTION.

Towerskay in Moscow.	Soldiers' Parade in Madrid.
Children—Cat and Dog.	Concorde Bridge, Paris.
The Disappointed Artist.	Lancers in Stuttgart.
Burmese Dance at the Crystal Palace.	Artillery in Barcelona.
	Fire Brigade Call, London.
Hamburg Bridge, Germany.	Charge of Cavalry in France.

AND

. A Remarkable Picture —"TOBOGGANING IN SWITZERLAND."

You would have to expend a large amount of money and time to obtain a
view of the Scenes of the above Programme in their Geographical situation, but
by the aid of this wonderful instrument in conjunction with Motor Photography,
they are brought before you exact in form and motion for the money and time a
visit to the Empire entails.

Tudor Printing Works, Cardiff. 14910

Figure 3. The first appearance of *Dracula* in London in the form of Stoker's novel takes place within a year of the arrival of Lumière's spectacular Cinematograph, England's first public projection of moving pictures.

in the year in which Bram Stoker was writing *Dracula,* a text that fore-grounds its own involvement—and that of its vampiric antihero—with the powers of mass media in the destruction and recovery of "characters" as well as with the invasion of the present by the past. The significance of this con-junction of events is most emphatically expressed, perhaps, by the fact that in this same year, the first vampire film was also made. Georges Méliès's two-minute silent film *Le Manoir du diable* (The infernal house) begins by showing a large bat flying into a medieval castle, which then transforms it-self into Mephistopheles. The demonic figure, presiding over a boiling caul-dron, conjures up a beautiful young woman, who is followed by a stream of phantoms, skeletons, witches, and cavaliers, until one of them brandishes a crucifix and thereby causes the demon to vanish in a puff of smoke. This film almost certainly played in London in 1896 or early 1897, because Méliès had already been signed by an English distributor who was bringing his films to London at this time. It is entirely possible, even likely, that the film was seen by Stoker (the manager and frequenter of another London theater, the Royal Lyceum). If so, this novel that has generated so many cinematic adaptations may itself (at least in some measure) have been adapted from the cinema. Regardless of whether or not that is the case, however, what is clear from this confluence of events is that the cinema and *Dracula* are the twin children of the same cultural forces: they arrive in London at the same time, each producing in the audience the same spellbinding effect under the cover of darkness.

The significance of this context for the novel is made quite explicit in Coppola's treatment of Dracula's arrival in London and his first encounter with Mina, a sequence that Coppola's film entirely invents. The sequence is provocatively crosscut with scenes of the dramatic medical intervention by Van Helsing's band of men upon the body of the already infected Lucy. Coppola has Dracula appearing in London first as a figure in old newsreel footage, emerging from the fluttering pages of a newspaper. He is shown as a dapper, bespectacled young man walking in the London streets in the jit-tery, speeded-up pacing and sepia color of an early silent film. These images are accompanied by the voice-over of an offscreen barker continuously urg-ing the public to come "See the amazing Cinematograph." Dracula arrives in London not only as the subject of the cinema, but as the transitional figure who signals a shift from the textual representation of a newspaper to the ar-tificial image of the cinema. Those antique cinematic images then dissolve almost imperceptibly back into the full-color image of the modern movie we have been watching—Coppola's movie—with Dracula spotting Mina and commanding her, subconsciously, to "See me now" (note that Dracula's command to Mina echoes the earlier injunctions of the disembodied voice-over spoken to the audience, an echo that identifies Dracula with the new medium of the cinema: "See the amazing Cinematograph"/"See me").

Dracula then contrives an encounter with Mina on the street and asks her if she can direct him to the cinematograph, the new invention he refers to as one of the "wonders of modern civilization." After cutting back to the scene of Lucy's receiving blood transfusions from her suitors, the scene dissolves from a close-up of the telltale bite wounds in Lucy's neck to the piercing eyes of a wolf and then, in a continuous dissolve, into the cinematographic theater where Dracula proceeds to assault Mina amid a confusion of projected images. One of those images is the oncoming train that Lumière famously exhibited at the Empire theater in 1896. The visual logic of the sequence suggests that Dracula's primitive inscription on Lucy's body, in the form of the textual trace of himself he leaves on her neck, is transformed into the even more penetrating medium of the cinema, through which he will seduce Mina. The medium is clearly meant to be the message here, as if Coppola has unearthed the unconscious of the other media that are so elaborately articulated in the novel and alluded to in his cinematic predecessors: Bram Stoker's *Dracula* arrives in London at the same time as the cinema, and his supernatural powers are identified with the effects of that magical medium.[24]

As is clear in its many film adaptations, *Dracula*'s potency for the screen is deeply related to the novel's intense interest in the power of the new media technologies that were transforming Victorian characters into modern subjects and with the privileged role of cinema in that process. Those media threatened to reduce their users to nothing more than, like Mina Harker, mediums for some transhistorical mechanism outside themselves—the powers of the ancient monster reconstrued in the authority of modern professional discourse, the hegemony of marriage, and so on. As the vampire produced in its victims the dehumanized, automatic response of the "undead," transforming the body into an erotically charged pleasure machine that ruled the mind, so the emergence of the magical pleasure machine of the cinema (also referred to variously in the 1890s as the "Vitagraph" and the "Biograph") not only held the audience in spellbound amazement, but implied in its lifelikeness that this may be all we are—the not-quite-living, not-quite-dead projections of the machinery of history that sucks the lifeblood of character from us. The backward glances at the threatened Victorian "character" in these cinematic Draculas offer the modern audience a fleeting specter of a desire that cannot be satisfied and of a possession that cannot be exorcised.

As a medium that was initially described as a form of magic and continues to be regarded as a kind of fantasy world or escapism, the cinema has managed—as Count Dracula did with his victims—to transform modern subjectivity and the modern sense of history into something that risks being as unreal and evanescent as the medium itself.[25] It is in this sense that the modern cinema exercises a vampiric power over these two principal orthodoxies of the nineteenth-century novel: the myth of historical progress and the fantasy of the authentic self. "The addiction that we have for the media," Jean Baudrillard has claimed, "is not a result of a desire for culture, communication and information, but of this perversion of truth and falsehood, of this destruction of meaning in the operation of medium."[26] Our modernist desire for a show, Baudrillard goes on to explain, our desire for this form of simulation, is also a desire for dissimulation, for the dissolution of demarcations of authenticity—an impulse that may in turn be regarded as a spontaneous resistance to "the ultimatum of historical and political reason."[27]

This analysis of mass media's social effect perfectly describes the transforming power that Dracula exercises upon his victims as well, an effect concretely manifested in their absorption by various technological media both in the novel and in its film versions. It also describes the effect that the movies exert on the notion of character as a coherent psychological entity as it is embodied in the nineteenth-century novel as well. Modern mass culture and its media, as Fredric Jameson has shown, should not be seen as expressions of "mere" false consciousness, then, but as forms of transformational work that are performed upon our anxieties and fantasies, and are managed by the production of compensatory narratives.[28] Not only is this the work done by every filmic resurrection, decapitation, and stake driven in the heart of *Dracula,* but it may be the achievement of every film adaptation of a Victorian novel. That is why the conventional objection to these films—that whatever their capacities for portraying the visual spectacle of the period, they are unable to represent the complex individual subjectivity or interiority of Victorian characters—should be understood as the medium's transforming effect on our understanding of persons rather than as a limitation of its representational powers.

Even within the novel itself, somewhere between the written text and the visual manifestation of Dracula the novel's characters go into a trancelike state and come out of it marked by some other identity. The most eloquent image of this process in the novel itself may be that of Mina Harker sitting at her desk, the "forked metal" listening devices of Seward's recording machine plugged into her ears, her fingers operating the typewriter, her foot working the pedal to stop and start the phonograph. "That is a wonderful machine, but it is cruelly true," Mina says to the doctor as she becomes the medium upon which information from one form is transcribed into another; "I think that the cylinders which you gave me contained more than you intended me to know" (222). As her consciousness is later taken over alternately by Dracula's telepathic powers and by Van Helsing's hypnotic trances, Mina is being made into a machine here, transformed by the forbidden knowledge of the "cruel" devices—the media—that contain more than they were "intended" to contain by their human agents. In this, Mina is a metaphor for us modern spectators, who watch the novel being projected before our eyes, hear it amplified in our ears, and participate in the artifice it projects upon us.

Like Dracula himself, the cinema erases the continuous interiority—or the "stream of consciousness"—that composes the individual "Victorian" character, replacing that more unified conception of the self with a sequence of post-Victorian "frames" of mind, a self composed of a series of discrete, fragmented mechanical images that engender a past to which the viewer cannot return and a future she cannot fully occupy. In this, the cinema converts the dilemma of modernity's impermanence and ephemerality into a source of pleasure and entertainment. In film, as Leo Charney put it, modernity's "shock, speed, and dislocation became editing, and the evacuation of presence, in the technique of cinema, became the means by which the viewer could find a place in the film's ceaseless movement forward."[29] By so explaining the allure of the cinema, Charney may also have been describing the temptations of Dracula's bite for Jonathan Harker or Mina Murray, when the vampire offers them the guilty pleasure of living as he does, somewhere in the afterlife of the Victorian novel, somewhere between the living and the dead. At the same time, Charney offers an explanation for the temptations of modern filmmakers to draw on the nineteenth-century novel in order to project for us phantom shadows of the Victorian characters we no longer can be.

Bram Stoker's Dracula, in other words, *is* the cinema, and the cinema of the 1890s (and 1990s) is a vampire that puts an end to what we mean by the Victorian era even as it keeps it animated (if not alive) for us—keeps its undead image projected tantalizingly before our eyes. Although Stoker's story derives from an ancient myth that has surfaced in many cultures in various forms, this late-Victorian version of that frequently told tale has its special power for us "moderns" because it functions in historically specific ways as a mechanism of reversion and preservation, one that both divides and connects our modern present and our Victorian past. Our desire for a show—or, to be precise, for the moving-picture version of a Victorian novel—does not manifest our desire for Victorian culture or even for Victorian character so much as it does a desire for historical dissimulation. Liberating us from the repressive hypothesis of the Victorian subject, this desire manifests modernity's attempt to participate in a performance in which the demarcations of difference between them and us may effectively be dissolved. What the cinematic incarnation of *Dracula* makes quite clear is that in the conflict between past centuries and modernity in which Jonathan Harker found himself suspended, Dracula is more an agent of the liberating, subversive powers of modernity than he is of the powers of the past. Those older forces, and the ideologies of the self they embodied, were more properly represented by the Victorian century that was reeling into the past as the novel was being published and cinema was being born.

Notes

1. Bram Stoker, *Dracula* (New York: Oxford University Press, 1983), 36. First published in 1897.

2. David Pirie, *The Vampire Cinema* (New York: Crescent Books, 1977), 6. See also James B. Twitchell, *Dreadful Pleasures: An Anatomy of Modern Horror* (New York: Oxford University Press, 1985), 105–59.

3. For a survey of Dracula films, see Alain Silver and James Ursini, *The Vampire Film from Nosferatu to Bram Stoker's Dracula* (New York: Limelight Editions, 1994).

4. D. A. Miller, *The Novel and the Police* (Berkeley: University of California Press, 1983), x.

5. Judith Halberstam has argued that the activities of reading and writing in *Dracula* are crucial to establishing a middle-class British hegemony annexed to the production of particular sexual subjectivities. See Judith Halberstam, "Technologies of Monstrosity: Bram Stoker's *Dracula*," *Victorian Studies* 36 (spring 1993): 333–52.

6. Regenia Gagnier has explored Stoker's linking of various boundary-defining cultural oppositions with eroticism and the machinery of everyday life. See "Evolution

and Information, or Eroticism and Everyday Life, in *Dracula* and Late Victorian Aestheticism," in *Sex and Death in Victorian Literature,* ed. Regina Barreca (Bloomington: Indiana University Press, 1990), 140–57.

7. Sergei Eisenstein, "Dickens, Griffith, and the Film Today," in *Film Theory and Criticism,* ed. Gerald Mast, Marshall Cohen, and Leo Braudy (New York: Oxford University Press, 1992), 395–402. First published in *Film Forum,* trans. Jay Leyda, 1944.

8. Marshall McLuhan, *Understanding Media* (Cambridge: MIT Press, 1995), 286. First published in 1964.

9. See, for example, George Bluestone's classic *Novels into Film* (Berkeley: University of California Press, 1961): "It is a commonplace by now that the novel has tended to retreat more and more from external action to internal thought, from plot to character, from social to psychological realities. . . . The rendition of mental states—memory, dream, imagination—cannot be as adequately represented on film as by language. If the film has difficulty presenting streams of consciousness, it has given more difficulty presenting states of mind which are defined precisely by the absence in them of the visible world" (46–47).

10. See, for example, Cynthia Ozick in a 5 January 1996 *New York Times* article on Campion's adaptation of James's *Portrait of a Lady*: "Henry James's 'Portrait of a Lady' explored the vibrations of the interior life. It's exactly the territory that movies have no use for." See also Daphne Merkin's review of *Wings of the Dove* (directed by Iain Sofley) and *Washington Square* (directed by Agnieszka Holland), a review subtitled, "Henry James's Unfilmable Passion for Renunciation" (*New Yorker* [10 November 1997]: 121–22).

11. Jean-Louis Baudry, "The Apparatus: Metapsychological Approaches to the Impression of Reality in the Cinema," in *Film Theory and Criticism,* ed. Gerald Mast, Marshall Cohen, and Leo Braudy (New York: Oxford University Press, 1992), 705. Baudry's essay was first published in 1975.

12. See David Glover, *Vampires, Mummies, and Liberals: Bram Stoker and the Politics of Popular Fiction* (Durham, N.C.: Duke University Press, 1996). Glover reads Stoker's career as a series of episodes in which "the Victorian era of equipoise" began to unravel, threatening the very ideologies that enabled individual subjects to "enact their own sense of agency": "At the core of this long transformation, lasting from the 1880s to the 1920s, lies a crisis in the character of British liberalism which put into doubt many of the received ideas regarding the proper relationship between the state and civil society, the public and the private" (5).

13. A number of critics have treated the subject of textuality in *Dracula* and noted the way the novel both represents and critiques processes of discursive production and circulation. See, for example, Rebecca A. Pope, "Writing and Biting in *Dracula,*" *Literature, Interpretation, Theory* 1.3 (March 1990): 199–216; and Geoffrey Wall, "'Different from Writing': *Dracula* in 1897," *Literature and History* 10.1 (spring 1984): 15–23.

14. Murnau's film essentially rose from the grave itself when, after an English

court ruled it to be an unauthorized use of Stoker's copyright, all known copies of the film were destroyed. Stoker's estate hunted down any surviving pirated copies while trying to sell the copyright to Hollywood. Copies of *Nosferatu* began to miraculously reappear after some years. See Roxana Stuart, *Stage Blood: Vampires of the Nineteenth-Century Stage* (Bowling Green, Ohio: Bowling Green State University Press, 1994), 219.

15. According to Sabine Hake, German Expressionist cinema commonly exhibited a "promotional self-referentiality that draws attention to the cinema and foregrounds its means," signaling "playful awareness of the apparatus and the simultaneous denial of its presence" (Sabine Hake, "Self-Referentiality in Early German Cinema," *Cinema Journal* 31.3 [1992]: 37–38).

16. Christian Metz, *The Imaginary Signifier,* trans. Celia Britton, Annwyl Williams, Ben Brewster, and Alfred Guzetti (Bloomington: Indiana University Press, 1982), 45. *The Imaginary Signifier* first appeared in 1975.

17. See, for example, Norman K. Denzin, *The Cinematic Society: The Voyeur's Gaze* (London, Calif.: Sage Publications, 1995); Mary Ann Doane, *Femmes Fatales: Feminism, Film Theory, Psychoanalysis* (New York: Routledge, 1991); Ann E. Kaplan, *Looking for the Other: Feminism, Film, and the Imperial Gaze* (New York: Routledge, 1997); Laura Mulvey, *Fetishism and Curiosity* (Bloomington: Indiana University Press, 1996); and Gaylyn Studlar, *In the Realm of Pleasure: Von Sternberg, Dietrich, and the Masochistic Aesthetic* (Urbana: University of Illinois Press, 1988).

18. Jennifer Wicke, "Vampiric Typewriting: *Dracula* and Its Media," *English Literary History* 59 (1992): 467–93; 475.

19. Garrett Stewart, "Film's Victorian Retrofit," *Victorian Studies* 38.2 (winter 1995): 153–98.

20. Metz, *The Imaginary Signifier,* 61.

21. Quoted in Rachel Low and Roger Manvell, *The History of the British Film: 1896–1906* (Old Woking: Unwin, 1948), 37.

22. Ibid.

23. See Low and Manvell, *The History of the British Film: 1896–1906,* 44–45.

24. McLuhan is careful to distinguish the "message" from the "content" of any medium; the "content" of a movie may be a novel or an opera or a play, but its "message" is better understood as the "effect" or force the experience has on the viewer. See McLuhan, *Understanding Media,* 7–21.

25. Méliès himself began his career as a magician, and the first cinema exhibitions were often billed together with (and as) magic acts. See Emmanuelle Toulet, *Cinema Is 100 Years Old,* trans. Susan Emanuel (London: Thames and Hudson, 1995), 13–27.

26. See Jean Baudrillard, "The Masses: The Implosion of the Social in the Media," in *Selected Writings,* ed. Mark Poster (Stanford, Calif.: Stanford University Press, 1988), 217.

27. Ibid.

28. Fredric Jameson, *Signatures of the Visible* (New York: Routledge, 1990), 24–26.

29. Leo Charney, "In a Moment: Film and the Philosophy of Modernity," in *Cinema and the Invention of Modern Life,* ed. Leo Charney and Vanessa R. Schwartz (Berkeley: University of California Press, 1995), 279–96; 292.

Postscript
Contemporary Culturalism: How Victorian Is It?

Nancy Armstrong

The essays in this collection indicate how pervasively postmodernism depends on the very conventions and critiques that modernism condemned as naive, authoritarian, mercenary, superficial, trashy, or commonplace. Moreover, the essays suggest why recycling these remnants should have resurrected a controversy over the very definition of culture that preoccupied the intellectuals of that earlier age. What the reader consequently takes away from this collection is a sharp sense of just how Victorian is the present-day identification of our nation with our national culture and the attendant fear that the strength of the nation is being sapped by an insidious erosion of national "values" and "identity" from within. It is a critical commonplace that Victorian intellectuals were concerned with defending their culture from without, against cultural objects and forms of behavior at once antagonistic to traditional Englishness and yet an integral part of imperial England. Indeed, the agents of empire who exported English ways around the world found that in the process both those agents and their English ways had undergone a self-alienating transformation. Flushed with the success of transplanting certain elements of their culture around the world, in other words, the British were among the first to think of themselves as a culture on the defense. Less obvious but just as essential as this first line of defense was the defense against a popular culture empowered not only by print but also by photography and all the technologies of spectacle that bombarded the national readership from within with sensations, images, narratives, and ideology.

The Victorian boom in culture criticism sought to protect a class- and gender-bound notion of Englishness against the tide of modernization accelerated by an information industry out of control, an international market in commodities, and the fabled mix of populations within the expanding parameters of empire. But the equation of nation with national culture not only accelerated the spread of English culture (according to Ian Baucom's essay, this holds true for Irish culture as well), in doing so, this same equation set off something like a quantum leap in the character and power of representation. The new primacy of national culture detached the nation from its traditional foundations in land, church, aristocracy, and those things made in England of English materials and instead subjected national identity to a new and profoundly unsettling order of discursivity. To the degree that postmodernism and the cluster of features associated with the degeneration of the national character can be said to have instigated and perpetuated what has been accurately termed "the culture wars," postmodernism is a consequence and acknowledgment of the Victorian redefinition of the nation. But objects and events postmodern do not stir up anxiety about the primacy of culture—its power to occlude, displace, or transform that which it purports to represent—simply because they reproduce the Victorian equation of the nation with a national culture. Postmodernism also extends that logic to the point where it arcs back upon itself to reveal a fundamental lack of any natural basis—whether geographical territory, historical events, or national character—for that entity we call a nation; it is strictly an imagined community.[1] In this respect, postmodernism simply acts out a contradiction uncomfortably but quietly nested within Victorian culture. By enacting that contradiction as a division within our culture over the definition of culture itself, contemporary culture defines itself as both very Victorian and not Victorian at all.

Not at All Victorian

Perhaps the most important accomplishment of *Victorian Afterlife* is its apparent disregard for European modernism's claim to have broken with the Victorian past. Contrary to the prevailing winds of literary and cultural criticism, the authors in this collection have no difficulty either describing postmodernism as a distinctive cultural phenomenon or determining the relation between postmodernism and an earlier moment in cultural history.

The collection as a whole establishes such an impressive range and variety of continuities between postmodernism and Victorian culture that it does the enormous service of rendering obsolete the whole question of whether postmodernism represents a break from modernism or just another version of it. What happens to modernism as a result requires a longer explanation than a postscript such as this would allow. But I do want to suggest that to consider postmodernism as an extension of Victorian culture—or more accurately, an extension of Victorian culturalism—is to expose modernism as an attempt at arresting the process of cultural modernization that shifts political action from government onto culture. Modernism would relocate identity—national and personal—from culture back to blood in the form of an authenticity that dwells on the other side of mediation where it had survived unnoticed from a mythical point in time. Whether one is English, Irish, Jewish, Indian, male or female, common or patrician, blood supposedly determines the quality and trajectory of modernist desire. Indeed, if we understand desire, as modernism does, as coursing along these ancient riverbeds, all historical changes in the objects, quality, and expressions of desire are by definition displacements, substitutes, and ultimately symptoms of an originary desire thwarted and suppressed by a culture bent on harnessing desire for its own narrow productive and reproductive ends. Written against the backdrop of a world at war, the circulation of theories of degeneration, the early signs of a crumbling empire, feminism, and an international workers movement, such literary works as *Women in Love, Ulysses, The Wasteland, Mrs. Dalloway,* and "The Second Coming" heralded the uncanny return of a nature that, if not adequately acknowledged and gratified, could easily spell the end of the West as it sought to define itself. For modernism, "nature" was neither blessing nor curse except that culture came along and made it so, but either way "nature" was the ultimate reality.

Being the compulsive imperialists they were, Victorian authors and intellectuals may well have intended not only to observe, but through observation also to regulate and even own the territories and populations within their imaginary domain. Hence the genres of expeditionary and criminal photography that grew up side by side with family photography and the parlor art of P. H. Robinson and Oscar Rejlander. But Victorian realism could not have succeeded in creating a "world picture" that allows "the observer" to position himself or herself at the center had it not required its consumers to believe in a world outside and prior to that picture.[2] The new technologies of representation we consider most Victorian—for example, scientific and social-scientific description, reportage, statistics, graphs, new cartographic methods, as well as photography, exhibitions, and displays— were all ways of bringing to the literate public chunks of the world that could formerly be seen only by traveling to various sites throughout that world. In that Victorian culture gestures toward a world of primary objects beyond itself, it cannot be called postmodern.[3]

Something like this distinction between Victorian and contemporary culture holds true in the domain of the subject as well. In transforming a hierarchical arrangement of stations based on blood and tradition into a differential system of instantly recognizable social stereotypes, a whole range of nineteenth-century social scientists and novelists sought to make individual interiority legible on that individual's face and figure. That they succeeded is not in question. Cultural history has called attention to the failures of such prominent figures as Francis Galton, Hugh Diamond, and Charles Darwin to find empirical justification for their respective typing systems. It is wise to remind ourselves, however, that this was the same period when fiction and photography became adept at using many of the same stereotypical features to indicate a whole range of personality types, and the new popular media were transforming interiority into a dazzling variety of material forms. Charles Dickens and William Makepeace Thackeray were joined by urban ethnologist Thomas Mayhew, psychopathologist Richard von Krafft-Ebing, urban photographers John Thomson and Paul Martin, and any number of social-scientific experts to bring the techniques of sensationalism to bear on the social underworld of industrial England and its primitive counterparts in Africa, Asia, and Polynesia.

Freud regarded the bodies and behaviors of his patients in the early *Studies on Hysteria* in much the same terms as a Dickens character—as outward and visible signs of an inward and psychological condition. If these women were paralyzed, unable to speak without impediment, and suffering from eating disorders as well as strange genital discharges, it was, Freud reasoned, their way of expressing reluctance to tell impolite truths, as well as their refusal to mature as women and reproduce. Obstacles—whether familiar or fantastic—were absolutely legible, when the body provided an allegory for their mental conflict as well as a means of preventing these women from achieving (hetero)sexual maturity. It did not require nearly as much ingenuity of the therapist to read those symptoms as to remove them. At some point in the *Studies on Hysteria,* however, Freud broke from his fellow researcher and coauthor Josef Breuer and decided that legibility required far more indirect and subtle reading procedures than his work had heretofore acknowledged. He came to the conclusion that although there were many ways of being man or woman, the individual did not make choices on the basis of what s/he desired. On the contrary, any expression of desire was more likely a way of disavowing identifications made and objects chosen on the basis of some natural appetite. Sealed off by compulsive disavowal, what Freud considered the "natural" core of individual identity came to exist as a buried city or dark continent within the individual, where it sought ingeniously to preserve its invisibility.

Using this shift in Freud's early work to illustrate the transformation of a Victorian into a modernist model of the subject, we can say that cultural conventions no longer express the truth of the subject as we cross into the twentieth century so much as misrepresent, block, and stigmatize that truth and in the process often render it monstrous. Commodity culture created a world in which virtually anything spontaneous and natural about national life could be bought up and resold in a predictable commercial package that would in turn elicit only canned responses. The result was an individual either repressed or hollowed out but, in either case, feminized, because lacking in natural (read masculine) desire. Hence the frequent representations of mass culture as a woman in the literature and critical theory associated with modernism.[4]

Postmodernism assumes that Victorian men and women were every bit as enchanted with the alluring surface of commodities as modernism claimed. But postmodernism rejects the modernist contempt for that enchantment by refusing to distinguish the achievements of the isolated erudite genius from the mass cultural spectacles that pandered to the populace for commercial purposes. Indeed, we recognize as postmodern traditional forms of art, architecture, film, and literature that display the staginess of nature, revel in the surface, and incorporate what is usually considered commercial, banal, repetitious, and lowbrow. Thus, as Sadoff and Kucich note, we have *Clueless,* a contemporary cinematic adaptation of the plot of Jane Austen's *Emma.* This movie distinguishes itself from anything Victorian not only by recasting the novel as a Hollywood blockbuster, but also by emphasizing clothes, cars, a precise use of a carefully crafted teenage slang, and the people with whom one hangs out. Such things as these, says the film, are the measure of a young woman's intelligence and good nature, as well as the basis on which she will value and be valued by others. Unashamed of its nineteenth-century heritage as it is of its contemporary commercialism, *Clueless* takes as its premise the idea that all relationships are versions of and require the same expertise as accessorizing. In a culture founded on this assumption, interiority is no more nor less than the cultural debris clinging to a body or a name. Such a subject cannot by any stretch of cultural-theoretical logic be called Victorian, because it has carried the logic of Victorian culture to the point where images create not only objects but the subjects who consume them as well. But *Clueless* would strike us as just another girl's coming-of-age film were there not also something very Victorian about it, devoid though it is of any indication of depth under the vibrantly colored celluloid surface.

Very Victorian

I have argued that Victorian realism—by which I mean all those technologies of representation that claim to bring the world in detailed veracity before the reader-observer—never relinquished its foundational assumption that the object was more primary and real than any representation. But I have also suggested that this did not hold true for popular culture. Far from it. Something was happening to the very idea that popular culture was produced by indigenous folk, artisanal practices, and regional customs. This idea of the popular was being pushed aside in the national consciousness, if not in fact by various technologies of mass mediation and the formal principle of repetition. Prompted, I believe, by England's crossover into a new information age, where the world one encountered was almost always mediated by print, photograph, illustration, or exhibition, John Stuart Mill began his *On Liberty* by sounding an alarm. "Apart from the peculiar tenets of individual thinkers," he explained, "there is also in the world at large an increasing inclination to stretch unduly the powers of society over the individual, both by the force of opinion and even by that of legislation."[5] Mill was particularly interested in explaining the potential of what he alternatively calls "public opinion," "popular belief," and "custom" to exercise something akin to the force of law over English citizens.[6] Mill sought to convince his readers that a radically democratized culture represented a threat to rather than a guarantee of individual freedom. "Unless a strong barrier of moral conviction can be raised against the mischief," he predicted, "we must expect, in the present circumstances of the world, to see [the power of popular culture] increase" (19).

There is a problem with this argument, however. What such intellectuals as Mill, Ruskin, and Arnold found so threatening was precisely the radical democratization of the public sphere: a situation where arguments could be made cheap and fast, come in many copies, and be authored by virtually anyone without so much as a moment's concern for good taste or the greater good. Not that these good Victorian men would say in so many words what troubled them about their culture, but there is no mistaking their disillusionment with a public sphere to which anyone could have access. Nor is there any mistaking the rhetorical lengths to which these men went to make an aristocratic past seem more conducive to the general good than the new forms of popular culture. It is through sheer redundancy, according to Mill, that modern culture acquires the power to limit individual liberty. With repetition, he explains, any opinion loses touch with the world of fact as well as with "the meaning of the opinion itself. The words which convey it cease to suggest ideas, or suggest only a small portion of those they were originally employed to communicate" (45). Behaving like any oppressive cultural institution, such opinions neither arise from nor speak to the individual but "remain outside th[at] mind," where they squelch any opinions that might be individually formulated. The implications of Mill's descriptive language are clear. Opinions that are mass reproduced, however popular, besiege the thinking individual and hold him prisoner until he is intellectually and emotionally starved. These opinions do not suffer "any fresh and living condition to get in," while they themselves do "nothing for the mind or heart, except standing sentinel over them to keep them vacant" (46). This reconception of popular culture as the semiotic equivalent of a barbarian hoard marks the turn away from liberal endorsement of an extended public sphere.[7]

In his well-known description of the commodity fetish, Karl Marx too blames popular faith in culture to represent the world faithfully and well. Much as he might disagree with the liberal intellectuals of his period on other issues, Marx joins them in contrasting Victorian culture unfavorably to an earlier epoch, when man had a direct relationship with the objects he made.[8] What, if not public willingness to consume the signs of things as if they were the things themselves, made it possible for signs to take the place of actual objects?[9] He warned that when the process of commodification separated the sign from the thing it represented, human identity would undergo a profound transformation as well. People would acquire their respective places in the social order, not on the basis of their needs or productivity, but through the objects they could or could not consume. Marx was of course neither the first nor the last to represent Victorian realism as a dangerously naive venture. How so many intellectuals could work so hard to develop ways of objectively representing the truth of the individual and so completely miss the boat was the subject of Woolf's comparison between Arnold Bennett's way of representing the conspicuously ordinary Mrs. Brown and Woolf's own version of that character.[10] It is certainly worth noting that Bennett can no more be described as a Victorian than Woolf herself could, even though she used him to exemplify everything that was obsolete about her predecessors. All she ultimately explained, however, was why one of her contemporaries could not represent individuated subjectivity to the satisfaction of a group of twentieth-century intellectuals who, along with Woolf herself, portrayed the Victorians as secret lovers of conventional surfaces. Postmodernism understands the Victorians rather differently.

In her essay "Where Have All the Natives Gone?" Rey Chow argues against the lingering modernist tendency in both feminism and postcolonial studies to counter objectifications of oppressed groups with descriptions of the interiorities that "objectification" has heretofore "suppressed." Indeed, she argues, "the problem with the reinvention of subjectivity as such is that it tries to combat the politics of the image, a politics that is conducted on surfaces, by a politics of depths, hidden truths, and inner voices. The most important aspect of the image—its power precisely as image and nothing else—is thus bypassed and left untouched."[11] This same difference between surface and depth is what made the difference between Charlotte Brontë's representation of "the madwoman in the attic" as a beast whose deranged interiority was entirely legible on her body in *Jane Eyre* and Jean Rhys's representation of that character by way of an extended interior monologue in *Wide Sargasso Sea*. Whereas Brontë believed that depth revealed itself on the body's surface, Rhys believed, as Woolf did, that such a surface obfuscated the interiority within, making each individual a mystery to every other. Postmodernism returns to the Victorian moment where an image displaces the object on which it depends for mimetic authority in order to collapse the surface-depth opposition itself.

Postmodernism does not consider repetition a lie so much as a fiction on its way to accumulating the historical sedimentation that it takes to become truth, and postmodernism consequently has no interest in peeling back the stereotype to discover an interiority that has been distorted or concealed from view. Indeed, postmodernism asks, what if the most oft-repeated and banal aspects of our culture—rather than the curious and inaccessible excavations of modernism—are the only basis for our selves? What if in seeking access to some more primary world of subjects and objects we do not approach those subjects and objects in all their premediated purity, but encounter instead just another cultural formation that we happen to consider most primary and real? To encounter such a nostalgic formation is to encounter culture rather than anything like unmediated nature. In doing so, moreover, we inevitably convert that chunk of an earlier moment of cultural history into modern stereotypical form. In this respect, postmodernism is perhaps more Victorian than even the Victorians were, and we must regard Cher, the heroine of *Clueless,* not as a shamelessly lowbrow parody of *Emma* but as an extension of the Austen principle that decorum—which for the novelist was the accumulation of rather small but absolutely appropriate details—is what we really are.

The Case for Resurrecting Culturalism

The Arnoldian equation of a nation with its culture inevitably raises the question of which culture is the authentic national culture. Once we are no longer so sure of an identity rooted in the land, or tied to ancestral sites, or prescribed by the metaphysics of blood, it begins to matter greatly what culture is revered, taught, displayed, and reproduced. If not our own, then we may cease to be ourselves. This is precisely what is at issue in the contemporary culture wars. Commentators tend to see this conflict as the result of the success of "women and minorities" in revising the traditional notions of where we came from and what characteristics make us American. Why else, for example, would Richard Rorty go out of his way to attack Leslie Marmon Silko for ending *Almanac of the Dead* "with a vision in which the descendants of the European conquerors and immigrants are forced back to Europe, thereby fulfilling Native American prophecies that the whites would be a temporary disaster, a plague that would last no more than five hundred years"?[12] In his recent collection of essays titled *Achieving Our Country,* Rorty slides comfortably into the defensive posture defined by Mill and

Arnold. Doing so allows him to reverse the position of colonizer and colonized, casting Silko as the interloper who prevents America from fulfilling its destiny. We have heard any number of claims of this kind from erudite white men who sincerely feel themselves marginalized simply because they have to share the privilege of representing "America" with a growing number of minority groups in addition to women and African Americans. I am less interested in why Rorty feels marginalized than in the reasons why he regards those emerging into cultural visibility under the umbrella of multiculturalism as so unfit to succeed him in representing "our country." From what, in other words, does he think he is protecting us?

The Victorian culture critics can help us answer this question historically. To a man, as I have suggested, they saw themselves defending traditional British culture against popular British culture. Rorty and his fellow defenders of a traditional white masculinist America do not classify the enemy as "popular" in a nineteenth-century sense, but a second look at his attack on Silko reveals that certain elements of Mill's argument nevertheless survive into Rorty's. After scolding her for producing an ending that imagines the collapse of the American government, "as the descendants of the Maya and Aztecs stream into California, Arizona, and Texas," he establishes a guilt-by-association relationship between her dark view of the present-day United States and theory:

> One does not need to know whether Silko has read Foucault or Heidegger
> to see her novel as offering a vision of recent history similar to the one
> which readers of those two philosophers often acquire. . . . Those who find
> Foucault and Heidegger convincing often view the United States of America
> as Silko does: as something we must hope will be replaced, as soon as possible, by something utterly different. (7)

Rorty himself remains relatively untainted by cultural theory because he failed to understand so much as a word of it.[13] For him, critical theory amounts to little more than brainwashing, much as television, popular cinema, and rap lyrics do for conservative Congressman Henry Hyde. "When young intellectuals watch John Wayne war movies after reading Heidegger, Foucault, Stephenson, or Silko," Rorty claims on the basis of no evidence or methodology but solely his own common sense, "they often become convinced that they live in a violent, corrupt country" (7).

The road to cultural politics is paved with theory:

We now have among many American students and teachers, a spectatorial, disgusted, mocking Left rather than a Left that dreams of achieving our country. . . . Members of this Left find America unforgivable, as Baldwin did, and also unachievable, as he did not. This leads them to step back from their country and, as they say, "theorize." It leads them to do what Henry Adams did: to give cultural politics preference over real politics, and to mock the very idea that democratic institutions might once again be made to serve social justice. It leads them to prefer knowledge to hope. (36)

According to Rorty, theory situates us in a world of discourse where signs are no longer attached to the world they represent. By condemning ourselves to concepts and terminology cut off from actual people and their problems, recent generations of intellectuals not only betray our traditional commitment to build a more democratic America, they also threaten the literary tradition that maintains that commitment from Lincoln and Emerson, to Whitman and Dewey, and presumably, to Rorty himself. "Even though what these authors 'theorize' is often something very concrete and near at hand—a current TV show, a media celebrity, a recent scandal— they offer the most abstract and barren explanations imaginable" (93).

Where Mill feared that popular culture was beginning to operate like the law and govern the nation, Rorty levels much the same charge against the present generation of intellectuals, who have abandoned American common sense for a critical perspective hostile in principle to an indigenous national culture. Although deliberately remote from the real world of politics, these theorizers, from his perspective, nevertheless serve the interests of minority groups within the United States and prefer popular culture to great American literature. Despite the apparent difference between his object of attack and Mill's, then, Rorty gives the enemies of traditional culture many of the same characteristics that Mill did; armed with theory and in league with multiculturalism, contemporary culturalism threatens to evacuate our national culture of all meaning and render it "barren." How can concern for minority groups possibly resemble the deadeningly mechanical effects of repetition that Mill described? How can a critical understanding of our national culture keep us from achieving our country? Like Mill, Rorty feels betrayed by a culture that has shifted the location of political action from labor, money, and law, or politics, onto the production and dissemination of information, or culture. His claims to this effect are based on the assumption that cultural politics amounts to the neglect of politics and the degradation of culture.

Postmodernism works the other side of Victorian realism. Postmodernism accepts the arbitrary relationship between signs and the things and people they represent and reassures us that we are who we are, not by some accident of nature, but because of the position we occupy in a differential system of such positions. In a modern mass-mediated social order such as ours, individuals understand themselves in relation to one of a number of utterly banal stereotypes that enable a wide spectrum of the public to read them. Under these conditions, one achieves individuality in the way he or she fails to meet or manages to embody contrary positions of this kind. The devout postmodernist would consequently say that no country, but especially not the United States, could cohere as such without a highly redundant, instantly recognizable, utterly banal method of social classification. If we begin with this as the primary social reality, then what would constitute responsible political action? Certainly some way of prying these categories loose from the flesh-and-blood bodies they presume to represent would be a start. Having done this, however, we would not seek out some more "original" object or subject behind the type but rather strive to understand the operations of the differential system itself: Why do some differences matter more than others? How do certain individuals become types unto themselves? How do new categories emerge and old ones reveal their artificiality? Who has the power to reproduce these categories? How would we change them for the better (because getting rid of them is out of the question)?

Political change has always taken more than "awe," "enthusiasm," faith in our ability to improve, and even courage and willing self-sacrifice, and I do wish that intellectuals with education and influence would stop indicating otherwise. Moreover, what it takes to effect political change is itself subject to change, and we have, as Rorty himself suggests, born witness to a major transformation in the theater of political action in the last half of the twentieth century. Even Rorty admits that the situation for women and minorities began to improve, particularly within American universities, once teachers and students began calling attention to the categories and kinds of people who happened to be excluded from the disciplines of knowledge. These minor changes in the demographic myth of who represents our country have reverberated across the culture. The ripple effects can be seen in the courthouse, hospital, pharmaceutical industry, publishing world, sports, military, and Wall Street, as well as the Congress and the university.

The 1960s can be regarded as the turning point. Where the war in Southeast Asia signaled a decline in the belief that to preserve democracy and the modern family we had to send heroic men to do battle against those who threaten to extinguish Western humanism, the war at home gave unprecedented and irreversible authority to spectacle. Refusing to attend university classes was fundamentally different from a General Motors strike. Throwing rocks at U.S. policemen and being carted off in a paddy wagon to the local jail was not at all the same as killing Germans, Koreans, or Vietnamese. The clothes of the 1960s were not the clothes of rebellious natives, migrant laborers, abused minorities, or the homeless poor but carefully crafted costumes. To regard this inaugural battle of the contemporary culture wars as anything other than a performance, a media event, or a spectacle is to imply that it was a disgusting parody of war, which is to ignore its profound cultural-historical importance. Precisely because the war at home displayed, for all the world to see, a generation out of control and acting out contempt for the values of their parents' generation, it was and remains a more bitter national embarrassment than the war in Vietnam itself. The antiwar movement was a willful violation of established social categories. This decisively violent renunciation of the prevailing categories of race, class, and gender was not a statement about a war going on somewhere else but an act of war in its own right, a war over how to represent this country and its ruling class.[14] Thus the most important achievement of "the sixties" was neither to deflect attention from the civil rights movement, which antiwar demonstrations certainly achieved, nor to bring an end to involuntary service in the military, which they also achieved, but to shift the theater of political activism from the plane of physical action, conflicts we call real, to the plane of discourse, conflicts over how our relation to the real should be imagined.[15]

Something got permanently turned around in the process, I am suggesting, and the outcome of military actions, hunger, trade policies, as well as elections and, yes, university search committees, began to depend on how those under consideration were represented, how well they managed the information about themselves, rather than who and what they were. Indeed, it is fair to say that modern cultures such as ours have moved so far in this direction that how people are represented may well be who they are. To come to this conclusion is to admit that any responsible political action depends on understanding the world so classified as the real and primary one, the one that must be changed if the material conditions in which people live and die are going to improve. Because our forebears were so successful in establishing their picture of the world as the world itself, cultural theory is not just a legacy they bequeathed to us, but one of the most effective means of intervening in the reproduction of that picture.

Notes

1. By this I mean not only those who had access to print culture but also the "imagined community" formed by their shared participation in a vernacular print culture (See Benedict Anderson, *Imagined Communities: Reflections on the Origin and Spread of Nationalism* [London: Verso, 1983]). I am convinced that this community underwent an important transformation during the nineteenth century with the advent of mass visuality, including photography, illustrated books and newspapers, public museums, and all the exhibitionary practices that accompany the imperialist phase of modernization. See my *Fiction in the Age of Photography: The Legacy of British Realism* (Cambridge: Harvard University Press, 1999).

2. In "The Age of the World Picture," Martin Heidegger explains that "world picture . . . does not mean a picture of the world but the world conceived and grasped as a picture. What is, in its entirety, is now taken in such a way that it first is in being and only is in being to the extent that it is set up by man, who represents and sets forth. . . . When, accordingly, the picture character of the world is made clear as the representedness of that which is . . . comes to stand as object and in that way alone receives the seal of Being. That the world becomes picture is one and the same event . . . of man's becoming [an observer] in the midst of that which is" (in Martin Heidegger, *The Question Concerning Technology and Other Essays*, trans. William Lovitt [New York: Harper and Row, 1977], 129–32).

3. See Mary Poovey, *The History of the Modern Fact: Problems of Knowledge in the Sciences of Wealth and Society* (Chicago: University of Chicago Press, 1998), 307–28. In concluding her definitive history of the problem of induction, Poovey notes how this epistemological problematic began, at some point in the nineteenth century, to open onto another: "Whether it takes the form of Ferdinand de Saussure's claim that signs are arbitrary, Jacques Lacan's definition of the ego as lack, Jean Baudrillard's fascination with simulation's ability to end all original reference, or Slavoj Zizek's celebration of the 'meaningless traces' that thrust meaning production onto analysis itself, the postmodernist conviction that the systems of knowledge humans create constitute the only source of meaning is gradually displacing both the problem of induction. . . . [J]ust as the Baconian fact did not suddenly or completely displace its ancient predecessor, so the postmodern fact has not wholly triumphed over either the production of modern facts or the longing for them" (327–28). This order of explanation as to why contrary epistemologies could achieve a synthesis during the Victorian period only to flare up in the culture wars during our own seems much more satisfying to me than modernist proclamations of great divides between then and now.

4. For the definitive articulation of this cultural paradox, see Andreas Huyssen's "Mass Culture as Women," in *After the Great Divide: Modernism, Mass Culture, Postmodernism* (Bloomington: University of Indiana Press, 1986), 22–62.

5. John Stuart Mill, "On Liberty," in *On Liberty and Other Essays* (New York: Oxford University Press, 1991), 19. Subsequent references to this essay are given in the text.

6. I will be suggesting that, by these terms, Mill meant something like "popular" culture, which had rather suddenly acquired a frightening capability to wipe out traditional culture. John Frow calls attention to how fraught a term *popular* is, and I will try to restrict its meaning, in discussing Victorian liberal defensiveness, as "the emanation of a homogeneous popular will, a singular politico-cultural impulse that feeds into and through the cultural forms adapted to its expression" (John Frow, *Cultural Studies and Cultural Value* [Oxford: Clarendon, 1995], 82–88). This limited usage is problematic, as Frow also points out, in that "the people," so conceived, are at once responsible for the tastelessness of mass culture and the hapless victims of it.

7. In *The Structural Transformation of the Public Sphere: An Inquiry into a Category of Bourgeois Society*, trans. Thomas Burger (Cambridge: MIT Press, 1989), Jürgen Habermas uses Mill to describe this reactionary turn against popular culture: "The political public sphere no longer stood for the idea of a dissolution of power; instead, it was to serve its division; public opinion became a mere limit on power. Mill's admission betrayed the origin of this reinterpretation. *Thenceforth* care had to be taken that the power of public opinion not swallow up all power in general. The liberalist interpretation of the bourgeois public sphere was reactionary: it reacted to the power of the idea of a critically debating public's self-determination, initially included in its institutions, as soon as this public was subverted by the propertyless and uneducated masses" (136).

8. Marx chooses Robinson Crusoe's island in the novel by Daniel Defoe to represent the moment before commodification begins, when objects still transparently reflected the value of the labor that went into making them so that even the most willfully naive individual could see: "All the relations between Robinson and these objects that form his self-created wealth are here so simple and transparent that even Mr Sedley Taylor could understand them" (Karl Marx, *Capital*, vol. 1, trans. Ben Fowkes [New York: Random House, 1977], 170).

9. More specifically, Marx claimed that there was something visually alluring about the commodity that prevented people from seeing what was real. "In the act of seeing," he explains, "light is really transmitted from one thing, the external object, to another thing, the eye." By way of contrast, "the commodity-form" has "absolutely no connection with the physical nature of the object itself." Moreover, because the traces of who made it from what and for whom disappear whenever a product becomes a commodity, the human relations that arise from making and exchanging products acquire "the fantastic form of a relation among things" (ibid., 165).

10. Virginia Woolf, "Mr. Bennett and Mrs. Brown," in *Approaches to the Novel: Materials for a Poetics*, ed. Robert Scholes (Scranton, Pa.: Chandler, 1966).

11. Rey Chow, "Where Have All the Natives Gone?" in *Writing Diaspora: Tactics of Intervention in Contemporary Cultural Studies* (Bloomington: Indiana University Press, 1993), 29.

12. Richard Rorty, *Achieving Our Country: Leftist Thought in Twentieth-Century America* (Cambridge: Harvard University Press, 1998), 6. Subsequent references are given in the text.

13. See ibid., 91–97. It is obviously not their work as philosophers that bothers Rorty, because he never once attacks the integrity of the arguments of cultural theorists but only their reading of "discourse" (Foucault) and "technology" (Heidegger) as the modern forms of political power. It is as if the traditional representations of the nation would adequately express the present-day United States, were we only to stop reading critical theory imported from Europe.

14. In "'Masculinity,' 'the Rule of Law,' and Other Legal Fictions," in *Constructing Masculinity*, ed. Maurice Berger, Brian Wallis, and Simon Watson (New York: Routledge, 1995), 221–37, Kendall Thomas argues that the establishment of law in the United States, from *The Federalist Papers* to the recent television series *Homicide*, is invariably imagined as an inaugural act of overthrowing the law. Given that ratification of the Constitution required nine states' approval, whereas the Articles of Confederation required unanimous approval by all thirteen state legislatures to alter those articles, it can be argued that the illicit procedures for approving the Constitution legitimated the law. In this respect, the ratification of the Constitution might be said to reproduce the inaugural act of revolutionary violence that at once established U.S. law and defined those who overthrew English law as masculine. It strikes me that the student movement of the 1960s observed precisely this paradox, not so much in violating the laws prohibiting disorderly conduct and defacement of public property as in staging spectacular displays of such unruliness. By taking the issue of the war to the streets, "the sixties" legitimated spectacle and public opinion rather than courts and congress as the means of henceforth thrashing out such policies.

15. Fredric Jameson offers a particularly clear analysis of the importance of this moment. Although, he regrets, "something is lost when an emphasis on power and domination tends to obliterate the displacement . . . towards the economic system, the structure of the mode of production, and exploitation as such," and the shift to discourse and spectacle identifying postmodernism, performed precisely that change in emphasis. But, Jameson continues, "when I am tempted to regret my complicity with [postmodernism], to deplore its misuses and its notoriety, and to conclude with some reluctance that it raises more problems than it solves, I find myself pausing to wonder whether any other concept can dramatize the issue in quite so effective and economical a fashion. 'We have to name the system': this high point of the sixties finds an unexpected revival in the postmodern debate" (Fredric Jameson, "Marxism and Postmodernism," in *The Cultural Turn: Selected Writings on the Postmodern, 1983–1998* [London: Verso, 1998], 48–49).

Contributors

Nancy Armstrong is Nancy Duke Lewis Professor of Comparative Literature, English, Modern Culture and Media, and Women's Studies at Brown University. She is the author of *Desire and Domestic Fiction: A Political History of the Novel* and *Fiction in the Age of Photography: The Legacy of British Realism*. She is also coauthor (with Leonard Tennenhouse) of *The Imaginary Puritan: Literature, Intellectual Labor, and the Origins of Personal Life*.

Ian Baucom is assistant professor of English at Duke University. He is the author of *Out of Place: Englishness, Empire, and the Locations of Identity*.

Jay Clayton is professor of English at Vanderbilt University and author of *Romantic Vision and the Novel* and *The Pleasures of Babel: Contemporary American Literature and Theory*. He is working on a book titled *Charles Dickens in Cyberspace; Or, Literature in an Age of Cultural Studies*.

Mary A. Favret is associate professor of English at Indiana University. She is the author of *Romantic Correspondence: Women, Politics, and the Fiction of Letters* and the coeditor of the anthology *At the Limits of Romanticism: Essays in Cultural, Feminist, and Materialist Criticism*. She is currently working on a collection of essays on reading Jane Austen.

Simon Gikandi is professor of English language and literature and director of the Program in Comparative Literature at the University of Michigan. His recent publications include *Writing in Limbo: Modernism and Caribbean Literature* and *Maps of Englishness: Writing Identity in the Culture of Colonialism*. He is also editor of the forthcoming *Cambridge History of African and Caribbean Literature*.

Jennifer Green-Lewis is associate professor of English at the George Washington University, where she teaches Victorian literature and culture. She is the author of *Framing the Victorians: Photography and the Culture of Realism*, as well as numerous articles on photography and nineteenth-century literature.

Kali Israel is associate professor of history at the University of Michigan, where she teaches modern British history. She is the author of *Names and Stories: Emilia Dilke and Victorian Culture* and is currently working on a study of the uses of Alices in contemporary culture.

John Kucich is professor of English at the University of Michigan. He is the author of *Excess and Restraint in the Novels of Charles Dickens, Repression in Victorian Fiction: Charlotte Brontë, Charles Dickens, and George Eliot*, and *The Power of Lies: Transgression in Victorian Fiction*, as well as numerous essays on Victorian culture and contemporary fiction.

Laurie Langbauer is professor of English at the University of North Carolina and director of graduate studies in the English department. She is the author of *Women and Romance: The Consolations of Gender in the English Novel* and *Novels of Everyday Life: The Series in English Fiction, 1850–1930*.

Susan Lurie is associate professor of English and associate dean for graduate studies at Rice University. She is the author of *Unsettled Subjects: Restoring Feminist Politics to Poststructuralist Critique* and has written essays on feminist theory, twentieth-century U.S. literature, film, and popular culture.

John McGowan is professor of English and comparative literature at the University of North Carolina, Chapel Hill. He is the author of *Hannah Arendt: An Introduction* (Minnesota, 1997) and *Postmodernism and Its Critics*.

He is coeditor, with Craig Calhoun, of *Hannah Arendt and the Meaning of Politics* (Minnesota, 1997).

Judith Roof teaches twentieth-century studies at Indiana University. She is the author of *Reproductions of Reproduction: Imaging Symbolic Change, Come as You Are: Narrative and Sexuality,* and *A Lure of Knowledge: Lesbian Sexuality and Theory,* and coeditor of *Feminism and Psychoanalysis, Who Can Speak? Authority and Critical Identity,* and *Staging the Rage: Misogyny in Modern Drama.*

Dianne F. Sadoff is professor of English and chair of the English department at Miami University, Ohio. She is the author of *Monsters of Affection: Dickens, Brontë, and Eliot on Fatherhood* and *Sciences of the Flesh: Representing Body and Subject in Psychoanalysis,* and the coeditor of *Teaching Contemporary Theory to Undergraduates.*

Hilary M. Schor is professor of English at the University of Southern California. She is the author of *Scheherezade in the Marketplace: Elizabeth Gaskell and the Victorian Novel* and the forthcoming *Dickens and the Daughter of the House,* a study of Dickens, the law, and female narrative. She writes widely on Victorian culture and cultural studies.

Ronald R. Thomas is professor of English at Trinity College in Hartford, Connecticut, where he also serves as chief of staff and vice president of the college. He is the author of two books on nineteenth-century fiction: *Dreams of Authority: Freud and the Fictions of the Unconscious* and *Detective Fiction and the Rise of Forensic Science.*

Shelton Waldrep teaches Victorian literature and critical theory at the University of Southern Maine. He is the coauthor of *Inside the Mouse: Work and Play at Disney World* and the editor of *The Seventies: The Age of Glitter in Popular Culture.* He has published essays in Victorian studies, cultural studies, and gender studies. He is at work on a book that resituates Oscar Wilde for the twentieth century (Minnesota, forthcoming).

Index

Abraham, Nicolas, 129, 130, 140, 144–45; *The Shell and the Kernel,* 129

Adams, Henry, 321

Adamson, Robert, 38, 39; *The McCandlish Children,* 38

Adelaide Gallery, 104, 119n.5

Africa: colonization of, 133, 167, 170, 172, 176, 314 (*see also* Colonism); culture, 168, 173; decolonization of, 160 (*see also* Postcolonialism); in discourses of slavery, 133, 142, 168; missionaries, 168–69 (*see also* Colonism: institutions of); and Victorian culture, 181–82; nationalism, 158, 168, 173, 178, 180

AIDS, 256

Albert, Prince, 107, 108, 227

Althusser, Louis, 5, 8

American Negro Academy, 169, 176

American Wake, 139, 140–43. *See also* Ireland: emmigration

Anarchism, 16

Annan, Thomas, 38

ANQ (journal), 192

Appiah, Anthony, 170, 173

Arendt, Hannah, 23; *Life of the Mind,* 23

Armstrong, Isobel, 4

Armstrong, Nancy, xiv, xxvii, 212, 220, 311–26

Arnold, Matthew, 3, 9, 12, 14, 161, 166, 170, 178, 182, 317, 319, 320; *Culture and Anarchy,* 14, 161, 166; "Stanzas from the Grande Chartreuse," 9; Victorian liberalism, 14

Arnold, Thomas, 166, 167

Arrighi, Giovanni, xvii, xviii

Atwell, David, 182

Auerbach, Nina, 257

Austen, Jane, ix, 19, 64–69, 73, 78, 80; *Emma,* ix, 315, 319; film adaptations, xi, xiv, 19, 30, 64, 67–80, 290, 315; *Persuasion,* 66, 72, 73, 77; and postmodern culture, xxiv, 65, 234; *Pride and Prejudice,* xi; *Sense and Sensibility,* 65, 66, 67, 69–70, 72, 77; sexuality, 66; in Victorian culture, xxiv, 66. *See also* Heckerling, Amy: *Clueless* (film);

Lee, Ang: *Sense and Sensibility* (film)

Austen-Leigh, James Edward, 66; *A Memoir of Jane Austen*, 66

Babbage, Charles, 186, 187, 188, 189, 190, 191, 192, 198, 200, 203, 205; Difference Engine, 186, 188; Silver Lady, 187, 188

Bakhtin, Mikhail, 23

Bammer, Angelika, 43

Banville, John, 130, 131; *Birchwood,* 130, 131

Barker, Pat, 234, 258; *The Ghost Road,* 258

Barrett, Andrea, 234

Barthes, Roland, 31, 37, 42

Bartlett, Neil, 60

Batten, Guinn, 144, 146, 147, 154

Baucom, Ian, xx, xxvi, 125–56

Baudrillard, Jean, xiii, 43, 305

Baudry, Jean-Louis, 293

Baum, L. Frank, 255; *The Wizard of Oz,* 255

Beauvoir, Simone de, 212

Bennett, Tony, 105

Berlant, Lauren, 90

Bernstein, Susan, 215, 226, 227, 229

Bhabha, Homi, 138

Bhutto, Benazir, 219

Blake, William, 195

Bloomsbury Group, 11

Blyden, Edward Wilmot, 177

Bolter, J. David, 192

Booker Prize, ix

Booth, Alison, 218, 219

Borges, Jorge Luis, 21; "Funes the Memorius," 21

Boyd, Blanche McCrary, 258; *Terminal Velocity,* 258

Bradbury, Ray, 188; *Something Wicked This Way Comes,* 188

Bradshaw, Brendan, 127; "Nationalism and Historical Scholarship in Ireland," 127

Branagh, Kenneth, 290; *Frankenstein* (film), 290 (*see also* Shelley, Mary: *Frankenstein*)

Breuer, Josef, 315

Brewster, David, 186, 187, 199

Bristow, Joseph, 58

Britain. *See* United Kingdom

British Broadcasting Company, 72, 234

Brontë, Charlotte, 235, 243, 290; *Jane Eyre,* 243, 290, 318 (*see also* Rhys, Jean: *Wide Sargasso Sea*); *Villette,* 243

Brontë, Emily, 76, 92; *Wuthering Heights,* xi, 76, 92

Browning, Elizabeth Barrett, 236

Browning, Robert, 166, 236

Browning, Tod, 292, 296–99; *Dracula* (film), 296–99

Brunel, Mark, 186, 187

Bullock, Dillman Samuel, 103

Bunyan, John, 182; *Pilgrim's Progress,* 182

Burke, Edmund, 195

Byatt, A. S., xi, xiv, 234–48; *Angels and Insects,* 235, 237, 239, 240–44, 247; *Babel Tower,* 236, 247, 248; *The Conjugial Angel,* 238, 243–45; *Morpho Eugenia,* 237–38, 240–43, 245; *Possession,* xi, 236; *Shadow of the Sun,* 236; *Still Life,* 236; *The Virgin in the Garden,* 236

Byron, George Gordon, 191, 198–99, 201; daughter of (*see* Lovelace, Ada); wife of, 201

Cameron, Julia, xi, 29, 38, 102; portrait of Mrs. Herbert Duckworth, 38; portrait of Sir John Herschel, 38; portrait of Thomas Carlyle, 38; *Whisper of the Muse (George F. Watts),* 38

Campion, Jane, xxi, 76, 83–98; *The Piano* (film), 76, 83, 91, 94; *Portrait of a Lady* (film), xxi, 83, 87, 89, 90–98; racism of, 91

Capitalism, xv, 18, 106; corporations, 19; economics, xiv, xv, xvii, xviii, xxv, 14, 18; history of, xvii, 12, 136; laissez-faire liberalism, 14; nineteenth-century British expansion of, xvii, 66, 104, 105, 112, 126, 137, 159; twentieth-century global, xvii, xxiii, xxvi, 12, 15, 18, 64

Carleton, William, 130; *The Black Prophet*, 130

Carlyle, Thomas, 3, 11, 13, 162, 166, 170, 171; *Past and Present*, 171

Carr, Caleb, ix; *The Alienist*, ix

Carroll, Lewis. *See* Dodgson, Charles Lutwidge

Casey, Edward S., 137

Cavell, Stanley, 73

Cazenove, Christopher, 57

Cellini, Benvenuto, 53

Charney, Leo, 306

Chase, Karen, 215

Chatterbox (magazine), 109fig.2

Chaucer, Geoffrey, 174, 244

Chow, Rey, 318; "Where Have All the Natives Gone," 318

Christensen, Michael, 195

Clayton, Jay, xxvii, 186–210

Clement, Joseph, 191, 192

Clifford, James, 130

Clinton, William Jefferson, xviii

Cohen, Morton, 253, 254, 260, 261, 262, 273; "Are You Kissable?" 253, 254

Coleridge, Samuel Taylor, 3, 191, 195

Colonialism, xvii, 161, 171, 173–74, 319; institutions of, 158, 166, 168–69, 177; Orientalism, 189; popular representations of, 53, 103, 180, 189; relationship to capitalism, xvii, 159, 312; struggles against, 158, 160; Victorian, xxi, 43, 76, 103, 104, 106, 112, 133, 158–60, 162–65; 177, 180, 314

Commodity culture, x, xviii, 7, 29, 66, 101, 110, 315; and mass media, xi, xxii, 29, 66, 114, 305, 316–17; and postmodernism, x, xii, xiii, xxv–xxvi, 10, 64, 66, 104, 112, 311; and women consumers, xvi; Victorian, 103, 105, 294, 301, 302, 312, 313, 321

Comaroff, Jean, 159

Comaroff, John, 159

Connolly, S. J., 128

Connor, Stephen, 34, 41, 42

Constable, John, 69

Contemporary Literature (journal), 192

Coppola, Francis Ford, 53, 292, 299–300; *Bram Stoker's Dracula* (film), 53, 292, 299–300

Country Living (magazine), 44, 47n.25

Cowper, William, 68

Crichton, Michael, 194; *Timeline*, 194

Cruikshank, George, 189; "Automaton Police Office," 189

Crummell, Alexander, xxi, 169, 170–81; *The Future of Africa*, 173, 174, 177; moral discourse, 179; Crystal Palace, 104, 108; "Exhibition of the Works of Industry of All Nations," 104 (*see also* Great Exhibition)

Cultural studies, xiii, xiv, 7, 12, 21, 44, 259; emergence of, xiii; film theory, 293, 296, 300–301, 306; mass media, 44, 289, 291, 300, 301, 302, 305, 316, 320–22; multiculturalism, 7, 319–21; relationship to Victorianism, xxv, 290, 314, 316; subcultures, 12

Culture wars, xii, 16, 311; and the

academy, 214, 228, 321–22; and
the canon, xiii, xvi, 61, 321; link to
welfare debates, xxixn.6; religious
fundamentalism, 15; threat of cultural erosion, xxvii
Cyberpunk, xi, 190, 193, 194, 255;
racism and sexism in, 193

Daguerre, Louis Jacques Mandé, 32;
Boulevard du Temple, Paris, 32,
33fig.3, 37; *Collection de coquillages
et divers,* 32
Daguerreotype. *See* Daguerre, Louis
Jacques Mandé
Dante, Alighieri, 244, 245
Darwin, Charles, 102, 115 , 116, 117,
235, 237, 239, 240, 247, 314
De Lauretis, Teresa, 259; *Alice Doesn't,*
259
Denfeld, Rene, 222, 223, 224; *The
New Victorians: A Young Woman's
Challenge to the Old Feminist Order,*
222
Derrida, Jacques, 21, 61
Diamond, Hugh, 38, 314
Dick, Philip K., 194; *The Man in the
High Castle,* 194
Dickens, Charles, 158, 164, 165, 166,
187, 188–89, 199, 240, 245, 247,
290, 292, 314; *Bleak House,* 24;
David Copperfield, 5; *Dombey and
Son,* 237; film adaptations, 290;
Great Expectations, 290; "Mudfog
Papers," 189
Dickinson, Emily, 260
Disney Co., Walt: Celebration
(Florida), 44
Disraeli, Benjamin, 190, 191, 195–96;
Sybil, 190, 191, 195
Doctorow, E. L., xi; *The Water-Works,*
xi
Dodgson, Charles Lutwidge (pseudo-
nym: Lewis Carroll), xi, xix,

252–66, 268, 276, 279; *Alice's
Adventures in Wonderland,* xi, 252,
256, 259; literary criticism about,
252–70; memoirs about, 258;
museum exhibitions, xi, xix, 253;
and pedophilia, 257, 261, 279;
photographs of Alice, 38, 252–54,
271; proliferation of Alice charac-
ters, xix, 254–65; *Through the
Looking Glass, and What Alice
Found There,* 252 (*see also* Liddell,
Alice)
Dollimore, Jonathan, 58
Domesticity: nineteenth-century, xvi
Douglas, Lord Alfred "Bosie," 49, 53.
See also Wilde, Oscar: gay lover
Drabble, Margaret, 234, 237; *The
Garrick Year,* 237
Du Bois, W. E. B., 168, 169, 170, 177;
The Souls of Black Folk, 168
Dunayesvskya, Raya, 157
Dusinberre, Juliet, 254

Eagleton, Terry, 51, 128, 140; *Saint
Oscar,* 51
Echeruo, Michael, 168; *Victorian
Lagos,* 168
Egypt: exotic representations of, 95
Eisenstein, Sergei, 292
Eliot, George, 3, 247; *Middlemarch,* xi
Elizabeth, I, Queen, x, 220, 221, 222,
236; films about, x
Ellmann, Richard, 55, 57; biography of
Oscar Wilde, 55
Emerson, Peter Henry, 38, 39;
Gathering Water-lilies, 38; *Osier-
Peeling,* 38; photograph of the
Norfolk Broads, 38; *Poling the
Marsh Hay,* 38
Emerson, Ralph Waldo, 85
Engels, Friedrich, 191
England. *See* United Kingdom
Epstein, Debbie, 223

Equitable Gallery, xi; exhibitions on *Alice in Wonderland,* xi

Evans, Frederick, 38; *The Sea of Steps— Wells Cathedral,* 38

Expressionism: German. *See* Murnau, F. W.: *Nosferatu* (film)

Faraday, Michael, 186, 187, 199

Favret, Mary A., xxiv, xxv, 64–82

Feminism, xxi, 84, 95, 174, 214; critiques of, 18, 224, 226; and eating disorders, 268 (*see also* Psychoanalysis: eating disorders); erotics of, 91, 97, 262; nineteenth-century emergence of, xiv, xxi; and postmodernism, 84, 86; scholarship, 211, 216–30, 268. *See also* Victoria, Queen: relationship to feminism

Fenton, Roger, 38, 39; *Valley of Death,* 38

Fetishism, xv, xviii, 53, 74, 80, 129; and postmodernism, xv, 43, 65, 66

Ford, Colin, 253

Forster, E. M., xi, 247; film adaptations, xi, 11–12, 19; *A Room with a View,* 11, 12

Foucault, Michel, xi, xii, xiv, xviii, xxvi, xxvii, 21, 38, 105, 220, 320; critique of, xii; *The History of Sexuality,* xi, xviii; panopticon, 105

Fowles, John, xviii; film adaptations, xviii; *The French Lieutenant's Woman,* xviii (*see also* Reisz, Karel: *The French Lieutenant's Woman* (film), xviii)

Foy, George, 191; *The Shift,* 191

France: social system, 18; French Revolution, 236

French, Nicci, 258; *The Memory Game,* 258

French, Sean. *See* French, Nicci

Freud, Sigmund, 119n.11, 128, 188, 217, 218, 244, 248, 314; *The Interpretation of Dreams,* 217, 293; *Studies on Hysteria,* 314–15. *See also* Psychoanalysis

Frith, Francis, 38, 39

Fry, Stephen, 49, 53, 54; as a gay actor, 51, 54

Fuchs, Elinor, 44

Fuller, Margaret, 260

Fuss, Diana, 71

Futurism, 178

Gael, Dorothy, 256

Gallagher, Thomas, 131, 141; *Paddy's Lament: Ireland 1846–1847,* 131

Gallop, Jane, 224, 225, 226

Galton, Francis, 314

Garland, Judy, 255

Gates, Bill, 102, 117

Gates, Henry Louis, Jr., 170

Gernsheim, Helmut, 253, 255

Gerrard, Nicci. *See* French, Nicci

Gibbons, Luke, 133; critiques of, 134

Gibson, Mel, ix

Gibson, William, xi, 186–87, 189–200; *The Difference Engine,* xi, 186–87, 189–200; *Neuromancer,* 193. *See also* Sterling, Bruce

Gikandi, Simon, xx–xxi, xxvi, 157–85

Gilbert, Sandra, xiv

Gilroy, Paul, 21, 134, 143; *Black Atlantic,* 143

Gingrich, Newt, xii, xxixn.6

Gleick, James, 202; *Chaos,* 202

Gogh, Vincent van, 236

Grace, W. G., 161, 164, 165, 166, 182

Grant, Stephanie, 268, 269–70, 272; *The Passion of Alice,* 268, 270

Great Exhibition, 106, 107fig.1, 108. *See also* Crystal Palace

Greenblatt, Stephen, 220

Greene, Graham, 181–82

Green-Lewis, Jennifer, xxiii, xxv, 29–48

Greuze, Jean-Baptiste, 69

Griffith, D. W., 292
Grolier Club exhibit, 253, 254
Gubar, Susan, xiv

Habens, Alison, 260, 268, 269–79;
  Dreamhouse, 260, 268, 269–70;
  276–79
Habermas, Jürgen, 17, 34, 325n.7
Halberstam, Judith, 307
Hall, Catherine, 174
Hall, Sir Peter, 49; *An Ideal Husband,*
  49
Hall, Stuart, 21
Hampton, Christopher, 258, 265, 266
Hardy, Thomas, 234, 290; *Jude the
  Obscure,* 290; popularity of, 234
Harrison, Harry, 194; *Tunnel through
  the Deeps,* 194
Hawarden, Clementina, 38
Hawking, Stephen, 202; *A Brief
  History of Time,* 202
Hazlitt, William, 195
Heckerling, Amy, ix–x; *Clueless* (film),
  ix–x, 315, 316, 319
Hegel, Georg W. F., 162
Heidegger, Martin, 137–38, 320; *Being
  and Time,* 137
Heinlein, Robert A., 194; "All You
  Zombies," 194; "By His
  Bootstraps," 194
Henson, Jim, 263, 264; *Labyrinth*
  (film), 263
Herder, Johann Gottfried, 8
Heterosexuality, xxii, 90, 95, 97; and
  autoeroticism, 88, 92; compulsory,
  83, 85, 86, 87; constructions of,
  69–70, 84, 98; eroticization of
  women of color, xxi, 84, 90, 186;
  and masculinity, 95
Hewett, Dorothy, 258; "Alice in
  Wormland," 258
Hill, David Octavius, 38, 39; *The
  McCandlish Children,* 38

Himmelfarb, Gertrude, xii, xiv, xvii;
  critique of, xii; moralism of, xiv
Hirsh, Elizabeth, 226, 227, 229
Hirth, Georg, 104
Hoffmann, E. T. A., 188; "The
  Automaton," 188; "The Sandman,"
  188
Hofstadter, Douglas R., 202; *Gödel,
  Escher, Bach,* 202
Hollywood, 9, 11, 256, 289, 315
Holliday, Billie, ix
Homans, Margaret, 211, 218, 219,
  220, 221, 222; "The Power of
  Powerlessness," 213; *Remaking
  Queen Victoria,* 212, 218; *Royal
  Representations: Queen Victoria
  and British Culture,* 211; "To the
  Queen's Private Apartments," 215,
  221
Homes, A. M., 268, 269, 270, 273–75,
  279; *The End of Alice,* 268, 273–75
Homosexuality: contemporary gay cul-
  ture, xiv, xix, 60, 61; gay liberation
  movement, 51, 54, 56, 57; homo-
  eroticism, 83, 84–85, 87, 88, 92;
  homosocial relationships, 11, 58,
  84, 86, 87; lesbians, 59, 225, 258;
  queer politics, 54, 57, 58–59;
  Victorian, xix, 50, 51, 60 (*see also*
  Wilde, Oscar: as gay martyr)
Hornbacher, Marya, 268, 270; *Wasted,*
  268
Howard, Elizabeth Jane, 234
Huff, Cynthia, 215, 227
Hughes, Thomas, 166
Hugo Award, 194
Hutcheon, Linda, xi, 42, 43, 194
Huyssen, Andreas, xvi
Hypertext, 102

Information technology, xxiii, 101,
  113, 114; in the global market,
  xxiii, 111, 113

In the Blood (Broadway play), xi
Ireland, 125–55; colonization of, 133, 134; emmigration, 125, 126, 133, 136, 139–43, 148, 151, 152, 153; Famine Museum, 127; nationalism, xx, 51, 58, 128, 136, 138, 139, 142, 143, 147, 154, 312; resistance to British colonialism, 128; Ulster, 127
Irons, Jeremy, xix
Israel, Kali, xix, xxvi, 252–87
Ivory, James, xi

Jackson, Michael, 243
Jacquet-Droz, Pierre, 186
James, C. L. R., xxi, 157–68, 180, 182; *Beyond a Boundary,* 157, 158, 161, 165, 167, 176, 180, 182; *The Black Jacobins,* 162; deportation of, 182; "Discovering Literature in Trinidad: the 1930s," 157
James, Henry, xxi, 11, 84, 85, 86, 87, 89–90, 93–94, 96, 290; Catholicism, 89; *Daisy Miller,* 88; film adaptations, 11–12, 84–98, 290; *Portrait of a Lady,* xxi, 85–86, 88–90, 92–94, 290; *Wings of the Dove,* 11. See also Campion, Jane: *Portrait of a Lady* (film)
Jameson, Fredric, x, xiii, xiv, xv, xvi, xvii, xxii, xxv, xxvi, 42, 239–40, 245, 248, 288, 326n.15; and authenticity, 43, 65, 239; critiques of, xxvii, xxviiin.3, 65; and Marxism, xiv, xv, xvi; *Postmodernism, or, the Cultural Logic of Late Capitalism,* x, 64, 71; *Signatures of the Visible,* 288
Jekyll and Hyde (Broadway play), xi
Jerinic, Maria, 219
Jones, Kathleen, 228, 229
Jonson, Ben, 69
Joyce, James, 143, 148; *Finnegans Wake,* 143; *Ulysses,* 313
Judas Kiss, The (Broadway play), 49

Kahn, Albert, 104; Museum, 103–4
Kaufman, Moises, 49, 50, 51; *Gross Indecency: The Three Trials of Oscar Wilde,* 49
Kavanagh, Patrick, 131; "The Great Hunger," 131
Keats, John, 191, 244, 245
Keller, Evelyn Fox, 216, 223, 225, 226; "Competition and Feminism: Conflicts for Academic Women," 216
Kempelen, Wolfgang von, 187
Kennedy, Adrienne, 217; *Funnyhouse of a Negro,* 217, 229
Kennedy, Ted, 14
Kidman, Nicole, 90
Kincaid, James, 274, 277; *Child-Loving,* 274, 277
Kinealy, Christine, 127, 128, 130, 135
Koetge, Noretta, 222; *Professing Women: Cautionary Tales from the Strange World of Women's Studies,* 222
Kolb, David, 44
Korean War, 323
Kostenbaum, Wayne, 57, 58
Krafft-Ebing, Richard von, 314
Kubrick, Stanley, 273; *Lolita,* 273 (*see also* Nabokov, Vladimir: *Lolita*)
Kucich, John, ix, xix, xxii, xiv, xxviii, 312, 315

Labouchère amendment, 49–50
LaCapra, Dominick, xxvi
Langbauer, Laurie, xxi, xxvi, 211–33
Laumer, Keith, 194; *The Other Side of Time,* 194
Lawrence, D. H., 247; *Women in Love,* 313
Lee, Ang, xi, 64, 67, 68, 72; *Sense and Sensibility* (film), 64, 67, 68–72, 77, 79–80
Leinster, Murray, 194; "Sidewise in Time," 194

Lessing, Doris, 247
Lethem, Jonathan, 255; *As She Climbed across the Table,* 255
Leverian Museum, 108
Levinson, Michael, 215
Lewinsky, Monica, 272
Liberia, 168, 171, 172, 175–76; nationalism, 175
Liddell, Alice (later Hargreaves), 252, 257–58, 260, 261, 263, 264, 269, 270, 274, 279. *See also* Dodgson, Charles
Lieber, Fritz, 194; *The Big Time,* 194
Lingua Franca (magazine), 214
Little Princess, A (film), 255
Liu, Alan, 129
Lloyd, Constance (later Constance Lloyd Wilde, then Holland), 49, 59; plays about, 49. *See also* Wilde, Oscar: wife of
Loeffelholz, Mary, 214
London, 169, 191, 294, 299, 304; Alhambra Theatre, 301, Empire Theatre, 301, 304; Lyceum Theatre, 303; Victorian, 52, 53, 60, 294, 299; West End, 57
Lovelace, Ada, 187, 193, 198, 199, 200, 201, 202, 203, 205
Lugosi, Bela, 292
Lumière, Auguste, 301, 302fig.3, 304. *See also* Technology: film
Lurie, Susan, xxi, xxv, 83–100
Lynd, Robert, 139
Lyotard, Jean-François, xxviii, 9

Macintosh computer, 112, 113
Marie Christine (Broadway play), xi
Martin, Paul, 314
Martineau, Harriet, 3, 199
Marx, Karl, 162, 317–18, 325n.8
Marxism, 162, 180; class consciousness, xii, 162, 164; critique of, 18; as a political program, 16; and post-

colonialism, 161; and poststructuralism, xiv, xx, 17; radical left, 16, 157
Maudsley, Henry, 186, 192
Mavor, Carol, 252, 253, 254, 257, 260, 273; *Pleasures Taken: Performances of Sexuality and Loss in Victorian Photographs,* 252
Mayall, John Edwin, 38
Mayhew, Thomas, 314
McClintock, Anne, xx, 129; *Imperial Leather: Race, Gender, and Sexuality in the Colonial Contest,* 129, 130
McGowan, John, xiii, xviii, xxv, 3–28
McHale, Brian, 192, 194
McLuhan, Marshall, 292; *Understanding Media,* 292
Méliès, Georges, 303; *Le Manoir du diable,* 303
Mercer, Kobena, 134; *Black Atlantic,* 134
Merchant, Ismail, xi
Metz, Christian, 298, 301
Michaels, Walter Benn, 21
Michell, George, 64, 72; *Persuasion* (film), 64, 72–75, 77–80
Microsoft Windows, 102, 112, 115
Mill, John Stuart, 3, 4, 9, 11, 12, 13–14, 316, 317, 319, 320, 321; *On Liberty,* 316; "The Spirit of the Age," 3; Victorian liberalism, 14
Millennialism, xiv
Miller, D. A., 290
Miller, Kerby, 131; *Emigrants and Exiles: Ireland and the Irish Exodus to North America,* 131
Miller, Nancy, 219, 226; "Emphasis Added: Plots and Plausibilities in Women's Fiction," 219
Milton, John, 174, 245, 258
Mitchel, John, 126; Young Ireland, 126
Modleski, Tania, 230
Moglen, Helene, 216, 223, 225, 226;

"Competition and Feminism: Conflicts for Academic Women," 216

Mohanty, Chandra Talpade, 129

Montrose, Louis, 220, 221

Mooney, Ted, 196; *Easy Travel to Other Planets,* 196

Moore, Ward, 194; *Bring the Jubilee,* 194

Morash, Chris, 130, 131

Morgan, Susan, 65

Morris, Meaghan, 225

Morris, William, xiii, 3, 236

Morrison, Blake, 259; *As If,* 259

Mrs. Brown (film), xi, 19

Muldoon, Paul, xx, 125, 143–55; *The Annals of Chile,* 148, 149–50, 151, 153, 155; "The Fox," 145; "Incanta," 149; *Madoc: A Mystery,* 151; "Meeting the British," 145, 146; "My Grandfather's Wake," 145; "Paul Klee: They're Biting," 125; "The Waking Father," 144; "Yarrow," 149, 151

Munich, Adrienne, 211, 213, 218, 219, 228; *Queen Victoria's Secrets,* 211; *Remaking Queen Victoria,* 212, 218

Murnau, F. W., 291, 292, 295; *Nosferatu* (film), 291, 292, 295, 297fig.1, 297fig.2

Murphy, Thomas, 133, 135; *Famine,* 133, 135

Nabokov, Vladimir, 252, 253, 260, 272, 273, 274, 279; *Lolita,* 252, 253, 257, 260, 272, 273, 274, 275 (*see also* Kubrick, Stanley: *Lolita*); proliferation of Lolita characters, 272–75, 279

Napoleonic Wars, 72, 79, 103

National Museum of Wales, 253; director, 253 (*see also* Ford, Colin)

National Portrait Gallery, xi, 253; exhibitions on Alice in Wonderland, xi, 253

Nationalism, xx; African (*see* Africa: nationalism); American (*see* United States: nationalism); Caribbean, 158, 161, 163; English, 108, 216; Irish (*see* Ireland: nationalism); in liberation movements, 181; Liberian (*see* Liberia: nationalism); nineteenth-century emergence of, xx, 84, 173; Pan-African movement, 158; postcolonial constructions of, xx, xxvii, 43, 157, 160; relationship to capitalism, xvii, 104, 114, 311; relationship to racism, 15, 84, 88, 90, 96, 173, 175; relationship to patriarchy, 88, 90; Scottish, 76; state power, 19

Neeson, Liam, 49

Neill, Kenneth: *Irish People,* 139

New Historicism, xiii, 220, 221, 246

Newman, Charles, 36

New York City, xi, 136, 168, 290; Broadway, xi

New Zealand, 76

Niven, Larry, 194; "All the Myriad Ways," 194

Noon, Jeff, 255, 260; *Automated Alice,* 255, 260

Nora, Pierre, 138

Nostalgia, xvi, 43; and consumerism, 40–41, 44; and photography, 30–31, 39

Novel: contemporary, 234; historical, xv, xxii; pornographic, 235; Victorian, 234, 235, 242

O'Connell, Daniel, 197

O'Grada, Cormac, 127, 130, 131, 132; *The Great Irish Famine,* 131, 132

Oldfield, J. R., 169

Ovid, 148

Paglia, Camille, 222
Paley, William, 243; *Natural Theology,* 243
Patai, Daphne, 222; *Professing Women: Cautionary Tales from the Strange World of Women's Studies,* 222
Paul, Robert William, 301; *The Soldier's Courtship,* 301. *See also* Technology: film
Philippines: Manila, 171
Photography, xxiii; American Civil War, 40; connection to referent, 31, 36, 37; contemporary, 36; Cottingley Fairy, 38; and the gaze, 87, 311; "Golden Age of British Photography," 39; market for Victorian, 29, 31, 34, 311; relationship to film, 53, 73, 299, 300, 301; stereoscope, 186; trick, 301; Victorian canon, 39–40, 45; Victorian pictorial, xxiii, 29–30, 31, 37, 38, 313; Victorian pornography, 39
Pierpont Morgan Library, xi, 253, 254, 255, 261, 262; exhibitions on Alice in Wonderland, xi, 253, 261
Pirie, David, 289
Pollit, Katha, 222
Polytechnic Institute, 104, 119n.5
Poovey, Mary, 5–7, 25n.4; critique of, 6–7; definition of ideology, 5
Pope, Alexander, 68
Postcolonialism: consciousness, 160; culture, xxi, 101, 160, 182, 318; decolonization and liberation movements, 164, 168 (*see also* Africa: decolonization of); First and Third worlds, xx; imperialist nostalgia, 43; and psychoanalysis, 129; relationship to nationalism, xx; theory, xx, 138, 320, 321
Poststructuralism, xiv, 21, 255, 305; deconstruction, 255; referent, 31; theory, 129, 293, 305

Potter, Dennis, 258, 263–68, 279; *Blue Remembered Hills,* 263; *Dreamchild,* 263–68, 270, 279; film adaptations, 263–68 (*see also* Wenders, Wim: *Dreamchild* [film])
Prostitution, 254; childhood, 254, 256, 261, 262; Victorian, 254, 256
Psychoanalysis, xx, xiv, 49, 61, 293; abjection, 152; disavowal, 129; eating disorders, 268; Freudian, 149, 217, 219, 244, 293, 314 (*see also* Freud, Sigmund); identification, 129; incorporation, 129, 139; introjection, 129, 130; Lacanian, 146, 255, 298; Law of the Father, 146; masochism, 95; melancholy, 65, 70, 71, 126, 129, 132, 139, 144–45, 148; mourning, 61, 129, 244, 248; Oedipal revolt, 146; primal scene, 53; psychosexual, 53; voyeurism, 296 (*see also* Cultural studies: film theory)
Pullman, Philip, 258–59; *The Golden Compass,* 258, 269; *His Dark Materials,* 258
Pynchon, Thomas, 188; *Mason & Dixon,* 188

Race: black power, 180; and gender, xxi, 84, 88, 175, 224, 225; miscegenation fears, 88, 89, 90; postmodern political struggles over, xx; racism, 163, 168, 173; relationship to nationalism, 15, 84, 88, 90, 96, 173, 175; slavery, 171; whiteness, 90
Raleigh, Sir Walter, 221
Reagan, Ronald: "Reagan era," xiv, 16
Rejlander, Oscar Gustav, 34, 38, 39, 313; *The Two Ways of Life,* 34fig.4, 35, 38; *Hard Times,* 38
Reisz, Karel, xviii–xix; *French Lieutenant's Woman* (film), xix